CAREER GUIDANCE AND COUNSELLING
Principles and Techniques

CAREER GUIDANCE AND COUNSELLING

Principles and Techniques

Shashi Prabha Sharma

KANISHKA PUBLISHERS, DISTRIBUTORS
NEW DELHI-110 002

KANISHKA PUBLISHERS, DISTRIBUTORS
4697/5-21A, Ansari Road, Daryaganj
New Delhi -110 002
Phones : 2327 0497, 2328 8285
Fax : 011-2328 8285
E-mail : kanishka_publishing@yahoo.co.in
kanishkabooks@gmail.com

Career Guidance and Counselling: Principles and Techniques

First Published-2005

Edition-2025

ISBN : 978-81-7391-711-6

PRINTED IN INDIA

Published by Madan Sachdeva for Kanishka Publishers, Distributors, 4697/5-21A, Ansari Road, Daryaganj, New Delhi-110002, Typeset by Sunshine Graphics, Delhi, and Printed at G.S. Printers, Delhi.

Preface

Though the concept of guidance, in practice, is as old as family and human civilization, but as an academic and professional subject of study, even in Western World is not even hundred year old, while in India it is still in infantile stage. Yet due to its utmost importance in the changing world of work and social pattern it has received much attention because educational and occupational is fast changing here and these everywhere.

Career guidance is largely considered as a branch of guidance but because of its very wide and complex nature it indirectly encompasses the concepts of educational, vocational, personal and all other forms of guidance in its scope because all these forms of guidances aim at, in one way or the other, enhancing the social image and status of the individual and develope his personality, which is the soul aim of career guidance.

The new world of work and its still growth oriented development has changed the concept and nature of careers, which are found to change in future, therefore, need and necessity of career guidance is found to multiply in our day to day life, but it is sad that in India literature on career guidance is very scanty and, thus, there is a great need of a good book on career guidance, particularly keeping in mind the changing nature of the new world of work.

The work at hand is an attempt to fulfill this need of our people for the good of our nation in the face of changing pattern of socio-economic, socio-political, socio-educational and socio-cultural systems, which are taking complex shape due to advancement in science and technology, which is instrumental in changing the existing world of work and effects the nature of human behaviour and his adjustment with his formality, community and society.

This book on career guidance and counselling: Principles and Techniques is a study of basic concepts, strategies and techniques of career guidance, methods of understanding the individual needing career guidance, avenues of career guidance in academic arena, need and methodology of discovering human resource and creative talent and having a forword look on the emerging careers in the new world of work and the nature of career guidance to face the problems of ever changing world of work.

The book contains 30 chapters and has been divided in six parts, captioned as follows:

1. Conceptual Aspects
2. Strategies and Techniques
3. Understanding the Counsellee
4. Avenues of Guidance
5. Discovery of Human Resource and Creative Talent
6. Emerging World of Work, Careers and Need and Nature of Guidance.

Among the several books, mostly western publications, on career guidance this book claims to be most comprehensive description and analysis of the concepts, principles, strategies and techniques of career guidance including techniques methods of understanding the counselee and averseness of career guidance in academic career, which discussed in part I, II, III and IV of this book respectively. It covers the syllabi of all the Indian universities on the subject in simple and lucid language.

The concepts covered in part V and VI of this book are the most distinctive and unique features of this book which are described hereunder:

Part five of this book "Discovery of Human Resource and Creative Talent" is an outstanding feature of this book. To the best of my knowledge—this concept does not find place in any Indian or Western publication on the subject as such, but since this aspect is of vital importance, therefore, we have devoted five chapters to discuss this vital aspect in this book, which are captioned as, 1. Basic Goal of Career Guidance—The Discovery and Utilization of Human Resource, 2. Creative Talent and Goals of Career Guidance, 3. Career Guidance—The Need for Identification of Creative Talent, 4. Career Guidance—The Process of Identifying Creative Talent, and 5. Career Guidance—How to Face the Problems of Maintaining Creativity.

A like part five part six of this "Emerging World of Work" Careers and Guidance, is the most outstanding feature of the work at hand. To the best of my knowledge—this concept does not find place in any Indian or Western publication on Career guidance, but since in the face of changing nature of the world of work this aspect is of Vital importance, therefore, to make this work as most outstanding we have devoted five chapters to discuss in Vital aspect in this book, which are captioned as, 1. Emerging Careers in the New World of Work and the Role of Institutions of Learning, 2. Forword Look—Prospects of Some Emerging Careers in the New World of Work Identified, 3. Some Low Profile Areas with High Profile Career Opportunity, 4. Forword Look on the Impact of Emerging World Work on Career Guidance and 5. Emerging World of Work—The Need of Guidance for Adults.

Thus, the concepts and aspects covered in this book, in # are not available any other single Indian or Western publications, hence, this book rightly claims to be most comprehensive in its nature and anylised.

Planned as a text book for the students and reference book for the specialists, scholars teachers and guidance workers this book is a critical and constructive appraisal of the subject and I have tried my best to make this book the best for the intellectuals, yet I feel that the reader are the best judge of its merits, therefore, suggestions to enhance the value of the work at hand will be gratefully received and attend to.

Shashi Prabha Sharma

Contents

PART II
STRATEGIES AND TECHNIQUES

PART IV
AVENUES OF GUIDANCE

PART I
CONCEPTUAL ASPECTS

1

Guidance and Counselling: A Historical Perspective

Guidance as a concept in practice in human society is and old as family and community and thus the principles of guidance are deep-rooted in the our socio-educational system and they have always influenced human behaviours and personality.

There always have been and will continue to be people with an occasional need for the help of older or more experienced associates in meeting problem situations; nor is it difficult to find someone who is more than willing to respond to requests for such assistance. In fact, every family or community group probably includes at least one person who delights in offering gratuitous advice to his fellows. The 'adviser' considers himself well qualified to direct the behaviour of others, to serve as mentor or guide in the conduct of their daily affairs.

The guidance movement is a young one, perhaps but a freshet in the longer view, having a history of only a little over eighty years. But this is enough to create many pools and eddies in the current of what does, or should, constitute the main stream. The role of the guidance worker is changing and it will continue to do so. Change is the guidance way of life. Much depends on the person's orientation, his self-concept, and his response to the challenges and opportunities of kaleidoscopic change. Whether he will drift along like a twig on the Columbia or swim, sail, or harness the power and check the flow depends on his choice and his abilities. Such are the choices and considerations dealt with in this chapter.

HISTORY OF THE GUIDANCE MOVEMENT

In 1908, Frank Parsons, working in a Boston settlement house, became sufficiently concerned about the rapidity of social change that he proposed and developed an occupational counselling programme for young people seeking a job.

His plan embraced educational and moral aspects which recognized the need for and nature of, the division of labour, the growth of technology, the need for extending vocational education, and the implications of our democratic orientation.

Parsons believed that vocational counselling would lead to greater individual fulfilment as well as to more efficient and humane industrial system. Within a year his Vocational Bureau began to work in cooperation with the Boston schools to guide children and adolescents into suitable schools and curricula. No longer were the young people following faithfully in the footsteps of their parents; and Parsons' insight into the resultant perplexities and his subsequent action led to his being called the "father of the guidance movement."

The enduring out come of Parsons' work is the development of occupational information. Today counsellors are moving away from the concept of studying jobs to one which emphasizes the willingness and ability of the individual to change and meet new demands as the culture develops. There is even the further rather frightening prospect, postulated by some, that automation and cybernation may render it unnecessary for many persons to work at all-in the traditional sense of the term.

And thus arises the need for concern about the individual's total life and future. Perhaps for different reasons, this sort of thinking was what led Davis, working in. Grand Rapids, Michigan, in 1908, to add to vocational guidance such aspects as moral guidance, course selection, counselling regarding cocurricular activities, and respect for the social side of complete living by using group guidance. Other school systems in New York, Chicago, Cincinnati, and Philadelphia began comparable programmes at about the same time.

The psychological cupboard did not remain bare for long. Walter Dill Scott and Robert M. Yerkes helped develop tests for the armed services. The inclination to use tests gained much impetus during World War I. The Q (qualification) card was developed at that time and was used extensively during World War II. Parallel developments in the School were the cumulative folder or the cumulative record, and the introduction of intelligence tests.

A steady stream of occupational information has continued since the days of Parsons and the counsellor today receives almost daily some pamphlet, brochure, booklet, or advertisement of a book about some phase of occupations and occupational orientation.

Similarly, there is experimentation, improvisation, and re-examination of tests so that one of the largest volumes in the counsellor's stock of resources in the *Mental Measurements Yearbook* which is published at intervals of five to ten years and the contents are not repeated. The Yearbook describes newly developed tests of intelligence, personality, and subject areas and evaluated them in terms of utility and scholarly construction.

The growth of information and tests, inventories, and questionnaires has been accomplished by a stocking of the cupboards of psychological information regarding the nature of the individual and measured with much more statistical accuracy.

No exact date for the emergence of the importance of the individual in the guidance process can be selected but by 1930 the emphasis was clearly discernible. Test data about the individual were part of the clinical study of him—the other major part was the information which could be obtained by the skilled counsellor about interests, values, prejudices, hopes, and aspirations.

Whether test data or interview data are more significant is one of the disturbing eddies in the course of personnel work. It is to be hoped that counsellors will see the value of both tests and interviews and set a course rather than to dissipate their energy in the discussion of which should receive priority.

The mental hygiene movement and the introduction of child guidance clinics—reflecting concern for the individual—were other influences in shaping the nature of guidance in the school. The mental hygiene movement began in 1909 with the establishment of the National Committee for Mental Hygiene.

The Committee's definition of mental health might well state the concern which counsellors have for their pupils in the school. "Mental health may be defined as the adjustment of individuals to themselves and the world at large with a maximum of effectiveness, satisfactions, cheerfulness, and socially considerate behaviour, and the ability to face and accept the realities of life."

The first child guidance clinic was an outgrowth of the 1909 experiences of a husband and wife medical team, Drs. Healy, when working with children in Chicago slums. Today the school counsellor finds frequent occasions when he can work, to the mutual benefit of the clinic, the school and the child, with local child guidance clinics now existing in both small and large communities throughout the nation.

The National Vocational Guidance Association (NVGA) was founded in USA in 1913, at which times three guidance needs were identified: economic—more efficient use and distribution of workers in industry, educational—appropriate courses for pupils, and social-the preservation of societal values.

The Association was reorganised in 1920, at which time the importance of grass-roots emphases was recognised. Seven branches were used as the elements of a federation. By 1952 the number of branches had grown to eighty-six. Members were guidance workers in elementary and secondary schools, college counsellors, and personnel from government, industry, and business.

The federal government has played an increasingly important role in the development of guidance since 1936. At that time the President's Advisory Committee on Education made recommendations for guidance on the national level. The George-Dean Act of 1936 re-emphasised the purpose of the Smith-Hughes Act of 1917 in supporting vocational education in schools.

The George-Barden Act of 1946 expanded federal activity by lending support to the guidance services. The National Defense Education Act of 1958 provided, under Title V-A, support for local school districts in providing better facilities, testing programmes, and for secondary school guidance activities. Title V-B provided for the establishment of Counselling and Guidance Institutes, with stipends for enrollees, for those who wished to prepare, or upgrade their qualifications, for secondary school counselling.

In 1964 the act was revised to make similar provisions for elementary school and personnel. The federal government has published, or encouraged publication of, materials on the gifted child, the dropout and the potential dropout, and on the culturally disadvantaged with particular emphasis on the role of counsellors.

In 1966 there was a strong surge of interest in establishing a position and policy for the role and preparation of elementary school counsellors.

In 1952 the NVGA, because of varied interests and insights into the ramifications of vocational guidance, merged with several associations having similar concern. The new organisation. The American Personnel and Guidance Association, consists of the following divisions, with the title of the corresponding publication being indicated:

- American College Personnel Association, *Journal of College Student Personnel* (bimonthly),
- Association for Counsellor Education and Supervision, *Counsellor Education and Supervision* (quarterly),
- National Vocational Guidance Association, *Vocational Guidance Quarterly,*
- Student Personnel Association for Teacher Education, *The SPATE Journal* (3 issues yearly),
- American School Counsellor Association,*The School Counsellor* (quarterly),
- American Rehabilitation Counselling Association, *Rehabilitation Counsellor Bulletin* (quarterly),
- Association for Measurement and Evaluation in Guidance newsletter (frequency open to need) *National Employment Counsellor Association.*

OBJECTIVE OF THIS STUDY

Presentation of this brief history of guidance is done to achieve three objectives. One of these is to begin the establishment of a rationale for the many emphases which now comprise guidance programs. Thus, we have seen in this preliminary chapter the origin and reasons for focus on vocations. It has been shown how the testing movements become *a part* of the guidance programme.

The gradual emergence of the focus on the individual, rather than on a problem such as vocational orientation or facile adjustment to school, has been at least implied. More and more people are realizing that a vocational choice is a personal problem involving family, friends, future, economics, and ethics—hence a cultural matter.

A second reason for the significance of the historical presentation is to show that guidance workers are not alone. The frustrations and disappointments inherent in the helping relationship are shared by others. On the other hand, the accomplishments and the gratifications one experiences are enhanced as they are seen to be helpful to others.

The third reason for studying the history may be but an extension of the second—the study of the many threads of history and the emergence of new ideas may serve to warn the individual against encapsulation. In a field developing as rapidly as guidance and counselling it can only be assumed that the next few years will yield many insights, suggest new emphases, and present more opportunities for innovation.

History warns against the danger of becoming arrested at the stage of vocational guidance—as some have been. It warns against overemphasizing tests—as some do. It warns against the temptation to accept all the 'folklore' presented in a counselling interview—as some so accept.

Paul Mort is credited with asserting that it takes forty years for a proven idea to be accepted in the schools. Today with 50 per cent of elementary students having no footsteps, parental or any others, to follow it is well that over forty years have passed and the idea of guidance has been accepted.

Today the problem is one of getting enough qualified counsellors to do the job, and enough inspired counsellors to envision the paths that have not as yet been clearly blazed.

Thus we see that officially in USA, guidance gained national recognition in 1936 but due to World War II much efforts were not made by the government to develop it, which was done in 1946 and re-emphasised in 1958. Following USA's example other nations also recognised national, social and educational importance of guidance and accordingly introduced some programmes.

We in India accepted this concept in theory after 1962 and thereafter too the guidance programmes are just a official formality. We need to do a lot to have the benefits of this programme for the good of the nation.

QUESTIONS FOR ANSWER

1. *Write a brief note on the history of guidance movement in USA, which has become a world movement at present.*
2. *Write short note on the following:*
   (a) Objectives of the history of guidance.
   (b) Why Parsons is called 'father of guidance movement'.
   (c) Divisions of American Personnel and guidance Association.

2

Guidance Movement in India: A Brief Review

INTRODUCTION

In the ancient Universities of our country like Nalanda and Taxila, we are told, the learned monks were sagacious and wise in their handling of students. They were occupied with the process of guidance and counselling, of course informal and incidental—right from admission of students to these seats of higher learning to seeing them through to enter the world of work and face life. The process was highly successful as these monks knew the students through and through and no undesirable element could either enter or stay in the universities.

Even the old Gurukula system of this ancient land was very healthy and led to harmonious relations between the teacher and the taught. All this was possible because the number of students was small, courses of study were simple and job opportunities were limited and world of work was more or less stable and students had few problems.

Now with the tremendous increase in the number of students in the institutions of higher learning, extremely wide range of courses of study and job opportunities, rapidly changing world of work and great complexity of students' needs and problems, there is a definite need for providing a fine nucleus for an *organised programme of professional help*, in the form of guidance and counselling by mature, experienced and professionally qualified persons for the development of all the unique potentialities of the students for individual fulfilment in particular and social and national uplift in general.

COUNSELLING IN MODERN INDIA

During the past few decades, attempts have been made to set up counselling centres at various universities.

Patna University is said to be the first institution in India to pay attention to the problems of college students. In 1945, the Department of Psychological Research and Services was established with the dual purpose of providing counselling service to the students as well as conducting research in psychology. Counselling of college students was one of the projects of the university.

In 1955, St. Xavier College, Bombay, started counselling students with an emphasis on *religious counselling*. Later, in 1960, it shifted its emphasis to the *personal and social problems of* students. The college also published a useful brochure—*Success in College,*— which gives guidance to the students for tackling varied problems which they might face in college life.

The credit for establishing the first full time counselling service for college students goes to the MS University, Baroda. In 1958, at the invitation of the University Grants Commission, the University of Baroda prepared a plan of a counselling center with full time staff to cater to the needs of its students. The plan included practical service to students with educational and vocational problems, research related to guidance and counselling and training of guidance personnel. The plan was approved by University Grants Commission and the Student Counselling Centre of the university was set up in 1959. This Centre did following commendable works:

(*i*) conducted a study of student problems and developed an adjustment inventory on the basis of the study;

(*ii*) published a series of pamphlets devoted to typical case studies;

(*iii*) prepared some measuring tools like Family Attitude Test for use with children and young adolescents; the Gujarati version of Wechsler's Adult Intelligence Scale; Abstract Reasoning Test; Selection Test for the Faculty of Engineering, etc;

(*iv*) prepared a handbook for developing guidance and counselling for the in-service school teachers, and;

(*v*) organised some seminars for teachers in small towns and villages.

The centre became well-known in India therefore, some consultants from USA visited the centre and often helped in its organisation and development.

In 1961, Allahabad University also organised a Counselling Centre for its students with the assistance of the United States Educational Foundation in India. From 1961-65, the Foundation placed one exchange professor either on full-time basis or to be shared between the Departments of Education and psychology, with the specific assignment to help developing a student counselling centre.

The Foundation and the UGC collaborated in the noble venture. For example, if the UGC were to support one post of a counsellor, the Foundation would match it with another post entirely supported by the Foundation. Unfortunately, the centre was closed down in 1966 and very useful work done by the centre came to an end.

In 1963, Wilson College, Bombay set up a counselling centre for its students. Later, the college set up an office of the Dean of Students with a comprehensive programme of student services.

In 1964-65, Delhi University informally started a programme of counselling in the Department of Psychology under the care of a lecturer in Psychology. A paper in counselling was also introduced as a part of the curriculum for the Master's degree in Psychology. A survey of student problems, too, was conducted by the Department. Unfortunately, the work did not continue for long.

In 1965-66, Annamalai University also started a counselling centre for its students with the help of a Full-bright Professor. But this did not succeed as the administration could not decide whether the counselling centre should be placed in the Department of Education, Psychology or philosophy. The SNDT Women's University, Bombay, has appointed a dean of students who is providing student personnel services on a modest scale.

In 1967, a student counselling centre was started for the students of the Panjab University, Chandigarh, on the recommendation of the Mental Health Expert Group of the Indian Council of Medical Research. The centre undertook a study of mental health of failed students of the Panjab University. It was also hoped that the centre would fulfil a long felt need to attend to the psychiatric problems of university students. The centre offers counselling facility to students in need of adjustment and also helps in the orientation and placement programme.

In 1952, the Vocational Guidance Association of Bombay was formed to help in the co-ordination of the work done by individuals in Bombay. Later at the initiative of Dr. Barnette, effort was made to co-ordinate the individual work all over the country. Barnette brought all the guidance workers together in a seminar in 1952 in Central Institute of Education, New Delhi. An opportunity was provided to guidance personnel to exchange ideas and problems with their colleagues and others interested in guidance. Later, in 1954, another seminar was conducted which took the decision to form an All India Educational and Vocational Guidance Association. Two years later, in 1956, the association was formed during a meeting held at the M.S. University of Baroda.

Bombay was the next to give official recognition to guidance programme. The Bureau of Vocational Guidance, Bombay was set up in 1950. Since 1957, the Bureau has been renamed and is functioning as the Institute of Vocational Guidance, Bombay. It gave a much wider interpretation to guidance, selection and training of guidance personnel and planned emphasis on collection and dissemination of occupational information.

GUIDANCE MOVEMENT IN INDIA

Guidance as an organised professional activity is more than four decades old in our country. While in America the guidance movement started as an attempt to fulfil the practical needs of employers and teachers, in India it began as an academic discipline. Calcutta University enjoys the privilege of being the first Indian university to introduce guidance as a section of its Department of Applied Psychology in 1938.

The main aim of the section was to conduct research in the field of educational and vocational guidance. Later, the Department also started the work on occupational information. Certain occupations were analysed and major occupations were classified into four categories according to the level of intelligence and the type of abilities required to fill these jobs.

Bombay did not lag behind in initiating programme of guidance. In 1941, Baltiboi a retired accountant working in Calcutta, realised the implications of guidance. With the help of a psychologist—Mr. Mukerjee from Calcutta University, Baltiboi set up the Baltiboi Vocational Guidance Bureau in Bombay with the sole purpose of providing guidance services to the community.

Guidance movement received another push forward when Trustees of the Parsi Panchayat Funds and Properties in Bombay decided to establish a guidance services bureau-Parsi Panchayat Vocational Guidance bureau-for the Parsi community in Bombay. This bureau worked on meagre resources and scanty staff but with the help of devoted workers it was able to do a great deal of useful pioneering work in guidance. It was this bureau which organised a career conference for the first time to disseminate occupational information. It was also the first institution to organise a course for career masters.

The bureau also started publishing the *Journal of Educational and Vocational Guidance* which provided the guidance workers with a professional organ of communication and interchange of ideas and information regarding research and practice in the field. Another step forward was taken by the Government of Uttar Pradesh, when it gave official recognition to the movement by setting up a Bureau of Psychology at Allahabad in 1947.

EDUCATIONAL GUIDANCE

The Ministry of Education, Government of India realised the need and importance of providing educational guidance for the deserving students. It set up 13 students' Advisory Bureaux which are functioning at various universities. These bureaux were set up to render services to the students pursuing higher studies in England for I.C.S., F.R.C.S., Bar-at-law, etc. Later on, their scope was widened to include other countries and the work of finding suitable employment for those who returned from foreign countries.

These bureaux.

(*i*) help in creating among students keen desire to know and plan their future;

(*ii*) encourage them to increase their knowledge about

educational developments, activities and facilities in India and abroad;

(*iii*) disseminate information on higher education, research and training in India and abroad to the students;

(*iv*) maintain educational information libraries for the use of students;

(*v*) supply application forms for admission to educational institutions and universities in foreign countries; and

(*vi*) hold orientation courses for the benefit of students passing out of the university.

The Academic advisers who head the students advisory Bureaux are under the Dean, University Instruction.

VOCATIONAL GUIDANCE

A Study Group on Educated Unemployed, in 1956, recommended the establishment of the bureaux in the universities to provide their alumni with *employment information* and *career guidance,* Later, in 1957, the scheme for the setting up of the bureaux was prepared by the Directorate General of Employment and Training. The scheme envisaged bureaux to be primarily *employment counselling agencies* but they could also function as *placement agencies* for professional and highly qualified persons.

It was also intended that bureaux would cater to the needs of all students of the universities whether still pursuing studies or about to leave after completing their education. Some universities are having both the Students' Advisory Bureau and University Employment Information Bureau.

The vocational guidance programme, under the supervision of the Directorate of Employment, Training and Rehabilitation, is being carried on by the employment exchanges. There is a State Vocational Guidance Officer in each state and a network of employment exchanges.

The programme has been further strengthened under a national policy formulated by the Ministry of Labour and Employment, Government of India. Regarding this policy, the Ministry has received both moral and material support from the International Labour Office (ILO). The Central Institute of Research and Training in Employment Services (CRTES) has been set up to further strengthen the programme through research training and career study.

The UGC in consultation with the Ministry of Education and Social Welfare and Ministry of Labour, feeling the necessity of career guidance for college students, recommended that career advising units should be established in all colleges. As a result of this recommendation, career advising units were set up in selected colleges of the country.

At this time, vocational guidance literature is prepared by various agencies as Central Institute of Research and Training in Employment Service, D.G.E. and T., Ministry of Education and Social Welfare, Ministry of Health, Family Planning, Works, Hosing, Urban Development, National Council of Educational Research and Training, University Grants Commission, Central Statistical Organisation, Council of Scientific and Industrial Research, Indian Council of Agricultural Research, State Guidance Bureaux, University Employment Information and Guidance Bureaux, Ministry of Information and Broadcasting, State Directorates of Employment and Training, etc.

It is obvious that the necessity for vocational guidance was felt by various ministries and institutions and they made efforts to impart vocational guidance in their own way. It is also clear that vocational guidance programme has a structure, a policy and a programme for both the colleges and the universities.

GOVERNMENT POLICY ON GUIDANCE

(A) The Education Commission 1964-66

The Education Commission (1964-66), while lamenting on the inadequacy of provision for student welfare in the institutions of higher learning, recommended the inclusion of guidance and counselling including vocational placement, among student services. It stressed:

A guidance and counselling programme which would assist the students in the choice of courses, indicate the lines of remedial action and help in dealing with emotional and psychological problems, should be an integral part of the educational facilities provided in institutions of higher education.

For an effective guidance service, the Commission recommended:

(*i*) There should be at least one counsellor for every one

thousand students on the roll. Smaller institutions may share a counsellor who should work in each of the institutions on a part-time basis;

(*ii*) A project for the training of professionally trained counsellors should be organised in some university competent to do; and

(*iii*) The Students Advisory Bureaux and University Employment and Guidance Bureaux should be combined to form an information and employment centre which should function directly under the Dean of students.

(B) The Draft National Policy on Education, 1979

The Draft National policy on Educational of the Ministry of Education, Government of India, does not contain any thing on guidance and counselling service either in schools or in institutions of higher learning. The words 'guidance' and 'counselling' are nowhere mentioned in the National Policy Note.

The UGC, too, has not earmarked any funds for this important student service.

COMPARATIVE PATTERN IN DIFFERENT COUNTRIES

Student Personnel Services is the name given to guidance for college students in USA and it covers the areas of help and guidance in housing, in securing adequate financial aid including part-time jobs, placement in an appropriate job after graduation, psychological help with personal and social problems, participation in co-curricular activities ands advising in academic and non-academic matters as well as under residential conditions.

These services have evolved gradually in American, British Canadian and Australian universities, over the last many years. They grew out of the deep conviction that education involves the whole person as an individual with his own problems which must be resolved if he is to derive the greatest possible benefit from the academic aspects of his college and university experience.

The student personnel programme involves the faculty and the administrative officials as well as the counselling specialists. The universities and colleges are generally well-equipped for assisting their students in achieving the best development of their potentials through effective and efficient of the resources of the institutions.

The guidance and counselling services have the following pattern in these universities:

1. *Career placement services* which is usually done by our employment exchanges.
2. *Career counselling* which includes career information services, career information library, administration of aptitude tests, etc.
3. *General counselling services* which include assistance in solving personal, social and other general problems of confidential nature related to the students-their emotional adjustments, their relations with parents, the teachers and others, etc.
4. Other services include:
   (*a*) Health service,
   (*b*) Union activities which offer legal protection, and
   (*c*) Student housing.

All the above activities are dealt by separates divisions headed by educationists. Almost all the western universities or colleges have each of this division or a combination of these divisions. The services are well utilised by students. This has helped a lot in the control of students problems.

The Present Position in Our Country

At this time, Students Advisory Bureaux under the Ministry of Education, and University Employment Information and Guidance Bureaux under National Employment Service are imparting educational and vocational information and guidance respectively to the students. Both these are working under different deans in the same university.

There is a lack of central direction and co-ordination resulting in a lot of duplication effort and wastage of resources. The career advising units in colleges, too, are existing in name only. They have not made their presence felt in the institutions due to a lack of sense of commitment in the Liaison officers, and patronage and support on the part of administration on the one hand and lack of latest occupational information material on the other.

The *integrated* programme of guidance composed of vocational, education and other important and desirable aspects of guidance and counselling for dealing with emotional and psychological problems of students, has not been introduced anywhere. Of late, there has been an emphasis on student welfare services.

Unfortunately, guidance and counselling do not occupy an important place in these services. Some universities have created the post of a student counsellor. A few serious minded counsellors are doing useful work, but their number is very small. Most of these counsellors are not well qualified. It has also been observed that these counsellors are busy with odd jobs assigned to them by the Dean, Student Welfare Services.

So far we have not taken any steps of train counsellors for working in universities and colleges. Here we are confronted with a dilemma. If we start producing trained counsellors, we do not have job opportunities for them.

The said Commission had also recommended that some competent university should take up the task of training the counsellors, but unfortunately, no university has felt so far the urgency of starting a training programme at the post-graduate level because there is no immediate plan before the universities to introduce counselling service as one of the major programmes under student services.

There is no national organisation which could handle effectively the entire guidance and counselling programme. The Ministry of Education, the Ministry of Labour and Employment, the University Grants Commission, are all singing different tunes-the net result is not very significant. There is lack of a coordinated well-knit picture. The concept of guidance in colleges and universities is narrowed down to one aspect of guidance, namely *vocational guidance*.

This may consist of taking intelligence, aptitude and interest tests and imparting some occupational information. This type of guidance is very good, and it should be available to students in every college. It certainly means a step forward in the right direction. But at the same time, it is essential in the present context, particularly to focus our attention on personality counselling and this is what is missing now.

There is an unfortunate absence of a national policy, clear-cut, straight-forward and viable on guidance and counselling. There is lack of direction and coordination, supervision and planning, administrative support and finances. That an urgent case for the introduction of this service exists was emphasised by the Indian Education Commission (1964-66) and convincingly brought to light by an empirical study undertaken several years ago by the All India Educational and Vocational Guidance Association. Its report was printed (1965) and circulated but nothing happened.

Time is ripe that in the wake of innumerable student needs and problems and an urgent need to channelise the national talent, we evolve a clear-cut policy regarding the introduction of this essential service in our colleges and universities. The earlier we do the better it will be.

QUESTIONS FOR ANSWER

1. *Write brief note on the guidance and counselling movement in India.*
2. *Write short note on the following:*
   (a) The Education Commission (1964-66) on Guidance and Counselling.
   (b) Comparative Pattern of Guidance in Different Countries.

3

Guidance: Some Conceptual and Basic Features

INTRODUCTION

The person who has ability or sense enough to work as befits his status in society is the one who wins the acclaim of society and its approval as well. It is in the performance of these various roles and duties, which conform to his differing statuses, that he needs guidance. In this way, the psychologist's guidance helps the individual fit into his role and status in society. Every individual is not fit to take up any and every position in society. Teaching, doctoring, advocacy and a variety of other professions are not jobs that require the same individual qualities from the person occupied in doing them.

Introducing fitness in an individual to occupy some position is a matter that has two aspects. The first is that his ability should be commensurate with the requirements of the jobs and the second that he should try to become qualified to occupy that position. The second of these aspects has some limitations.

Whatever the effort expended every person cannot become an artist or author, because every individual does not have the ability or quality to adopt any and every profession. Even every individual cannot become a successful trader as that requires a definite shrewd and calculating mentality that is not possessed by every one. Hence, in order to prove able for some particular position a person should choose the position that concurs with his capabilities and qualities.

The Indian cultural traditions since the inception of human civilization bear a mark that elder members of the family, teachers and wiseman of the community always guided the budding generations to achieve the maximum as per their capacities and abilities and make intelligent choices and adjustments in the family, community and society.

To some extent this is appreciable to each and every society in the world. But formally the concept of guidance in the academic Western World is not even hundred-years old and as a formal academic concept for study in educational institutions not even fifty years old, thus though this concept is very new yet its field is very wide and its nature is very comprehensive, therefore, it is not possible to define the concept of guidance in a universally accepted manner. The nature of the concept of guidance may be discussed and understood as follows:

BASIC FUNCTION OF GUIDANCE

To define guidance in clear-cut words is not easy. It has been defined in varied ways: Crow and Crow write, "Guidance is not direction. It is not the imposition of one's point of view upon another. It is not making decisions for an individual, which he should make for himself. It is not carrying the burden of another's life. Rather, guidance is assistance made available by competent counsellors to an individual of any age to help him direct his own life, develop his own point of view, make his own decisions, carry his own burdens."

Hamrin and Erickson define guidance as "that aspect of educational programme which is concerned especially with helping the pupil to become adjusted to his present situation and to pupil to become adjusted to his present situation and to plan his future in line with his interests, abilities, and social needs."

Guidance is the assistance given to individuals in making intelligent choices and adjustments. It is based on the democratic principle that it is the duty and the right of every individual to choose his own way in life in so far as his choice does not interfere with the rights of others. The ability to make such choices is not innate but, like other abilities, must be developed. One of the functions of education is to provide opportunities for the development of such abilities.

Guidance is an integral part of education and is centered directly upon this function. Guidance does not make choices for individuals; it help them make their own choices in such a way as to promote to stimulate the gradual development of the ability to make decisions independently without assistance from others.

The basic function of guidance is, of course, to help individuals who need or seek assistance in the meeting of problem situations. The kind and amount of help provided by individuals or groups depend upon their understanding of the guidance concept.

BASIC AIM OF EDUCATION AND GUIDANCE

Basic aim of education is all round harmonious development of individuals, which may be understood as follows:

P_D = Physical Development
S_D = Spiritual Development
I_D = Intellectual Development

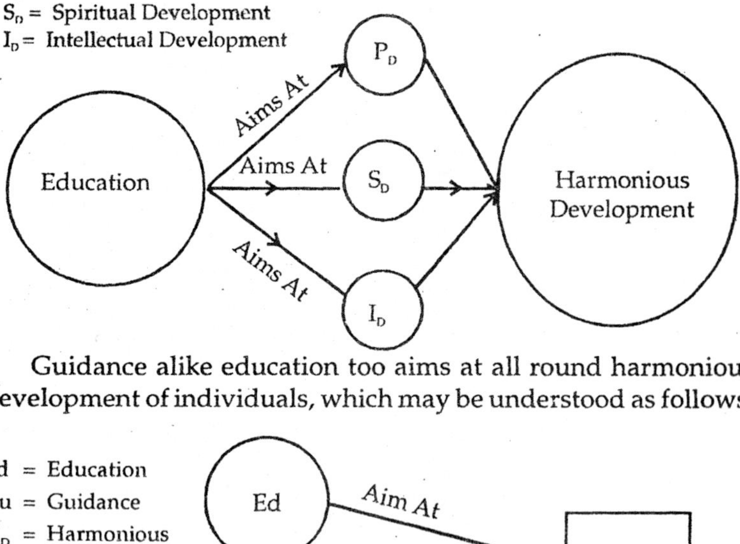

Guidance alike education too aims at all round harmonious development of individuals, which may be understood as follows:

Ed = Education
Gu = Guidance
H_D = Harmonious Development

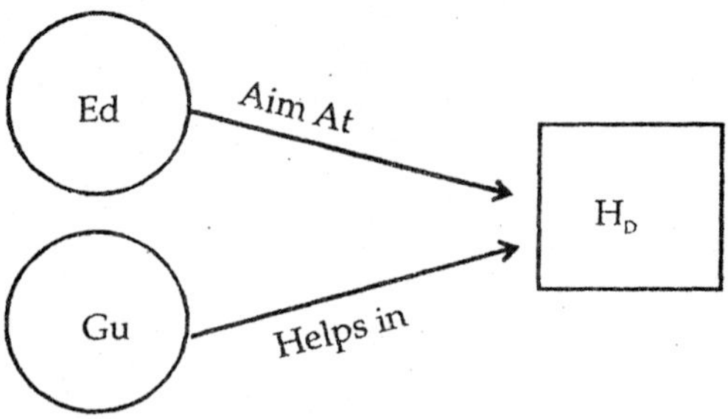

MEANING AND DEFINITION OF GUIDANCE

The above discussed nature of basic function of guidance and basic aim of guidance and education gives a clear picture to enable us to understand the meaning and definition of guidance, which we will discuss, in detail, as here under:

MEANING OF GUIDANCE

In its beginnings guidance was centered on problems related to vocations. It was largely concerned with getting jobs for young people. One of the reasons for this was to reduce juvenile delinquency. Teen-age boys and girls, many of them not in school, had nothing to do; they had time on their hands. Such a situation breeds delinquency.

Even in its beginning, however, the purpose of guidance was more than just for finding jobs for youth. Much attention was given to a 'wise' choice, that is, one that was suited to the abilities and needs of the individual.

Although the vocational aspect has always been stressed, guidance has gone far beyond this; it is now concerned with the entire individual, in all aspects of his life, and with the interrelation between the individual and society. It helps youth to attain a life that is individually satisfying and socially effective.

When we stress the fact that everyone, at one time or another may be in need of guidance, we must be sure that we understand to thoroughly just what it is that he needs and should have made available for his use. Guidance is not giving directions.

It is *not* the imposition of one person's point of view upon another person. It is not making decisions for an individual, which he should make for himself. It is not carrying the burdens of another's life.

Shirley Hamrin's definition of guidance as "helping john to see through himself in order that he may see himself through" is a simple and practical but challenging concept of guidance. This statement represents much more than a facile arrangement of words. Once the guidance worker has led an individual to see the extent of his guidance needs, any further help given him in solving his difficulties or problems requires patience, understanding, and experience combined with training, if the individual is to receive the kind and amount of assistance that will bring about desirable adjustment.

Whenever a person is aided directly or indirectly by another person in gaining in knowledge, emotional fitness, mental acuity or stability, social and civic adjustment or occupational efficiency and job satisfaction, guidance of one kind or another is functioning. It will be noted that guidance, thus conceived, increases the individual's power to think and perform. It should not be considered an activity having for its purpose the lessening of an individual's ability to act independently or to follow his own initiative.

Guidance is operating whenever a child, adolescent, or adult is helped in any way by another person or persons to come to a decision, improve his behaviour, or change his attitude concerning people or things.

Adults are constantly guiding the life of a young person, either by precept or by example. This is accomplished many times without specific purpose or even awareness on the part of the person who is responsible for the guidance.

The young person who has benefited from his association with a fine adult, who has imitated his behaviour, or who has been influenced by his words may be equally unaware of the eventual effect upon him of what he has observed or heard.

DEFINITION OF GUIDANCE

Mathewson believes that "guidance is the systematic professional process of helping the individual through education and interpretative procedures to gain better understanding of his own characteristics and potentialities and to relate himself more satisfactorily to social requirements and opportunities in accord with social and moral values."

Traxler considers guidance as a help which enables "each individual to understand his abilities and interests, to develop them as well as possible and to relate them to life-goals, and finally to reach a state of complete and mature self-guidance as a desirable member of the social order."

According to Jones, "Guidance involves personal help given by someone; it is designed to assist a person to decide where he wants to go, what he wants to do or how he can best accomplish his purpose; it assists him to solve problems that arise in his life." This is one aspect only.

"Guidance is an attempt to individualize education. Each pupil should be helped to develop himself in the maximum possible degree in all respects." —*Kitson*

"Guidance is a service designed to help one individual or group of individuals in making necessary adjustment to environment whether that be within the school or outside it."

—*Proctor*

"Fundamental of all the guidance is the help or assistance given by one competent person to another individual so that the latter may direct his life by developing his point of view, make his own decisions and carry out those decisions." —*Crow and Crow*

"Effective education is guidance, and realistic guidance is self-guidance." —*Carmicheal*

"Guidance is inherent in education and as such should be done largely by classroom teacher. He should try to help pupils set up dynamic, reasonable and worthwhile objectives for themselves."

—*Cox*

"Guidance involves personal help to promote the growth of an individual in self-direction. The help may be given to the individual alone or in a group; it is the individual who is the focus of attention and not the group. Also this attention is to be paid to the individual and not to the problem." —*Jones*

"Guidance involves the difficult art of helping boys and girls to plan their own future wisely in the full light of all the factors that can be mastered about themselves and about the world in which they are to live and work." Quoted by Indu Dave in a paper 'The Initial Interview' published in '*Siksa*', October, 1958.

'Guidance is the process of assisting the individual to choose, to prepare, to enter upon and progress in course of action pertaining to the educational, vocational, recreational and community services." —*Manual of Educational and Vocational Guidance*: Ministry of Education, Government of India.

"Guidance is process of helping individuals through their own efforts to discover and develop their potentialities both for personal happiness and social usefulness." —*Labh Singh*

"All guidance is education, but some aspects of education are not guidance, the objectives of both education and guidance may be the same viz., the development of individual, but the methods used are different." —*B.B. Taneja*

"Assistance given to an individual in solving problems related to occupational choice and progress with due regard for the individual's characteristics and their relation to occupational opportunity." —*The General Conference*, ILO, 1949.

THE SCOPE OF GUIDANCE

The term guidance represents a concept that is neither simple nor easily understood. The complexity of human nature, developmental differences even among offspring of the same parents, personal and social problems associated with changing environmental conditions and cultural mores—all require that many and various guidance approaches be utilized.

Guidance is a process. As such, it defies exact definition. A former students of the authors, now la full-time school guidance counsellor, was asked to define guidance. Her reply was, "What is guidance? To me it's a twenty-four-hour job!" Indeed, for anyone who sincerely desires to meet his guidance responsibilities, the challenge of offering effective guidance services is broad and deep.

The scope of guidance and counselling is extremely comprehensive. As the life is getting complex day by day, the problems for which expert help is required are increasing proportionately. The scope of guidance, per necessity, is extending horizontally to much of the social context, to matters of prestige in occupations, to the broad field of social trends, and economic development.

Guidance is assuming more and more responsibility for the individual in every direction-it helps in the selection of educational courses, and profitable occupation, in job placement; placement in the next stage of education and training; occupational surveys; improvement of study skills, maintenance of mental health; counselling regarding personal adjustment problems; identifying the gifted, the backward and help them achieve the maximum. In short, educational, vocational, avocational, social, personal, moral and even marital problems of individual are the concerns of guidance and counselling. Their scope is indeed very vast.

THE NEED AND IMPORTANCE OF GUIDANCE

Life problems are becoming more and more complex. Traditional mores and personal convictions concerning rightness and wrongness of attitude and behaviour are breaking down. The black-and-white analyses of our Puritan ancestors on matters dealing with human relations are fast giving way to neutral grays. No longer are we able to affirm, unchallenged, that one mode of conduct is completely right and another wrong. Nor are thinking people willing to assert didactically that any person must necessarily behave in the future in a manner similar to his past or present behaviour.

Many diverse factors inherent within our home, school, and social and occupational activities and relationships pull us in different directions. We often find ourselves in such a state of confusion or bewilderment that it is difficult to steer unaided the course of our conduct toward ends which will be satisfying to ourselves and to those about us.

Too often the recognized need for advice or guidance leads us to become the victims of those who set themselves up as authorities in areas of guidance for which they have little or no capacity beyond the power to speak convincingly in a 'patter' of glittering generalities. These generalities may satisfy the listener for the moment, but they do little toward building within him the power to face reality courageously or to gain strength to meet the problems which arise in his life.

According to a statement prepared recently by a representative group of Virginia educators, guidance is necessary in meeting the following needs:

- For each person to find a place in which he enjoys personal happiness.
- To develop a sensitivity for moral and spiritual values.
- To be recognized and respected as an individual.
- For each person to feel that he is making a contribution to any group of which he is a part.
- To understand himself, his abilities, his limitations, and his potentialities.
- For the opportunity to develop and use his abilities and experiences.
- For warmth, affection, and understanding.
- To develop resourcefulness and self-direction in adapting to changes in society.

These statements are based on the belief that "each person is an individual in his own right and has within him the power for change and development. He has capabilities for making desirable choices that will lead to continuing adjustment."

In an annual report to the Superintendent of Schools, the Director of the Department on Guidance and Placement in Medford, Massachusetts, said:

The Objectives of the guidance and counselling programme are to provide services which will meet certain needs in the growth and development of young people, namely:

1. Personal development and adjustment.
   Self-understanding: the discovery of potentialities, special aptitudes, and interests.
   Recognition and development of favourable attitudes and habits, and the elimination of undesirable traits. Self-direction.
2. Educational process and adjustment.
   Selection of appropriate courses in line with individual needs, interests, abilities, and circumstances.
   Choice of the right type of advanced training, college or otherwise.
3. Occupational development and adjustment.
   Information on occupational opportunities and trends.
   Knowledge of occupational fields toward which individual aptitudes and interests may best be directed.
   Help in finding suitable employment.
4. Follow-up after leaving school.
   Research with respect to needs of pupils and the effectiveness of the secondary school curriculum.
   Evaluation of the guidance programme.

The fulfilment of the basic needs as given above for which guidance has assumed the major responsibility will help greatly to meet our present-day situation without damaging freedom of choice.

Guidance functions whenever choices are to be made and where help is needed in making intelligent decisions. Even when there is no choice possible, guidance may help the individual understand and accept the situation; that is, it may enable him to "co-operate with the inevitable."

Guidance may also operate when the individual is not conscious that a choice is possible by pointing out the avenues that are open to him. In still other circumstances the time may not be favourable for making a choice because of fatigue, emotional strain, or influences that will make an intelligent decision unlikely. In such situations the best help may well be to suggest that only those decisions be made which are mandatory, leaving open as many as possible until a later, more favourable, time.

A survey was conducted by the All India Educational and Vocational Guidance Association (1960-61) for gauging college students' needs. Three thousand students from seventeen Indian universities responded. The survey revealed students' felt needs. Eleven problems were marked by more than 50 per cent of the respondents:

1. I cannot do as will in my studies as other people expect me to do.
2. I do not know enough about the qualifications needed for different kinds of work or careers.
3. I worry too much about what my future will be after I have finished my studies.
4. Even though I force myself, my attention will not remain on my assignments long enough to finish them.
5. I do not know how to make friends among the opposite sex.
6. I do not have sufficient information about matters on sex.
7. I do not know enough about my aptitudes and abilities for different kinds of work or careers.
8. It is difficult for me to get the books I need for study.
9. I cannot read fast enough to complete my studies in time.
10. I do not know proper methods of study.
11. I have more difficulty in forgetting my mistakes than I believe I should have.

The eleven areas may be summarised under four headings- *Study habits and skills, Career choice, knowledge of aptitudes and abilities, Sex education.*

The respondents reported that their *parents were the only source of help the received, if any, along these lines and practically no help had been forthcoming from college personnel.*

Eighty per cent of respondents expressed the need of such assistance from their non-parental source. The bigger the college, the bigger the campus, the more the need for personalised student services, else the student will merely feel a small cog in a huge machine.

Another survey of the educational, vocational and personal problems was conducted by Umrudin and Gadri (1964). Widespread maladjustment was rated among hostel residents who showed much concern over problems connected with *study habits, vocational choice, family relationship and mental hygiene.*

All these emerging issues and problems make it obligatory for our educational planners and administrators to build into our higher education an appropriate guidance and counselling programme for the development of the individual student into an adult personality, imbued with social and occupational awareness, intellectual and functional proficiency, discipline and confidence. We can sum-up-the need and importance of guidance with following observation:

"It would not be too much to say that on the success or failure of our guidance programme hangs in all probability, the success or failure of our system of education."

Conant, Former President of Harvard University.

MAIN CHARACTERISTICS OF GUIDANCE

An analysis of above view points and factual considerations concerning need, importance and significance of guidance bear out its following main characteristics:

(*i*) *It is a process.* It helps every individual to help himself, to recognise and use his inner resources, to set goals, to make plans, to work out his own problems of development.

(*ii*) *It is a continuous process.* It is needed right from early childhood, adolescence, adult-hood and even in old age.

(*iii*) *Choice and problem points are the distinctive concerns of guidance* as here the individual's unique world of perceptions interacts with the external order of events in his life context.

(*iv*) *It is assistance to the individual in the process of development rather than a direction of that development.* The aim is to develop the capacity for self-direction, self-guidance and self-improvement through an increased understanding of his problems and his resources as well as limitations to solve the problem.

(*v*) *Guidance is a service meant for all.* It is a regular service which is require at every stage for every student, not only for awkward situations and abnormal students. It is a positive programme geared to meet the needs of all students.

(*vi*) *It is both generalised and a specialised service.* It is a generalised service because everyone-teachers, tutors, advisers, deans, parents—play a part in the programme. It is a specialised service because specially qualified personnel as counsellors, psychiatrists, psychologists join hands to help the individual to get out of his problem.

GOVERNING PRINCIPLES OF GUIDANCE PHILOSOPHY

According to Hollis and Hollis, there are eight principles on which any guidance programme should be based. They can be modified to fit locally accepted beliefs. The principles are:

(*i*) The dignity of the individual is supreme.
(*ii*) Each individual is different from every other individual.
(*iii*) The primary concern of guidance is the individual in his social setting.
(*iv*) The attitudes and personal perceptions of the individual are the bases on which he acts.
(*v*) The individual generally acts to enhance his perceived self.
(*vi*) The individual has the innate ability to learn and can be helped to make choices that will lead to self-direction consistent with social improvement.
(*vii*) The individual needs a continuous guidance process from early childhood through adulthood.
(*viii*) Each individual may at times need the information and personalised assistance best given by competent professional personnel.

GUIDANCE AS AN EDUCATIONAL CONCEPT

Too often informal advice, given without a clear understanding of the problem involved, is likely to be not only ineffectual but harmful and misleading.

During the recent past the term *guidance* has become increasingly popular among laymen and school people. It is one of the most recent catchwords to stir the imagination of men and women eager to improve human welfare.

Popularity of Educational Slogans

Current public interest in guidance is not something entirely new. The first half of the present century was noteworthy for its extensive and intensive research into human development and effective learning. As educators attempted to apply research findings to school situations, certain basic concepts came to be expressed in catchwords or phrases: "education of the whole child," "homogeneity of grouping," community school," "learning by doing," "project method," "core curriculum," "social promotion," "areas of living," "broad fields," and so on. Present emphasis seems to be given especially to "education for world co-operation," and "guidance and personnel service."

GUIDANCE: ITS RELATION TO EDUCATION

Very early in the guidance movement Brewer, a consistent advocate of vocational guidance, recognised the close relationship between guidance and education. Throughout the years the nature of this relationship has been a source of much concern and controversy. The different points of view are largely owing to differences in the meaning of the term 'education'.

'Education' may be used to mean (1) the process of changes that take place within the individual, (2) instruction, or (3) the conscious effort of society to guide and direct the physical, mental, emotional, and moral growth of the individual so that he will be able to live a life that will be socially effective and individually satisfying. To make clear the relationship between guidance and education each of these meanings needs to be examined more closely.

"In actual life, however neither occupations are designed to suit individuals nor are individuals made in order to fit into specifies vocations. It is an educational process in which learning experiences provided in the school, home, and near neighbourhood help to bring about adjustment between the individual and an occupation."

—*Kocher*

Education is the Process of Changes that Take Place within the Individual

From this point of view education is essentially a process; it is something that takes place *in individuals*; It is the process by which changes are made in the individual or, better, by which the individual makes changes in himself.

At birth human beings are the most helpless of all animals. They are absolutely dependent upon others for their very existence. For long years they must be fed, cared for, and protected in order to preserve life and ensure normal growth and development.

Although man essentially has not changed, the structure of society has become tremendously complex. Social demands have so far outstripped man's physical nature that the gap between the social plane of the infant and that of the adult is very wide-impossible to cross, in fact without assistance. As civilization advances, the gap is ever widening.

The method by which the infant is enabled to bridge this gap, to raise himself from the social plane of childhood to that of manhood, is education. This is accomplished by certain changes that are made by the individual so that he acts in appropriate and desirable ways to situations that confront him.

The number of changes and their quality are such as to require long years and special techniques for their development. Education is, then, the process by which the individual makes these necessary changes.

From this point of view education is essentially and wholly an *individual* process. It is some change that takes place in the individual as a result of something that *he* does. It is "the up-building of a world in feeling or consciousness.

Each individual builds for himself the world in which he lives. His images, his memories, his thoughts and feelings, his ideals are formed from his own experience—what he himself does. They are his own, and no one can share them; nor can anyone take them away against his will.

When we view education from this standpoint, there can be no guidance, for guidance implies assistance given by someone to the one who is educating himself. In so far as the individual is really self-educated, there is no guidance; however, if we think of education as resulting only from what the individual himself does—if he is the active agent—what is the relation of instruction to this process?

EDUCATION IS INSTRUCTION AND GUIDANCE

Situations in the classroom are not simple. They are composed of many different stimuli; some of these are the selected stimuli provided by the teacher, but others are supplied by many factors in the immediate environment of the pupil, including the pupil himself.

The child can and often does choose from among the stimuli that make up the situation the one to which he responds. He may single out the teacher's prominent nose, her gaudy dress, the wasp in the window, or any one of a dozen things to which he gives attention and to which he responds, rather than the words of the teacher or the material in his textbook.

Efficient education requires not only that a person respond to a stimulus but that he select the desirable groups of stimuli to which he responds-desirable, that is, from the standpoint of education.

Again, even though he singles out the desired stimulus, he may respond to it in many different ways. Suppose the topic he is studying is the products of South America. He reads the words in his book describing them; these words are the stimuli.

Whenever, in the process of accomplishing the ends (that is, in learning,) the pupil needs help, it is the teacher's function to give it. This help is usually stimuli in the form of outlines, references, suggestions, leading questions, expressions of approval and disapproval, incentives, and anything else that may help the pupil to learn. This is teaching or instruction; it may or may not be guidance. Teaching conceived of as assisting the learner to choose ends or methods is guidance.

Education is a Function of Society

It is a conscious effort on the part of society to guide and direct the physical, mental, emotional, and moral growth of the individual so that he will be able to live a life that will be socially effective and individually satisfying. In this broader concept of education, guidance and education are closely related.

This concept of education might seem to make guidance and education synonymous both when we stress the development of the individual for himself as an end and when we emphasize the needs of society, for education is thought of as the conscious effort of society to assist the individual.

It should be noted, however, that the important words in this sentence are not "the conscious effort of society," but "assist the individual," and the role of society in the education of individuals may not be 'assistance' in the real sense.

When society merely determines what shall be taught and does nothing to assist the individual-when the individual is thought of as passive-guidance is not present except in a very indirect and remote way. In a sense the entire conscious effort of society to see that the individual reaches certain goals set up by society is assistance.

The physical and social environment, which is selected and organised by society for the purpose of making sure that the child will develop properly, the curriculum, the textbooks, library, and laboratories, the organized life of the school, all are instrumental in making sure that the pupil develops in certain ways.

This broader concept of education includes guidance only when the modern, progressive viewpoint of the place and function of the individual is accepted. When only the goals of society are considered, we may have education but not guidance, for guidance implies assistance in making choices.

These choices are individual ones and imply a compromise between, or a synthesis of, the needs of society and the needs of the individual. There are certain situations in education where the element of choice by the individual is prominent, and there are others in which it is not.

Guidance and Purposive Living

If one views the life of the individual as a whole, guidance may be said to have as its purpose helping the individual to discover his needs, to assess his potentialities, gradually to develop life goals that are individually satisfying and socially desirable, to formulate plans of action in the service of these goals, and to proceed to their realization.

This statement clearly identifies the purpose of guidance with that of education. It places major emphasis upon the development of the whole individual who is now functioning and who will function in the future in a social environment.

It is a useful concept because it stresses the unity of one's life and shows the impossibility of separating one aspect of life from another. It is based upon the belief that each of us builds up, step by step, a life purpose or goal which serves or should serve as a center of integration for our desires and ambitions and as a guide for our plans.

One of the most vital elements in our efforts to educate individuals is the assistance we give in connection with choosing and developing these life purposes or goals. Form this point of view guidance and education are seen to share the same purpose and sometimes the same methods.

EDUCATION DIFFERS FROM GUIDANCE

The guidance is found in that area of educational endeavour, which involves assistance given by agencies or persons to the individual in making choices and in helping him choose a line of action, a method of procedure, a goal. It is not choosing for him or directing his choice; it is helping him to make the choice.

Education deals with the entire scope of human development. From one standpoint it is the conscious effort of society to change and develop the individual so that he may conform to society, take his place in it, improve it, and in doing this secure his own optimum development.

Another standpoint is the conscious effort of the individual to adjust himself to his physical and social environment, to improve it, and so to secure his own highest development.

Here are two forces, the individual and society, working for the same ends. When society merely determines what will be learned and how it will be learned and does nothing to secure the cooperation of the individual in the choice of things to be learned or methods to be used, guidance is not present, for there is no choice by the individual.

Society in general and the teacher in particular may need to influence or direct the growth of the individual since wise choices in later life are dependent to a large extent upon habits and attitudes formed in early years. This might be considered good education, but it is not guidance. On the other hand the individual may consciously attempt to establish a goal without help. When he does this, guidance is not present.

Although education may, and often does, take place through the effort and initiation of the individual alone, the same thing is true as above: this is education but not guidance. It is only when the cooperation of the individual is secured and assistance given him in choosing his goals or his methods that guidance is present.

All guidance is education, but some aspects of education are not guidance; their objectives are the same-the development of the individual—but the methods used in education are by no means the same as those used in guidance.

GUIDANCE: ITS RELATION TO OTHER EDUCATIONAL SPECIALITIES

One of the most important developments in the field of education during the past century has been the increased specialization in educational services. Among the first specialities to emerge were the four large areas of teaching, counselling, administration, and supervision.

These characteristics and requirements have given a clear and definite professional status to the many educational specialities. Such specialisation has some disadvantages and dangers, but there can be no doubt that it has greatly increased the effectiveness of the entire educational system.

Although each of these areas has a definite responsibility for certain services and uses characteristic techniques and thus makes its own contribution to the overall programme of education, the lines separating one area of service from another are not entirely clear and distinct.

The interrelation and overlapping in objectives and techniques may be seen by a brief discussion of the four large areas of service previously mentioned. Teaching is concerned with helping students to learn.

Counselling deals with helping students to develop the ability to solve their own problems. Supervision is responsible for providing leadership in improving instruction. Administration is concerned with the control, direction, and management of the school, that is, the provision of conditions favourable for learning.

Guidance and Counselling Differentiated

Very few terms have been more loosely or inter-changeably used than the terms 'guidance' and 'counselling'.

According to Tolbert, "Guidance... is the total programme or all the activities and services engaged in by an educational institution that are primarily aimed at assisting an individual to make and carry out adequate plans and to achieve satisfactory adjustment in all aspects of his daily life. Guidance is not teaching but it may be done by teachers. It is not separate from education but is an essential part of the total educational programme. Guidance is a term which is broader than counselling and which includes counselling and as one of its services."

Butler makes a logical separation of the counselling process discerned as having two phases called 'adjustive' and 'distributive'. In the *adjustive* phase, the emphasis is on the *social, personal* and *emotional* problems of the individual; in the *distributive* phase the focus is upon his *educational, vocational* and *occupational* problems.

According to Arbuckle, Butler's *distributive phase* can be most aptly described as 'guidance' whilst the *adjustive phase* can be considered as the description of 'counselling'.

GUIDANCE: ITS RELATION TO DISCIPLINE

A peculiar phobia appears in some guidance leaders when they consider the relation of guidance to discipline. Apparently they fear that any contact with discipline will interfere with the success of guidance workers. This fear is quite unwarranted and arises largely from misunderstandings. Guidance functions in all sorts of problem situations, past, present, or future.

It is a help given or received by all personnel in the school system—superintendent, supervisor, specialist, teacher, custodial worker, student. It is found wherever there are problems to be solved in teaching, in supervision, in discipline. In fact discipline offers one of the most useful and rewarding areas for guidance.

The confusion of these leaders is best resolved by examining the meanings which may be attached to the term 'discipline'. Discipline has two different but related meanings. First, discipline is a planned series of activities or exercises considered necessary for the attainment of a certain goal. An example is the training of an athlete for a race or for some other athletic contest. This meaning would include the development of regular exercise, eating, and sleeping habits as well as certain restrictions.

Another example of this meaning is the college curriculum leading to a degree. In this first sense discipline also means a set of rules or laws affecting conduct such as the discipline of the church, the law, or medicine. This meaning may be called 'positive' discipline.

Second, discipline means punishment for conduct that is considered undesirable. Failure to achieve a required standard in school, for example may result in punishment or 'discipline.' The punishment may also be the natural result of undesirable conduct.

This meaning may be called 'negative' discipline. Its purpose is to prevent conduct that is undesirable. It is intended to help the individual understand what is necessary to attain the goal and to motivate him to keep to the exercises and the rules, that have been set up.

It will be seen that the two meanings of discipline are closely related and that guidance has a unique function in both of them. Guidance helps set the goal and develop a programme of activities leading to it. It also encourages and motivates the individual to keep at the activities and exercises that are essential in attaining the desired end.

Guidance as Punishment

When discipline means punishment by some authority for unacceptable behaviour, guidance may help the student to understand why the behaviour is unacceptable. High school is not too early to help students to understand the function of punishment as seen in the history of human society and to comprehend what their community would be without laws leading to the punishment of offenders.

The responsibility for assistance to students in cases of discipline, in both its positive and its negative meanings, may rest upon any school personnel.

They must provide the motivation necessary for the attainment of the objectives and administer such punishments as may be necessary for failure to study or to achieve academically. In addition each teacher is responsible for the behaviour of the children in his class and to a large extent for their attendance and health. Without a doubt the chief responsibility for all these guidance services rests upon the teacher.

Preventive Guidance

By far the most effective discipline is that which operates before the crisis occurs and help the student to understand and accept the type of behaviour that is demanded by the school. In most cases discipline of this kind helps the student to realise what is required and therefore makes punishment unnecessary.

Here the teacher is the most important factor, but the counsellor may also be of real assistance. This type of discipline is not always possible, however, because one cannot always foresee the approaching crisis.

Furthermore, not every crisis can be prevented. When a crisis does come, the student is in dire need of help, and the counsellor has a clear responsibility to give him help.

Role of the Counsellor in Discipline

Just as the counsellor should not be involved in the actual punishment of the student, neither should he be the "lawyer for the defense" and seek to free him from punishment. If he has established rapport with the student, however, he may be able to find out why the misdemeanor was committed. He may discover what the student wished to accomplish by the act and help him to understand why his purpose was undesirable and what the effect of such behaviour would be on other students and on the school.

The counsellor can often help the guilty student to realise and frankly confess that his act was undesirable and to accept his punishment as well deserved. Thus it can be seen that the counsellor may have a definite responsibility in cases of discipline and may be able to make a real contribution to the student and to the school by helping the student to understand and modify his antisocial behaviour.

In summary, guidance and discipline are closely related, and the counsellor's role, even though it does not involve the administering of punishment, is both clear and unique.

EXPERIENCE AS A SOURCE OF GUIDANCE

Choices are often made on the basis of a person's own past experience or that of others. A person may call to mind some choice that he or one of his friends made in a situation that seems similar to the present one.

If what was done before was satisfactory, he might choose to make the same choice again; if the result was unsatisfactory, he might decide to do something else. Such a decision may result in a good choice or in a poor one.

The two situations although similar in some respects, may be very different in others. The choice may have been a good one once, but with the passage of time and with changed conditions, it may be quite unsatisfactory now.

Guidance may help here by assisting the individual to examine the two situations carefully to see in what ways they are alike and in what ways they are different and by helping him to get a broader view of the possible choices.

With youthful enthusiasm and undue confidence in their ability, they often make hasty and unwise decisions. Other avenues of life work may begin to make a strong appeal to them in later years. They may realise too late that these avenues might will have offered success and satisfaction. The necessary training cannot now be secured without great financial sacrifice that would jeopardize the comfort and welfare of the family.

Although they may realise that their early choices were unfortunate, they can ao nothing about it now. Wise guidance could have been of great value by making them realise that their experience was too limited to give them proper perspective. It could have helped them review carefully the entire range of occupations within their interest and capabilities.

THREE-FOLD FUNCTIONS OF GUIDANCE AND COUNSELLING

Guidance and counselling have three-fold functions: *adjustmental, orientational* and *developmental.*

Guidance and counselling are *adjustmental* in the sense that they help the student in making the best possible adjustment to the current situations in the educational institution and occupational world, in the home and the community.

Professional and individualised aid is given in making immediate and suitable adjustment at problem points. At the same time, the adjustive attitude in the spirit of Reinold Neibuhr is to be developed in the individuals:

> God grant me the serenity,
> To accept the things, I cannot change,
> The courage to change the things I can
> And the wisdom to know the difference.

Guidance and counselling have *orientational* function also. They orientate the students in problems of career planning, educational programming and direction towards long-term personal aims and values.

Awareness of the need to plan in the context of the complexity of the world of work is an essential prerequisite of going through education and preparation for after-education career. Guidance and counselling have another important function—*developmental function.*

They should try not only to cure when the problems have occurred and done their damage, rather they should begin before the problems arise and maladjustments occur. If unsolved problems are allowed to accumulate, their total effect may lead the student to the point where his capacity for growth is blocked. In such cases, guidance and counselling may be of little or no help.

That way guidance and counselling have a very important developmental function for helping the students achieve self-development and self-realisation. Guidance and counselling also have to discharge the important function of furthering the welfare of the society and be important instruments of national development.

QUESTIONS FOR ANSWER

1. *"Effective education is guidance, and realistic guidance is self guidance" Carmicheal. In the light of this statement write a note on the concept and aim of guidance and education.*
2. *Write a note on the need and characteristics of guidance.*
3. *Write short notes on the following:*
   (a) Scope of guidance.
   (b) Principles of guidance philosophy.
   (c) Guidance—Its relationship with education.
   (d) Guidance—Its relation with discipline and punishment.

4

Career Oriented Guidance: The Objectives

The scientific and technological developments have changed the structure of the society, which includes the careers primarily, therefore, we need to plan the careers of our children as per abilities and capabilities from the very early stages of education, hence we must understand the objectives of career oriented guidance and counselling programme in our schools, colleges and universities. Such programme has following objectives as per need of our educational system and as per future needs of respectable career and status in the society:

1. *To help in the total development of the student*: The emphasis on intellectual development through the teaching of subjects alone cannot help in the total development of the students. We have to evolve some method of helping students understand themselves and helping teachers understand the students.

There has to be a basic and fundamental change in our entire system of education, change which recognises that no matter how well a human being is educated in chemistry, physics, economics, history or literature, he remains a barbarian unless he knows something about himself.

Self-knowledge in depth which has been the forgotten factor in our educational system must become its primary focus—and this is what can be done through a programme of guidance and counselling.

Total development of the students necessitates that individual differences among students are expected, accepted, understood and planned for and all types of experiences in an institution are so organised as to contribute to the total development of the student.

All that a student needs in an educational institution is good teaching, is an exploded myth. Something much more and beyond this is needed to produce competent, mature and well-rounded citizens.

2. *To help in the proper choice of courses*: Everyone knows that so far our educational system has grown up in a higgledy-piggledy fashion. The subjects which are the least wanted—humanities and the liberal arts—have been those most frequently offered and taken, both in the colleges and the universities because they were the oldest and relatively inexpensive areas of knowledge, taken because they require no specified intellectual equipment.

The problem is grave in another way also. In an article on 'Unrest on Campus', Piloo Modi, M.P. wrote, "Our student population reaches the university level, having made up their mind broadly about the courses that they may have a decision, which in almost all cases, is taken by unthinking and unsympathetic parents and relatives with an eye on a more lucrative profession. It is a great tragedy when a potential poet becomes a chemical engineer... Many a mute inglorious Milton is languishing in the dark engineering world".

This entire process of herding our youths into educational disciplines unconnected with their aptitudes needs to be checked through a scientific process of guidance and counselling for the best development of individuals and growth of society.

3. *To help in the proper choice of careers*: We are living in a highly complex and rapidly changing world of work. There are changing requirements in industrial jobs, altered market conditions for professional manpower, the development of para-professional occupations and many other labour market trends which make occupational selection more difficult than ever.

The young students in colleges and universities need to be informed about various jobs and openings available to them and the requirements, responsibilities and the nature of work involved in them so that they could measure themselves upto them and develop and crystallise their occupational goals.

They need to be helped in making meaningful occupational selection and preparation for an entry into them to have a fulfilling and rewarding career.

The need for helping the students in the choice of a proper career is further enhanced due to the fact that majority of our students in colleges and universities are the first generation learners. In their family, they have no one with an experience of college or university education background to guide them in the choice of a career.

With a right to the best education available, and a wide range of jobs open to them, these students need mature help in making a judicious occupational choice. Hence the need of adequate guidance and counselling arrangement in our colleges and universities.

4. *To help the students in vocational development*: The process of vocational development covers almost the entire span of life of an individual. It begins quite early in one's life and continues till sometimes after retirement. In this process, the individual passes through various stages—*growth, exploration, maintenance and decline.*

Guidance services need to be provided to the colleges and universities to help the students in the process of vocational development—particularly the stages of *growth and exploration*, by making it possible for them to gain knowledge about themselves—their abilities, interests and needs on, the one hand and knowledge about the world of work on the other.

By providing them opportunities for self-exploration as well as exploration of the world of work while they are still in an educational institution, their transition from education to work can be facilitated.

5. *To develop readiness for choices and changes to face new challenges*: In a paper entitled *The Need for Counselling in Higher Education*, presented at the Third International Round Table of Educational Counselling and Vocational Guidance, Miss Newsome, Counselling Officer at the University of Keels, North Strafford Shire, England, writes, "For the students of higher education the demands of life are likely to be great, in a most different way from the exacting demands of education itself. On graduating he will be called upon to make use of the kind of person he has become as much if not more than what he has learnt in his course of study—not only to make an initial choice of what he is to do on graduating but will be called upon to change his occupation several times in a life time. Readiness for these choices and changes is essential, not only to the student himself but to the society as a whole. To the extent to which he is able to capitalise on his experience and face new challenges with a realistic expectation of success, to that extent

he will benefit society. If he is unable to meet the changing demands, not only of the working world but also of his other roles of life, to that extent he will be a liability and will fail to fulfil the expectations which society has for its most able people".

Guidance services are needed to develop in the students the ability to cope with their new problems and concerns in such a way that they become more competent to meet the demands which will continue to be made upon them in the future.

6. *To minimise the mismatching between education and employment and help in the efficient use of manpower*: The latest analysis (1981) done by Planning Commission reveals that the educated youth between 15 and 29 years of age constituted 11.5 per cent of the corresponding labour force but they accounted for 33.2 per cent of the total unemployment in the country. According to the Planning Commission's labour force projections, the total number of educated unemployed at the beginning of 1980 was estimated at 3.47 million. If there is no further deterioration in the unemployment rate, this number was 4.66 million in 1985. And this is the challenging situation we have to face as now we have 10 million such youth.

It needs to be pointed out that the hiatus between education and employment has rarely been as wide and as disturbing as it is today. Higher academic education, as very well pointed out by Mr. L.K. Jha, Chairman of the Economic Administration Reforms Commission, is far too general and diffused to be of practical value to the vast majority of youngmen and women. Most of our young men and women have no clear objectives of career targets. They amble through university courses of learning without acquiring much knowledge of preparing themselves for an uncertain future.

Every year, our colleges and universities disgorge thousands of hopeful youngsters into the labour market who are virtually *unemployable*—despite their fancy degrees and diplomas. In fact, employers often complain that of the hundreds of applications that come in response to a single vacancy, at least 80 per cent have no relevance to the job specifications whatsoever. Few students pursue their education with a clear idea as to what they would eventually like to become.

7. *To motivate the youth for self-employment*: Considering the magnitude of educated job-seekers flowing into the job market in

India every year, it is essential that a sizable fraction of enterprising youth is initiated into careers of self-employment.

Some arrangement needs to be instituted in the colleges and universities to identify the deserving cases fit to take up self-employment, educate them on how to proceed about the job of setting up a venture, help them through the cooperation of the concerned agencies in this sphere to prepare technically sound and economically viable projects; sponsor their cases to the banks for loan assistance and guide them to overcome the teething troubles through effective follow-up after the commencement of the venture.

8. *To help freshers establish proper identity*: In our country the youngmen entering colleges and even universities are comparatively young in years. Young adolescents as they are, they are passing through a stage between childhood and adulthood, between the morality learned as a child and the ethics to be developed by the adult. They find it extremely difficult to establish a satisfactory identity.

Such failure or delay leads to what can be called "role diffusion". This crisis in role identity is perhaps very acute today. The uncertainties of the future, the conflicts in languages, culture, regions, castes, etc., and the erosion of traditional values has rendered Indian youth rootless.

Guidance and counselling programme is needed to help students deal effectively with the normal developmental tasks of adolescence and face life situations boldly.

9. *To identify and motivate the students from weaker sections of society*: Students from weaker sections have their own problems and needs. They experience difficulty in adjustment with the peers, teachers and the environment. To communicate, make friends, utilise the time profitably, make the best use of lectures, make an effective use of library and other facilities available—all pose problems for them. Guidance facilities are urgently needed for such type of students to enable them to adjust and utilise the available facilities properly.

10. *To help the students in their period of turmoil and confusion*: The students undergo a great deal of turmoil and searching to give meaning to their lives. They have their conflicts and anxieties. They feel disillusioned regarding higher education. They find that colleges and universities, instead of imparting them education,

just enable them to pass examinations—they feel sunk and cheated. When this education does not enable them to get immediate employment, they feel lost and bewildered.

Similarly, they have their personal conflicts and anxieties. They have the problems about their parents and family, their relations to boy and girl friends. They have the problems of adjusting their personality to the world of people, of ethical ideas and of goals and situations.

For tackling all these situations successfully, they need someone to sort out the strands—they need some strong, tactile presence of a hand guiding the anxious and enabling them to develop realistic expectations.

11. *To help in checking wastage and stagnation*: The average pass percentage at the graduate and post-graduate level is about 50 to 60. Thousands of our students, unfortunately, drop out, get pushed out, and fall out of the system. This problem is becoming more serious day by day.

There is another unfortunate side of this problem—majority of our students pass in second and third division, which is a low qualification for the world of work.

A study concludes that *sizeable percentage of alumni obtaining professional qualifications have to work as clerks. The report also gives evidence of much aimless and unrealistic vocational choice.*

Higher education is a very costly enterprise. Much of the money wasted on these poor and low achievers could be saved by a policy of prevention. Just as preventive medicine is sounder economically and more humane than remedial medicine, so too is preventive education more sound economically than remedial education.

There is thus a clear need for developing better professional services of a counselling kind—to check the huge wastage of student time and money and also huge state expenditure on education.

Miller, in this connection, said so well, "If one counsellor could prevent the wastage of only four student years each costing £800 to £1200, he would be earning his keep. Similar savings of graduate salaries foregone as a result of failure or delay would benefit student as well as the taxpayer".

12. *To identify and help students in need of special help*: There are such students as the gifted, the backward the handicapped who

need special opportunities. Some arrangement needs to be provided in our colleges and universities to identify them and provide them with help according to their requirements.

13. *To ensure the proper utilisation of time spent outside the classrooms*: It is common knowledge that students in the colleges and universities spend two to three times as many hours outside classrooms as in them. And the manner in which students spend their non-class hours clearly affects their success in achieving both academic competence and personal development of all types.

It is, therefore, essential that institutions of higher learning provide positive direction to students by influencing how they can use those non-class hours. The programme of guidance and counselling can meet this need.

14. *To help in tackling problems arising out of student explosion*: Increased demand for higher education is outstripping the growth of facilities in the seats of higher learning. Resultant unfortunate qualitative changes in the nature of entire educative experiences are creating innumerable problems.

The students population is highly heterogeneous students from a variety of sections—highly affluent and extremely poor, educated in convents and ordinary schools and colleges, rural and urban areas, students from our own country and different foreign countries are attending colleges and universities.

When students from a broad range of families and educational and social backgrounds meet in classes for instruction, in hostels for housing, in cafeterias and mess halls for eating, numerous problems crop up. Guidance and counselling facilities need to be provided for helping them tackle these diverse and complex problems.

15. *To check migration*: There is an unhealthy trend among the youth of migrating from rural to urban areas and from our own country to foreign countries. Unless migration is checked by proper guidance and counselling, cities will continue to swallow the rural talent and foreign countries the national talent and thus render both unproductive.

16. *To make up for the deficiencies of home*: A large number of students come to institutions of higher learning from homes which are not able to assist them adequately in dealing with their life problems. Because of various factors such as rapid industrialisation, political and social changes in the occupational

structure of the country and the growing complexity of life there are greater pressures and strains in the family.

The home is not able to provide the kind of support and help it did in earlier days. Also, there is a gap in the range of sympathetic adults who could be turned to in need, which formerly was filled by adult brothers and sisters, friendly aunts and grand parents when communities and families were more intimate.

Also our homes are not equipped to be the source of information concerning the qualifications required for different kinds of courses or careers. Such information can come from agencies which make a full time job of supplying adequate and up-to-date materials. Similarly, home is not equipped for studying future labour shortages and the labour supply and demand situation. Besides, many parents are not trained for helping their grown up children to develop sound study techniques, and obtain reliable information in matters of sex etc.

Seth (1962) collected a sample of students at Allahabad University. The parents were indicated as the most usual source of help. Forty per cent of student respondents said that they could not discuss their problems with their parents. There is a strong evidence that professional help could be well-used.

17. *To minimise the incidence of indiscipline*: Majority of our students lack a sense of direction, a sense of purpose and a sense of fulfilment. They indulge in destructive activities which lead to social damage and loss. This educated proletariat, so to say, is a time bomb in the heart of the nation that can explode any time if immediate care is not taken to inactivate it.

Adequate guidance and counselling facilities is the only answer—to help and guide the youth to worthwhile channels and help them realise the goal of optimum academic, personal and social development.

NEED AND OBJECTIVE OF GUIDANCE IN A SURPLUS ECONOMY

New interpretations of our way of life have resulted in changes. The concept of society as an organised group of individuals bound together by similarity of interests and activities is enlarging not only geographically but also ideologically. Traditional mores and customs are breaking down.

Yet newer concepts of human interrelationships are still in a state of flux. Today more than ever before, every man, woman, and child is expected to utilise his abilities and experiences for the benefit of others, as well as for his own advancement.

Any philosophy of life that sets an individual against the group or that permits him to disregard the welfare of his fellows is becoming increasingly untenable. The newer concept of society is that of a group wherein no one should have rights or privileges that he has not earned or that are denied to any other worthy member of a world fellowship.

The realisation of so broad a goal of world democracy cannot be achieved entirely through the efforts of world leaders. More and more, people—no matter how narrow and limited their sphere of experience—are beginning to recognise their personal responsibility for effecting desirable social changes. Unfortunately, however, some individuals still seem unable or unwilling to accept this responsibility.

The climatic conditions growing-out of world unrest affect practically every phase of human experience. Adjustment to or improvement of the many current challenging situations is in part an individual responsibility which can be met by some people with a minimum of outside assistance. For others, effective counselling services should be available to prevent their becoming the victims of social, economic, and political changes.

But there are persons who advocate as follows:

> "What is the use of guidance and counselling—particularly educational and vocational—in an economy where labour is too abundant and jobs and opportunities are too few? What is the use of this service in a country which is groaning already under the weight of unemployment of the educated?"

These are the oft-repeated questions asked when a case is built up for the introduction of guidance and counselling in our colleges and universities.

The logic in these arguments against the introduction of guidance and counselling is too simple to be true. It needs to be remembered that *guidance and counselling have a challenging role to play in every developing economy, much more so if it is labour intensive.*

Selection of a job from a multitude of alternatives, although a very important objective of guidance and counselling, is not the be-all and end-all of guidance and counselling. The core aim of these services, let us remember, is to help our job-seeking youth from realistic career notions, in conformity with their capacities, aptitudes and social settings, so that they do not, in their adult life, end up as career 'failures'.

The fact that wrong career decisions eventually make a big drain both on the emotional health of the individuals and the productivity of the society can hardly be disputed. Therefore, helping the youth to build up a desirable self-concept to achieve an ever larger measure of self-appraisal and choose a proper career line is the need of the hour—and provisions of guidance and counselling service is our immediate requirement.

The guidance and counselling service worth its name should enlighten the job-seeking youth on "new" careers coming up on the job horizon. Whether the economy is labour intensive or the one characterised by over-all man-power dearth, so long as it continually organises developmental endeavours and strives for economic self-sufficiency, it will bring about inevitable, permeating and permanent changes in its occupational matrix. In a developing economy, such as ours, new explorations are constantly attempted, social values gradually change, scientific break-through eventually revolutionises consumption and productive patterns; new industries spring up, technological applications modify production process; consumer tastes are shaped and cultivated.

All these growth-induced changes in the society accelerate the demand for the hitherto 'unheard' of skills, at the same time eclipsing certain traditional occupations. It is very necessary that some arrangement is there in our educational institutions, particularly the institutions of higher education, which keeps track of these changing facets in the occupational matrix and educates the youth appropriately and adequately. Hence the need of guidance and counselling even in a surplus economy as ours!

In colleges and universities, we deal with the development and growth of the nation's greatest asset—its youth. Neither India nor any other country—big or small—can endure or prosper with inadequate and third rate out-dated educational experiences for its youth. And we cannot, rather should not, rest with the place where we stand as far as the quality of products of our higher education is concerned.

We have to make concerted all-round efforts to make our students fit enough to play the vital role in nation-building. The myth that our college and university students do not have any problems or "all that is needed to set everything right is good teaching" or that services as guidance and counselling are "frivolous additions" to higher education, stand exploded today.

In fact, there is a great truth in the words of Conant that on the success or failure of our guidance and counselling programme hangs, in all probability, the success or failure of our system of education. It is high time we realise this hard reality.

QUESTIONS FOR ANSWER

1. *Write a note on career oriented programme of guidance and counselling in our educational institution and give an account of its basic objectives.*
2. *Whether the economy is labour intensive or the one having over-all man-power dearth equally need proper guidance for effective and productive use of man-power". Justify this statement.*
3. *"Guidance and Counselling have a challenging role to play in every economy, much more, so if it is a labour surplus one". Justify this statement.*

5

Approaches, Fundamental Aspects and Areas of Guidance and Counselling

Basic knowledge of approaches, functional aspects and areas of guidance and counselling is essential for effective career guidance and counselling, because understanding of fundamental guidance approaches is very essential. These approaches help individuals to discover their potentialities. Hereunder, we will discuss these approaches, very briefly.

GUIDANCE APPROACHES

Following are the guidance approaches based on more recent guidance practices as per results of researches in natural and social sciences:

Pseudoscientific Guidance Approaches

Non-scientific 'prediction' took many different forms: numerology, astrology, graphology, palmistry, phonology, physiognomy, occultism, spiritualism, dream-interpretation, 'fortune telling' by means of tea leaves, coffee grounds, and playing cards, and the application of one or another superstition peculiar to the traditions of a people.

Dream analysis has received considerable attention from people in all walks of life. The more credulous still consult "dream books", which assign specific meanings to the content of dreams. For others the works of Brill and his associates in dream analysis offer a fruitful field for probing into the lowest depths of the subconscious and uncovering hidden urges and desires.

The fact that many people are still adherents of these pseudoscientific practices indicates their great need for help. Such individuals seem to be groping blindly for a means of building personal morale or developing self-realisation.

Changing Concepts of Psychology

Among the psychological principles evolved, the following are basic to an understanding of the functions of guidance:

1. Physically, mentally, emotionally, and socially an individual may develop at different rates, achieving mature status in these several phases of his development by different steps, at different times, and to differing degrees.
2. Members of the human family share elements of likeness in their general pattern of development; but factors of biological inheritance and social heritage combine to bring about individual differences which must be taken into consideration when we are dealing with any group of persons.
3. The principles of learning that have evolved from much study and experimentation in the field have been of service in helping us appreciate the value of practice in learning, the place of motivation in arousing interest, and the extent to which satisfaction or annoyance with the learning process affects learning success.
4. Through the combined efforts of psychologists and educators, significant advances have been made during the twentieth century in the construction of techniques for personality evaluation.

Consequently, an important aspect of guidance has become the utilisation of standardised tests of physical status, mental ability, and specific aptitude; interest inventories; achievement scales; prognostic and diagnostic techniques; behaviour scales; and other means of evaluating emotional and social status.

Industrial and Scientific Progress

The invention of machinery and the rapid increase of industrialism have led to a degree of occupational specialisation unheard of in earlier times. Increased production, distribution, and consumption of goods have increased the number of special jobs to be performed; they also have led to the development of many other forms of service occupations to meet the complexities of urban life and to provide for the leisure-time activities of workers.

The rapid strides made by researchers in various fields of science have almost completely revolutionised modern living. The discovery of atomic energy, its uses in warfare, and its application to peacetime activity, require carefully selected and thoroughly trained workers.

Furthermore, youth no longer can be expected to limit his interests and activities to the community in which he was born and reared since many opportunities are becoming available to him in other lands. These can so stimulate his spirit of adventure that he needs intelligent guidance toward the attainment of effective life goals.

Changing Educational Objectives

Twentieth-century educational emphasis on the learner rather than the materials to be learned has done much to further interest in guidance. Schools on every level evidence an interest in all phases of the individual's development. Formulated objectives of education exemplify this trend.

In 1918, the Commission on Secondary Education of the National Education Association of the United States (NEA) recommended that the goal of educational theory and practice be to provide adequate means for helping young people meet life needs in the following areas; which are applicable to India as well:

1. Health
2. Command of fundamental processes
3. Worthy home membership
4. Vocations
5. Civic education
6. Worthy use of leisure
7. Ethical character.

These *seven cardinal principles of education* have influenced teaching and learning at all levels.

The cardinal principles are basic to later formulations of educational objectives. For example, in 1938, the Educational

Policies Commission of the NEA offered the following four general objectives:

1. The Objective of Self-Realisation,
2. The Objective of Human Relationship,
3. The Objective of Economic Efficiency, and
4. The Objective of Civic Responsibility.

As a result of their findings, we are convinced that American education, without neglecting study in mathematics, science, and other fundamental curriculum areas, must:

(*a*) give attention to life problems throughout the world,
(*b*) develop the ability to communicate with other peoples in their own language,
(*c*) achieve skill in working with these peoples, and
(*d*) interpret to them the democratic way of life.

Increase in School Population

Publicly supported schooling through the secondary level is accepted generally as a state responsibility. In some states public support is provided through at least four years of higher education. Moreover, to ensure for every young person his educational rights, each state has enacted compulsory attendance laws which set minimal dropout ages. These age requirements range from a low of 14 to a high of 18.

The increase in the number of children and adolescents who are expected to be receiving formal school training has caused serious consideration of the problems of administration, organisation, and guidance. There are budgetary difficulties involved in the matter of providing buildings and school personnel sufficient to meet the needs of such large numbers of pupils. Hence, proper guidance is our prime need.

THE FUNCTIONAL ASPECTS OF GUIDANCE

As now interpreted, guidance touches every aspect of an individual's personality—physical, mental, emotional and social. It is concerned with all of an individual's attitudes and behaviour patterns. It seeks to help the individual integrate all his activities, using his basic potentialities and environmental opportunities. In any one situation, guidance services may be aimed at helping a person achieve adjustment in a particular area of activity, such as curriculum adjustment. The emphasis then will be placed on educational guidance.

A satisfactory adjustment of the study programme, however, necessitates consideration of other factors which may include all or many of the following: the pupil's health, his intellectual capacity, his attitude toward study in general or toward one area of learning, his industry, the amount of time that he can or will devote to studying, his post-graduate plans, and the kind and extent of parental cooperation.

The Function of Guidance in Education

In a real sense, guidance pervades all of education. It expresses the concern of the school for individualising the educational programme. This means that it is every teacher's responsibility to understand the interests, abilities, and feelings of every child and to adapt the educational programme to meet those needs.

In another sense, guidance is a series of special services. These include activities which make the school programme effective in meeting the needs of each child. Among these are plans for:

1. discovering the real needs and problems of students,
2. using information collected about students to adjust instruction to meet individual needs,
3. developing among teachers a greater understanding of child growth and development,
4. providing such specialised services as orientation, individual inventory, counselling, occupational information, group guidance, placement, follow-up of graduates and drop-outs,
5. conducting research which evaluates the success of the programme.

Although the guidance point of view touches every aspect of school activity, the fact should be stressed that education and guidance differ in purpose and process. Education, interpreted either *as process or product*, is an *individual* matter. The child, adolescent, or adult himself must make the changes within himself which he recognises to be desirable.

The function of the teacher can be no more than to make available to the learner opportunities of value to him in his self-education. He needs to be stimulated to want to learn, to be helped to discover what things he should learn, and to be encouraged to progress satisfactorily in his learning. The educational process takes place within the individual, and educational products are evidenced in his behaviour.

What then is the relation of guidance to education? Guidance constitutes those factors *outside* the individual that are made available to him in his search for self-development. In its broadest connotation, guidance can be regarded as a form of education. In its more specific interpretation, it includes all those techniques of counselling and all those bodies of information that can help the individual help himself.

It should be remembered, also, that young people receive much informal guidance from their elders. Because of their close relationship with the growing child, parents and teachers exert a significant influence on his attitudes and behaviour.

This kind of guidance is constantly in action. Hence whatever kind of persons we want our young people to become, we ourselves must be. The parents who tells lies in the presence of the child cannot admonish the child to be truthful.

The teacher in charge of a study hall who engages in conversation with a fellow teacher does not dare ask pupils to refrain from talking so as not to annoy others who are studying. It is imperative that all of us recognise that general concept of guidance and that we be ever on the alert to have our actions serve as worthy guides.

Identification of Basic Guidance Goals

In an attempt to achieve a tenable point of view concerning the various aspects of the guidance concept, one difficulty encountered is that of clear terminology. The expansion or modification of guidance functions has been accompanied by semantic changes that can be extremely confusing.

For example, certain pairs of terms, such as *guidance and counselling, guidance worker and guidance counsellor, guidance services and personnel services,* or *guidance and personnel services,* too often are used indiscriminately as identifying the same functional aspects of the guidance concept.

The terms *pupil personnel, personnel work, pupil personnel worker and personnel services* are finding their way into the literature of guidance. Apparently the term *personnel work* originated in industry to describe administrative activities aimed at better management-worker relations and improved utilisation of industrial manpower.

The term *student personnel work* came to be used on the college level to identify administrative management of student life. Later, lower-school administrators employed the term *pupil personnel* in much the same way as it is used in industry and on the college level. Thus we may conclude:

> Guidance is the outgrowth of a philosophy of education that every child in a school system should have an opportunity for full growth the development in order to achieve his greatest potential...
>
> We consider the guidance function, therefore, as consisting of two integral phases, (1) the guidance concept of teaching, (2) pupil personnel services available to give assistance to the teacher, the school, and the pupils and parents to aid in the implementation of the educational programme. An effective child-centred programme of education cannot be accomplished without both phases of guidance, each supplementing the other; neither can function effectively without the other.

GUIDANCE AS A CONTINUOUS PROCESS

The rapid and widespread development and application of the guidance concept during the past fifty years have given rise to many questions and various controversial issues, but the real situation is as follows:

Not only do growing boys and girls need to be helped to meet their growing-up experiences satisfactorily, but they also should be led to realise that no matter how well a person is adjusted to the challenges of childhood and adolescence, he is likely to be confronted as an adult of any age with problems which may be beyond his power to meet successfully.

In such situations, he should know where he can go for help, be willing to utilise the resources available, and learn to solve his problems in the light of his own best judgement after he has had the suggestions of those who, through training and experience, are qualified to interpret the situation.

In an increasing number of communities, attempts are being made to provide some guidance assistance for both young and older persons. Actually, however, little has been done to establish and implement programmes which would make for continuity of guidance.

AREAS OF GUIDANCE AND COUNSELLING

The period of student life plays a very vital role in the formulation of the individual's career, therefore, proper care as well as proper guidance and counselling is needed to plan each and every activity during this period and development of proper attitude to face each and every situation, which we discuss hereunder:

The student life is getting complex day by day. It is common knowledge that the students have to face many types of difficult situations, make a wise curricular and co-curricular choice; acquire basic study skills for optimum achievement; live with and share facilities with students from varied social and economic backgrounds; adjust to the peers and parents, teachers and administrators; secure adequate financial aid to carry on the studies; spend leisure properly; adjust to hetero-sexual relations satisfactorily, etc.

The students need expert help for optimum achievement and adequate adjustment in these varied life situations. For the sake of convenience and clarity, we will group these situations under seven major heads.

1. Education

Educational problems head the list of student problems—hence education is an important guidance area. Today, curricula offered by colleges and universities have increased tremendously. Vocations in many forms are penetrating colleges and universities.

Competitive examinations for entry into institutions and services have become a normal phenomena in our country as elsewhere. Naturally, expert help is required by the students in making wise choices and be successful in competitive examinations.

Expert assistance is also required for enabling the students in making proper adjustment in relation to general academic life at college or university to effect maximum intellectual, emotional and physical development, as discussed earlier in this chapter.

2. Vocation

This is another important guidance area. There are vocations as there are persons, and certainly all persons are not suitable for all vocations. Every vocation needs a certain educational and professional background and preparation and only those having them can succeed. Hence the need for guidance to the students for a right choice of a vocation!

Arrangement has to be made to assist the students to have a reasonable estimate of their abilities and limitations, strike a balance between their aspirations and those of their parents, between their interests and the availability of opportunities.

They have to be assisted in making decisions and choices involved in planning a future and building a career. They have also to be helped in developing an integrated and adequate picture of themselves and of their role in the world of work.

Occupational world is also changing very rapidly. Fresh and new occupational outlets undreamt of before are emerging. It, therefore, becomes essential that students are also helped to acquire clearer perspective of the changes that are taking place in the job world.

The primary aim of vocational guidance is the promotion of *personal satisfaction with life as a whole*. As such, the process of vocational guidance will consist of the following factors:

(*a*) Enabling the students to discover information about themselves—their abilities, interests, needs, ambitions, limitations and their causes;

(*b*) Providing them information about their environment, the advantages and disadvantages of different occupations and educational courses, the qualifications necessary for entry into them, and the range of opportunities available to them;

(*c*) Providing them with a *frame of reference* in which to see themselves in relation to these educational and vocational opportunities; to orient them to the helping agencies available to them, and to alert them to future decision-making points in their careers;

(*d*) Disabusing the minds of students of any romantic or vague notions about certain jobs;

(*e*) Providing *counselling* in order to promote self-understanding and to develop educational and occupational plans;

(*f*) Providing *placement service* to help them to implement those plans; and

(*g*) Providing a *follow-up service* to help them, if necessary, when faced with future decision-making situations.

3. Avocation

Woodrow Wilson said so well, "The real intellectual life of a body of undergraduates, if there be any, manifests itself, not in the classroom, but in what they do and talk of, and set before themselves, as their favourite objects between classes and lectures". If that be so, responsibility of any college or university does not end with the syllabus and the teacher's performance.

We must be keenly concerned with the nature of that day-long learning aside from books or lectures. We need to remember that the student spends only 5 or 6 hours of a 24 hour day in classes. What goes on the rest of the time is the area of student services—the intellectual efforts outside of class, physical activities, social interaction, emotional experiences, cultural programmes etc. We must realistically recognise where learning is going on, help the students plan for them and actively participate in them.

There is hardly any doubt about this fact that avocational pursuits in which the students engage themselves are no less important in giving a direction to their lives. This is all the more important as our college and university students get so many holidays—spring break, autumn break, long summer vacations, and so many scheduled and unscheduled holidays in between.

Students in Arts subjects particularly have got much spare time. How to ensure that vacant hours are profitably utilised is one of the problems which we have to face boldly. Avocational needs of the students need to be met before they grow to troublesome proportion rather than being left to drift on a sea of confusion, doubt, anxiety, aimlessness, get exploited by others, or indulge in destructive acts or in unwholesome activities.

The students need to be properly guided for effective participation in varied types of avocational pursuits so that they are able to shape their interpersonal behaviour in desirable direction and widen their outlook.

4. Social

Social relationships constitute a problem area for most of the students. For example, they come from a school which served a particular linguistic or socio-economic group. Friendship had been formed casually and spontaneously. In a city college/university, student body is heterogeneous and drawn from many linguistic and socio-economic groups. It consists of adolescents who are self-conscious and tend to formalise their relationships; they seem to need a structured situation within which to socialise, be it the classroom or the college gymkhana, an extra-curricular interest or a class picnic.

Some shy students find themselves friendless even after an entire term at college or university. There are others who want to be effective as individuals in their groups. Very often, they have to work with people they dislike. All such situations necessitate that students are guided to live as socially well-adjusted individuals. They need to be helped in making friends and improving their style of conversation.

It is of utmost importance that the students are helped in acquiring the feeling of security and being accepted by the group; in developing a social poise; in becoming tolerant towards the behaviour of others; in achieving individuality and freedom from the slavish imitation of the adults or 'heroes'.

5. Health

Society has a special stake in the health and physical well-being of the college and university students who are or should be the elect of the rising generation and in whom it has to invest large resources and to whom it looks for the advancement of national interest. Total health of the student should be our goal; both the preventive and restorative measures are needed to ensure the achievement of the objective.

The basic responsibility for the health programme must rest with the Health Officer in charge of Student Health Centre. The physician should set a tone of acceptance for student problems.

This climate of acceptance is particularly important in the case of early detection of disorders, since students may be afraid to reveal symptoms like those of venereal diseases, tuberculosis, etc.

It will be desirable to have a medical check up of all the students in the beginning of the academic session and reports may be sent to the parents or guardians and a written report of the action taken may be insisted.

For early diagnosis and treatment of illness these measures may be taken up:

(*i*) An adequate physical examination of every student upon entrance to the college or university;
(*ii*) Follow-up treatment of detected disorders;
(*iii*) Reference of students to other medical resources when necessary; and
(*iv*) Maintenance of confidential files and health records to keep track of mind and body's harmonious functioning.

There are some disabled students; efforts have to be made for their rehabilitation in collaboration with psychologists, educators and social workers. Remedial measures have to be taken with students suffering from speech and hearing defects.

6. Moral

Students face so many awkward situations at home, college/ university or in their peer groups. They find it difficult to get out of them. They tell lies; try to dodge and indulge in so many undesirable practices. Some guidance needs to be provided to such students to keep them on the track and lead noble lives.

7. Personal

This is another very important area where guidance is very much needed. Students face many personal problems related to themselves, their parents and family, their friends and teachers, their educational achievement and social adjustment.

Students often have memories related to home or family which create feelings of disappointment in them. Their parents may be expecting too much of them which leaves them with a feeling of incompetence and insecurity when they fail to live up to their expectations. Many parents nag their children, thus creating an unfavourable atmosphere at home for studies.

Students at times find difficulty in understanding the materials of the lectures; they may find the lectures lousy and the educational institution a dump; they may not be liking the teacher and his/her methods of teaching, thus landing in poor achievement. Guidance needs to be provided to such students to enable them to adjust to the situation which they cannot change.

Some students are obsessed with problems such as lack of friends; loneliness; feelings of inadequacy; inferiority and the like. They feel a sense of chaos and despair around. They need counsel to overcome their difficulties.

Students also at times see a danger to their self-concept. Help needs to be given to such students to emerge successful out of this crisis of identity, by perceiving more accurately their self with all its assets and liabilities and identification of this self with the more achievable goals.

Students at times find difficulty in concentration, learning and recall. They feel tense, anxious and depressed. They need to be guided to get relief from all these.

Some students also find adjustment to heterosexual relations difficult. They are not well-equipped regarding knowledge about sex. Parents generally do not make a good job of it. The lack of proper sex knowledge creates social and emotional conflicts. This is particularly so in co-educational colleges and universities.

Generally, the students enter colleges and universities at an age when biological sex impulses are new and strong but the consummation of sex has to be delayed till one is able to earn and marry. Sex guidance has to be given to the students; they have to be educated regarding masturbation, nocturnal emissions, etc. and the educational programme has to be so planned that sex urge of the students finds healthy outlets.

Some students are hard-pressed for finances. They need to be guided regarding the freeships, fee concessions, scholarships, stipends, etc. available in the institution or offered by other welfare agencies and how and when to apply. The provision of financial assistance has to be ensured so that no meritorious student is denied education for lack of financial assistance.

Students are also faced with the problem of accommodation, particularly in big universities and almost all professional institutions.

The Dean of Students Welfare with his panel of advisers can study the possibilities of securing 'healthy' accommodation with landlords of standing and good reputation in the location around the college or university.

Many landlords are willing to accommodate students in spare rooms and guest houses at comparatively cheaper rates if these students are recommended by the college or university authorities. The landlords may be requested to keep a protective eye on the students staying in the house and to contact the authorities if they need help.

Thus, the students can be helped in avoiding the spending of disproportionate amount of time seeking adequate, cheap accommodation.

QUESTIONS FOR ANSWER

1. *Write a note on functional aspects of guidance and its importance in social and educational field.*
2. *Write a note on recent guidance practices.*
3. *Write short notes on the following:*
   (a) Changing concept of psychology and guidance.
   (b) Guidance as a continuous process.
   (c) Functions of guidance in education.
   (d) Identification of basic guidance goals.
4. *Write a note on the areas of guidance during student life.*

6

Principles and Fundamentals of Guidance and Counselling

Basic knowledge of principles and fundamental and nature of guidance and counselling services equips the professional career counsellor to provide effective and proper guidance to the needy person.

Maladjusted behaviour of any person reflects that he has adjustment difficulties, which effects his career, functional aspects of this have been discussed in the earlier chapter. Hereunder, we will discuss various aspects which may help in ensuring better adjustment and fine career in life at various stages from the period of schooling till death:

Community planners attempt to provide the kind of housing facilities and educational, recreational and health services, that will help community members achieve and preserve good physical, mental, emotional, and social adjustment.

We already have mentioned that effective education is guidance-pointed. An individual's educational progress depends on the motivation he receives from parents and school personnel toward optimum development of his innate potentialities. Hence, regardless of school level, guidance services include specific aids provided by qualified members of the school staff to help learners understand themselves and their responsibilities, and to assist them in the solution of learning problems.

Guidance as a Profession

Some notions about guidance and its functions are the outgrowth of a realisation and the general public that self-direction in the management of one's own affairs is becoming increasingly difficult.

Interest in giving assistance or in guidance-pointed activity is the prerogative of any sincere, well-intentioned, capable individual.

Correctly interpreted, guidance as a profession is one that:

1. operates within the framework of a total educational programme,
2. requires its practitioners to have appropriate professional preparation, and
3. offers needed services which are organised in the form of an appropriate, flexible guidance programme.

We subscribe to Mathewson's succinctly stated definition of guidance as "the systematic, professional process of aiding individuals in making their choices, plans, and adjustments, in undertaking effective self-direction, and in meeting problems of personal living related to education".

Guidance activities are based upon the recognition of individual differences, the basic concepts of human growth and development, the diversity of present-day educational opportunities, the complexity of modern occupational life, the importance of human relations, the right of the individual to make his own choices, and the realisation that the adjustment of an individual to his life situations is an ever changing process.

KINDS OF GUIDANCE

Before discussing the principles of guidance let us understand the kinds/types of guidance as advocated by eminent educators. According to Proctor:

1. Educational guidance
2. Vocational guidance
3. Guidance in civic and social activities
4. Guidance in health and physical activities
5. Leisure time guidance
6. Guidance in character building

According to Johns guidance was initially of six types but later he opted for the first four only.

1. Course curriculum and school guidance
2. Vocational guidance
3. Leisure time guidance

4. Leadership guidance
5. Civic and Moral guidance
6. Social guidance

Koos and Kefauver has given five types of guidance as follows:

1. Educational guidance
2. Vocational guidance
3. Recreational guidance
4. Health guidance
5. Civic, social and moral guidance

Patterson and Williamson too has given five types of guidance as follows:

1. Educational guidance
2. Vocational guidance
3. Personal guidance
4. Health guidance
5. Economic guidance

Bureau of Psychology, Allahabad and Central Bureau of Educational and Vocational Guidance, Delhi has classified guidance into three parts as follows:

1. Educational guidance
2. Vocational guidance
3. Personal guidance

BASIC PRINCIPLES OF GUIDANCE

When disturbing or unhealthful conditions interfere with satisfactory patterns of behaviour, it becomes the responsibility of teachers and members of the guidance personnel to supply whatever service is needed. Whatever the function of the guidance supplied—prevention, preservation, or attempted cure—certain assumptions are basic to its achievement.

Significant Guidance Principles

1. Every aspect of a person's complex personality pattern constitutes a significant factor of his total displayed attitudes and forms of behaviour. Guidance services which are aimed at bringing about desirable adjustment in any

particular area of experience must take into account the all round development of the individual.

2. Although all human beings are similar in many respects, individual differences must be recognised and considered in any efforts aimed at providing help or guidance to a particular child, adolescent, or adult.
3. The function of guidance is to help a person (*i*) formulate and accept stimulating, worthwhile, and attainable goals of behaviour, and (*ii*) apply these objectives in the conduct of his affairs.
4. Existing social, economic, and political unrest is giving rise to many maladjustive factors that require the cooperation of experienced and thoroughly trained guidance counsellors and the individual with a problem.
5. Guidance should be regarded as a continuing process of service to an individual from young childhood through adulthood.
6. Guidance service should not be limited to the few who give observable evidence of its need, but should be extended to all persons of all agents who can benefit therefrom, either directly or indirectly.
7. Curriculum materials and teaching procedures should evidence a guidance point of view.
8. Although guidance touches every phase of an individual's life pattern, the generally accepted areas of guidance include concern with the extent to which an individual's physical and mental health interfere with his adjustment to home, school, and vocational and social demands and relationships, or the extent to which his physical and mental health are affected by the conditions to which he is subjected in these areas of experience.
9. Parents and teachers have guidance-pointed responsibilities.
10. Specific guidance problems on any age level should be referred to persons who are trained to deal with particular areas of adjustment.
11. To administer guidance intelligently and with as thorough knowledge of the individual as is possible, programmes of individual evaluation and research should be conducted, and accurate cumulative records of progress

and achievement should be made accessible to guidance workers. Through the administration of well-selected standardised tests and other instruments of evaluation, specific data concerning degree of mental capacity, success of achievement, demonstrated interests, and other personality characteristics should be accumulated, recorded, and utilised for guidance purposes.

12. An organised guidance programme should be flexible according to individual and community needs.
13. The responsibility for the administration of a guidance programme should be centered in a personally qualified and adequately trained chairman or head of guidance, working co-operatively with his assistants and other community welfare and guidance agencies.
14. Periodic appraisals should be made of the existing school guidance programme. The success of its functioning should rest on outcomes that are reflected in the attitudes toward the programme of all who are associated with it—guiders and guidees—and in the displayed behaviour of those who have been served through its functioning.

Application of Guidance Principles

Wise and experienced leadership in guidance is extremely important. It is often said that "As the principal is, so is the school". This statement holds equally for organised guidance programmes. Completeness of organisation; elaborateness of equipment; multiplicity of records, guidance forms, and reports; and specialisation among guidance personnel—these do not constitute the whole of a programme of effective guidance. Necessary as these adjuncts may be, the core of guidance lies in the spirit in which the services are rendered—the cooperativeness of effort and the earnestness of purpose that motivate the attitudes and behaviour of all who are participants in the guidance activity. These include administrators, teachers, and specialists, as well as the recipients of personal help and counsel.

Intelligent application of the basic principles to the operation of a school programme of guidance services has value not only for the young or older pupils for whose benefit the programme has been organised but also for their parents, the members of the school staff, and the community at large. This fact is not always recognised by the government leaders who provide money for educational purposes or the school administrators who allocate budgetary allowances. Yet, because so many other aspects of education demand financial support, available guidance services often are inadequate.

FUNDAMENTAL PROPOSITIONS

The general organisation and implementation of guidance services and the special procedures employed on the various school levels are discussed in succeeding chapters. At this point attention is directed to certain fundamental assumptions.

Attitudes Toward Guidance Programme

A school guidance programme consists of the co-ordinatedservices of the school faculty, including administrators, teachers, professional guidance workers, and other school personnel in cooperation with appropriate community agencies. All of the services are aimed at encouraging individual and group welfare.

The relative effectiveness of a school guidance programme depends, in part, on:

1. understanding and acceptance by administrators of its functions and goals,
2. well-trained, experienced and personally qualified guidance workers,
3. recognition of pupils' guidance needs, and
4. parent and community cooperation.

An adequately functioning programme of guidance services can be established in any school if the staff members are sufficiently interested to develop it. A programme that is superimposed by the administration how ever, is rarely successful.

Implications of a Guidance Programme

If one is convinced of the value to individuals on any age level of help received through an intelligently conceived and appropriately conducted guidance programme, the formulation of basic principles of guidance procedures is relatively easy. A more difficult task is that of organising and implementing the programme in such way that everyone concerned will receive maximum benefit.

A school guidance programme is concerned in a broad sense with the mental and physical health and personality development of each child with whom the school comes in contact. Guidance is inherent in the total process of education. One of the ultimate goals of guidance is a well-integrated personality. The guidance programme should concern itself with the problems of all youth.

Every teacher on the school staff has a responsibility for aiding in the guidance of boys and girls. Every person who accepts responsibility for a share in the guidance programme must aid in discovering the needs and problems of each child and help the child in resolving his problems. The guidance programme includes both the helping of each child [to] adjust to an established or required pattern, and the adjusting of the pattern to better meet the needs of the individual child.

The acceptance of the responsibility for a guidance programme as defined above suggests the following implications for the school:

For the Individual Child

1. To provide conditions that will give every child a maximum opportunity to feel socially secure, free from abnormal fears and anxieties, happy in the belief that his best achievements are worthy and acceptable.
2. To provide opportunities for each child to find success.
3. To develop those understandings and attitudes that foster sound physical and mental health.
4. To understand himself in terms of his abilities, aptitudes, interests, and achievements.
5. To develop fundamental attitudes toward good social behaviour—behaviour appropriate for various places and times.
6. To develop poise, resourcefulness, and increasing self-direction.
7. To develop interests of intellectual, social, and recreational value.
8. To acquire educational, vocational and personal-social information necessary in making decisions concerning present and future plans.
9. To aid in the selection of a worthy, satisfying vocation which is compatible with the individual's interests and aptitudes.

10. To develop self-control in terms of the best interests of the group and the attitudes and abilities of cooperating successfully with others—a sense of personal responsibility for group welfare.
11. To develop an understanding and a wholesome respect for the acceptance of one's own capabilities and limitations, as well as those of other people.
12. To develop confidence in and respect for one's self.

For the Organisation and Operation of the School

1. To place the needs of individual personalities above most other considerations of school procedure.
2. To provide a curriculum and working conditions where each child may work successfully to fully capacity.
3. To provide information concerning pupils which is necessary for determining appropriate instructional materials and experiences.
4. To provide conditions where children actively participate in planning and successfully carry through group activities.
5. To provide teachers whose classrooms have an atmosphere of good will and kindly understanding.
6. To provide professional service to aid teachers in developing the attitudes, skills, and techniques necessary for successful counselling in the classrooms.
7. To provide health services that will aid in detecting physical conditions that may be causing maladjustment.
8. To provide materials for testing and recording data necessary to understand the individual child's needs, aptitudes, and interests.
9. To provide counselling with parents where it is needed in order to help in the adjustment of the pupil.
10. To provide specialised services for those individuals who cannot be adjusted through group procedure or through the individual efforts of the classroom teacher.
11. To provide an opportunity for an organised cooperative approach to the solution of staff problems.
12. To provide an opportunity for staff planning so that a common point of view and goals may be developed.

There can be no valid objection to the implications suggested in the foregoing. Again, in the words of Mathewson, a guidance programme should possess the following characteristics:

1. The guidance activity (incorporating process of appraisal, adjustment, orientation and development) will be *continuous* from nursery school and kindergarten to, and through, adult education, including the college and university level and including, also, community services for out-of-school youth and adults.
2. The guidance process will be *perversive;* it will be infused in every school activity and will be conducted by teachers as well as specialists.
3. The guidance programme will be *definitive* and will be identifiable as a set of procedures and activities toward definite objectives, practiced in most intensive form by professional specialists.
4. All phases of the guidance programme will be *coordinated,* including community activities, in a systematically organised personnel service, all component functions being directed at the same objectives.
5. In its primary focus, the programme will *center upon the needs and problems of the individual student;* it will seek to foster self-understanding, development, and direction, socially oriented.

Each of the five characteristics listed contains many implications that are both broad in scope and detailed in application. In the light of the materials presented, it is probable that the reader now realises that:

1. guidance is more than giving direction,
2. counselling does not begin and end with a single face-to-face interview,
3. guidance is a continuous process that touches every aspect of an individual's life pattern, and
4. effective programmes include numerous activities and involve the series of many persons.

ADVICE AS GUIDANCE

Another very valuable source of help which is frequently used is the experience of others expressed through advice. The value of this source of guidance is clearly seen in the history of mankind. Man's superiority over the lower animals is due, in large measure, to his ability to profit not only from his own experience but from that of others; without this ability there would have been little progress. Such experience may be utilised either directly, through advice given by others, or indirectly, through a knowledge and understanding of history.

Although advice is an old and widely used method of guidance, some guidance authorities condemn it in any form, maintaining that it is harmful. They even go so far as to say that the only time it is safe to give advice to others is when you know they will not use it. This statement grossly exaggerates the dangers of advice and is plainly untrue.

Industrial firms spend millions every year on advice, and it pays. Older men who have had years of experience either in the industry that employs them or in similar industries are used as consultants or advisers. The value of their services is evident in the large salaries given to such men. Throughout history sages have been singled out for great honour and reverence.

All aspects of the past—social, industrial, economic, scientific, artistic, and religious—have much to teach us. Such sources of understanding are too little used in our present programmes of guidance. To be of any use the lessons of history must be read and interpreted not only in terms of the past but also in terms of the present. Teachers of English, history, science, art, and music can open up these sources of help and interpret them as well.

The lessons of the past that are of the greatest value are those that state fundamental values of life and general principles of conduct. These lessons will help in many different situations because they usually do not indicate exactly what one should do but leave it to the individual to determine what definite action will be best.

This is in accord with the principle that the purpose of guidance is the development in the individual of the ability to solve problems without the help of others. Conditions may have changed so much that the present problem is quite unlike the old one, and what was once a desirable solution may no longer be satisfactory.

Advice is usually received best and carries more weight when the one who seeks it comes voluntarily to the counsellor because he feels the need for help. Gratuitous advice is usually of little value because most people regard such proffered help as an intrusion on what they consider to be their own affair. Such advice is also often given without knowledge or consideration of the needs of the person advised.

In summary, one's own experience as well as that of others may be very valuable in guidance, but it may not be a safe guide in itself. To be of real value, experience must be interpreted in relation to the particular problem that is at hand. Is this problem the same as the one previously faced? Is the solution that was made in the past as satisfactory now as it was then?

There may be differences, even though slight ones, in the present situation that may be very significant, thus making the solution that was once satisfactory quite unsatisfactory now. For example, action taken fifty years ago based on a certain religious belief may have been useful then, but it may be quite useless or even undesirable now. Even now two persons may have the same beliefs regarding the worth of the individual and his relation to God and yet be on opposite sides of such a social problem as segregation.

One may honestly believe that the best interests of the Negro can be secured by segregation; the other may believe just as sincerely that they can be attained only by desegregation. The previous family and social experience and the background of each person have a powerful influence on the belief which is held.

Guidance must help young people to develop techniques of utilising their own past experience and that of others for the solution of the problems facing them in making their adjustments in life.

QUESTIONS FOR ANSWER

1. *Write a note on the kinds of guidance.*
2. *Discuss in detail basic principles of guidance.*
3. *Explain fundamental propositions of guidance.*
4. *Write a note on implications of guidance programme.*
5. *Write a note on 'advice as guidance'.*

PART II
STRATEGIES AND TECHNIQUES

7

The Nature of Guidance and Counselling Services

All forms of human activities in one way or the other directly or indirectly effect the career of the individual because career is a very wide and complex term. Similarly, guidance of any form regarding any aspect of individual's personal, family, vocational or social life effects his image which in wider sense means his career in society, therefore, for proper and effective career guidance, the structure of guidance and counselling services, particularly at institutional level needs to be properly understood for organisation and effective use of these services. Hereunder, we will, very briefly discuss this aspect for effective application these services for career guidance:

Since guidance programme is concerned with meeting student needs, it can be structured properly only as a *service*—to aid the student in the identification of his abilities, aptitudes, interests and attitudes; to help him to understand, accept and utilise his traits; to provide him with opportunities for learning about areas of educational and occupational endeavours; to help him in obtaining experiences which will assist him in the making of free and wise choices; to assist him in developing his potential to the optimum so that he may become the individual he is capable of becoming and to aid him in becoming more and more self-directive.

To achieve these manifold objectives an effective guidance programme will have to be organised in the form of a constellation of services comprising of the following specific services:

1. The Pre-admission Service
2. The Admission Service
3. The Orientation Service

4. The Student Information Service
5. The Information Service
6. The Counselling Service
7. The Placement Service
8. The Remedial Service
9. The Follow-up Service
10. The Research Service
11. The Evaluation Service

It needs to be pointed out that different labels have been given to the different services for practical considerations only. A good guidance programme, in fact, is a unified programme—all the specific services woven into it. The various services have to be supportive of one another for best results.

1. The Pre-admission Service

After completing high school education, students aspiring for higher education join colleges or universities. To enable the students to get admission in the right course, the pre-admission service is needed to ensure that:

(*i*) the occupational aspirations of the students are correlated with their scholastic achievement;
(*ii*) the occupational aspirations of the students are in consonance with the economic condition of their families;
(*iii*) their social bearings are also in tune with their job aspirations;
(*iv*) there is a positive relationship between the subjects of education and their job aspirations; and
(*v*) the students are familiar with the repercussions of choosing a particular course of study.

It is very essential that the students are acquainted with the present supply and demand position in various occupational fields, estimation of manpower requirements, projected picture of employment opportunities, shortages and surpluses of occupations so that they plan to follow these occupations where shortage of manpower exists.

This service may be arranged in collaboration with the Employment Exchanges, University Employment Information and Guidance Bureaux, Student Advisory Bureaux, and local resource persons. Facility should be provided to those students who might feel the necessity of further guidance and information before deciding a line of action.

It may be provided in the form of meetings with faculty advisors, employment officers, academic advisors and deputy chiefs of the University Employment Information and Guidance Bureaux.

2. The Admission Service

Admission service is one of the important links in the chain of guidance services. This service is needed to:

(*i*) admit the right persons for the right course for the maximum advantage both to the individual and the society;
(*ii*) select those candidates most likely to succeed to keep wastage figures and dropout rate at the minimum level.

Admission service, to be effective, will comprise a carefully framed criterion of admission, some entrance test and interview. For admission to the various professional institutions—National Defence Academy etc.—this triple measure is adopted. The same needs to be adopted for admission to all the colleges and universities.

3. The Orientation Service

A very heterogeneous population gets admitted to a college or university—students coming from cities, towns and villages, from happy and unhappy homes, from highly educated parents and totally illiterate parents, from well-established peer groups and isolated individuals, from convent schools and colleges and ordinary schools and colleges.

Adequate arrangements need to be made in colleges and universities for raising efficiency of all these students not only in scholarship but also in citizenship, social skills, vocational skills, sense of responsibility, courage and poise.

The orientation service may include issue of printed material like:

(*i*) A leaflet containing campus map and the names of the Heads of Departments and staff members;
(*ii*) Time Table for the Welcome Day;

(*iii*) Calendar of events for the whole year—which should include all important dates like the last day of registration, examinations, holidays etc;

(*iv*) Students' handbook which should include a welcome letter by the Principal/Vice-Chancellor, summaries of courses, degrees and certificates offered, and qualifications for each; academic information such as whom to consult regarding selection of compulsory and optional courses; timings and locations of such consultations; whom to contact for change of a subject; registration—when and how; fees—scholarships and fee concessions; classroom procedures; library and its service; the availability of various student services, how to make optimal use of the same, etc.

Orientation Day

A day may be fixed for giving all types of information to the students regarding the clubs and societies, cultural activities open to freshers, financial counselling, health services, student centre, honorary organisations, athletic teams, recreational facilities, special interest clubs, hobbies, hostel accommodation, student Government, rules of conduct, etc.

The members of the faculty may also give their self-introduction. In big colleges and universities, the orientation day may be celebrated faculty-wise—Arts Faculty, Science Faculty, etc. In small colleges, the whole of the student population may be gathered at one place for the programme.

The orientation day programme must not become a series of talks but must be punctuated with humour and liveliness.

Orientation service must organise following activities for better understanding and results:

1. Campus Tour
2. Welcome Desk at the Entrance
3. Social Evening

Special efforts need to be made for orienting the foreign students in particular. They need orientation at two stages:

1. *Prior to their arrival*: They need general information about the country they are about to visit; the city they are going to live in; and the college/university they are about to join;

2. *On arrival*: They need specific information such as local transportation, hostel, the whereabouts of organisations and individuals who are in a position to assist them with special services and opportunities. Such students also need to be oriented to the culture and society of the host country.

Comprehensive printed information should be sent to them before coming to India and specific and detailed information given to them when they come to our country. The foreign students may be advised to study the two booklets published by the Indian Council for Cultural Relations—*Studying in India and Toward understanding India*. Some universities have a post of Dean, Foreign Students. He and his staff can take up this job.

If the orientation service is well-organised, the students will surely get off to a good start.

4. The Student Information Service

A proper choice of courses and careers can be made if the student not only knows the opportunities available and the requirements of particular courses and careers but also what he has to bring to any course or career that he may choose. The Socratic dictum "Know Thyself" is fundamental to a wise choice.

The student information service is intended to:

(*a*) assist the student to obtain a realistic picture of his abilities, interests, personality characteristics, college/university achievement, level of aspirations, state of health, etc;
(*b*) enable the student to know himself on a socio-comparative basis;
(*c*) provide a record of the student's progress; and
(*d*) help the guidance workers and others to understand him more adequately.

The service involves:

(*a*) Collecting essential data about the students;
(*b*) Orderly maintenance of records to assist the students as well as their advisers/tutors in making important decisions.

5. The Information Service

Information is an essential part of virtually every guidance programme, whether we want to assist the student to make better choices, help him in better adjustment or optimum development. This is the reason that information needs to be organised and utilised as a distinct guidance service so as to:

(*a*) develop in the students a broad and realistic view of life's opportunities and problems at all levels of training;
(*b*) create an awareness of the need and an active desire for accurate and valid occupational, educational and personal-social information;
(*c*) assist in learning the techniques of obtaining and interpreting information for progressive self-directiveness;
(*d*) promote attitudes and habits which will assist in the making of choices and adjustments productive of personal satisfaction and effectiveness; and
(*e*) provide assistance in narrowing choices progressively to specific activities which are approximate to aptitudes, abilities and interests manifested and to their proximity to defined decisions.

Information provided by this service can be divided into three categories:

(*i*) Educational Information;
(*ii*) Occupational Information; and
(*iii*) Personal-social Information.

Here are some examples of the various types of information within each of the three major categories:

(i) Educational Information

(*a*) Prospectuses from different colleges, universities, professional colleges, institutes of technology, polytechnics, etc.
(*b*) Directories of various types of colleges and universities.
(*c*) Books/brochures containing information on scholarships and loans.
(*d*) Books, pamphlets, brochures, leaflets on developing study skills.

(e) Illustrative material as films, filmstrips, posters, charts etc. regarding educational facilities and processes.

(ii) Occupational Information

(a) Occupational abstracts, briefs, guides, monographs and pamphlets.
(b) Occupational files and dictionaries.
(c) Career information manuals.
(d) Illustrative material as films, film strips, posters, charts, etc. regarding different jobs and job processes.

(iii) Personal-Social Information

(a) Booklets for increasing self-understanding.
(b) Mental health material.
(c) Personal hygiene material.
(d) Illustrative material as films, filmstrips, posters, charts, etc., regarding personal-social adjustment.

6. The Counselling Service

The service is intended to establish a relationship between guidance worker and the student in which the former attempts to assist the latter in achieving optimum educational, vocational and personal-social development and adjustment. The service may be performed by the counselling officer, liaison officer, teacher, administrator, etc. provided they are adequately trained.
The service involves helping the student to:

(a) understand what he *can* do and what he *should* do;
(b) understand the choices he faces—the opportunities open to him and the qualifications he possesses for the goal he has chosen;
(c) handle his difficulties in a rational way and strengthen his best qualities;
(d) make his own decisions and plans on the basis of self-understanding, accept responsibility for the decisions and take action on the plans developed.

Counselling is helpful in crystallising the problem and reaching a reasonably good solution. That way counselling is one of the most distinctive of all the guidance services.

7. The Placement Service

This is another important service in the guidance programme. It is intended to help the student in:

(*a*) situating himself in the proper scholastic track in the proper course;
(*b*) finding a proper place in the post-college or university or post-university environment;
(*c*) the proper choice of co-curricular activities available in college/university;
(*d*) the choice of job-oriented courses;
(*e*) getting admission in a college or professional institution or university; and
(*f*) getting part-time jobs, during working session and whole-time jobs after getting education and training.

The service is useful to all types of students—the normal, the intellectually gifted, the emotionally disturbed, the artistically talented, the mentally retarded etc., to find their appropriate place in an educational or vocational setting.

8. The Remedial Service

There is no doubt about this fact that the defects in speech, hearing, reading and study habits can seriously impede the functioning of many able students and restrict the contributions which may be made by otherwise adequate personalities. Arrangements for remedial help in these and similar other areas need to be made in colleges and universities.

Almost all students could profit by some training in study skills. But efforts should be made to identify those whose reading skills and oral speech competence are below average; special arrangements may be made to enable them to overcome these handicaps.

Speech articulation at low cost can be arranged with the help of tape recorders. This help is particularly needed by pre-university or first year of TDC students who are exposed to lectures in English for the first time. Similarly this service is of great value to students going abroad for further study.

9. The Follow-up Service

Follow-up is that review or systematic evaluation which is carried out to find out whether guidance service in particular and educational programme in general satisfy the needs of the students.

It has to be seen to what extent have the students been able to achieve according to their abilities and aptitudes, to what extent curricular and co-curricular choices have been wise, and how are the students adjusting with the part-time or whole-time jobs. The students need to be followed in order to determine the nature and extent of their need for assistance.

The typical follow-up technique employs one or more of the following techniques—*interview, post-card survey*, or *questionnaire*. Each approach has certain advantages and limitations. For example, the interview results in the most valid information but it is time-consuming and expensive.

The post-card survey is inexpensive and easy to conduct, but the results are extremely limited. The questionnaire accomplishes some of the objectives of the other techniques and also overcomes, in part, the limitations of the other approaches.

Information obtained through follow-up techniques can be used for improving the curriculum, stimulating better teaching, increasing the value of the guidance services and establishing better college/university and community relationships.

For the success of this service, it is necessary that all the members of the staff join hands. There should also be some means of bringing about coordination in follow-up activities.

10. The Research Service

Research, naturally, is one of the most important guidance services. It is needed for a better understanding of students as well as for a working knowledge of college/university needs and resources and for evaluation of achievement in relation to goals. The findings of studies form the basis for curricular enrichment and/or redirection and also reorientation of other services.

The service is intended to examine both the personnel in the college/university guidance programme and the techniques of guidance used by them so as to discover their strong and weak points and ultimately strengthen the whole of the programme.

Research can give the guidance staff greater psychological security because of a knowledge of the effectiveness of its efforts. It can also provide a basis for guidance development programme.

Research has to be a continuous process, it cannot be "done" and "forgotten". It would be advisable if one part of a student counselling centre should function exclusively on research activities.

11. The Evaluation Service

The evaluation service completes the entire process of guidance. It is essential to evaluate the use and application of information to established activities in order to determine their effectiveness (i.e., the degree to which they satisfy needs) and their efficiency (i.e., how well time, money and personnel are utilised). This can be done by finding out:

(*i*) Degree of harmony between educational and vocational plans and capacity of the students;
(*ii*) Agreement between subjects taken or planned and the entrance requirements of the college/university the student plans to enter;
(*iii*) Extent of participation of students in co-curricular activities;
(*iv*) Extent and nature of shifts in vocational choices;
(*v*) Amount of maladjustment among students; and
(*vi*) Extent to which students are aware of the type of information to be considered in making an occupational choice and the source of such information, etc.

Guidance and counselling programme in a college/university can work effectively if all these services are organised in an efficient manner. If organised well and implemented effectively, these services will facilitate good teaching and efficient learning and thus prove as necessary supplements to academic achievement which is the primary responsibility of educational institutions.

They will also help in decreasing wastage, improve student performance, lower class absenteeism, create favourable faculty opinion, eliminate student indiscipline and unrest and, on the whole, create congenial atmosphere in the institution.

QUESTIONS FOR ANSWER

1. *Write a note on the significance of guidance and counselling services in educational institutions and discuss the aims of these services briefly.*
2. *Write short notes on the following:*
   (a) The follow-up service.
   (b) The orientation service.
   (c) The information service.
   (d) The evaluation service.

8

Guidance Strategies: The Counselling Techniques

INTRODUCTION

Guidance, like all other services of the school, uses and should use many different techniques suited to the special need, the special situation, and the abilities of the counsellor or the teacher. In this respect it is like teaching. Effective teaching is not dependent on any one technique since the one that is most effective for the dull student may not be suited to the bright student.

The effective counsellor will study each student, each problem, each situation, and then select from the many techniques available to him the one that, in his judgment, will be the most effective in helping the particular student to solve his particular problem.

Counselling is the component of guidance, which includes various aspects to serve the people who need it individually or collectively in groups. It is a service that should be above all the activities of the school.

The concept of counselling has radically changed in the past twenty-five years and even now is undergoing considerable modification. It is still centered upon the individual, but the ways in which the help is given are being reconsidered and new methods explored.

The guidance service of the school will be effective only if we keep constantly in mind the individual student and his need. We must keep an open mind regarding the particular techniques to be used and not use one just because some authority has praised it.

COUNSELLING

One of the standard techniques of guidance is counselling. There does not seem to be any specific definition of counselling which is acceptable to all authorities. A well-organised attempt by a group of clinical psychologists to develop such a definition is described in *Roles and Relationships in Counselling*. A careful analysis of counselling and developed principles and techniques are important for effective counselling.

What is Counselling?

On the basis of these considerations the following definition was constructed by Gustad:

> "Counselling is a learning-oriented process carried on in a simple one-to-one social environment in which the counsellor, professionally competent in relevant psychological skills and knowledge, seeks to assist the client by methods appropriate to the latter's needs, and within the context of the total personnel programme, to learn more about himself and to accept himself, to learn how to put such understanding into effect in relation to more clearly perceived, realistically defined goals, to the end that the client may become a happier and more productive member of society".

It would be much more useful to formulate a simple definition that would apply to all counselling, good and bad, and then to list the conditions and principles that are essential for effective and desirable results.

The following definition by Bordin is an excellent example, although not entirely complete: "Counselling is the process of aiding an individual to solve his problems through the medium of the interview".

"Therapy is a process in which an individual is helped to free himself from trying conditions and hardships in the environments and from his own inner conflicts, anxieties, or a sense of inadequacy and gains courage to live again to face life positively instead of negatively". —*J.C. Agrawal*

"Therapy is the development of a satisfactory solution to a personal problem". —*Hemphre*

"Psychotherapy or treatment aims at restoring of mental health and at making a person more mature, flexible, and adaptable; so that he is submissive or aggressive, cooperative or resistant according to the requirements of the situation". —*Udai Shankar*

Webster's dictionary defines counselling as "Consultation, mutual interchange of opinions, deliberating together".

Wren (1962) says, "Counselling is a dynamic and purposeful relationship between two people who approach a mutually defined problems with mutual consideration of each other to the end that the younger or less mature, or more troubled of the two is aided to a self-determined resolution of his problem".

James Michael Lee and Nathaniel J. Pattan say, "Counselling is the relationship between two persons in which one of them attempts to assist the other in so organising himself as to attain a particular form of happiness, adjustment to a life-situation, or in short, self-actualisation. Counselling always involves a one-to-one relationship, that is one client and one guidance worker in a formal or an informal interview situation".

Merle M. Ohlsen (1977) writes, "Counselling is an accepting, trusting and safe relationship in which clients learn to discuss openly what worries and upsets them, to define precise behaviour goals, to acquire the essential social skills, and to develop the courage and self-confidence to implement desired new behaviours".

According to Arbuckle (1965), "Counselling is helping a person to come to see who he really is, what he has and does not have; what he can do easily, what he can do with difficulty and what he probably cannot do at all... (It) is a close sharing of a human relationship with one who has for him a high regard; one who can offer him unconditional acceptance, but one who has no guarantees, no answers".

Pepinsky and Pepinsky (1954) feel, "Counselling relationship refers to the interaction which (*i*) occurs between two individuals called "counsellor" and "client", (*ii*) takes place within a professional setting, and (*iii*) is initiated and maintained as a means of facilitating changes in the behaviour of the client. The Counselling relationship develops from the interaction between two individuals, one a professionally trained worker and the other a person who seeks his services".

Hahn and Maclean (1955) define "Counselling as a process which takes place in a one-to-one relationship between an individual beset by problems with which he cannot cope alone and a professional worker whose training and experience have qualified him to help others reach solutions to various types of personal difficulties".

Blocker (1966) explains it as "helping an individual became aware of himself and the ways in which he is reacting to the behavioural influences of his environment. It further helps him to establish some personal meaning for this behaviour and to develop and clarify a set of goals and values for future behaviour".

ELEMENTS OF COUNSELLING

An analysis of the above viewpoints will reveal the major elements of counselling:

1. Counselling involves two individuals—one seeking help and the other, a professionally trained person who can help the first.
2. There should be a relationship of mutual respect between the two individuals. The counsellor should be friendly and cooperative and the counsellee should have trust and confidence in the counsellor.
3. The aim of counselling is to help a student to form a decision, make a choice or find a direction at some important fork in the road such as that of planning a life career, a programme in college or university, or a campaign to obtain employment.
4. It helps the counselee acquire independence and develop a sense of responsibility. It helps him explore and fully utilise his potentialities and actualise himself.
5. It is more than advice-giving. Progress comes through the thinking that a person with a problem does for himself rather than through solutions suggested by the counsellors.
6. It involves something more than the solution to an immediate problem. Its function is to produce changes in the individual that will enable him to extricate himself from his immediate difficulties.
7. It concerns itself with attitudes as well as action.

8. Emotional rather than purely intellectual attitudes are the raw material of the counselling process. Information and intellectual understanding have their place in the counselling process. But it is the emotionalised feelings which are most important.

Counselling has proved to be very useful wherever the development of an individual student is cared for. It helps an individual to know himself better, gives him confidence, encourages his self-directiveness and provides him a vision.

The main objective of counselling is to bring about a *voluntary* change in the client. For this purpose, the counsellor provides facilities to help achieve the desired change or make the suitable choice. *The client alone is responsible for the decisions or the choices he make, though the counsellor may assist in this process by his warmth and understanding relationship.*

Counselling and Psychotherapy

Counselling and psychotherapy are different. Although the psychotherapist uses counselling as one of the techniques of treatment, psychotherapy is concerned mostly with individuals whose behaviours are neurotic. It deals with repressed individuals but counselling is concerned mostly with normal anxieties. Psychotherapy operates in a medical setting whereas counselling operates in an educational setting.

Psychotherapist uses play therapy, psychodrama, socio-drama, etc. as techniques; in counselling, such techniques are used as can be employed in educational institutions, industrial establishments etc. Psychotherapy is deeper in scope whereas counselling is broader in scope. A counsellor cannot be a psychotherapist, a psychotherapist can be a counsellor, being better and specially qualified.

Scope of Counselling

Counselling has a vast scope. According to Williamson, "The techniques of counselling individual students may be observed in greatly modified form, in the individualised service; granting loans and scholarships; handling discipline cases; assignment of rooms and selection of room-mates in dormitories; advising on student activities and programmes; helping students choose vocational objectives; selecting optional courses of study; learning to read at college rate and comprehension".

Concerns about educational progress, course programme planning, financial and health matters, and problems of family, social and emotional adjustment are commonly expressed in the context of counselling.

Very often, many of these are closely intertwined in experience of the same student. In such instances, terms such as 'vocational problem' and 'emotional problem' are nothing more than convenient labels which serve as tentative and approximate methods of classifying counselling cases.

It often happens that a problem which is initially expressed by the student as simply one of learning how to study better or of making a suitable vocational choice turns out to be much more complex than that.

Levels of Counselling

Counselling is a term that is used quite loosely for face-to-face interviews in which the counsellor attempts non-coercively to help the counsellee or client, or a group of clients, to make personal decisions.

It may be helpful to differentiate three levels of activity related to training:

1. *Informal counselling*—It is any helping relationship by a responsible person who may have little or no training for the work. For instance, ladies helping patients in hospitals through friendly conversations with them.
2. *Non-specialist counselling by professionals*—It is the help provided by physicians, lawyers, teachers, ministers, and others who do a great deal of face-to-face work with psychological problems in the course of their other work. Sometimes, special titles are used like "religious counselling" or "financial counselling".
3. *Professional counselling*—It is helping another person with decision and life-plans, whether personal or educational-vocational, by a person specially trained for this work.

Professional counsellors are usually psychologists, or educational psychologists. 'Professional' means among other things, the possession of master's or doctor's degree with at least a year of supervision by a trained professional and the acceptance of a professional code of ethics. Training for psychologists, among other things, emphasises test interpretation, research, the psychology of personality, occupational information and experience with a variety of clients.

PURPOSES OF STUDENT COUNSELLING

Dunsmoor and Miller are of the view that the core of student counselling is to help the student to help himself. From this point of view they describe the following purposes of student counselling:

1. To give the student information on matters important to success.
2. To get information about student which will be of help in solving his problems.
3. To establish a feeling of mutual understanding between student and teacher.
4. To help the student work out a plan for solving his difficulties.
5. To help the student know himself better—his interests, abilities, aptitudes and opportunities.
6. To encourage and develop special abilities and right attitudes.
7. To inspire successful endeavour toward attainment.
8. To assist the student in planning for educational and vocational choices.

It is obvious that the goal of counselling is problem clarification and self-directed needs. The counselling officer helps the student to understand the problems and helps the student to help himself.

In this process, the role of the student is objective self-assessment of the situation and the role of counselling officer is to formulate the decision making process and to act as the stimulator of insights and sensitivities of the student.

Counselling does not solve the problems but helps in solving and if solution is not possible to help face challenges and to live with them.

Classification of Counselling

Counselling can be classified according to the *nature of the problem, the complexity of treatment, and the competence of the counsellor.*

Some writers classify counselling in terms of several factors. Lloyd Jones and Smith, for example, describe various levels of counselling with respect to the depth of the problem, length of contact, degree of need, and the skill of the counsellor.

At the *Surface level* is the counselling offered when the student wishes only some item of information. The counselling given may be casual; it is brief, and it may be superficial in that it is not extensive or intensive. The need for help is important even though slight, and the relationship maintained through the brief contact should not be less than that maintained during the long counselling session.

Counselling at the *next level* requires a more prolonged contact because the counselee needs more and complicated information. He may, for example, wish assistance in planning a programme of study for a two or four year period. As the problems became more complicated and as more intensive study of the case is required, and more specialised help is needed, counselling at deeper levels becomes necessary.

When the student is seriously disturbed, *therapeutic counselling* may be needed. Williamson feels that counselling is needed not only for helping individuals to gain insight into their emotional conflicts but also for helping them with problems stemming from lack of information, such as information about vocational aptitudes and interests or about work opportunities, so that they may conduct their future adjustments in such a way, that a 'minimum of maladaptive repressions' occur.

Conditions Essentials for Counselling

It is generally accepted that rapport is a necessary precondition for counselling. Rapport between counsellor and counselee is thought to be present when the counselee feels the need for help, when he comes to the counsellor willingly because he feels that the counsellor can help him, and when the counsellor is deeply understanding and sympathetic and has only one purpose—to be of assistance to the counselee.

There seems to be a difference of opinion regarding the place of rapport in counselling. Some authorities feel the rapport is essential for counselling, that is, that it is necessary to establish rapport before counselling can function.

If this is true, then the great majority of high-school students, being sent by teacher or principal, cannot have any counselling until rapport is established. Establishing rapport is a function of counselling, therefore the counsellor's effort to attain rapport is itself counselling.

When Counselling is Required?

The following are some of the situations in which counselling is needed:

1. When the student needs not only reliable information but an interested interpretation of such information as meets his own personal difficulties.
2. When the student needs a wise, sympathetic listener with broader experience than his own, to whom he can recount his difficulties and from whom he may gain suggestions regarding his own proposed plan of action.
3. When the counsellor has access to facilities for helping in the solution of a student's problem to which the student does not have easy access.
4. When the student is unaware that he has a certain problem but for his best development, must be around to a consciousness of that problem.
5. When the student is aware of a problem and of the strain and difficulty it is causing, but is unable to define and understand it, and is unable to cope with it independently.

Who should be Counselled?

The following type of students are in urgent need of counselling:

1. Students who have a consistent record of under-achievement.
2. Students whose scholastic achievement drops suddenly.
3. Students who need financial aid in order to continue their studies.

4. Students who find it difficult to participate in class and extra-class activities.
5. Students who use exhibitionism for gaining recognition or attention in class.
6. Students who find it difficult to adjust to the college/ university.
7. Students who suddenly decide to drop out of college/ university.
8. Students who display unusual ability in any direction—intellectual, artistic, musical, etc.
9. Students who have behaviour problems such as drug addiction, aggressiveness, bullying, stealing, shyness, timidity, etc.

Who Should Do Counselling?

This question leads inevitably to the rapidly growing belief that counselling should not be confined to the counsellor but should be used, as far as possible, by the entire school staff, especially the teacher. In fact, counselling is basically a teaching technique. Guidance is more and more considered as a *learning* activity by an increasing number of authorities.

It is important to recognise the fact that this close personal relationship between counsellor and counselee and between teacher and pupil is not achieved quickly; it may be long in developing and may be present long before the pupil is conscious of the problem.

Because he often is not aware of the developing problem, the pupil's feeling that he needs help may often be slow in emerging. If the counsellor or teacher sees in advance what the problem of the student will be, he can be of maximum assistance by preparing the student to meet it as it appears.

It should also be kept in mind that all people are not equally able to develop the necessary rapport. The ideal relationship is that of father-son or mother-daughter. This is not to say that the father-son or mother-daughter relationship is always ideal, but it has all the elements that make possible such rapport. Parents are with their children day after day and year after year as they grow up and are in the best position to see and understand problems due to growth and developing maturity.

Counselling is a combination of science and art. It involves an intimate relationship between counsellor and client. This relationship depends in large measure on the counsellor. He must like people as people and must have the ability to show that he likes them and to act really interested in them.

He must also be a person whom people like and in whom they can trust. He must at the same time be objective in his attitude toward the client and not allow his liking for him to warp his understanding; he must be able to see the client as he is. In deciding who should do counselling, one must keep in mind the above considerations.

Does Counselling Help?

It is apparent that good counselling does not necessarily provide solutions to the problems of the client. The provision of such solutions is not only difficult but often undesirable. The value of counselling cannot be measured by the ability of the counsellor to discover what is the best choice of occupations or college for the client or by his ability to influence him to accept this choice.

Even if he could do this, there is no statistical procedure that would enable us to find whether the choice made was the best one. Even if the student were successful in the college he chose or in the occupation he entered, there is no way of determining whether he could not have been equally successful if he had made another choice.

We cannot relive our lives with all conditions the same. The fundamental purpose of guidance is not merely to bring success to the client but to help him develop the ability to choose wisely. Initial success may lead to satisfaction with lesser goals, and initial failure may stir one to greater effort in attaining more adequate goals.

TYPES OF COUNSELLING

Some authorities have attempted to distinguish between such types of counselling as counsellor-versus client-centered, directive versus nondirective, controlled versus permissive. The distinction client-centered versus counsellor-centered reveals an entire misconception of counselling. All service activities are, by their nature, centered on the person to be helped. All teaching is pupil-centered even when the teacher has fifty pupils in his class.

The services of the physician and the nurse are patient-centered. What is really meant by client-centered versus counsellor-centered is the relative activity of the counsellor and the counselee in the guidance process or in the interview.

Directive versus nondirective indicates also the degree to which the counsellor attempts to direct the discussion along the lines that he thinks profitable as compared with encouraging the counselee to determine the direction of the discussion. The nondirective technique is based on the belief that the client has the resources within himself to solve his own problems without direction from others.

Client-Centered Point of View

The nondirective, permissive, client-centered approach is more effective when 'emotional' problems are present. It is clear, however, that many problems of students who come to the counsellor have few if any such emotional conditions. Many cases merely call for information or some other routine help.

Without any intention to detract from the real value of the client-centered technique, it should be pointed out that the "slight suggestion or interpretation" made by a counsellor when he is in the 'semitrance' of feeling as the counselee feels may be as purely directive as a similar suggestion made by a directive counsellor.

The value of the suggestion or interpretation in such a case comes from the counsellor's wide experience which enables him not only to understand the present feeling of the student but to see more clearly than the student the steps that must be taken to arrive at a suitable solution of the problem.

Directive Point of View

In contrast to the client-centered technique it is often said that the directive counsellor is more interested in the problem than he is in the counselee, but this belief is an exaggeration. He is concerned with the student *and* his problem—the two cannot be separated.

The directive counsellor, however, is apt to be more active, to make use of tests and other records, and to be freer in giving advice and information. It is likely that most school counselling could be classified as directive.

Contrast and Comparison

Although the differences between the client-centered and the directive point of view may be more theoretical than practical, it will be valuable to examine some of the claimed point of opposition.

Differences in Emphasis between Directive and Client-centered Techniques

Directive	*Client-centered*
Centre of Interest	
Counselee with the problem; problem is very important.	The counselee; the problem is incidental.
Need for Assistance	
Counselling is a learning process. Counselee needs help. Counsellor can see the problem and the solution better than the counselee.	Counselee has within himself the power to solve his own problem. The counselee can see the problem and the solution better than the counsellor.
Use of Records	
Tests, records, past history are very important in finding the origin of the problem.	Past history, tests, and records often interfere with the solution of the problem. Counsellor sees the counselee *as he now is.*
Emotional Aspects	
Interfere with the solution of the problem. Intellectual element of most importance. Many problems have few if any emotional conditions.	Emotional condition very important as an element in the situation.
Interview	
Rapport important, but in many cases not essential.	'Empathy' essential. Counsellor must understand the state of mind of the client but not feel as the client feels.

ECLECTIC COUNSELLING

The process of eclectic counselling proceeds somewhat along the following lines:

1. Counselling may be preceded by an intake interview.
2. During the opening phase of counselling, the counsellor tries to establish rapport and may have to do structuring so that the client understands what to expect of counselling.
3. Often a tentative diagnosis is made which may include the collection of a case history and a plan for counselling is formulated.
4. To enhance the client's self-understanding, information, about him and his background may be gathered from various sources. The client needs to be helped to assimilate this information.
5. Educational, occupational and social information, if needed by the client, may be supplied to him.
6. The client achieves emotional release and insights, alters his perceptions and attitudes about himself and his situations.
7. During the closing phase, the client makes decisions and plans, modifies behaviour, solve his problems.
8. There may be follow-up contacts, if needed.

No matter what method or view-point—directive, non-directive or eclectic is employed in the practice of interviewing and counselling, counselling should have *developmental preventive* and *remedial* values.

It is obvious that counselling process is viewed differently by different approaches. But in spite of the diversity in approaches to counselling, there are some common factors which are:

1. All counsellors accept the importance of ideal counselling relationship.
2. Interview is the basic tool of counselling.
3. The counselling relationship is built during interviews.
4. All counsellors realise the importance of acceptance of and respect for the counsellee.

5. "Honesty", "Sincerity", or "Openness" of the counsellor is another common element with all counselling approaches. How the counselee perceives the counsellor is more important than even the skills and the knowledge of the counsellor.

FORMS OF COUNSELLING

Counselling can be divided in the following two categories:

1. Individual counselling
2. Group counselling.

We shall discuss individual counselling in the next two chapter, first individual counselling—the interview technique and second counselling individual situations. Therefore, hereunder, we will only discuss the concept of group counselling.

GROUP GUIDANCE AND GROUP COUNSELLING

Guidance is concerned with help given to individuals. This leads some authorities to conclude that there can be no such thing as group guidance or group counselling.

But teaching is also concerned with the individual, and yet we use the term "group testing", meaning testing pupils in groups, but in each case it is the individuals in the group with whom we are concerned.

We can, in the same way, speak of group guidance. By this we may mean either one of two things:

1. that group procedures may be used when they are thought to be more effective and economical for helping individual pupils, or
2. that group guidance means the guidance of a *group*.

Guidance in Groups

This is the term used by Bennett to indicate the value of group procedures in helping individuals in the solution of their problems. The therapeutic value of group procedures has long been generally accepted. The knowledge that others in the group have the same problems helps the individual to realise that he is not the only person who is faced with this difficulty.

The opinion of the group regarding the best method of solving this problem is a powerful influence on the acceptance of the solution by the individual. The results of experiments in the use of group methods indicate that in many cases they are more effective than individual counselling.

Group Counselling

The values of group guidance are generally accepted, but the term "group counselling" is still rejected by many guidance authorities. Some believe that group counselling is an 'anomaly' and say that "it is as silly to speak of 'group counselling' as "group courtship".

Many other clinical psychologists take the same position because they accept the definition of counselling as a "face-to-face", "one-to-one" relationship, as in the interview. Such definitions automatically exclude any notion of the group; but this is merely circular argument and leads nowhere.

Psychologists and sociologists recognise that there is a group 'entity'; the group is different from the sum of all the individuals in it. There is a group purpose or objective that is not the same as the objective of any individual in the group. There is a definite group psychology.

Mob psychology is not only real but terribly effective for good or evil. Its power is seen not only in men but also in animals. The stampede of horses and cattle and the "death march" of a herd of cattle around the body of a recently killed member are striking examples of mob psychology. Many times the individual in the mob is not even conscious of his existence as an individual—he is just a part of the mob.

In everybody life, in community, in the home, in the school, problems appear which can be solved more effectively by the group. In the school especially problems of a group often arise, that is, a problem common to the whole group and not merely to any one individual.

The group presents its problem to the principal who listens and stimulates discussion. Different members suggest methods that might be helpful in solving it, and a decision is reached. A *group* interview is held because the problem is a group problem and the solution a group solution.

Case Conference Procedures

A technique that combines the techniques of "counselling in groups" and "group counselling" was used by Allen and practiced in the public schools. The method has much to commend it.

The purpose of this method was to provide the counsellor with an approach to the discussion of personal and social relationships by means of *group thinking* in order to obviate the need for 'preaching'. Common problems of young people in the group were presented for study and discussion.

After the problem had been stated concretely by way of a case, each pupil reviewed his own experience in a similar situation. Then the leader guided the group away from the more immediate and temporary advantages to be gained and toward more remote and permanent values.

Consideration was given to the effect of the proposed line of action upon others and to possible exceptions or other conditions that should be considered in deciding upon a plan of action. Finally, conclusions were summarised in order to see what generalisations could be formulated which would be helpful in other situations. The entire process was really an experience in social thinking.

Allen makes several suggestions to ensure the success of his method. The attitude of the conference leader must be different from the typical attitude of the teacher in that the teacher knows the answers to the questions which he asks, and the pupils know that he knows. A good leader never, under any circumstances, enters into the discussion by expressing approval or disapproval of any opinion or attitude or by voicing his own opinions.

On the contrary, the leader, without losing control, must be an impartial, open-minded, tactful, tolerant and courteous presiding officer who must see that all points of view have a hearing, especially the 'wrong' attitudes.

While care must be taken not to waste school time by aimless discussion, it must always be kept in mind that the conference cannot be hurried without loss of effectiveness since any conference is a leisurely procedure.

The counsellor need not always follow any particular order of questioning, for in some of the most successful conferences most of the questions have been asked by the pupils.

A good conference leader occasionally restates and summarises the group thinking at various stages. Sometimes conclusions may be noted on the blackboard, sometimes written by a secretary, and sometimes not recorded at all.

It is clearly the leader's function to keep the case discussion moving forward a solution and to keep the members informed of the progress of the thinking.

Lastly, a conference group should be large enough to represent a diversified range of opinions but not so large as to prevent each member from taking an active part in the discussion.

Allen believes that many important results can be expected from this procedure. One result is that students get the view of the majority on personal and social problems. A pupil is taught to think for himself and to defend his opinions. Everyone is so interested that even shy pupils get excited and talk.

The problems are real live topics of today and therefore have meaning for the participants in the case conference. Because the facts sink in deeper when the same things are said by pupils, the conference helps determine the policy of a pupil who is debating the subject within himself.

Boys and girls discuss these things privately; why not bring them out into the open for frank debate in a situation where the teacher can learn much about the pupils? When the teacher keeps his views out of the discussion, the pupils give more honest opinions and learn what is best for the group, not merely for the individual. The method keeps pupils to the point by using specific examples of modern problems.

It makes them more tolerant of the opinion of others, brings them "out of themselves", and helps them analyse subjects that they might not otherwise think out. It is a good test of one's beliefs to stand up for them in the face of opposition. These and other values convinced Allen that the case conference method was a useful group guidance technique.

Multiple Counselling

Froelich has suggested the term "multiple counselling" to indicate the utilisation of group methods in the counselling of individuals. The purpose of such counselling is to assist the individual in the solution of his problems by utilising the group setting. This is not essentially different from the "case conference problems" of Allen or the "guidance in groups" of Bennett.

There seems to be no logical reason for calling this group method "multiple counselling" just because many (multiple) problems are considered by many (multiple persons in one group).

The chief reason given by Froelich for the term 'multiple' is to avoid the criticism centering on the terms "group guidance" and "guidance in groups". It also serves to emphasise the function of the group itself in the guidance of individuals through the utilisation of group therapy.

A modification of Bennett's "guidance in groups" to "counselling in groups" might well be accepted. This modification recognises that counselling of individuals may take place in a group setting and that the group can be used effectively both for problems of the individuals in the group and for problems of the group itself. This term, however, can never be accepted by those who still insist that counselling is a one-to-one, counsellor-client relationship.

QUESTIONS FOR ANSWER

1. *Explain the conditions essential for counselling.*
2. *Write a brief note on the merits and demerits of various types of counselling.*
3. *Briefly explain the differences between directive and client-centered techniques of counselling.*
4. *What do you understand by Group Guidance and Group Counselling? Explain case conference procedures in particular.*
5. *Define counselling and write a note on its major elements.*
6. *Write short notes on:*
   (a) Levels of counselling.
   (b) Classification of counselling.
   (c) What should be counselled?
   (d) What should do counselling?

9

Counselling: The Techniques of Interview, Rational-Emotive Therapy and Behavioural Therapy

Irrationality is the product of emotional problems and need rational-emotive therapy. While other behavioural disorder need behavioural therapy to ensure better personality and career. This is a form of counselling as done through interview technique. We discuss all these aspects, briefly, hereunder:

THE INTERVIEW TECHNIQUE

Interview is a give and take of views between the interviewer and the interviewee. It consists of consultation, mutual interchange of opinions and deliberating together. It can be used to get information, to give information and to change behaviour.

Its purpose, thus is three-fold—it involves gathering all available pertinent facts, making a diagnosis on the basis of all the evidence and formulating an appropriate plan of action.

All problems may not be settled in the interview but to be successful, it should lead to some plan of action. Its aim should be to serve the individual even though the counsellor may do no more than present the facts in a more objective light, thus enabling the student to see himself, his assets, his liabilities and his opportunities more clearly than he could see them unaided.

The interview may be used for any of several purposes, but a purpose it must have. It may be *introductory, fact finding, informative, evaluative, therapeutic* in nature and its use for any of these purposes should be clearly recognised by the counselling officer and his subject.

What are some of the specific practical questions which are likely to come up for consideration during an interview? There are a great many such questions, of course and they are as varied and as individually coloured as the interviewee who seeks answers to them.

The student who feels a need to be better informed about his scholastic and vocational prospects may want estimates of his aptitude for college work, his intellectual promise for special fields of training, his disposition to favour or avoid various spheres of activity (vocational interests), and his emotional adjustment tendencies (traits of personality and temperament).

He may wish to consider with his counsellor the questions as whether he should remain in college, how much additional training he should take, what course he should take and whether he should transfer to another institution. He may decide to ask about the duties and services performed by workers in a particular occupation and about employment requirements and opportunities in that field of work.

There might be some difficulties at home or harassment by other students or he might find difficulty in his adjustment with room-mates in the hostel.

It is obvious there is no simple answer to the question 'what problems should be discussed in an interview?' Perhaps the best rule of thumb is that any personal problem that generally concerns the interviewee or any question that bears upon his personal planning and decision making activities is a legitimate matter for interview.

What is a proper counselling topic for one student may not be suitable for another. There are a number of problems of the students—*academic, disciplinary, economic, educational, emotional, residential, social,* etc. which necessitate the use of this tool.

The fact that a student comes to a teacher occasions a meeting and may result into an interview.

For some problems, interview may have to be arranged and the interviewee may have to be called for, as stated earlier, under the heading 'Who should be counselled?'

TYPES OF INTERVIEWS

Introductory Interview

The first interview with a subject should be designed for the purpose of getting mutually acquainted and building rapport, so that follow-up conference and procedures will be welcomed and appreciated. The counsellor may introduce himself, state the purpose of the interview and advise the subject about the procedures that will be used later.

The short ten-to-fifteen minute introductory interview may end with an invitation to the subject to drop in at any time, with making a second appointment, with informing him about the time of the next conference, or with setting the date of the first administration of tests or of any other procedures that are to follow.

Expending of whatever time is necessary to establish happy relationship in this introductory interview, is justified. On the part of the counsellee, it involves developing a feeling of ease, born of growing confidence in the counsellor's competence, interest, knowledge, and skill, and a feeling of freedom to reveal both facts and emotions. On the part of the counsellor, it entails treating the student as a responsible adult, being considerate of all attitudes and feelings.

The introductory interview should be held very soon after the student enters the college. If the first interview is delayed until the student runs into difficulty, fails in some subjects, breaks a rule, has trouble with other students, or the like, the counselling officer may not find it easy or possible to establish good relations with the students.

The counselling officer should make notes about this introductory interview after the subject has left the conference room. It is not advisable to take or recommend any action on the basis of data obtained in the introductory interview, as there will usually be little information to justify action.

Fact-finding Interviews

These interviews may be designed to discover the intensity of a counsellee's attitudes towards persons and situations which he cannot or will not reveal in writing or in response to formalised questions which do not allow for indications of strong feelings.

Thus interview may reveal interests that had not previously been noted, and it may allow the counsellor to determine their strength and their source. It can be used to obtain information concerning relationships with other persons and about activities that are carried out with them.

Informative Interviews

A counsellee may be interviewed for the purpose of informing him about data that have been obtained from other sources, for providing information to answer questions that he has raised or of passing on some decision that has been made about him by a person in a position of authority.

The counselling officer may also inform a student about such matters as his performance in tests and their interpretation; the acceptance or rejection of an application for a position or for permission to a change in courses, the decision of the principal/head of the department concerning his success in an examination.

Many educational-vocational problems of the students are solved by acquisition of new and accurate information about themselves and the world of work or by discovering a different orientation to information which they already possess.

Therapeutic Interviews

Interview may be used for therapeutic purposes. All of us like to discuss our problems, dreams and aspirations with others in whom we have confidence and with whom we have rapport. Interview gives a chance to the counsellee to talk about himself, his past, his wishes and fears, his hopes and aspirations.

The process of talking things over brings new clarity of thought, relief from over-tension, and a new objectivity. We can know a lot from what the counsellee says, from how he behaves in the interview situation, by noting what the student is not inclined to talk about, what he speaks of with the most satisfaction and the most distress, what are the topics which when mentioned cause him the most embarrassment or inhibition.

In other words, it often happens that *how* a thing is said, seems just as important as *what* is said and it is only in the interview that this aspect of the counsellee's revelations can be appraised. When through interview the counsellee is permitted to "think aloud" in the presence of a sympathetic listener, it can give a clue to a number of problems of the counsellee.

INTERVIEW PROCEDURE

It is four stage procedure:

1. Preparation

Interviewing is an art that requires careful planning and

preparation for satisfactory performance and good results. Before the interview, the counselling officer needs to work out the entire interview procedure.

He needs to be sure as to how is he going to initiate it, what responses are possible to his opening statement, which one of these responses does he want, how he can eliminate the unwanted responses and achieve definite objective.

The following hints can prove useful:

A. *Decide what is to be accomplished*: The interviewer knows the problem, when the interviewee comes for the interview, he has his own expectations and objectives. It is, therefore, important for the interviewer to be clear about what is to be accomplished. It will be desirable to write them down.

B. *Know the interviewee*: It is necessary to know the interviewee before he comes for the interview. This could be done from college records, test records, cumulative records, activity reports, from his friends and, if necessary, from his parents/guardians, etc.

   This will help in two ways—in giving a good start to the interviewer and in establishing rapport and in solving the problem. Such data can furnish a framework within which the students' problem can be advantageously surveyed.

C. *Make appointments:* When appointments are made, both the interviewer and the interviewee are prepared. It saves time.

D. *Provide for privacy:* Privacy is an essential condition of interviewing. It is necessary that the student is in a proper frame of mind induced by privacy and respect for the counselling officer's competence. Interruptions during the course of the interview should not be there.

E. *Practice taking the interviewee's point of view:* The interviewer must learn to step in the shoes of the interviewee. He must be able to see the interviewee's point of view, how he looks at the problem, how he reacts to the interviewing.

F. *Know your own personality:* The interviewer needs to be objective. He must be able to introspect, overcome or at least control his opinions, convictions, attitudes, preconceptions, prejudices, notions, etc.

2. The Process

A. *Establish rapport*: The interviewer should make all out efforts for establishing rapport—a relationship of confidence, trust and mutual appreciation which helps the counsellee to express himself without inhibitions and resistance. Building of this relationship is helped by the atmosphere of the counselling officer's room, his attitude and the initial reception he gives to the counsellee. The room should be attractive and pleasing.

   The general atmosphere should convey an impression of friendliness and informality. By rising to meet the student as an expected guest, the interviewer may give an impression that he is welcome. By giving him full attention and avoiding a preoccupied manner, he can give to the student the impression that the conference is the most important thing he could be doing at the moment.

B. *Help the interviewee feel at ease and ready to talk*: The interviewer should begin with topics which are easy to talk about and thus warm up the interviewee. After getting on to the main topic, the counselling officer should make the interviewee talk freely. It is essential that the interviewee feels free to express his own ideas unhampered by the ideals, values and preconceptions of the interviewer.

   He should give advice only sparingly. Even when advice is sought, it would be better to avoid assuming responsibility for the decision which rightly should rest on the student himself.

C. *Help the interviewee obtain and organise into a meaningful pattern the information he needs in his choice-making activity*: Especially in cases of educational and vocational decisions, the interviewer and the interviewee may discuss and agree on aptitude tests or interest inventories. The interviewer may also obtain information from college records or from an intake questionnaire which the interviewee has filled out at the time of application.

D. *Ask unambiguous questions*: The success of an interview depends a good deal on the form of questions. Questions should be simple and easily understood, even if the reply they call for is difficult. Only one question should be asked at a time and the questions asked should carry the interview a stage further.

E. *Learn to listen:* The interviewer should develop the skill of listening. The interviewer should not only listen but listen with the third ear. He must go behind the words of the interviewee to the hidden feelings, the half-expressed or unexpressed ideas and reactions. He should also be able to see if the interviewee has used any of the dynamics of personality like repression, sublimation, projection, identification, rationalisation, suppression, etc.

F. *Keep control of the interview*: Sometimes the interviewee does not want to reveal himself—he may say irrelevant things. At times, this may be allowed—it may help the interviewee feel relieved of tensions and anxieties. The interviewee should be brought back to the topic without allowing much time to be wasted. Attempt should be made to eliminate the unwanted responses and get only the ones which he seeks.

G. *At the close of the interview, watch for additional information or new leads in the casual remarks of the interviewee*: The interviewer should be alert to catch the change of expressions which may drop after the interview has ended. When the tension has been released and he is off guard, he may say things which he may have wanted to say earlier but which seemed to him irrelevant or too trivial to mention. The interviewer must always remember that the interview has not yet closed even when he has asked all his questions.

3. Interpretation

What the interviewee says is often a mixture of facts, his view of the situation as he sees it, and his feelings. Unless the interviewer has information from other sources, he is often unable to distinguish between fact and fiction.

There is another difficulty arising out of the interviewer himself—his tendency to project his ideas and attitudes upon the interviewee. Without interpretation the counsellee may remain on a superficial level of self-understanding. The interpretation to students of the varied aspects of their emotional life is essential and it requires great skill and understanding.

4. Developing Insights and Putting them to Work

The process of clarifying and gaining insight naturally leads to the making of decisions and the planning of courses of action. The successful interviewer is resourceful in making the counsellee reach his decisions and put them into practice.

Termination of the Contact

Instead of having an abrupt break, the termination of the contact should be a stage in the process. It should be planned, not sudden, clear-cut, not indefinite.

5. Recording

There should be an efficient system of recording and maintaining the interview notes. If a complete record is desired, it may be necessary to keep a tape-recorder in the room. In cases, where good rapport has been established, the necessary notes can be taken without disturbing the subject.

In general, however, the interview will proceed better if no notes are taken. A summary must, however, be written immediately after the interview, to make sure nothing of importance is forgotten.

Limitations

(*i*) The validity of data obtained from interviews is always suspect because the results are contained in judgments made by one person.

(*ii*) The validity and reliability of this technique varies with how well and skilfully the interview has been structured and who is conducting it.

(*iii*) Interviewer's bias is another limitation of this technique. Researchers have pointed out the fact that the interviewers report a particular phenomenon according to their own interpretations, understandings, beliefs and attitudes.

The validity studies of interviews have revealed very low statistical measures of validity when interview predictions have been compared with the actual performance of the person.

THE RATIONAL-EMOTIVE THERAPY

Rational-emotive therapy was developed by Albert Ellis.

According to him human being is both rational and irrational. Irrationality is the cause of emotional problems, such as guilt, anxiety, anger and depression. Emotional problems cannot be separated from ideas.

Ellis thinks that the mistake most people make is rating themselves against other people and then labelling themselves. This prevents them from accepting their natural fallibility and almost always results in self-contempt or in a defensive pose of superiority.

Ellis has developed his own model of behaviour which is called A, B, C, model. 'A' is the activating event, 'B' is the belief system and 'C' is the emotional consequence. Here mode 'A' is not the cause of 'C' rather 'B' is the cause of 'C'.

According to Ellis 'every human being who gets disturbed really is telling himself a chain of false sentences. That is the way humans seem almost invariably to think in words, phases, and sentences and it is these sentences which really constitute his neurosis. Ellis has identified the following eleven irrational ideas which lead to neurosis:

(*i*) It is absolutely essential for an individual to be loved or approved by every significant person in his environment.

(*ii*) It is necessary that each individual be competent, adequate and achieving in areas of interest, if the individual is to be worthwhile.

(*iii*) Some people are bad, wicked or villainous and these people should be blamed and punished.

(*iv*) It is terrible and catastrophic when things are not in the way an individual wants them to be.

(*v*) Unhappiness is a function of events outside the control of the individual.

(*vi*) If something is dangerous or harmful, an individual should constantly be concerned about it.

(*vii*) It is easier to run away from difficulties and self-responsibility than it is to brace oneself up to lean on.

(*viii*) Petty events in an individual's life determine present behaviour and cannot be changed.

(*ix*) An individual should be very concerned and upset by other individual's problems.

(*x*) There is always a correct and precise answer to every problem and it is catastrophic if it is not found.

The Goal

Regardless of what happened to the individual in the past, the therapist assumes that the person is solely responsible for the way he feels about himself and this is responsible for his happiness. The goal of rational emotive therapy is to show the client how his misinterpretation of events are causing him problems and to teach him to see things in a more rational manner and aid him in the process of adjustments.

The Process

In the initial interview the responsibilities of the counsellor and the client are defined. The client is responsible for practising any learning acquired during the counselling sessions. Practising means home work.

Techniques Used

Rational therapists use a wide variety of techniques to correct the illogical and self-defeating goals and beliefs of the client. These include persuasion, confrontation, challenge, command, even theoretical arguments.

They do not 'baby' their clients. He may go so far as to give 'home work' assignments encouraging the clients to risk arguing with their boss, patting a dog that frightens them. In short, rational therapists are very directive.

THE BEHAVIOURAL THERAPY/COUNSELLING

Behavioural counselling is one of the most modern methods of treating disorders of behaviour. In this overt symptoms are considered important. Symptoms are determined by individual differences; faulty learning is considered the cause of maladjustment; cure is achieved by treating symptoms without going into the past.

Behavioural counselling is based on laboratory of conditioning for describing behaviour and specifying the conditions under which it is acquired, maintained and eliminated. Behaviourists reject the idea that behaviour disorders are symptoms of hidden emotional conflicts that must be uncovered and resolved.

They argue that the behaviour disorder is the problem, not a symptom of the problem. If a therapist can teach a person to respond more appropriately, they feel he has "cured" him.

Behaviour therapies are based on the belief that all behaviour, normal and abnormal, is learned. For instance, the hypochondriac has learned that he gets attention when he is sick; the catatonic has learned that he is safe when he withdraws entirely.

The therapists' job is to extinguish such inappropriate responses and to teach the person more satisfying ways of behaving. He does not need to know how or why the person learned to behave as he does.

Behavioural counselling as a technique is based on the principle of learning. The most important contribution to behavioural counselling has been made by Pavlov, Skinner, Wolpe and John D. Kumboltz who believed that neurotic behaviour is acquired and is subject to the established laws of learning.

Goal

The goal of behavioural counselling is to change particular behaviour efficiently and specifically.

The Counselling Process

Blackhom and Silverman have suggested the following steps of behavioural counselling:

(*i*) *Problem definition*: The counsellor should specifically define the problem—all the circumstances regarding the inappropriate behaviour should be identified.

(*ii*) *Development and social history of the problem should be prepared.*

(*iii*) *Specification of the counselling goals*: The client and the counsellor should come to an agreement as to what the problem actually is. It is the counsellor's responsibility to decide if the goal is within his realm of expertise and in accordance with ethical behaviour.

(*iv*) *Selection of methods*: The techniques used in the counselling, consistent with the client's goals, need to be selected.

TECHNIQUES OF BEHAVIOURAL COUNSELLING

Behaviourists use a variety of techniques to build new habits:

A. *Operant conditioning*: It is based on the idea that a person will learn to behave in a different way if the new behaviour is rewarded and the old behaviour is ignored.

B. *Aversive conditioning*: It is a technique for eliminating specific behaviour patterns. The therapist teaches the person to associate pain and discomfort with the response he wants to unlearn. This form of behaviour therapy has been used successfully to treat alcoholism, homosexuality, obesity and smoking. Dent treated alcoholics by giving them a drug that produces extreme nausea when mixed with alcohol in the stomach.

The people were encouraged, in fact, instructed to drink, and each time they did they became violently sick. Gradually they began to feel sick everytime they even saw a bottle of whisky.

Desensitisation: It is another technique for reducing irrational behaviour. In this technique, if a client has described several anxiety producing situations, those situations are ranked from the lowest to the highest in terms of disturbance. The client is instructed in relaxation technique.

When this is accomplished each anxious situation is presented starting with the one that produces the least anxiety. As the situation is recalled by the client he is reinforced by the relaxation process until there is no anxiety. Behaviourists have used decentralisation to cure phobias about snakes, heights, closed rooms and sex.

Reciprocal Inhibition: There are individuals who feel anxious and unhappy most of the time. Wolpe feels behaviourists can treat diffused anxiety. Here the therapist establishes a hierarchy, from the least to the most anxiety provoking situations. Next he teaches the client to clear his mind, release tense muscles and relax.

In some cases, he may use drugs or mild hypnosis to produce relaxation. Once the client has mastered the technique of deep relaxation, they begin at the bottom of his anxiety hierarchy. The therapist asks the person to imagine the least threatening scene and to signal when he begins to feel tense.

At the signal, the therapist tells him to forget the scene and concentrate on relaxing. After a short period, he instructs him to return to the scene. This process is repeated until the person feels completely relaxed.

Gradually they move up the list until the client is able to imagine the situation he most feared without anxiety. Wolpe is of the opinion that the clients learn to inhibit anxiety responses with incompatible, deep muscle relaxation.

It is obvious that the success of behavioural counselling depends upon the following:

(*i*) establishing a valid hierarchy by the client and the therapist;

(*ii*) discovering an adequate reinforcer (cooperant conditioning) by the therapist; and

(*iii*) lack of counter conditioning outside the therapy sessions.

Some psychologists are critical of behavioural counselling. They feel that by concentrating only on behaviour, it presents an over-simplified version of human psychology.

These psychologists feel that an individual's mental behaviour is just as important in therapy as his overt behaviour.

It is also felt that the behavioural counselling is symptom-oriented. Effort is made to smother the neurotic symptoms, no effort is made to remove the conflict that caused them. There is always a danger of the client relapsing into his original condition.

Wolpe defends his approach with follow-up studies of 249 people he treated for neurotic problems, only four developed new symptoms.

QUESTIONS FOR ANSWER

1. *Discuss interview as a tool of career counselling and write a note on the basic features of the interview process.*
2. *Define 'Rational-Emotive Therapy' on its goals and techniques.*
3. *'Discuss the utility of Behavioural Therapy' as a tool of career counselling and write a note on the techniques of behavioural counselling.*
4. *Write short notes on the following:*

   (*a*) *Types of Interview.*

   (*b*) *Irrational ideas which lead to neurosis.*

   (*c*) *Therapeutic Interviews.*

10

Guidance and Counselling: Individual Situations

We have stated earlier that every action or behaviour pattern of the individual effects his image and status, which in other words career. Similarly various situations in human life do have a bearing on the career of the individual. Counselling as a component of guidance helps individuals to face the situations effectively so that their adverse effect on the personality or to say career of the individual is minimised or negativated and the career of the individual gets a boost. Hereunder, we will discuss this personal and situational aspect from the career point of view:

SITUATIONS NEEDING COUNSELLING

Following situation are more serious, requiring individual counselling by a skilled counsellor:

Personal and Situational Influences

An individual's need for assistance in making decisions, planning courses of action, and making adjustments to life situations may be centered in any of his present or future areas of experience. Very few problems are confined to one area. An individual's attitude toward situations requiring decisions and his ability to meet them usually are the result of many factors.

The purpose to be served by counselling is directly related to the age, interests, and experiences of the counselee. Moreover, one of the responsibilities of the counsellor in individual counselling situations is to help the individual discover the fundamental causes of his problem. The difficulty may stem from his experiences in the home or the school, on the job, or in his social relationships or recreational activities.

Home experiences: It is not unusual for a child occasionally to resent what he considers to be unjust treatment by his parents, to be jealous of apparent privileges granted a brother or sister and denied him, or to be embarrassed by the fact that his home compares unfavourably with that of his classmates.

If the mother as well as the father is working and is thus away from home, the child is likely to engage in unsupervised after-school activities that get him into trouble with the parents of neighbourhood children and elicit consequent punishment from a work-weary mother when his misdemeanors are reported to her.

These are but a few of the many problem situations that are likely to arise in the home even when the father and mother try to be good parents.

The effect on a child or a young adolescent of real or fancied home difficulties may be such that it necessitates individually-received assistance from a counsellor. In some instance, the situation lends itself to help that can be given by a member of the school guidance staff. If inner resentments and conflicts become too serious, the situation may require clinical or psychiatric attention.

During later adolescence and adulthood, matters dealing with plans for establishing a home of one's own become extremely important.

Choosing a mate, marrying, selecting and furnishing a home, budgeting the home finances, and rearing children give rise to questions that may cause the young person considerable concern. The older adult also needs help toward the solution of problems of marital adjustment and parent-child relationships.

School experiences: During his elementary-school years, the child usually can be helped to meet his problems of adjustment in group situations through the efforts of an alert and guidance-minded teacher. It usually is best not to place too much emphasis on the personal difficulties of the child by subjecting him to individual counselling situations that will seem to set him apart from his schoolmates.

Secondary-school pupils and college students may require individually received help in planning their courses or in adjusting to them. An individual may have academic difficulties or his attendance record may be unsatisfactory. Personality differences between a student and an instructor often cause difficulties. Ineffective study habits or too little time for or lack of interest in home study will interfere with school success.

The questions often asked by young people about their school experiences indicate their concern over matters that may not seem important to the adult but that are extremely significant in the lives of high-school and college students.

Vocational and occupational adjustment: Many problems in this area can be taken care of by guidance in group situations. There are times, however, when the pupil should receive specific information about his particular situation, or when the solution of a problem is made difficult because of his attitudes or the behaviour of other people.

It is in situations like these that the individual should be able to avail himself of the services of a counsellor; who will help him think through the problem and arrive at a reasonable conclusion. The specific questions raised by an individual about vocational choice, preparation, and job satisfaction are extremely important to him.

Feelings of insecurity or of personal ineffectualness and expressed or implied criticism of one's course of action are likely to arouse one emotionally to the point where clear thinking and unbiased judgment are almost impossible. In situations like these, an individual feels the urge to talk over his problems with someone in whom he has confidence.

Social and leisure-time adjustment: Not all of an individual's waking hours are spent in meeting his home, school, or business responsibilities. Everyone should take time off to play, preferably in the company of others who have interests similar to his. Personal inadequancies, lack of opportunities, and pressures of duty can give rise to more or less serious problems of adjustment.

A problem is intensified if the individual is unable or unwilling to recognise the fundamental cause of his difficulty. He may place the blame on elements in the situation outside himself rather than recognise that the fault lies within him.

Many of the questions asked counsellors give evidence of this shift of responsibility for personal adjustment from one's own shoulders to those of one's friends and acquaintances.

INFORMAL COUNSELLING

The Counselling Process

Counselling, as a process, has been defined variously by authors and professors for nearly fifty years. While no single definition has stood the test of time, most contain some reference to difference in role of the student (who is to be assisted or helped) and the counsellor.

Also, mention is generally made of the objective or goal in terms of improved adjustment, higher functioning, and greater happiness. Finally, focus is usually placed upon the process involved, the learning that occurs, and the assistance that is given.

Four basic assumptions must be accepted if counselling is to be successful.

First, it is assumed that the student is willing to participate in the process. He may have a concern, a wonderment about the world around him, or curiosity about what he is experiencing. While the process may be unfamiliar to him and he may display resistance at moments, counselling will not be successful unless he participates fully.

Second, the counsellor must posses appropriate training, experience, and personal attitudes to function effectively. He must be able to relate easily with the student, assist him in establishing objectives and goals, and employ any ethical means that will assist the student to change or learn behaviours necessary to cope with his environment and work toward the objectives they mutually have established.

Third, an appropriate environment is necessary. Depending upon the nature of the interview, this environment must provide assurance of confidentiality, a mood of contemplation, and/or adequate information resources.

Finally, as the term is used in school settings, counselling must provide a relationship that allows for meeting both immediate and long-term needs. The counsellor must be available at moments when the student needs him for specific assistance.

Another objective toward which the counsellor works is *assisting the student to examine the psychological dimensions of what he is thinking and saying*. The counsellor's approach in this regard is quite the opposite of that of a person engaged in social conversation. In social situations we react to remarks of self-doubt or anxiety by attempting to "close down" the display of emotion. We may interject mirth, change topics, give words of comfort, or suggest that things really couldn't be as they seemed.

The counsellor must be mindful of limits in time and his ability to assist the student. Assisting the student to *open up* carries with it the obligation, on the part of the counsellor, to have the time and skill to follow through and terminate the interview successfully.

During the course of practice, counsellors find themselves operating at various points along our dimensions. The nature of the relationship of the student's awareness may determine, in part, the counsellor's behaviour. However, the counsellor's basic philosophy concerning human development and the translation of this philosophy into a theoretical approach to counselling also influences his behaviour.

Examination of these dimensions is not made to determine which is appropriate and which is inappropriate; rather, they are stated here to help the counsellor order his thinking and understand the meanings and purposes of the four continua.

1. *Diagnostic-developmental*: Our problem-solving nature sometimes causes us to attempt to 'diagnose' and 'prescribe' in the best tradition of the family doctor. The counsellor's insight may prove immediately helpful to the student. He may be able to make a specific observation that causes the student to view himself more clearly. More than one-shot problem solving is involved in counselling, however. Concerns frequently are of a developmental nature. The student may wish to explore subtleties of his environment and culture or learn how to relate effectively with peers. In these instances, he will learn more effectively through experiencing than being told.

2. *Cognitive-affective*: Both intellectual content and personal feeling are the substance of counselling, and a relationship seldom develops in the absence of either. Again, it is the responsibility of the counsellor to assist the student in focusing upon facts and descriptive content at one moment and their affective meaning to the student at another.

The counsellor can sometimes combine both in his response. He may say, "You see that you're not accepted, can understand why, but feel pretty angry about it".

3. *Observer-participant*: The counsellor must, at all times, view himself as operating in two distinctly different ways. A part of him must remain the detached, scientific observer who takes account of student behaviours, formulates thoughts as to their implications, and subjects these thoughts to tests by questioning the student or observing whether or not behaviour is consistent.

However, the counsellor is fully involved in the relationship, must act and react, and cannot remain a stoic observer if the relationship is to be marked by involvement and movement.

4. *Ambiguity-structure*: Stress has previously been placed upon the need for structure within the interview. That the student may need some assistance in understanding the purpose of counselling and what is expected of him in general terms is not argued. At the same time, he needs freedom to decide what he feels is important and how he wishes to proceed. The counsellor, therefore, may vacillate from stimulating student responses through general, ambiguous leads.

BASIC ASPECTS OF A COUNSELLING RELATIONSHIP

The help of a counsellor is sought or accepted because the counselee has perceived that his own resources are not entirely adequate to resolve the difficulty or to surmount the developmental task. If the problem tends to be one which is particularly disturbing, the counselee is likely to feel that he is very much alone—that his difficulty, thoughts, and feelings are unique.

Many come to the counsellor, not with any great degree of hope, but with a willingness to pay for companionship. For these and countless similar reasons, the core of counselling is an interpersonal relationship. The quality of relationship is what determines the effectiveness of the therapist, teacher, counsellor, social worker, and the parent.

It is Rogers' belief that the quality of the relationship is much more important than is one's knowledge of theoretical issues, the availability and use of assessment data, the nature of his professional training, or the technique and orientation of the counselling process to which he adheres. There are several aspects of this relationship which, because they are susceptible to development, are worthy of attention.

Bearing in mind that the counsellor must help as well as to understand, it is important to distinguish between sympathy and empathy. One can feel sympathy without comprehending the meaning of another's behaviour. Rogers suggests that empathy is a matter of sensing the counselee's private world as if it were the counsellor's own world; but the "as if" must be preserved.

Empathy is an essential part of an effective interpersonal process because it gives access to the counselee's perceptions, feelings, and behaviours. The concept is limited in the sense that we can never share completely the feelings, attitudes, and actions of another—through it does seem that identical twins often come very close to it.

Rogers asserts that empathy is rarely received and rarely offered because one runs the risk of being changed in the process. But the effort to be empathic is appreciated.

Counsellor-education programmes are increasingly coming to recognise that empathy can be enhanced by experience when "sensitivity training" or "process sessions" are part of the programme. This is but another way of saying that the counsellor's personality development should be a central focus of counsellor education.

The value of the counsellor's being congruent, real, genuine is such that it can be reiterated that counsellor preparation programmes should place strong emphasis on the understanding of oneself. Counsellors should be involved in sensitivity sessions, interpersonal dynamics, self-examination. It may be called a variety of names and should entail a variety of approaches.

Involvement, as was suggested in the discussion of empathy, is perceived by many to be essential to an optimally productive counselling process. Being subjectively involved tends to keep the counselee emotionally involved. It is a matter of being keenly interested in helping another resolve some of his difficulties; it involves human warmth and psychological closeness. Subjective involvement must, however, be balanced by professional objectivity.

Skill in listening is an essential aspect of the counsellor's effectiveness. It is a difficult skill to teach because

1. people think they know how to do it,

2. there has been no distinction made between hearing and listening, and because,
3. one is in such haste to help another that he must speak his words of wisdom—to which the counselee will probably not listen because of limitations quite similar to those listed.

Listening as a technique has two advantages in a counselling milieu. One is that we can become aware of—and formulate hypotheses, if not draw conclusions from—changes in speech rate, accompanying breathing patterns, levels of intensity, and varying choices of words.

But the technique is much less important that is the process of counselling, in which the matter of feeling becomes ascendant. Meanings flow from the 'feeling' which is aroused in the counsellor.

In addition to the mechanics of being objective one must also listen with his "inner ear" by his willingness to make a subjective investment, to become personally involved. Listening might conceivably include giving attention to visible signs such as clenched fists, finger twisting, facial mobility, posture and leg and arm movements.

Attentive listening, to *the person* and not just to the words, will be an approach to the understanding sought. The other advantage is that listening provides assurance to the counselee that he is not alone, that there is someone who will give him time, and share feelings, without criticism or moralising.

Even the experienced counsellor will do well to recall those numerous instances in which he did not give suggestions or hints but was only mentally exploring possible ways to help.

Nevertheless, at the end of the session the counselee would say, "This has helped me so much". Even if no plans were formulated the ventilation was helpful, psychoanalysts use the word *catharsis* to indicate what has taken place.

The assurance aspect of listening is related to another element of counselling—that of encouragement and support. This does not necessarily mean endorsing the things a person does, though there are occasions when one persisting in the face of devastating odds deserves that endorsement.

It also implies an emotional acceptance of the counselee as a person with whom fellowship is established. It suggests that it is understandable that one would react to situations as the counselee had been doing.

Persons who look for therapeutic counselling are quite frequently lacking in ego strength. Support is afforded by calling to attention, in some way, a particular trait or behaviour of the individual which is commendable. We have found that support can be expressed merely by allowing children and teenagers to be with us—taking them out for a hamburger, letting them walk to the parking lot with us, or giving them some minor chore or errand to perform in the office.

Spontaneity is to be sought as a goal of counselling because the goal is to free the individual to become his own best self. He must then get from behind his blinding masks. We are, however, not talking about discarding all one's defenses. The concern is to help the individual appreciate his unique qualities and aptitudes—to see that he is unique and also that he possesses much in common with others.

Because spontaneity is sought in the counselee's behaviour it is advantageous for the counsellor to be spontaneous—to be real. It has been noted from observations of numerous counselling sessions that when the counsellor is trying to play a role he and his counselee are ill-at-ease and the session is not characterised by flow.

Spontaneity leads to consideration of the need for the counsellor to be himself as a basic aspect of counselling. It was mentioned above that some persons, or introspection, find they like to counsel with athletes, honour students, poor readers, potential dropouts, or those interested in art, music or some other special interest area.

THE NATURE OF COUNSELLING PROBLEMS

There has been and still is considerable discussion about the kind of problems with which the school counsellor should be concerned. Many counsellors have been firmly instructed to recognise that there are some emotional and personal problems that should be avoided; that they should be ready to refer the individual to a psychiatrist or consulting psychologist.

They have been told that there is a danger of doing the person harm, although the specific danger and harm have not been delineated.

A dictionary definition of psychotherapy may be reassuring to those who doubt the wisdom of the counsellor's becoming involved in difficult cases. Psychotherapy is the treatment of maladjustment by any psychological technique including faith cure, hypnosis, or psychoanalysis. Therapy may also include activities in which counsellors routinely employ assurance, advice, suggestion, and psychodrama.

The big difference between counselling and psychotherapy appears to be a matter of structure. It has been indicated that in psychotherapy the approach is general and initially vague while in counselling, as typically viewed, the relationship involves a specific problem. It is a simple matter to demonstrate that very frequently a specific problem of vocational choice is an excuse the counselee uses to deal with a general problem of dislike of parents, distrust of teachers, and fear of one's peers.

It must also be admitted that aversion to psychotherapy on the part of the counsellor is an indication that he lacks the skill and knowledge that will give him sufficient self-assurance to function in a situation lacking the comfort of discernable structure. The final fact is that making a vocational choice often does call for an examination and evaluation of personal problems.

We have previously stated that the counsellor's skills define his role. Those who are inadequately prepared must necessarily seek comfort in those conceptualisations which limit the range of their counselling activities. Those who are well prepared in theory and laboratory experience find it difficult to limit their work to an information-giving role similar to that of a classroom teacher. Their perception of the bearing which the counselee's attitudes, prior conditionings, and personal self-defeating behaviours have on all decision-making makes it difficult to avoid their assumption of psychotherapeutic roles.

FREEDOM AND RESPONSIBILITY IN COUNSELLING

Earlier chapters have shown that our concept of the essence and purpose of counselling is rooted in the basic characteristics of man and the nature of the culture in which he lives. Thus in many contexts the belief has been expressed that man becomes free as he develops his talent potentials, knowledges, skills, and his uniqueness.

It is the purpose of individual counselling to try, by the approaches which seem appropriate for the counselee and the counsellor, to help the person enlarge his vision, to make choices, to define goals that will enhance his freedom.

What is appropriate may in a specific case be developing of a new skill, seeing a situation in a new light, or taking a new view of himself as a person. For healthy children these developments probably are a natural concomitant of their burgeoning strength and wisdom. For less healthy children such growth and appreciation of one's self is by no means automatic. These are the ones who need the help of prolonged counselling.

It should be noted, however, that if the counsellor assumes the burden (responsibility) for indicating that new skill, for revealing the new perception of a situation, or for presenting the new view of self, then the responsibility is wrongly located. It is the individual who must assume responsibility.

Counsellors do a disservice to individuals if they "dredge up the past" for a counselee and create the impression that he is the unfortunate victim of foul circumstances.

Pierson points out that in much of counsellor education there is an issue regarding the nature of society—where it is deterministic or indicative of freedom. Most counsellor educators believe that although there are deterministic factors (cultural demands, availability of jobs, racial discrimination, geographical location), the individual has choice. He has the chance of controlling his future by the choices he makes of developing flexibility and versatility.

The developing individual needs help in achieving the degree of freedom which might characterise his life; and he needs help in maintaining it. The world is too complex to win the freedom by rebellion alone. But neither will freedom be won by those who are led by the counsellor to dependent relationship. The counsellor must aim at the counselee's assumption of responsibility and thus establish and/or maintain his thrust toward freedom.

FORMAL COUNSELLING ACTIVITIES

(*A*) Clinical Procedures

The clinical approach is employed as a guidance technique for those cases of emotional disturbance which are serious in nature, in which many maladjustive factors both within and outside the individual appear to be operating. The study and treatment of these cases may require a relatively long period of time.

Method of Approach

Clinical procedures involve the following activities:

1. recognising the presence of an apparently serious adjustment difficulty,
2. gathering extensive data on the client and recording them in the form of a case history,
3. interpreting and evaluating the data in relation to observed symptoms,
4. recommending appropriate treatment,
5. applying therapies, and
6. following up the case for the purpose of determining the kind and extent of adjustment effected.

The client is referred to the psychiatrist or the clinic when it is believed by the person or institution making the referral that his maladjustment is such as to require expert care. It is usually the responsibility then of a social worker to accumulate relevant data on the immediate situation and background history.

If the study is being made by a clinical staff, the psychiatrist, paediatrician or physician, psychologist, and social worker hold staff meetings at which the findings are discussed.

Expert interpretation and evaluation of available data is extremely important. Usually it is found necessary to supplement data resulting from the administration of tests, scales, and inventories with the utilisation of evaluating techniques peculiarly suited to clinical purposes.

Appraisal Techniques

The techniques of appraisal include individually administered measurements of sensory acuity and muscular coordination, mental capacity, learning achievement, and personal qualities. One of the most valuable techniques of evaluation for clinical purposes is the *projective method*, mentioned earlier, through the utilisation of which one may gain insight into the individual's unconscious or fantasy life. The Rorschach method of ink-blot interpretation and thematic apperception tests are widely used by clinicians.

Another approach to the study of young children is that of *play therapy,* in which children are supposed to give vent to their unconscious desires, animosities, and conflicts as they play with "doll families" and other toys. In their behaviour with these objects they express their attitudes toward the adult or situation which appears to be the cause of their difficulties.

Effecting Changes

Changing or removing maladjustive elements in the individual's environment, of course, is important. More significant, however, are the desirable changes that can be effected in his own attitudes and patterns of behaviour. This purpose can be served best through a series of therapeutic interviews conducted by skilled persons.

A 'case' should not be closed when the individual has been led to gain insight into his difficulties, as a result of which he starts on an improved course of action. He needs help during his adjusting process, and he should continue to have the services of the clinical staff and any others who have participated in the remedial procedures until his adjustment is satisfactory to himself and his counsellors.

Unfortunately, clinical treatment often ceases too soon, leaving an individual who is still mentally half-sick to continue unaided in his struggle toward complete adjustment.

(*B*) Interview Procedures

We have discussed interview technique as a tool of counselling, therefore, hereunder, only in brief some aspects of interview technique in respect of individual situations as per needs of this chapter:

Personal Qualities of the Interviewer

The interviewing phase of counselling for personal adjustment is an art; for it the interviewer must have certain specific personality qualities, thorough training, and experience under expert guidance.

It is important that the interviewer possess those desirable personality qualities stressed in this book as requisite for dealing with people in any guidance situation. No matter what the purpose of the interview may be, the teacher, the school counsellor, the employer, or the staff member of a guidance clinic should give evidence of being an understanding and personally well-adjusted human being. In adjustment interviews, especially, possessing these qualities is imperative.

According to practically all state requirements for school counsellor certification some teaching experience is needed. The reason for this is easily understood.

Before a person can undertake the responsibility of counselling an individual pupil wisely, he needs the experience of working with individuals in classroom groups.

The counsellor's behaviour should be friendly but dignified. He must avoid a sentimental or a 'kidding' approach that is supposed to set the counselee at ease.

An individual seeking help from a counsellor needs to have sufficient confidence in the latter's acceptance of him so that thoughts and feelings can be expressed freely, without fear of recrimination.

Initial Interview Procedures

Most counselling within a school setting is, in a sense, initial interviewing. School counselling is not marked by a long series of weekly or biweekly interviews.

The student visits the counsellor, for example, in November for one or two interviews, and they may not have another conference until spring of the following year.

Although the counsellor follows the student's progress and may have several brief chats in the corridor or at an athletic event, their next meeting starts the process all over again.

Quite likely, the objectives established for the first interview or interviews will bear no relationship to those established at a later date. The school counsellor, therefore, must be particularly skilled at initial interviewing. Basic procedures are presented and commented upon.

1. *Preparing for the interview and getting started*: Counselling can hardly be expected to be effective unless both counsellor and student are prepared for what is to take place. The counsellor may need to review background data concerning the student or read notes made after the last meetings. He may know of some materials or information sources that he could have readily available. The student, if he is aware of the purposes of counselling, should consider, how he can best use the time available.

As described earlier in the chapter, the counsellor uses his skill in communication to draw upon what the student wants, what he is attempting to say, and what he considers of current primary importance.

2. *Developing opening structure*: The student needs to know who the counsellor is, what he is able to do, and what he expects of the student. This should be done briefly and simply. Experienced counsellors know how to communicate quickly and effectively.

3. *Establishing the objectives*: As a product of his training and experience, the counsellor will be aware of objectives he can set for himself in counselling. These stem from his professional value system and the way he conceptualises human development. They are manifested in the ways that he can effectively behave and communicate with students.

During the opening minutes of the interview, the counsellor and student need to establish objectives or goals toward which they can work in the time available. The objectives are not of a fixed nature and may be revised as the interview develops. An objective must be attainable and realistic in order to be a goal worth pursuing.

4. *Building the relationship*: As the interview progresses, the counsellor must continue to build upon the relationship that has been established. His honesty, expression of interest, humanness, and perceptiveness will allow the student to realise that the counsellor is fully committed to assisting him.

At times, however, the novice counsellor needs to remember to let a little of himself out. A warm smile, a touch on the hand, a nod of understanding, any act of caring that is shown will help the student to invest a little more of himself and be more honest in his communication.

5. *Helping the student to talk*: The counsellor may perceive that the student is reluctant to discuss some concerns or some aspects of concerns even though a sound, trusting relationship has been developed. When this occurs, the counsellor may need to give particular assistance to get communication going.

The threatening nature of the concern probably prohibits approaching it frontally. The counsellor must therefore rely upon spontaneity and sensitivity in (*a*) assisting the student to express his feelings, (*b*) understanding why the student is experiencing difficulty, and (*c*) helping the student to recognise feelings of which he is unaware or has difficulty accepting. The counsellor's own relaxed and reassuring manner will convey more than the words he uses.

6. *Terminating the interview*: The counsellor must use his skill in developing closing, as well as opening, structure. He initiates this phase of the interview by pausing longer between responses, focusing more upon cognitive than affective aspects of the student's concern, and not encouraging further exploration of subtleties or tension-producing areas. His sensitivity assists him in determining when the focus might be changed to the summary and plans for subsequent meetings.

This may be initiated by his suggestion that "our time is all but up". The counsellor asks the student to summarise those aspects of the interview that were most meaningful and assists him, as necessary, in reviewing the objective and whether or not it was achieved. Plans for the future must then be made.

Will there be another interview? When? Where? Or should there be a referral? Should tests be taken? Information sources tapped? When counsellor and student have reached an understanding concerning how they might handle matters such as these, the counsellor stands up (an excellent way to prevent a reopening of concerns) and sees the client to the outer office.

7. *Planning the follow-up*: After each interview the counsellor should make some brief notes as a check upon his own faulty memory and in order to keep a running record of what has transpired through the series of interviews.

This informal, individual follow-up can be structured to give the counsellor some evidence of whether or not he was effective. A more comprehensive, mass follow-up is conducted separately as a guidance service to study groups such as all seniors, all recent graduates, or all students now in technical schools.

Some Interviewing "Do's"

1. Be objective, keep your own value judgments to a minimum.
2. Know your student!
3. Practice taking the student's point of view.
4. Gain *and* deserve the student's confidence.
5. Render your student a real service during the interview.
6. Be a good listener, a taker as well as a giver.

7. Practice an exchange of ideas.
8. Accept the student as he is.

Some Interviewing "Don't's"

1. Don't dominate unnecessarily; it's the pupil's interview
2. Avoid the role of teacher; be a *counsellor* in the interview
3. Be truthful and frank; not unkind and blunt
4. Avoid the use of sarcasm, impertinence, criticism
5. Don't try to reform the pupil
6. Avoid punitive discipline in an interview of this type

QUESTIONS FOR ANSWER

1. *Explain more serious situations which require counselling by skilled counsellor.*
2. *Write a note on the importance of counselling relationship between the counsellor and the counselee.*
3. *Discuss the need of clinical approach as a guidance technique in the case of emotional disturbance.*
4. *Write a note on the basic procedures of Interview Technique in Counselling.*
5. *Explain "Do's" and "Don't's" of Interview Technique of Counselling.*

11

Guidance and Counselling: The Group Approach

The concept group approach in guidance and counselling is as old as the concept of education, because the teacher always wants that all his students should behave and conduct themselves in a socially accepted manner and should have high career and life goals. Since group approach is the basic characteristic of democratic way of life, therefore, group approach or group process in guidance is increasingly become more popular as it is cost effective and in certain situations it yields better results. Hereunder we mention necessary details concerning group approach in guidance.

GROUPS : MEANING

A definition of 'group' should include at least the number of persons (size), the type and quality of interaction (transactions), and the potential learning or changes in the members (purposes). A group is always a means, never an end. The individual is the end or 'product' of a group.

The individual human being is the living end of a group. Schools and guidance counsellors will gain unique opportunities to build new learning environments and enhance existing ones by getting acquainted with current knowledge of groups and by acquiring skills in capitalising on group action.

The power of a group lies in the behaviour of its individual members. An individual becomes a member of a group as a matter of his own choosing, or assent. A person chooses a group because he agrees with the values it supports and the purposes it purports to achieve. Groups are natural phenomena in our culture.

The dynamics of any group may be described if one has access to individual members and/or if one can observe the process of the groups. The process of the group is the interaction pattern, or who talks to whom under what conditions.

The dynamics of a group may be described by labelling the roles within the group. Leadership development for management of task-oriented groups use labelled roles.

Issues such as study skills, human relations, drug abuse, sex education, etc. can be discussed in a group.

After the student has attended group counselling sessions, individual interviews may be scheduled to answer any questions a client may have about group counselling; to help the counsellor get to know the student better in order to determine—how he can best be helped and with whom he would best fit in a counselling group; to give the student a chance to discuss the problems with which he hopes to obtain assistance in the group and to assess the readiness for group counselling and commitment to change his behaviour.

The counsellor often supplements the information obtained in the individual interview with a teacher or parent conference and by carefully examining the students' cumulative record.

Physical arrangement of the room: The room for group counselling should be warm and inviting with fairly comfortable chairs.

Composition of the group: Sometimes it is felt that a homogeneous group consisting of students of the same age, or sex, or students who seem to have similar problems is the most helpful, while other counsellors find that the wider talents of a heterogeneous group make for a better counselling situation.

Size: A group of six to eight students is probably the best size for maximum group interaction.

USES OF GROUP COUNSELLING

1. It helps in the understanding of self and expression of his real feelings about other persons and himself.
2. The student feels that the counselling officer accepts him and wants to understand him.
3. The student realises that his peers had problems too.
4. The student feels that in spite of his faults, which his group-mates wanted to help him to correct, his peers accept him.

5. The student feels that he was capable of understanding, accepting and helping others.
6. The student realises that he could trust others.

Group counselling, in fact, is an experience which uses peer group support and identification in the social setting of the group to encourage students to accept and to learn more about themselves and at the same time to learn to accept and help others.

Group counselling is characterised by *experience not by words, by being something not by talking about it*. If one can experience a sense of reality about one's self in the presence of others then a step forward has been taken in the realisation of emotional maturity and security.

FUNCTIONS

1. Groups to be Served

Guidance in group situations usually is thought of as referring to those guidance services that are made available by school personnel to large or smaller groups of pupils. Yet, though the welfare of every member of a school's pupil population is the major concern of its guidance personnel, it must be remembered that successful functioning of a programme of services involves the guidance of parents and of members of the school staff, as well as of the young people themselves.

The achievement of self-understanding; and understanding of others is the ultimate objective of all guidance-pointed activities. Those persons who are the recipients of help from others in managing their affairs certainly need to gain these understandings.

Unless parents, teachers, and counsellors also posses the same understanding attitudes, it is difficult for them to provide effective assistance. In this chapter, we shall consider the purposes and operation of programmes intended to offer guidance services to the various kinds of groups.

2. Group Leadership

To be a stimulating and effective group leader a person must (*a*) have creative imagination, (*b*) be willing to devote time and thought to the activity, and (*c*) possess the ability to encourage leadership from among the members of the group.

Whatever is attempted in the way of guidance through group activity should focus on the vital interests of the participants. This is a fundamental principle that should be adhered to strictly.

Whether the group consists of school pupils, teachers, parents, other community members, or a business or industrial group, its guidance objectives probably will include one or more of the following:

1. dissemination of helpful information,
2. solution of common problems,
3. gaining of an understanding of the group's general attitudes and points of view, or
4. analysis and reconciliation of differing interests, policies, or points of view.

Leadership in a group situation can be more direct if the purpose to be served is that of giving information. Of course, individual interests and needs still are of primary importance. Those who are supposed to benefit from the information which they receive must recognise the value of the information to themselves.

A more indirect leadership approach is needed when the topic under consideration deals with the personal interests, attitudes, or problems of the group. This form of leadership often is difficult to achieve. For the most part, the discussion consists of a give-and-take among the members of the group.

A successful group leader listens with courtesy and interest to the comments of any member of the group, aids in the clarification of ideas, brings about harmony in group thinking and planning, and encourages the less vocal members to express their ideas.

It also is the responsibility of a group leader to initiate and guide the organisation of a group activity according to individually expressed interest. It may be necessary for him to summarise ideas expressed by others, but his remarks are brief and to the point. Perhaps, most important is the leader's ability to accept objectively and expressed disagreement with own ideas, suggestions, or points of view.

3. The Group Situation as a Supplement to Individual Counselling

Programmes of guidance in group situations that are related to the specific functions of the guidance services of an institution should be planned and sponsored by the members of the guidance staff. Although counselling represents a personal relationship between the counsellor and the counselee, time can be saved, and perhaps better results achieved, if the counselling is conducted with small groups of individuals whose problems or questions are similar.

The question of one member of the group may stimulate the thinking of another, or the shy and retiring person may be motivated by the group situation to ask questions or to seek help more easily than he would in a face-to-face conference with a counsellor.

THE NATURE AND TECHNIQUES

Group guidance is that relationship in which a guidance worker attempts to assist a number of students to attain for themselves satisfactory development or adjustment to their respective individual or collective life situations. It occurs in a setting in which one or more guidance workers encounter students as a group.

Groups are best suited for discussing educational and vocational plans, problems relating to adjustment to college and social situations, problems relating to choice of options and choosing a career, economic and occupational problems, personality adjustment problems, etc.

A number of techniques can be used for imparting group guidance:

1. *Informal discussions*: Informal discussions, if done under the able and skilful leaders, can prove very helpful. These discussions should centre around desirable objectives and should be so guided as to result in conclusions that may be helpful to the group as a whole.

2. *Group reports:* If the students are divided into groups which have certain specific problems to tackle and later these reports are presented in larger groups, they can help all the members of the group in gaining awareness of a number of problems and their solution.

3. *Lectures*: Lectures delivered by experts on certain problems too can impart group guidance in an effective way.

4. *Dramatics*: This is another good technique of group guidance. If certain interesting topics are dramatised, the students can be given guidance in an interesting way. How to appear for an interview, how to prepare for an examination, how to prepare notes—all these can be dramatised and guidelines suggested to the students in an interesting way.

5. *Question box*: "Question-box" says Jones, "If carefully organised and not too frequently used, is also a desirable technique, for it gives the shy and retiring pupil an opportunity to propose a question that is bothering him without revealing that it is his question".

Most of the times, we find the shy student remains buried with his problems as he is not vocal. It is also possible that there are quite a few students having the same problem. So if the question could be proposed in a silent way, the same could be discussed in a group and valuable guidance provided to the students.

6. *The case conference*: Here the problem faced by the majority of the group is stated concretely by way of a case. Each member of the group reviews his own experience in a similar situation. The group is guided away from the more immediate and temporary advantages to be gained toward more remote and permanent values. Then the effect of the proposed line of action is considered upon others. Possible exceptions may be discussed.

Some other conditions that should be considered in deciding a plan of action are also gone through. Some generalisations are also formulated which may prove helpful in other situations. According to Jones, the entire process of the case conference is an experience in social thinking and it has positive and unique values in the group guidance programme.

OBJECTIVES OF GROUP GUIDANCE

The objectives of guidance in groups vary with school level, pupil needs and interests, administrative philosophy, and available school personnel qualified to lead group activities.

In those institutions which provide group programmes, children, young people, and adults can receive the following benefits through participation in them:

1. Information that will assist them in adjusting to their various areas of experience, including:
   (*a*) educational progress,
   (*b*) occupational opportunities and vocational preparation,
   (*c*) leisure-time activities,
   (*d*) social and civil conditions.
2. Experience in cooperative living leading to the development of:
   (*a*) initiative,
   (*b*) good sportsmanship,
   (*c*) consideration of others, and
   (*d*) self and social understanding.
3. Development of individual abilities and interest through:
   (*a*) participation in group projects,
   (*b*) organisation of pupil-initiated activities,
   (*c*) special services and programmes in and out of the school.

A young adolescent, sometimes a child, or an older adolescent, is prone to believe that he is experiencing problem situations and conditions that are peculiar to himself. Often his parents do not understand him; he is the prey of conflicting urges or interests; his teachers expect him to obey certain class or school rules which to him seem foolish; he is bothered by physical and physiological changes which he does not recognise as symptomatic of the growing-up process; he has difficulty in peer-age group relationships.

Too often the young person keeps his worries and anxieties to himself. He gradually builds up resentments or feelings of insecurity that may continue to be unnoticed by adults unless his difficulties are recognised by an insightful parent, teacher, or counsellor.

When young people, in appropriately organised groups, are given the opportunity to discuss their respective interests, ambitions, attitudes, or emotional reactions, they come to realise that many of their supposedly personal 'troubles' are experienced by all or most of their age peers.

A wise group leader, who has earned the confidence of the group, then can motivate a boy or girl having a special problem of adjustment to seek individual counselling.

SIGNIFICANT ADVANTAGES OF GROUP GUIDANCE

Group guidance should have an important place in a college or university's total guidance programme because of its significant advantages. Some of them are:

1. *It is both economical and efficient*—Through meetings with a group of students, the Counselling/Liaison officer can convey information in much less time than if he gives the same information to each student individually.

The time thus saved can be utilised for the more difficult and complex problems of the students. Also, it is economical to collect general background information about the students and their problems in a group, more specific information about the student can be collected individually.

2. *It aids the normal student*—As colleges and universities are organised today, counselling will continue to be largely remedial and deal with problems after they have arisen.

No matter how well planned the counselling programme is, there is need for group guidance for the normal student to give him information and the direction that he needs and wants. With such assistance, he can go on from there to manage his own affairs better.

3. *It helps in having more contacts with students*—The Counselling/Liaison officer can have many more contacts with a large number of students through group guidance.

During these contacts, he observes each student's behaviour in the group situation and thus increases his knowledge of that student.

4. *It offers students the opportunity to discuss common problems*—Under expert leadership, students within a group can determine what their common problems are.

They can then work toward general agreement as to the best ways to solve them.

5. *It helps improve student's attitudes and behaviour*—Group discussion provides opportunities for free exchange of opinions and realistic analysis of attitudes.

All these can help the participants of the group to achieve better and balanced judgments and more desirable behaviour.

6. *It focus collective judgement on problems that are common to the group*—Students are often willing to discuss in group problems

that they are unwilling to discuss in individual interviews. It gives them an opportunity to express their anxieties and relieve their pent up feelings. Group suggestions may help them resolve their problems.

7. *It provides an admirable opportunity* to the guidance workers to observe each student as he reacts in a group situation and to know some elements of his personality not revealed in any other way. This helps in the thorough understanding of the student.

8. *It helps in the development of wholesome and helpful awareness of unrecognised needs and problems of the students.* This lays the foundation, develops the need and prepares the way for individual counselling.

TYPES OF GROUPS SITUATIONS AND ACTIVITIES

In the broader connotation of the term guidance, every group teaching-learning situation possesses guidance implications.

Schools vary in the number of guidance-pointed group situations and activities provided and in the efficacy of the ones that are included in the programme of guidance. The more prevalent types are:

1. The school assembly,
2. The home-room programme, especially in junior and senior high schools,
3. Guidance courses,
4. Interest and service clubs,
5. Organised programmes of school government and management, and
6. Special small-group conferences.

Some of the general functions and organisational patterns of these media of guidance are considered here briefly.

1. The School Assembly

The school assembly is a form of group participation common to all educational levels. The weekly schedule is so arranged that one or more opportunities are afforded for bringing together.

Non-school institutions recognise the value of assembling their personnel for the purpose of encouraging an attitude of oneness among them and of bringing to the attention of the group certain matters of interest to them.

Many business houses, industrial plants, professional groups, and social and civic organisations have regular meetings which are attended either voluntarily or under requirement by all who are associated with the institution or the group.

At such meetings, instruction is given, operational plans are discussed, or management and worker problems are considered. The assembly on any level or of any group is extremely worthwhile in the programme is related to the interests of the participants and is well organised and well presented.

Various values have been attached to the school assembly. It affords opportunities to:

1. Help pupils develop attitudes of oneness and school loyalty.
2. Integrate and broaden classroom learnings through various media; guest speakers, motion pictures or television showings, and educational programmes prepared and presented by pupils and teachers.
3. Provides practice of good audience habits.
4. Encourage the development of self-expression and poise through pupil-conducted programmes.
5. Acquaint pupils with voting-procedures as applied to the selection of school government officers.
6. Give recognition to individuals and groups for good academic achievement and other phases of school performance.
7. Alert pupils to school and community standards of behaviour.
8. Inform pupils of special school and community activities and opportunities.

2. The Home-room Programme

Much has been written concerning the benefits to pupils of participation in home-room activities. During the home-room period, certain administrative details must be taken care of. These include recording attendance, making reports, and reading notices.

Such activities are time-consuming, since they may give rise to pupils questions and discussions. No matter how efficient a home-room sponsor may be, he often finds the period slipping away before little if any of a planned programme has been reached.

In addition, the home room should be what its name implies, a *home* situation in which individual pupils can settle many of their school or personal problems with teacher assistance.

3. Guidance Courses

The home-room period then can remain a time during which the class engages in informal but teacher-led activities of immediate interest to the group. The scheduled guidance period is not a regular recitation period; no marks are assigned for performance.

Although the content of the course usually is 'structured' so that the topics for discussion fit into a sequential framework.

As an individual progresses through succeeding school levels, he needs to learn the "know-how" of adjusting to the various areas of his present and future life experiences. At least a part of this learning process takes place in his regular study programme.

Factors closely associated with one or another particular area of adjustment probably can be dealt with more adequately in special group situations or guidance classes. The areas most commonly included in such courses stress educational and vocational opportunities and human relationship or mental hygiene.

4. Interest and Service Clubs

Young people like to participate in activities with similarly minded schoolmates in which they can give expression to their interests and display initiative and self-direction.

Although they often appear to be extremely self-centered, they also welcome opportunities to do things for other people. Interest and activity clubs are excellent media for the satisfaction of these youthful urges.

Clubs may either be an outgrowth of regular classroom work or stem from personal interests and school or community relationships. For the purposes of our discussion, they are included in these out-of-class activities.

The point of view of some educators is that all co-curricular clubs should be included among curricular offerings. The advocates of this policy stress the idea that recitation-class sessions then would be conducted in the same informal manner that characterises club activities.

This would seem to be almost impossible in some areas of studies, especially on the secondary level. The teacher's approach is restricted according to the demands of a course of study.

Class activity is work, even though it should be a pleasant experience; club activity, no matter how great its educational value and how seriously the club members participate in the completion of projects, still is regarded by them as interesting 'play' or recreation.

5. Pupil Participation in School Government and Management

Organising and carrying out a programme of pupil-teacher school government and management offer excellent opportunities for guidance in democratic living. Such programmes can be found on all school levels. As young people grow in maturity and the power of decision-making, they may be permitted to assume added responsibility for the management of school affairs.

However, they should not have complete control. Since members of the faculty are as much a part of the school community as the pupils, the former should have a voice in matters which concern the welfare of the entire school.

The administrative head of the school is responsible for whatever is done in the school; hence he has the veto power over activities of the student council.

In schools where teacher members of the school government council exercise tactful and indirect guidance over pupil enthusiasms, the principal rarely needs to exercise his veto power.

For every member of school's pupil population to participate actively in school government would constitute an ideal situation. Counsellors sometimes find it difficult to motivate even a few young people to assume responsibility for helping, initiate and carry on certain pupil benefits resulting from student government action.

Yet all pupils want to avail themselves of privileges achieved. In many instances, non-participating individuals are reflecting the citizenship attitudes displayed by the adult members of the family. The worthwhile outcomes of participation in student-school government include:

1. Development of friendliness and cooperation between pupils and staff members.

2. Training toward good citizenship and the assumption of civic responsibilities.
3. Encouragement of pupil self-discipline.
4. Development of leadership qualities.
5. Gaining of an appreciation of individual responsibilities in relation to the rights of others.

6. Special Small-group Conferences

In addition to guidance rendered through general school-sponsored group activities, counsellors and teacher-counsellors often are called on to lead small-group projects or confer with small groups of pupils concerning immediate problem situation involving the interests or welfare of the group.

Such group-guidance conferences usually represent emergency needs, require little preparatory planning by the counsellor, and need no more than a few sessions to accomplish their purpose.

Small groups of pupils having similar educational or vocational interest, or school-life problems may wish to meet with a staff member to receive information about opportunities for specialised education, specific business or industrial openings, learning difficulties in a particular field of study, teacher-pupil relationships in a particular situation, pupil-pupil relationships, or any other area of interest or difficulty common to the group.

When a counsellor discovers that a small group needs special guidance of one kind or another, he arranges for conferences with them as a group. The degree of success attained in any small-group conference depends on the pupils' recognition of the counsellor's sincerity, co-operative attitude, and ability to be helpful.

GROUP ACTIVITIES OF COUNSELLING AND TEACHING PERSONNEL

A teacher's or counsellor's growth on the job usually is regarded as an outcome of individually received supervisory assistance and personal experience in learning from one's own mistakes. At present there is a trend toward attaining professional efficiency through experience in the group process.

Teacher and Counsellor Orientation

In many school systems, beginning teachers and teachers newly appointed to a school meet as a group with the principal or an assistant for orientation purposes. They are briefed on the school's policies, organisational plan, composition of the pupil population, school standards, curricular offerings, and pertinent aspects of school and class management.

One or more such group sessions may be needed. A 'new' teacher may be paired with an experienced member of the faculty for individual briefing.

Attitudes and Skills of Group Counsellors

The attitudes and skills which a counsellor finds effective with individuals closely parallel those desirable for group counselling as well. Ethical behaviour, flexibility, intellectual competence, acceptance, understanding, and sensitivity are among the basic attitudes and skills of the group counsellor. Each was described in some detail in previous chapter.

Individual counselling, although the best single background experience, may cause problems for the counsellor who attempts to apply this experience directly in the group situation. Communication within a group is far more complex.

Experience in counselling individuals may well have taught him to be aware of the student's every verbal and nonverbal act. Those who choose to continue the intensive one-to-one interaction learned from the previous counselling experience are forced to treat the group as a succession of individuals.

His intensive personal interaction with a single member deprives the counsellor of the opportunity to be sensitive to the needs of others, and their participation cannot be properly encouraged. Other than its observational value for group members, the counsellor is essentially conducting a series of individual interviews.

Group counselling is built upon the assumption that members are assisted by helping others as well as being helped by them. The counsellor, therefore, must facilitate student-student communication as well as counsellor-student interaction.

Linking, further, helps the individual to feel a common bond with other group members. As each member, in turn, attempts to link his comment to what has previously been said he feels more inclined to assist his fellow member.

The experienced counsellor, then, is able to enlist the efforts of group members so that the individual receives help from many members as well as the counsellor.

Procedures in Group Counselling

Counselling, individual or group, can be effective only when an objective or terminal behaviour has been identified and is understood by both counsellor and student. Group counselling further implies the involvement of other group members in assisting the individual.

Procedures that follow are those which the counsellor must understand thoroughly and be able to implement before he involves students in group counselling.

1. Identifying Each Member's Objective

Group counsellors frequently organise a group and then expect members to find group and individual purpose while participating. The wide range of interests and purposes that an individual may express diminishes the likelihood that sufficient time can be concentrated upon a given objective to ensure its attainment.

2. Organisational Decisions

The counsellor needs to consider the optimal size, physical site, and length and frequency of meeting for each group with which he works. Too often the counsellor applies the same alternative to all groups.

Ample conjecture and some research indicates that a group of five or six is optimal for counselling purposes. As group size increases, the leader tends to become more dominant and addresses himself to group rather than individual needs, members become more dependent and talk less, and feelings of frustration, threat, and inhibition concerning participation increase. They may well be cases, however, where a larger number would actually be advantageous to the group.

The counsellor may vary the length and frequency of sessions, also, in order to enhance goal-directed behaviour. During the early stages of a group, he frequently finds that two or three meetings each week are beneficial.

As more intensive attempts are made by the individual to reach his objective outside the group setting, formal group meetings may be reduced to once weekly.

3. Forming the Group

Two potential sources of group members exist for the counsellor. First, he might make the opportunity for joining a group available to students with whom he or his fellow counsellors are working individually. Second, he could make announcement of the opportunity to students more generally.

As an example, he may be working with two students who are unable to communicate effectively with members of the opposite sex and might benefit from working on this objective with a group.

The counsellor may, on the other hand, consider it advantageous to have a group composed of people with *different* primary concerns. A girl who has trouble conversing with boys might well gain more insight from an effective communicator than from another like herself.

The critical issue for the counsellor is in determining the group composition that will maximally benefit each member. The complexity and unpredictability of human behaviour may force him to rely more on hunch than scientific observation. His knowledge of people from previous counselling contacts may guide him.

4. Getting Started

The counsellor can get the group started by giving a brief but clear description of his role and clarifying the role of members. Some counsellors place primary emphasis upon counsellor-student communication and discourage extensive contributions from members.

Students should be aware of the counsellor's preference and reasons for his choice of primary communication pattern.

Care must be exercised that the time and place of subsequent meetings is agreeable to members' schedules. Cautionary words must also be given concerning the importance of confidentiality and the opportunity provided for setting any other rules or procedures that seem appropriate.

As is the case in individual counselling, the counsellor must be able to assist the group in starting to talk. Attention to natural difficulty in getting started may release tension a bit. To state, bluntly, "Where shall we get started?" may be threatening and cause members to be needlessly uneasy.

From prior contact he may be able to identify a member who has little difficulty in communicating and encourage this student to begin. The use of open-ended leads rather than specific questions will assist the individual as he begins to speak. Concurrently, the counsellor must be sensitive to other members and encourage them to participate.

5. Building the Relationship

The counsellor's transparent honesty and sincere interest will allow the student to realise that the counsellor is fully committed to assisting him. The counsellor, through the linking function, must assist other members to participate effectively also. The pooling of insights and mutual encouragement will help members to attempt new behaviours outside the group as they gain more confidence.

In some instances a member may be accompanied by another in order that he might have immediate reinforcement for attempts at changed behaviour. Other circumstances may suggest that this is unwise or that the member is able to act more independently.

6. Terminating Group Membership

The rate of development varies greatly among group members. Some will attain one objective, then identify and attain another before others have made much progress. Inevitably, some will have exhausted the group's potential, and the counsellor must concern himself with terminal alternatives for the group and probably will wish to involve the members in discussion of the alternatives prior to reaching a decision.

A primary decision concerns whether members will leave the group singly or whether all will stay until the entire group is terminated. To ask members to remain after their purposes have been served may seem to be an imposition.

These members, however, have a commitment to assist their peers and frequently will be among the more active contributors. If they are allowed to leave some of the most beneficial helping relationships may be eliminated and the effectiveness of group counselling may be reduced.

7. Evaluating Outcomes

The effectiveness of counselling, individual or group, can only be measured by observing how successful the student is in attaining the objective outside of counselling that he established at its outset. Observations of a counselling group at work or members' ratings of their peers are not indicative of effectiveness.

Assessment is not a difficult task if the objective has been stated in terms that are measurable. This explains the need for counsellor assistance in developing a specific objective prior to entering the group. "I hope to generally get along better with people" represents an objective that could only be measured by inference. No direct way exists of measuring attainment.

An objective that states the conditions for attainment might be: "I am shy and awkward with strangers. My objective is to be able to carry on a five-minute talk with a stranger in the student union in which I introduce myself, reveal my thought on at least two current issues, and recall the stranger's name after he leaves".

A simpler, yet equally measurable objective might be identified by a person whose nervousness in tense situations causes him to stutter. If, as the result of group counselling, he could deliver a two-minute speech to a class without stuttering, counselling would have been effective.

Evaluation conducted in this manner allows the group member to know immediately and specifically whether group participation has been effective. He may identify new objectives or continue present efforts based upon the outcome.

His efforts and those of the group are not consumed in repeating ineffective procedures. Those that are helpful are continued. Those that are ineffective or inefficient are replaced.

GUIDANCE OF PARENTS IN GROUPS

During his early childhood, the child is at the mercy of whatever parents can and will do in the way of guiding his attitudes and behaviour. Throughout the developing years, an individual is influenced greatly by his experiences in the home. Social and occupational activities are closely tied to parental interests and activities.

Educational progress depends to a great extent on the co-operative endeavours of parents and school personnel. The school, the community, and the home are tending to work together more closely for the welfare of the child and adolescent than they did in former years.

Parent-Teacher Associations

Each school chapter holds monthly meetings for the purpose of considering, as a group, the ways in which the organisation can be of service to the school. It is becoming customary to invite guest speakers to some of these meetings with whom the attending group members discuss particular aspects of child-rearing and guidance.

On occasion, the principal, a member of the guidance staff, or another qualified person is asked to attend a meeting in order to clarify school policy and procedures, such as curricular offerings, instructional techniques, promotions and class placement, available guidance services, and similar matters of concern to parents.

In addition to these monthly meetings, small committees serve in specific areas. These functional meetings often are led by a member of the school guidance staff. Such sessions offer excellent opportunities for informally administered guidance of parents.

Child-Study Groups

We have referred to these groups earlier. A small group of parents meets once a week, usually between one and three o'clock in the afternoon. During a period of from four to six weeks, the group is led by a counsellor in the study of an aspect of child development and adjustment chosen by the parents.

Difficulties Encountered

The various approaches to parent guidance in group situations have great potential value. Counsellors often find that when they are dealing with a young person's problem, it is the parent, not the child who needs guidance.

When parents avail themselves of opportunities to improve their own attitudes and behaviour in relation to their child, many of the latter's maladjustive experiences can be avoided.

School counsellors sometimes are faced with a difficult situation. Often a mother devotes considerable time and energy to cooperating with the school in every way possible in order to become a better parent. Her intent is to learn how to utilise preventive measures as the helps guide her child's activities.

This type of parent takes her responsibilities so seriously that, without meaning to, she intimidates the child. Hence it becomes the counsellor's task, in group sessions or in individual conferences, to try to teach the parent the difference between sympathetic guidance and too-strict discipline.

Most discouraging to the counsellor is the attitude displayed by a father or mother who evinces no interest or concern about the child's school progress.

AIDS TO GUIDANCE IN GROUP SITUATIONS

Various types of supplementary materials are now available to aid leaders in motivating group interest in pertinent topics of discussion. These materials need to be used with discretion, however. Supplementary group guidance materials include appropriate books, motion pictures and film strips, radio and television programmes, and tours or visits. Added to these can be "try-out" experiences for young people, especially on the junior-high-school level.

Reading Materials

Much reading material for use with young people has been published. National Forum, Inc., has prepared a series of books and eye catching charts for guidance classes, grades seven through twelve.

Many pamphlets or handbooks, some for young people and others for teachers and counsellors can be obtained from Science Research Associates, Inc. Individual books and pamphlets as well as journals and magazines are available for use by young people, teachers, and counsellors, or parents.

School people are beginning to recognise the value of utilising appropriate reading matter in connection with group-guidance projects. Some schools prepare their own pamphlets. Student handbooks are common in educational institutions from junior high school through college. They also can be found in a few elementary schools. These handbooks include information of value to both the young people themselves and their parents.

A series of leaflets dealing with elementary-school counselling contains pen-illustrated, tersely stated information about the guidance services in the elementary schools of Tacoma, Washington. Some of the titles are: "Ways to Use the Elementary School Counsellor", "The Teacher as Counsellor", "Teachers and Counsellor Work Together", and "How Counsellors Work with Parents".

Audio-visual Aids

Motion pictures films depicting life situations offer excellent approaches to guidance in group situations for pupils and parents. Also available for group sessions of teachers, teacher-counsellors, and counsellors are films in which ways of using guidance-pointed techniques in and out of the classroom are presented.

In the utilisation of motion picture films or film strips it is important that the members of the group be prepared for their showing and the subsequent discussion.

The leader of the group (1) selects an appropriate film and previews it, (2) makes certain that the running of the film goes smoothly and that the time consumed in its showing does not prevent immediate discussion of it, (3) alerts the group to the purpose of showing and suggests points to be considered during the showing, (4) after the showing, asks a few pertinent questions about what has been viewed, and (5) then encourages free discussion. Unless the group is properly prepared for the viewing of a film, some individuals may concentrate on unimportant details and miss the film's purpose. This situation is likely to occur especially in film-viewing by children.

Some of these programmes and recordings have guidance value. Like appropriate films, they can be used to pinpoint discussions in guidance class sessions. Similar programmes presented on commercially sponsored radio and television networks can be recommended for viewing by parents as a basis for child-study group meetings. The suggestions offered for showing motion picture films should be followed here as well.

Other Group Guidance Media

Visits by young people or parents to community agencies, such as health centers, local institutions of higher learning, or business houses and industrial plants, serve as aids to programmes of guidance in group situations.

The leader of the group or a member of the agency visited conducts a discussion on the agency's offerings.

Try-out courses, especially on the secondary-school level, give young people an opportunity to observe, participate in and discuss in group sessions various occupational fields.

In some junior high schools, interested pupils may engage in several of these group-guidance experiences during the course of a school term or year. It is the counsellor's responsibility:

1. to recommend to groups of pupils the kinds of courses for which they seem to be fitted by inter groups of pupils the kinds of courses for which they seem to be fitted by interest and special aptitude,
2. to follow them through their try-out activities, and
3. in group sessions, to discuss with them whatever they need or want to know about the occupations.

CLINICAL APPROACH OF GROUP GUIDANCE

By clinical approach is meant the use of scientific method for the diagnosis and treatment of individuals. The coordinated action of the group is tried here to help the individual in difficulty.

The teacher, the parent, the counselling officer, the psychologist, the psychiatrist, the physician, all join hands to help the individual with the problem.

The causes of trouble are identified, the treatment is prescribed and then the case is followed up through the appropriate agencies of correction.

Clinical method does not take the place of individual counselling but does aid very materially in getting a picture of the student that is more nearly complete than can be obtained by any one individual, however capable, when working alone.

The method can be used in any educational institution to increase the effectiveness of the guidance programme.

There are certain guidelines which clinical counsellors must always bear in mind.

Hahn and MacLean have suggested some principles which can prove useful:

(*i*) Counsellors should work within the limits of their professional competence.
(*ii*) Counselling should not be forced on individuals with problems.
(*iii*) Counselling must strive to develop client-understanding of self and of environment.
(*iv*) The counsellor should act as a special type of corrective mirror.
(*v*) The counsellor should aid the counselee to accept himself as the mirror shows him to be.
(*vi*) The counsellor should not close educational-vocational doors without opening others.
(*vii*) The counsellor should help the counsellee to consider practical educational-vocational alternatives.
(*viii*) Final educational-vocational decisions must be made by the counsellee.
(*ix*) Counsellors must search out all the angles of a counsellee's problem and use all pertinent tools and techniques in its solution.

QUESTIONS FOR ANSWER

1. *Explain general functions of Guidance in Group Situations.*
2. *Explain the purposes to be served by the Guidance of Pupils in Group.*
3. *Write a note on the activities and importance of various Group Situation Programmes.*
4. *Explain the importance of Guidance of Parents in Groups.*
5. *Write short notes on the following:*
   (*a*) *Aids to Guidance in Group Situations.*
   (*b*) *Role of Interest and service clubs in Guidance.*
   (*c*) *Role of Leadership in Group Guidance.*
6. *Write short notes on the following:*
   (*a*) *Uses of group counselling.*
   (*b*) *The concept of clinical approach in group guidance.*
   (*c*) *Significant advantages of group guidance.*
7. *Discuss the nature and techniques of group guidance and write a note on the objectives of group guidance.*

PART III
UNDERSTANDING THE COUNSELLEE

12

Career Guidance: The Need for Individual's Evaluation

Effective career guidance can only be provided if the counsellor has full and upto date knowledge about the abilities and capabilities, attitudes, interest and aptitudes as well as personality traits and behavioural pattern of the individual. This is possible by correct evaluation of the individual, therefore, this chapter is devoted to discuss this aspect of career guidance.

THE CONCEPT OF EVALUATION

The term *evaluation* rather than *measurement* is coming to be used generally in the field of education and guidance. *Evaluation is* more inclusive in its scope than *measurement*, though the two terms often are used interchangeably.

Evaluation comprises at least two major phases:

1. Determining the extent of change, and
2. Judging the desirability and the adequacy of the change.

By means of data obtained through the application of one or another technique of measurement, the individual's gain in knowledge, development of attitudes, growth in interests, and achievement of emotional controls are interpreted.

Function of Evaluation

Teachers and guidance personnel constantly are studying the extent to which changes are taking place within an individual as a result of his experiences in school and elsewhere. Since subjective personality factors tend to affect an individual's behaviour in any situation, it often is difficult to evaluate adequately all phases of the individual's development. Some aspects of progress are measured easily and can be interpreted objectively.

Other more subjective aspects may require that the interpretation of objected data represent the mature and trained judgment of two or more experts. Since teachers differ in their standards and in their attitude toward individuals or toward the process of evaluation, the judgment of only one teacher concerning an individual's developmental status in any area of his personality may be insufficient or inaccurate.

If an individual does not perform as he should in reading, in displayed attitudes, or in any other area developed through learning, what is the cause? The discovery of the answers to these questions is the responsibility of guidance workers—teachers or specialists.

Evaluating Approaches

Pupil evaluation includes:

1. A more or less informal study by teachers and counsellors of an individual's displayed attitudes, behaviour patterns, and learning performance in the classroom, and
2. The utilisation of more *formal* evaluating techniques.

Our educational objectives are aimed at providing for every learner, within the limits of his innate capacity, whatever plans, materials, and procedures that are needed to help him develop adult status in all area of life.

Hence one of the primary responsibility of teachers and counsellors is to discover a person's innate capacities, his learning needs, and his own attitudes toward adequate achievement of constructive life goals.

Some of the most common programmes of pupil evaluation are given, hereunder:

INFORMAL STUDY APPROACHES

Most teachers are confronted daily with a feeling of inadequacy whenever they attempt to evaluate the behaviour of their pupils and to guide the learning process. As a result of experimentation, certain procedures have been found to be helpful to teachers and counsellors as ways of studying young people.

These approaches include:

1. Observation of learner behaviour, accompanied by writing anecdotal reports of significant behaviour deviations,
2. Pupil-submitted autobiographical sketches,
3. Sociograms,
4. Teacher-pupil interviews, and
5. Some other pupil-study approaches:
   (*a*) individual or group projects,
   (*b*) oral recitations and short quizzes,
   (*c*) learners' notebooks, reports, and themes, and
   (*d*) displayed creativity.

Although all of these approaches have value as giving indices of pupil characteristics, we shall discuss some and refer only briefly to the others.

Observation

Observation is a continuous process. Some persons are careful observers and report more reliably than others. Parents observe in the home, the counsellor observes during an interview, the test administrator observes during the giving of a test, and the teacher observes during his daily teaching. The supervisor makes planned observations so as to help the teaching and the learning process.

In the past, teachers came to know pupil leaders through casual observations; today we are more concerned with developing attitudes of careful observation of the behaviour of all individuals and recording facts *at the time of their occurrence or shortly thereafter.*

No matter how strongly anyone believes that he will remember what has happened, he can be sure of its recall only if he makes an immediate record of it.

During their observation and study of individual learners, teachers and counsellors can look for the exhibition of the following characteristics:

1. Desire to get attention and recognition or approval from associates,
2. Tendency toward mastery or submission,
3. Display of rivalry, teasing, curiosity, or desire to play,
4. Desire to co-operate in class and to participate in discussion,

5. Habits of study,
6. Speed of reading and completing special assignments,
7. Quality of expression in answering questions,
8. Social adaptability,
9. Leadership qualities,
10. Kind and number of questions asked,
11. Extent of interest in school work,
12. Speech difficulties or other physical deviations,
13. Attempts at cheating, and
14. Promptness in coming to attention.

If the observer is trust-worthy, is known for his ability to assess facts and to report them correctly, and is experienced in a given situation, his observations can be accepted as valid.

Among the limitations of observation as an evaluating techniques are these:

1. The observer may have a strong bias and not be able to overcome it.
2. The observations may be limited in time and number.
3. The items reported may be out of proportion to the total situation.
4. The observer may not be accurate in his reporting.
5. The observed behaviour may be misinterpreted, resulting in unfair or inaccurate conclusions.

Anecdotal Records

If a plan is inaugurated whereby each teacher uses cards or sheets of paper to report incidents that occur in the classroom, eventually data will be collected that can be of service to the counsellor.

Many forms of behaviour can be reported, both those that are commendatory and those that need adjustment. For example, the teacher may report acts of helpfulness as well as acts of discourtesy.

If teachers are encouraged to write such anecdotal records, they tend to observe behaviour more carefully and to evaluate it in the light of its background.

The cumulative effect of these records can be startling. If they are taken seriously by the teacher, they can be helpful to him as well as to the counsellor and the learner.

Autobiographical Sketches

An interesting device for obtaining data concerning an individual's routine behaviour and his attitudes, interests, and ideals is to have him write a comprehensive autobiography.

This may provide an insight into his personality not only through what it includes but also by what it fails to include. If this is planned as an assignment in an English class rather than given to a group in a special room and at a definite time, the results may be more satisfactory.

Writing an autobiographical sketch motivates the individual to evaluate himself and his behaviour in a more objective fashion than he might otherwise employ.

A number of variations of this activity may be used, such as including areas of experience in an account of "My Most Interesting Experience" or writing a detailed diary of one's activities over a definite period of time.

Sociograms

Some teachers find the use of sociograms helpful in discovering those pupils who have not yet established satisfying peer relationships and who need assistance in developing habits of good social living. The construction of a sociogram is not difficult but care must be exercised in its utilisation.

In a sociometric study, the teacher asks each pupil to write the names, in order of choice, of his three best friends in the class, for example, or perhaps the names of three classmates he would like to have as co-workers in a class project. The teacher then constructs a sociogram based on these pupil choices.

Teacher-Pupil Interviews

A face-to-face talk between a teacher and a pupil is not an interview according to the correct definition of the term. A pupil may seek out a teacher in whom he has confidence before or after the regular school session, during the lunch period, or at any other time to speak to him or her informally concerning an immediate interest or problem.

Similarly, a teacher may want to obtain information from or give information to a particular young person. Such informal, on-the-spot, talks can be very enlightening to the teacher and can give the young person a feeling of security in pupil-teacher relationships.

Keeping a pupil after school, incidentally, for the purpose of scolding him or otherwise *talking at him* rather than giving him an opportunity to express his thoughts and feelings has little value for either the teacher or the pupil.

Some Other Pupil-Study Approaches

The ways in which a teacher can utilise oral recitations, short quizzes, projects, and pupils' notebooks and reports are self-evident. Study habits, attitudes toward neatness and care in the execution of assigned tasks, and ability and willingness to cooperate in a project are pupil characteristics that usually do not go unnoticed by an alert, understanding teacher. Often a teacher can use his insight constructively.

A young person may possess some creative ability, for instance, yet fail to give evidence of it except through teacher encouragement. One English teacher had the rare gift of motivating his students to express their thoughts in poetic form. Writing the poems was not a homework assignment, and the students showed him their work whenever they wished.

Not only did the teacher and the school counsellors learn a great deal about the students' feelings and attitudes, but the teacher also encouraged those who showed some talent for writing to develop it further.

This man's approach characterises that of many teachers who are interested in the various fields of creative expression. Children tend to reveal their needs and cravings in their drawings, dancing, singing and similar forms of expression. The differences among individuals displayed in their responses can stimulate teachers to gain some understanding of the causes for them and to guide learning accordingly.

FORMAL EVALUATING TECHNIQUES

Scientific measurement is becoming one of the most valuable tools of education. It is a technique which serves the teacher, the principal, and the guidance staff in trying to evaluate the learning readiness, attitudes, interests, aptitudes and achievement of their pupils.

Anyone interested in guiding a young person must have a means of discovering the kind of person with whom he is dealing, his quality of thinking, his likes and dislikes in vocational and avocational areas, and the extent of his achievement, as well as his capacity for achievement.

Value of Standardised Instruments of Measurement

Each activity in which the school staff engages to help the individual learner adjust to the school and its curriculum, to adjust to other people, or to make a vocational choice is a guidance function.

The information needed for counselling comes from all kinds of sources. The teachers and others in the school help to build cumulative records which include anecdotal records of classroom or out-of-class behaviour.

In fairness to learners, all available sources of information should be used, since seen separately they may be inaccurate or some may be misinterpreted. If more precise information about an individual or a group is needed than can be obtained through somewhat subjective methods, tests may be given.

The success of a programme of pupil evaluation depends on the kinds of tests used, the efficiency of administration, the accuracy in scoring, the skill in interpreting the results, and the facility in utilising the results for the benefit of the individual concerned. A testing programme that is administered for guidance purposes should:

1. test for instructional purposes,
2. test for interests, and
3. test for individual needs.

Tests are considered to be useful to counsellors when they accomplish these purposes:

1. Furnish valid and reliable information with which to help a pupil, along with his parents and the school staff, to make wise curricular choices and to assist the administrators of the school to place him with a group of pupils or teachers with whom he can grow at optimum rate and to the maximum level of his ability.
2. Assist in arranging continuous, sequential, and integrated

learning experiences for an individual pupil, as well as for groups of pupils.
3. Establish a basis for comparative estimates of status in a given characteristic from pupil to pupil.
4. Serve as a meaningful framework in which to interpret data concerning an individual.
5. Supply scientific, objective data about each pupil, which the counsellor can use in helping the individual to understand his strengths and weaknesses.
6. Provide comparable data concerning all pupils with whom a counsellor works.
7. Facilitate counsellors' follow-up studies of the relationships of school experiences and counselling services to the after-school adjustment of graduates and drop-outs.

Utilisation of Formal Techniques

Standardised measuring instruments and other tools of evaluation function as a *means to an end.* The background of knowledge concerning an individual that is obtained from the administration of teacher-made tests and of formal instruments of evaluation, in addition to classroom study approaches, constitutes the basis of understanding on which are built effective teaching and counselling procedures.

Hence the application of as many appropriate evaluating techniques as are available is needed for:

1. motivation of successful learning,
2. educational, vocational, and personal guidance, and
3. character development.

Included among the commonly used and more or less adequately standardised evaluating techniques are the following:

1. Standardised tests, scales, and inventories:
   (*a*) Intelligence tests for general classification,
   (*b*) Differential aptitude batteries,
   (*c*) Tests of special aptitudes,
   (*d*) Scholastic achievement tests—comprehensive, special areas,
   (*e*) Personality tests and scales, and

(*f*) Interest inventories.

2. Projective techniques,
3. Situational tests,
4. The interview, and
5. The case history.

In most school systems, all or many of the various kinds of standardised group and individual testing material listed above are utilised according to a planned programme of testing or as the need arises.

Usually they are administered by the classroom teacher or the teacher-counsellor under the supervision of a trained counsellor. With some training a teacher can become proficient in the selection, administration, and scoring of tests.

Intensive preparation and long experience are required for the development of skill in interpreting test results and in stimulating a pupil to make the most of his assets, no matter how meager these may be.

As we have intimated earlier, much can be learned about an individual in the face-to-face *interview*. The purposes served by using this technique are discussed in chapter 10. A case history is not strictly speaking an instrument of evaluation.

Rather it does represent an attempt to bring together as much of the data concerning an individual as can be obtained from various reliable sources. Its construction and the application of its findings usually are utilised in the diagnosis and treatment of seriously maladjusted individuals.

MEASUREMENT OF GENERAL AND SPECIAL ABILITIES

Tests of general intelligence or classification tests, differential aptitude batteries, and aptitude tests are utilised by school guidance personnel to serve the following purposes respectively:

1. General intelligence tests results are used to organise learners into *relatively* homogeneous teaching-learning groups. For example, though there is value in "social promotion" (permitting pupils to advance from grade to grade in peer-age groups regardless of scholastic achievement), complete heterogeneity of grouping can

interfere with the learning progress of both the mentally superior and the slow learners who are in the same class).

2. Differential aptitude batteries are administered to discover the area or areas of learning in which individual pupils are likely to be most successful. The utilisation of these batteries is especially valuable to a senior-high-school or college counsellor as he attempts to help students decide on their major field of study in college.
3. The results of the administration of a special aptitude test can indicate the potentiality possessed by a young person to acquire superior proficiency in a particular area of performance.

The measurement of individual's personality, ability and capability for a job or a situation can best be done through psychological tests, which can be administered by a trained psychologist or by a trained and qualified guidance counsellor. The details of these tests such as intelligence, aptitude, attitude, interest, achievement and personality tests may be read in any book of educational or experimental psychology, or educational and vocational guidance published by this publisher. Therefore, as per requirement of this chapter we will discuss some of the tests with regard to their utility for evaluation of the individual. A brief account of this aspect is as below:

INTELLIGENCE TESTS

The utilisation of well-standardised intelligence tests has value in educational and vocational guidance. In high school and college, successful mastery in courses such as advanced mathematics and science requires a high degree of mental alertness.

Learners who are mentally slow usually experience learning difficulties if they are permitted to elect those courses. It also has been discovered that success in certain vocational areas is dependent on a high degree of intellectual ability.

The results of intelligence tests assist the counsellor in recommending the selection of those courses which may have value toward occupational competency.

The teacher and the pupil should remember, however, that the intelligence quotient is not the sole determining factor in educational, social, or vocational success.

DIFFERENTIAL APTITUDE BATTERIES

As a result of factor-analysis, based on the multiple-factor theory of trait relationships, some psychologists have constructed intelligence tests according to what are termed the *primary mental abilities*. Included among these abilities are verbal comprehension, word fluency, number, space-associative memory, perceptual speed, and reasoning.

A differential aptitude battery differs from general intelligence tests since it comprises a battery of tests each of which is designed to measure one of the primary mental abilities.

SPECIAL APTITUDE TESTS

A quality or ability that all people possess to some degree can be regarded as an aptitude. A person who possess, as one aspect of his total personality pattern, a superior ability to profit from study in a particular, limited area of activity can be considered to have a *special aptitude* for it.

Whether this superiority is inherited or environmentally induced still is uncertain. According to the dictionary, aptitude is "natural or potential capacity or ability".

Measuring instruments have been constructed to determine the degree to which an individual shows an innate readiness for superior performance. Some aptitude tests are designed to discover better-than-average possession of a quality that is favourable to success in various occupations. Other tests attempt to measure special aptitude for vocational training in fields, such as mechanics, teaching, law, and medicine.

Controversy exists as to whether innate aptitude is basic to superior performance in the graphic arts or design, music, literary production, teaching, or other areas of specialisation. It probably is a fact that years of patient, conscientious practice alone will not produce a virtuoso, or that taking many courses and reading many books will not guarantee a person's becoming a legal genius, an insightful diagnostician of physical ills.

Although attempts have been made to measure special abilities, the construction of worthwhile aptitude tests has not proceeded far. Many of the available instruments are unsatisfactory largely because of the kinds of items included and the widely different populations used in their standardisation. Moreover, an aptitude test is designed to measure the quality of performance *at the time the test is given.*

The results of these tests may indicate future superior achievement in the particular ability or skill tested. Whether or not a potentiality attains realisation depends on various factors:

1. the willingness of the individual to engage intensively in appropriate study and practice,
2. the kind and amount of training available to him,
3. the pressure of family or other responsibilities and obligations, and
4. public interest in and demand for the exercise of his special ability.

Nevertheless, aptitude tests should have a place in the guidance programme. If used in conjunction with other means of evaluation, they can offer the school counsellor some information concerning one of the many aspects of a young person's developing personality pattern.

ACHIEVEMENT TESTS IN A GUIDANCE PROGRAMME

Academic achievement is one of the areas in which guidance counsellors can obtain relatively accurate information. The guidance personnel need this type of pupil appraisal.

Teacher-made tests have value, and many standardised tests are valid and reliable.

Achievement tests can be helpful in two important ways:

1. by furnishing the individual himself with scores that help him appraise the progress he is making toward the achievement of his goal;
2. by furnishing the counsellor with information on the amount of knowledge the individual has in a given field of learning.

Areas of achievement tests. Many valid and reliable achievement tests have been developed for the elementary schools. There are available both batteries of tests that include various subject areas and tests in single areas, such as arithmetic, vocabulary and word usage, spelling, reading, penmanship, science, health and safety, and social studies.

Hundreds of achievement tests have been constructed for subjects on the elementary and secondary levels and more tests are being constructed.

Some batteries also are available. For the most part, these batteries include supposedly fundamental knowledges, skills and appreciation of relationships.

THE EVALUATION OF PERSONALITY

Personality is dynamic integrated behaviour resulting from the interaction between inherited potentialities and environmental influences. It is, in other words, the resultant of the interrelationship among all phases of an individual's behaviour.

The personality pattern includes innate potentialities, motivating needs, urges, interests and ambitions; emotionalised attitudes toward any given situation; overt acts.

Hence "personality" evaluation includes the measurement of intelligence, aptitudes, and achievement, as well as of certain other qualities or characteristics of an individual of any age.

Significance of Traits

The many qualities or trait clusters (general categories of related traits) that comprise an individual's total personality do not function in isolation. There is a constant interplay among them; the functioning of one trait may affect the activity of another.

However, under certain conditions or in specific situations, one or another trait or trait cluster may become so dominant that others seem unable to function adequately.

There are times, however, when parents, teachers, counsellors, and even the individual himself are unable to explain his overt acts or his inner state. Underachievement in learning, delinquent behaviour, or emotional disturbance may have its roots in failure to recognise the value of adhering to school or community standards, conflict among offering urges and interests, or confused thinking.

In order to help a young person achieve self-understanding and consequent self-realisation coupled with self-discipline, counsellors need to discover the underlying causes of difficulties.

Various study approaches are utilised to evaluate inner motivations of overt behaviour. In addition to the methods of evaluation described earlier, there are following things available:

1. Paper-and-pencil tests, questionnaires, and inventories to measure personality traits, and
2. Projective techniques and situational tests, the administration of which supposedly yields functional analysis of the integrated 'whole' personality.

Measurement of Personality Traits

An individual's specific traits can be studied by means of

1. *Questionnaires* or *inventories*, to the various items of which the individual himself responds, and
2. *Rating scales*, in which one or more persons evaluate specific forms of behaviour or attitudes that seem to be habitual characteristics of the subject.

Although attempts have been made to standardise personality questionnaires, inventories, and scales, established norms may not be reliable. The responses of either the self-rater or another rater are subjective. The former may give evidence of self-deception or wishful thinking; the rating of the latter may reflect personal bias or opinion rather than fact.

Self-administered interest and attitude inventories are concerned with the way an individual feels about people, objects, conditions, and situations. They include many areas, such as:

1. attitude toward various vocational fields,
2. opinions on political, social, economic, or religious issues, and
3. attitudes in relation to school, home, or community conditions, or toward family members, school personnel, supervisors, co-workers, or other associates.

Personality tests and rating scales tend to place emphasis on habits, expected reactions in specific situations, and other aspects of behaviour.

The effective utilisation of all these measures depends on the attitude displayed toward them by the members of a guidance-minded faculty and the inclusion in the guidance staff of a counsellor trained in the use of the various techniques listed. Discretion is needed in the selection and interpretation of these measuring instruments.

To *know* is not always *to do*. Responses to test items may show a knowledge of accepted patterns of behaviour, but the subject's actual behaviour may differ greatly from his reactions on paper.

Projective Techniques and Situational Tests

A test or inventory dealing with specific personality traits contains "structured" material. It consists of definite items according to an assigned pattern of response from which the subject or rater selects that which seems to be most appropriate.

Responses are thereby restricted. The "unstructured" situations or tasks presented in a projective technique permit the subject to respond freely and informally. A test usually is individually administered and the administrator does no more than ask occasional questions or offer informal suggestions.

In the utilisation of these techniques, the subject can give free rein to his imagination. He is encouraged to *project*, through his responses, his hopes and aspirations, his fears and worries, his likes and dislikes, his opinions, and his aggressive, submissive, or other expressive attitudes.

Because of the informality of the evaluating experience and the ambiguity of the stimulation, objective interpretation of responses is difficult to obtain. No one except an intensively trained clinical psychologist should attempt to administer a projective technique or interpret the resulting data.

A situational test is intended for the observation of an individual's behaviour in a disguised or partially disguised "lifelike" situation. An example of a "structured" situational test might be that of having pupils correct their own spelling test papers (which already had been rated by the teacher but not marked) in order to discover incidence of dishonesty as evidence by changing incorrectly spelled words.

The setting up of adequate situational tests is difficult and costly. Unless an individual, participates in many such situations, one cannot be certain that the displayed behaviour is habitual.

Moreover, all that is discovered is that the subject acted in a certain way; the *reason* for the behaviour is not necessarily apparent.

THE SCHOOL TESTING PROGRAMME

A. The Planning of a Testing Programme

An adequate testing programme involves cooperative planning by counsellors, teachers, parents, and pupils, as well as administrative encouragement and approval. School administrators and supervisors must recognise that the pupils, not the teachers, are the ones to be evaluated. Sometimes teachers believe that when standardised or other school or school system tests are administered, it is the teacher and not the learner who is the chief concern of the school administrator or supervisor.

Pupils should know the purpose to be served by a particular test. They should be given an opportunity to have the test results interpreted to them. Parents also should know that their children are to be tested and that this is being done for the benefit of the pupils.

The testing programme should be a long-range one. For example, the testing programme for the schools of Shaker Heights, Ohio, includes tests in appropriate areas from the second grade through the senior year of high school.

The tests selected should be appropriate to the purpose to be served. Other things being equal, they should be easy to administer, to score, and to interpret. Since the cost of tests is relatively high, care should be taken that they are selected carefully and intelligently.

Until experience is gained with standardised tests, no more than one or two tests should be used at one time.

A test worth giving is worth scoring and having its results recorded, interpreted, and applied. The counsellor should be more concerned with the score made and what it means regarding the next step to be taken in the guidance of a particular pupil than with whether the score is high or low.

B. The Administration of a Testing Programme

The teachers selected to administer group tests should meet with the person in charge to study the test and the test manual.

They should learn the exact procedures to be followed and should be alerted to some of the problems and questions likely to arise. Emphasis should be placed on:

1. the importance of following the directions exactly as given in the manual, and
2. the necessity of preparing test materials ahead of time, so that once the test starts there are no interruptions.

Equally important are the provisions to be made for scoring the tests. Many tests now can be scored by machines, but this method is expensive. When tests are scored by individuals, the first scoring should be checked. Even if capable pupils help with the scoring, the final responsibility is the teacher's.

All scores should be recorded. A recording system that includes, besides the individual's score, the standard norm for the test and the median for the local group is helpful in the interpretation of individual results. This involves extra clerical work but aids in the interpretation of individual performance.

C. Value of Test Scores

Test scores do not show absolute possession of the trait or ability tested, but they do represent the *measurable degree* to which the individual possesses it. Usually a high rating on an intelligence, aptitude, or achievement test, or on an interest inventory is an index of good potential.

When the scores are translated into percentile ranks, they should not be regarded as absolute, even though they are then more meaningful than as raw scores.

Guidance counsellors have time to rely on the results of valid standardised tests for assistance in analysing the behaviour and potential ability of individuals. Every counsellor is aware, however, that he needs to know more than the score that the individual earns on a particular test.

For example, a raw score of 72 on an intelligence test made by a six-year-old boy represents a much higher degree of mental ability than the same score on the same test made by a fifteen-year-old boy. The scores are the same, but the ages are different, and so are the age norms established for the test.

CONSTRUCTION OF A CASE HISTORY

The case history is *not an instrument of evaluation*. Rather is it a compilation of all available data on an individual who requires intensive study and special therapy. For a case history to be valid, all items of information must be accurate.

Not having any reported information about an aspect of personality is better than having incorrect data if the case history is to serve as an adequate basis for intelligent evaluation of client needs and appropriate treatment.

When an individual is referred by the school or another community agency to a psychological clinic for special remedial treatment or rehabilitation, a trained member of the clinic staff, usually a psychiatric social worker, accumulates and arranges the various kinds of information needed for clinical study. A complete case history includes the following:

Identifying data: name, age, sex, etc.

The specific problem condition or situation, including observable symptoms:

- Health history
- Family history
- School experiences
- Occupational experiences (if an adult)
- Social adjustments
- Examinations
- Physical
- Mental
- Psychological
- Psychophysical
- Educational

This outline can be adapted to meet the needs of the particular person or situation being studied. One point concerning the construction of a case history cannot be stressed too strongly.

The term *case history* should not be applied loosely to any body of information about an individual. For example, one area of college study for persons preparing for teaching or counselling is that of human development and adjustment.

Often in connection with this course the student is expected to observe, over a period of time, the behaviour of a developing young person and then report of his findings, including any available data on school achievement, results of tests administered, and similar pertinent items of information.

THE CASE STUDY

The case study goes beyond the case history. The data of the case history are interpreted, the client's difficulty is diagnosed, appropriate treatment of therapy administered, and a follow-up continued until satisfactory adjustment is evidenced.

Conducting a complete case study is a task for specialists. It represents a clinical approach to serious problems of maladjustment which go beyond the training and experience of teachers and school guidance staffs.

Although the school guidance personnel are responsible for supplying pertinent data to the social worker for inclusion in the case history, interpreting the data and applying needed therapy are the functions of the psychiatrist and his assistants, a guidance clinic, or a hospital for the mentally ill.

Besides supplying information to be included in the case history, the members of a school staff have the responsibility of applying any remedial measures suggested by the specialists.

THE GUIDANCE FOLDER

Recording information is just as important as obtaining it. Significant facts should be recorded in such a way and kept in such a place that they can be used efficiently. The work involved in recording and filling is tedious and un-interesting yet most important.

The record should be cumulative and, in addition to up-to-date identifying data, should include important items concerning a pupil from the time he enters the lower school until he is graduated from high school.

Development of a Cumulative Record

The term *cumulative* record is a recent addition to the terminology used in identifying the various types of records that have been used through the years. The cumulative record is constructed and interpreted differently in different schools, but it usually represents an attempt to begin with certain basic information to which data are added as they are accumulated.

An individual's record may be kept either on a card or in a folder. It is regarded as a *permanent* record, and it is designed to cover a period of years.

The specific items of information usually included in a cumulative record (some to be corrected from time to time, such as address) are the following:

1. Identifying data,
2. Home conditions and background,
3. Economic possibilities and limitations,
4. Health record,
5. Academic record,
6. Record of out-of-class activities,
7. Character and personality development record,
8. Record of individual potentialities,
9. Record of happenings of special significance,
10. Record of special interests and achievements,
11. Educational plans,
12. Vocational interests,
13. Work experiences,
14. Plans for after-school life, and
15. A small picture of the pupil, placed with the record when the individual enters the school. Other pictures of him can be added at later stages of his development.

Entering on a cumulative record card all of the additions or changes that may be needed to keep items 9 through 14, for example, up to the minute for every pupil would constitute a time-consuming chore.

Consequently, some schools use as envelope or folder for each pupil in which is placed the cumulative record card indicating pupil progress, and separate cards containing information concerning, respectively, significant happenings, teacher's or counsellor's comments, vocational interests, work experiences, and similar notations. In other schools, various areas of information are filed separately and kept in different offices:

1. complete health record in the office of health and physical education department,
2. factual identifying information and yearly attendance and achievement records in the general office, and
3. less objective, personal data in the guidance office.

Moreover, in most school systems, the school on each level elementary, junior high, and senior high—keeps its own set of cumulative records which remains in the school and pertinent data are copied from it for transfer to the next higher school a pupil will attend.

There is a trend toward placing all pertinent data on one card which travels with the pupil from one school level to another.

QUESTIONS FOR ANSWER

1. *Differentiate between evaluation and measurement.*
2. *Describe the various types of measurements of individuals that can be utilised as aids to good guidance.*
3. *What are the important conditions to be considered in administering a testing programme for guidance purposes?*
4. *What is the value of the case-study technique in pupil evaluation?*
5. *Enumerate the important uses to which the guidance folder can be put.*
6. *What is the value of cumulative records of student activities to the student? the employer? the school? the college?*

13

Self-Understanding: The Prime Need for Effective Career Guidance

The value of self-understanding, of the individual and effort made by the counsellor to help the individual for better self-understanding, is much more than the guidance is given for any other purpose. This concept is briefly, discussed below:

The concept of self-understanding has come to prominence through the studies of Rogers, Snygg and Combs, etc. It is an interesting and stimulating approach to guidance. It is just the modern version of old Greek motto 'know theyself'. It is essential that the youth seeking guidance must tell his good and weak points to his Counsellor and the Counsellor must help him in knowing his abilities and capabilities properly. This concept also known as 'self-image', 'ego' and 'self-concept'.

The importance of the self-concept in guidance stems from the fact that individuals live in separate and constantly changing worlds which constitute the only reality they can ever know. The individual is the center of his world, and we can never completely share his view of things since we can never join him in his private world.

To understand our behaviour we need to assume that all of us have drives to actualise, maintain, and enhance ourselves and that what we do constitutes an attempt to satisfy our needs in the world as we see it. We all behave in ways that are consistent with our view of ourselves and our world.

It is impossible to overestimate the importance of self-understanding. A well-formulated self-concept that takes into account the realities of the working world makes for an easier transition from school to work than does a hazy or unrealistic one. A major goal of education is the development of clear, well-formulated, and realistic self-concepts. Guidance workers also attempt to help people develop clear and consistent self-images not too opposed to social reality and not too distant from the ideal which we all hold up for ourselves.

DEVELOPMENT OF THE SELF-CONCEPT

We are not born with the ability to understand ourselves. The young child is not even conscious of himself as an individual; he is merely a part of his environment. Consciousness of oneself in some cases emerges suddenly, almost without warning.

To some it is electrifying and deeply satisfying; to others it is depressing, for it signifies that he is alone in the world. Such a dramatic experience is by no means common; but when it does occur, it may well be the beginning of real self-understanding.

For most youth the development of self-understanding is a slow and relatively unconscious process involving some degree of emotional maturity and readiness. It requires more than the collection of data about oneself. It calls for the ability to interpret these data in terms of self and environment.

The individual must come to see himself as he is in comparison with what he wants to be. He must come to grips with himself as he is, as well as with what he thinks he should be; that is, he should have a clear and realistic concept of himself, his surroundings, his obligations and opportunities.

Self-Understanding is Not Related to Age

A realistic self-concept, that is, accurate self-understanding, is not attained at any given age. Some attain it in early youth; some later; some never. An accurate self-concept usually begins to appear in early adolescence, becoming clearer with growth and experience.

It will usually be possible to share with the gifted youth all available data about his strengths and weaknesses early enough and fully enough so that he can develop or remedy them. He will certainly be able to use this information realistically in planning.

Making Decisions Helps Develop a Realistic Self-Concept

If the purpose of guidance is to help the individual solve his own problems and make his own choices as an adult, the responsibility for the choices he makes as a youth must also rest primarily on himself. If he is to make choices that are wise, he must understand himself, his needs, and the choices available to him.

In helping the student to understand himself, one must take great care that he does not develop the habit of morbid introspection to the extent that he either becomes the center of everything—the most important person in his world—or shrinks in importance so much that he feels worthless to himself and to others. Either result will make it impossible for him to assess correctly his abilities and aptitudes and will defeat his attempts to reach emotional maturity.

Information is Needed for the Development of a Self-Concept

It is difficult to decide how much, if at all, the individual should participate in gathering information about himself. The prevailing feeling is that the school counsellor is a person with special training in the methods and techniques of guidance and that he, with the other school personnel, is responsible for securing the necessary information about pupils and recording it in the cumulative folders.

After studying these records, he consults with teachers and with the pupil and, on the basis of all this information, helps the pupil to understand himself, to adjust to school, and to plan his future. This approach is quite logical if the counsellor is considered to be the center of the guidance process.

If, however, the individual student himself; he should participate in it and, through this participation, learn more about himself.

We should also remember that certain important data cannot be obtained without the cooperation of the pupil himself. The pupil needs information about himself as an aid to clear self-understanding.

Current Experiments in the Development of Self-Understanding

Sociograms may help in self-understanding by showing the pupil how he is seen by his fellow students. Even when the judgments of other students about an individual are incorrect, they may help him to ask, "What have I done that makes other students see me as they do?"

In one high school the students who were nominated for various offices were brought together in a number of conferences where they discussed the purposes and duties of the various positions and the kinds of ability and qualities essential for them. Each nominee was stimulated through these group discussions to examine himself and find out whether or not he had the attributes considered essential for the job for which he was nominated.

In another school a still more interesting and daring plan was used. A selected group of seniors engaged in a free discussion of the qualities and characteristics of different members of the group. The teacher sat in the rear of the room and took no part in the discussion except when he was asked for his suggestions.

One boy was selected as the subject for discussion, and a student evaluator gave in detail what he considered were the good and bad characteristics of the boy. When he had finished his summation, another student spoke in defence of the individual being discussed. Finally, the boy himself was given an opportunity to speak. However, there was not the slightest evidence of hurt feelings by any of the students.

The teacher in charge was confident that the plan was a very useful one in helping the student to understand himself and in helping fellow students and teachers to understand the individual. Perhaps the secret of the success of this plan was that the teacher had real sympathetic understanding of youth. He had not forgotten his own youth, as unfortunately is the case with many teachers, counsellors, and parents.

Such devices are useful in helping the individual to develop an understanding of himself, which is essential for adjustment and for the solution of personal problems.

He is a strange mixture of a boy and a man. The entire direction of his future depends upon choices that are made, and wise choices are determined by the degree to which he understands himself. Wise counsel by sympathetic and understanding teachers and counsellors can be of great help at this time.

MEASUREMENT OF SELF-UNDERSTANDING

By its very nature the self-concept is so private and deep that it probably cannot be completely communicated to others. Attempts are made, however, to disclose this core of the student's personality so that guidance may be based on the individual's 'reality'.

Autobiography

The autobiography has been previously mentioned as a device for developing realistic self-pictures, but it is also used for disclosing the self-concept. Through these life stories the student may tell how he sees himself and how the world looks to him. This instrument has especial value because it can be adapted for use at nearly all grade levels.

Interview

Perhaps the most useful method for disclosing the individual's level of self-understanding is the interview. If we give students a chance to talk in a non-threatening atmosphere, they will tell us much about themselves, and in the process they may be helped to clarify what they really think and believe. The feelings of the student will be expressed to his and our benefit if we take time to listen him.

Scales and Check Lists

There are a variety of scales and check lists on the market which are sometimes used to help teachers and counsellors understand the self-concept of their students.

Teachers may want to construct their own lists of incomplete sentences to be completed by the student. Such 'stubs' as the following may be useful: I am ...; People say that ...; I get nervous when ... These approaches should not be thought of as clinical tools but merely as stimuli which may help the student to clarify what he thinks about himself. Lists of adjectives are also used for this purpose. The student is presented with a list of flattering and damaging descriptive terms and asked to underline the ones which he thinks apply to him. So used, devices of this kind may provide us with gross measures of the student's concept of himself.

QUESTIONS FOR ANSWER

1. *Write a note on the importance of self-understanding in the process of guidance.*
2. *Explain the process of development of self-concept.*
3. *Write short notes on the following:*
   (a) *Measurement of self-understanding.*

14

Understanding of Individual's Personality Essential for Career Guidance

INTRODUCTION

We all have seen that every doctor not only asks some questions regarding the ailment of the patient but also some general questions about his physique and some times some questions about pathological and physiological condition of the patient which is complicated ailments, doctors see the reports of various pathological and other test. It is essential for effective and beneficial treatment. The same principle is applicable to teaching and guidance.

Guidance, like teaching, is a service given by one person to another. We often say the teacher is "teaching a class", but what he is really doing is teaching *each one* in the class—helping each pupil to learn. The counsellor often meets pupils in a group, but his purpose is to help each individual in the group.

This help cannot be effective unless the teacher or counsellor knows the problems faced by each pupil and his characteristics, his abilities, and his desires. On the other hand, if the help offered is to be accepted by the individual, he must know himself, his limitations, and his strengths. Successful guidance, like successful teaching, is predicted on the student's being understood by the counsellor and by himself.

IMPORTANCE OF UNDERSTANDING

It would seem to be self-evident that effective counselling toward specific goals is impossible without a clear understanding of the individual by the counsellor, the teacher, and the parent, and that guidance should not be attempted unless such understanding is present. But life is full of tragedies in home and in school because of the lack of such understanding.

Many parents try to determine the future of their children, especially that of their sons. If the family tradition for generations has been that the first-born son becomes a physician, a lawyer, a minister, then an attempt may be made to fit a boy into the tradition regardless of his abilities or interests.

It is often said that what the student does, what courses he takes in school or college, what occupation he chooses, should be based on the needs that he, himself, feels. There is no doubt that these are important, but the needs that one feels at any given time may not be based on a clear self-understanding.

We often feel a variety of needs at any given time, but some are quite superficial and relatively unimportant. Assistance in making choices should be based on as thorough an understanding as is possible of the individual, of his basic needs, and of the real circumstances surrounding his decisions.

MAJOR LIFE AREAS NEEDS TO BE UNDERSTOOD

Understanding an individual is dependent upon knowledge of how he acts in different situations. This understanding may come from observations by those who know him in school, at home, or in the community. These observations need to be combined and judgments made regarding the motives and reasons behind the observed acts.

This is by no means an easy thing to accomplish. It calls for sympathetic insight into the desires and needs of students and the unusual ability to put aside any preconceived ideas of what the individual may be.

One important key to such understanding is the physical and social environment of the individual. Careful, long-range studies are now being made of the relationship.

The Individual in His School

A study made recently indicates that the greatest prestige is often given to those students with organisational leadership ability—the ability to get other students to agree on what is to be done and to organise them so as to do it effectively, even if what is planned is not approved by the school authorities.

In some schools the value placed by students upon superior attainment is high, in others it is low. Such student values are of extreme importance and can usually be developed by the school itself with the support of the homes and community. This "climate" of the school often becomes traditional.

Recently a father took his son out of a public school that had a very low standard and secured his admission into one of the private schools which had maintained unusually high scholastic standards. In the public school the boy received high marks, but his achievement was low.

In the private school the boy was told that he would be dismissed at the end of the term unless his achievement improved. By hard work, and with the help of outside tutoring, he steadily advanced and eventually was doing the high quality of work of which he was capable. The improvement was due to the climate of the private school and his acceptance of it.

The Individual in His Home

Another life area that is important in our attempts to understand an individual is his home. The socio-economic level of the home may account for the academic ambition or apathy of the child. Generally speaking, the lower the level of the home, the less education is valued.

Subtle psychological forces such as acceptance, rejection, or domination may play important roles in shaping the child. The relationship between parents and children and sibling relationships may provide us with keys to the behaviour we observe. The home is often the most important element in the individual's life, and we cannot understand him without knowing about his home.

The counsellor may be an important bridge between the school and the home and thus help both the parent and the teacher to know the student more completely.

The Individual in His Community

Community conditions are of great importance in securing an understanding of individual students and in developing effective self-concepts. Such conditions are fully as significant as those in the home or in the school. Differences in the social status of families in a community often are reflected in the attitudes of different groups of high-school students toward one another.

Differences in dress, in habits of speech, in social manner, in points of view, and in values are often seen. In consolidated schools, rivalries and clanish customs often appear and cause feelings of hostility between groups.

In spite of efforts made by the school staff to overcome these unfavourable conditions, they often continue. In the school itself, students in the college preparatory course are likely to look down on those taking industrial courses.

Understanding cannot come merely from observation of what a person does, how he acts, and how he seems to feel. It is important to know the influences that were responsible for his behaviour, "how he got that way", what his purpose was in doing what he did. Many times he himself does not understand why he acted as he did.

PSYCHOLOGICAL BARRIERS TO UNDERSTANDING

A meaningful understanding of the individual is not always easy to secure. Certain psychological barriers may impede our progress toward understanding. Young people especially are reluctant to reveal themselves as they really are.

Because of the intensely personal nature of our lives, it is difficult—perhaps impossible—to have complete empathy for another person, that is, to feel what it would be like to be in his position.

Reluctance to Reveal One's Real Self

Adolescents often go to great lengths to keep another person from knowing what they really are. They are cruel to keep others from knowing that they are really tenderhearted; they pretend to dislike someone in order to conceal their inner feelings of respect and liking. Many persons, old and young, feel that it is indecent to "bare one's soul and dare the day".

It is almost as bad as being a nudist! They also feel that "it is none of your business". This attitude, in itself, reveals something about the individual. A wise and sympathetic counsellor or teacher, who has not forgotten his own youth, can look behind this bravado and learn much about the student.

Difficulty in Understanding Another Person

It is difficult for adults to understand the behaviour of adolescents; we so easily forget what we thought and did when we were "young and gay". A common danger is that we may read our own present motives, feelings, and aspirations into the expressions and activities of the student.

Another serious difficulty is that, although we can secure some information about the individual, what we get sometimes interferes with our understanding of him. "We cannot see the forest for the trees".

Real understanding of another person involves an unusual ability to put oneself sympathetically and intelligently in his place. At the same time one must stand apart and be impersonal. The privacy of the individual must be respected; we must not be in a hurry see what the student is not ready to disclose.

Individuals Change

One difficulty in dealing with the adolescent is that he is constantly changing, even from day-to-day. As a consequence, by the time data are obtained and recorded, he has changed, and the data are important only as they show a developmental picture of the student.

Such a picture is important, but it does not tell us what he is now. A current picture is very difficult to attain.

Cumulative records have great value in showing the development of the individual from year to year—his scholastic record, his changing interests, his attitudes toward teachers and fellow students, the changes in his personality patterns.

But more important is a truly understanding teacher or counsellor who can interpret the conflicting behaviour of the developing adolescent. Such understanding is absolutely essential.

The past must not be confused with the present. Records tell us what was; only the individual himself can tell us what is.

SOCIAL CHANGES ARE BARRIERS TO UNDERSTANDING

Great and rapid changes in our society increase the difficulty of understanding across the generations. Adults and adolescents live in truly different worlds. The meaning of work, the role of the family, religion, and morals, the philosophy of the schools have all undergone considerable transformation during this century. These changes impede the understanding which is so essential for the function of guidance.

The Family Changes

In any consideration of the present difficulty in the guidance of youth the changes in the home and community should be kept in mind. In most present-day homes there is no longer the same amount of intimate interrelationship that once was present. The increased tempo of life too often materially reduced or even eliminated the time or the opportunity for such relationships.

Because electrical appliances of all kinds—for cooking, dishwashing, laundry work, housekeeping, refrigeration—have materially reduced the time necessary for such responsibilities. There is actually more time available for home life and for closer relationships. In some homes this "free time" is being utilised to enrich home life and has resulted in closer relationships between parents and children, but in the typical home this is not the case.

There seem to be two main factors that are largely responsible for this situation. One of these is the increased participation of fathers and mothers in activities outside the home in social, civic, church, and political affairs. Such activities, for example, those of the parent-teacher association, are often very useful and desirable.

The second factor is the increased independence of children which results in a decrease in the feeling of need for help or even for association with parents. The many out-of-class activities in the school—athletic, musical, dramatic, school government, social—provide group satisfactions and reduce both the time and the need for companionship at home.

At home the children have the radio, the television, and the record player at their disposal, and they need no assistance from their parents to enjoy these facilities. The new kind of less-intimate family seems to have resulted in much juvenile delinquency.

If juvenile delinquency is ever to be eliminated, the home and the community must be improved. As a first step, there must be closer and more effective cooperation of home, school, and community in securing accurate and significant information regarding the conditions and influences that are responsible for the attitudes and purposes of youth.

Once identified, these conditions and influences must be changed to provide an environment more conducive to a wholesome life and respect for law.

Religious Beliefs and Morals: Yesterday and Today

Another area of great importance in the lives of young people in which there have been far-reaching and significant changes is that of morals and religion. The reasons for these changes are difficult to determine.

Developments in our social, economic, and industrial life probably have contributed to the change, as has the interaction of different beliefs, customs, and morals brought to India from all parts of the world.

Whatever the cause, we cannot fail to understand the great importance of different moral codes and religious beliefs to the development of young people, even though both these areas are considered to be the private concern of the family, the church, and the individual rather than of the school.

Many people believe that religion has a greater hold on people than it ever has had and point out that the growth in church membership in all denominations has steadily increased and many new churches are being built.

We are certain: religious customs have changed. The great majority of people are far more liberal in their beliefs and more tolerant of those who do not believe as they do. Young people are increasingly thinking for themselves and refusing to accept religious dogmas merely because they have been recognised for centuries.

In this atmosphere of controversy, of changing beliefs, and of lack of belief, it is small wonder that young people are confused and often unable to adjust properly and to distinguish between transient and permanent values. Wise assistance is needed. Much of this help must be given by the home and the church, but the school also has a responsibility here.

Racketeering, graft, and corruption are everywhere apparent, in politics, business, industry, government, and labour unions. Some men become wealthy and powerful not because of their contribution to society but because of trickery, clever dealing, influence, control of the political machine, or even theft, intimidation, or murder.

Our legal system is slow, cumbersome, and too often ineffective. Criminal sometimes escape just punishment because they have money or influence or because of the work of lawyers who specialise in helping criminals evade the consequences set up by the law. The old virtues of industry, thrift, and honesty have, in some cases, been the actual cause of poverty and suffering.

Men who have worked long and hard and who have been thrifty have sometimes been cheated by the unscrupulous and lost their money. They have found themselves poor and ruined not because they were dishonest or prodigal but because they were thrifty and honest.

Standards of good conduct are continually changing. Some conduct that was once considered acceptable is now unacceptable, and what was unacceptable is now acceptable.

Some research has suggested that youth indicate relatively little concern about problems of morals and religion or of home and family. Two opposite conclusions might be drawn from these findings. We might say that young people are well adjusted in morals and religion and to home and family since they apparently have few problems in these areas.

In other words, young people may not be conscious of problems in these areas because they have little sense of moral obligation and little restraint imposed on them. The mounting delinquency rate among youth might indicate that the second conclusion is correct.

The Meaning of Work is Changing

During the past fifty years there has been a marked change in the attitude of youth toward standards of accomplishment in schoolwork. In most schools the number of high-school students who have the ambition to do their best in studies is small.

Some think that one of the causes of this situation stems from the attitude of workers during the depression of the 1930s. Unemployment was high, and the government took the responsibility of providing jobs for all. It was difficult to find or create enough jobs for all who needed the income, and, as a result, much of the work was unnecessary, and there were more men on each job than were needed.

There was no incentive to do the job quickly or well. A very common sight was that of workers on road jobs leaning on their shovels. This unfortunate attitude toward work permeated nearly all kinds of public employment and society in general.

Still another factor related to this situation is the social pressure not to be different from other members of the group. "Who wants to be a brain?" "I want to be like other people".

To many students in high school it is no longer considered important or desirable to get high marks or to do one's best—getting by is enough.

The climate of the community will determine in large measure what kind of school it will be. Most young people will respond to whatever values are set by their companions, their school, and their homes.

To understand the changing meaning of work and accomplishment for our adolescents, we must remember that the adult society created the climate that helped these new and troublesome values to flourish.

The Changing Educational Philosophy

One of the most important social changes in recent years has been that in our philosophy of education as it concerns the place of the child in the teaching-learning process. This change is so intermingled with the changes in the home and in religion and morals that it is difficult to tell whether the changes in the philosophy of education are responsible for the changes in the home and society or the reverse.

Formerly, education was the process of passing on to the young the cultural heritage of the past. It was the process of inculcating in the young those habits, skills, ideas, and knowledges that were necessary to enable them to take their place in adult society.

The central figure in this process was the teacher. The student was the recipient and, as far as possible, passive and obedient. He was thought to be too young to have and voice in determining what he had to do or to learn. Discipline was the process of preventing behaviour that would interfere with this attitude of docility.

The new educational philosophy places the child at the center of the educational process and is concerned primarily with his development, that is, with what he is now rather than what he may become or what society may demand of him.

His needs for personal development, his own interests and desires, are dominant. His impulses for action are of extreme importance and should not be unduly restricted. He should have a large part in decisions regarding what he should do—even regarding what he should study.

The extreme of this position is that he should not be made to do what he does not want to do. Failures are considered undesirable and should be avoided.

Because punishments and restraints are negative, they should either not be used at all or at least be minimised. The rule of promotion for all is sometimes adopted.

Even though some of the extreme implications of this philosophy have not been generally accepted, its impact has been very great.

Probably its most important implication is the emphasis it places upon the enlarged place of the individual in choosing his own way of life and in selecting his own activities.

Even young children are allowed and often encouraged to make important choices for themselves. Many of these choices may be unfortunate; but when the choice seems undesirable, instead of arbitrarily refusing to allow the child to do what he has chosen to do, we try to help him evaluate the wisdom of his choice.

The underlying idea of this educational position emphasises the fundamental purpose of guidance—helping the individual to make wise choices. The necessity for adequate guidance in the very early years of life in order to develop this ability is emphasised. This emphasis is certainly desirable.

Some children have been quick to take advantage of this situation in the home and in the school and have become restive under old restraints. Formerly, it was expected that children, willingly or unwillingly, would do what they were asked to do, but now some of them argue about it and often win.

Some more effective guidance is absolutely essential. Many national and local agencies are working hard to solve the problem, and some of the suggested solutions seem to be hopeful. At the root of any successful plan must be some form of intelligent guidance.

The last few years have seen great changes in our society. Adults trying to understand adolescents must take account of the fact that the world of their own childhood is gone. It is not likely to return.

If you wish to understand today's youth, you must first understand his world—however much a stranger you feel in it, however much you may disapprove of some of its elements—for the youth and his world are so much a part of each other that they cannot be known separately.

AIDS IN UNDERSTANDING

Many techniques are needed to help us understanding youth. Such an understanding cannot be attained merely by watching what they are doing. We must know the reasons and motives that impel them to act as they do. This level of understanding requires close and sympathetic personal relationship over a reasonably long period of time.

Cumulative Records

A cumulative record is a collection of information about a student and constitutes a picture of his development—physically, academically, and socially. These records, which have great value in showing year-to-year development, include, as we have stated earlier, his scholastic record, his changing interests, his attitude toward teachers and fellow students, and the changes in his personality patterns.

Well-organised anecdotal records—objective statements of significant incident— may be very helpful if carefully made from time to time. Autobiographies often reveal characteristics and attitudes unsuspected even by the student himself. Valuable as they are, such records are quite inadequate to provide a real understanding of the pupil.

What is needed most is a sympathetic and understanding teacher or counsellor who can interpret the conflicting behaviour of the developing adolescent and look behind and beyond the records themselves to see him as he is. This is essential in any attempt to give guidance to the individual.

Cooperation in the School

The development of the self, the ego, is a gradual process which may continue throughout life, but for most people the period of childhood and youth is by far the most important time in the formation of the self.

Understanding of an individual comes from a knowledge of how he acts in different situations and why. It might be that the person best able to understand the youth would be the one who has the closest relation to him for the longest period.

Teachers see children four to six hours a day, for nine or ten months a year and observe their acts and judge their motives. Teachers, however, see the individual in a more or less restricted situation and are not completely qualified to understand him. Fellow students, on the other hand, observe their classmates in many types of situations which are more varied and lifelike than those seen by parents or teachers.

Although the counsellor is the person who is charged with the responsibility for bringing together all the data in the school records, including the observations and opinions of teachers and peers, he may have comparatively little personal contact with individual students. Often, however, he can judge more objectively than parents and teachers, even though he might not be able to develop a completely accurate understanding of the whole personality by himself.

Cooperation with the Home

The school and the family share the greatest responsibility for understanding. They are so closely related that there is every reason and need for cooperation, but effective methods to bring this about have as yet not been developed.

The major responsibility for initiating such cooperation rests upon the school system. During the past ten years a number of systems have been experimenting with different types of cooperation, some of which seem to be very promising.

Close personal relations are developed among teachers, parents, business and professional people so that they are known to each other as individuals. Through social occasions and professional meetings they come to know one another better and to realise the necessity for cooperation among friends in all areas, not only in the schools.

In many schools lay people have been invited to come to the school for a variety of reasons so that they can know and understand it better. Some schools are providing "parent" rooms where there are easy chairs and books and pamphlets on school matters and where desirable conferences with teachers, counsellors, and administrators can be arranged.

At present the chief means of cooperation with the home is through reports to the parents on the status and progress of the child, but it is difficult to make such reports meaningful to them. The primary meaning is conveyed by the grades received, promotion of non-promotion, and comments on the child's behaviour.

At times conferences are arranged between the teacher and the parents to discuss the status of the pupil. In most schools, however, this conference is held only when there is something wrong. If the pupil is getting along well in school, no need for a conference is seen.

The difficulty in providing these conferences is very great; but in the schools where such methods have been adopted, a very definite change has been seen in the relation between teachers and parents not only in their personal contact but also in their friendly cooperation in the solution of problems of pupils and in the improvement of school facilities.

Community Information

Teachers and counsellors should know their community if they are to be of maximum help to students. The school needs to know about the community activities of the students. Which ones are active in church work? Which ones are leaders in their neighbourhood peer groups?

Contacts with service clubs such as Rotary, Kiwanis, and Lions have been found to be very useful in revealing sources of assistance and also in securing information about students who are friends or relations of members of these organisations.

Many schools have found it helpful to initiate some type of community survey, which reveals the resources of the community, such as men and women who are leaders in business or industry and who are willing to talk with students about opportunities and qualities essential to success in life.

Such contacts will help students to understand social and economic conditions and to realise how they may prepare themselves for lines of work for which they are especially fitted.

QUESTIONS FOR ANSWER

1. *Write a note on the importance of understanding in guidance and the methods of understanding the individual.*
2. *Explain how social changes have effected the understanding of the individual and thus complicating efforts of effective guidance.*
3. *Explain the role of various aids is understanding the individual to ease the process of guidance.*

15

Guidance Toward Life Goals: A Road to Better Career

Socially accepted life goals guide an individual to do his best for better social and occupational career likewise an individual with socially accepted better career usually has better life goals. Thus both are interdependent. Every individual, particularly the wise one, has some life goals and he tries to realise them accruing to best of his abilities and capabilities.

The wise choice of an occupation is of extreme importance. It should be one that is suited to the abilities of the individual and that will enable him to fulfil his basic needs, to develop his "self-image".

The wise choice of leisure-time activities is also important not only to refresh and revive mind and body but also to minister to the aesthetic and spiritual side of life.

Life is more than the sum of all its parts. Some unifying principle is needed which will bind together all the aspects and activities of one's life into one consistent whole. This is found in the concept of the life goal.

This being the case, the choice of a life goal is, perhaps, the most important choice in one's life. The process of selecting a suitable life goal is one of the most essential and complex experiences in the area of guidance.

THE MEANING AND IMPLICATION OF LIFE GOALS

A goal is a dynamic concept. It is not merely an end to be reached so that some activity can cease. It is not an ideal which is to be worshipped but which will remain beyond one's reach. A goal involves something that the individual believes is valuable and feels a compulsion to make an effort to attain it. It is "a-something-of-value-that-I-am-trying-to-attain".

A life goal is one that permeates all the aspects of one's life at any given time. To attain it may involve all the areas in one's life. It may be reached in a short time or never. The important element is the effort to attain, not the attainment.

A life goal is based upon and determined by a set of values that govern, bind together, and give meaning to all the activities of a person's life. It provides a center for the gradual integration of all the physical, intellectual, and emotional factors in life.

A valid life goal must take into consideration the worth of the individual himself and his obligation to society. Such a goal is a rejection of the idea that a man's job is the most important thing in his life and that all his activities should be centered around it.

A job is not an end in itself but merely a means to a larger and more important goal. This point of view, while generally accepted as an ideal, is often forgotten in practice.

The implication of this position is that the life of an individual should be considered as an organic whole, not as a mixture of more or less unrelated and often conflicting elements.

Therefore, in considering the usefulness, effectiveness, or desirability of any job or any aspect of life, the entire pattern of life should be taken into account, not merely one segment of it.

One should take into consideration how a given job will contribute to the attainment of one's life goal. While there are other elements of value that must be considered—working conditions, wages, chances for advancement, etc.—the life goal itself is the crucial element that ties together and serves to complement and give meaning to the job as a part of the life of the individual.

There is, for most persons, no one best, predetermined avenue through which the life goal may be realised. Any one of a number of different avenues may be equally effective and satisfactory in getting an individual to his goal. The particular avenue that we take is influenced by many different elements in our environment.

One does not always need to change jobs in order to make his occupation more useful in achieving his goal. In most occupations there is some opportunity for a personal adjustment that may make it possible to use the job in such a way that it will be more helpful in the attainment of the life goal.

Life is full of illustrations of men and women who have so interpreted their jobs and so governed their activities as to make them avenues through which they have attained their life goal. The lives of individual we know—carpenters, plumbers, nurses, lawyers—constantly remind us that any job that is not in itself antisocial may be used in such a way as to contribute to human welfare when making such a contribution is the worker's life goal.

Examples of Life Goals

There are as many life goals possible as there are value systems and different social contexts in which the values can find expression. Some may devote themselves to working for the equality of opportunity for all Americans.

Some may think that the highest goal is the achievement of peace and good will among nations.

"To make two blades of grass grow where only one grew before" may be a life goal. Others wish to emulate Schweitzer, Gandhi, or Lincoln. These and other purposes can give meaning to life and help the individual make choices of all kinds as they are related to this goal.

Difficulty of Choosing Life Goals

It is often very difficult to select a life goal that is suited to the abilities, needs, and interests of the individual and that has a reasonable promise of attainment. After the choice is made, it is sometimes difficult or impossible to reach the goal.

Both choice and attainment often require assistance from others. The process of so clarifying our values that we know what we stand for is a lifelong task.

Many live confused, shallow lives unable to differentiate the important from the trivial. While we should not expect most students to have clear and expressible life goals, we should assume some responsibility for helping them to learn the dimensions of this human problem and to have some acquaintance with the major tools useful in its solution.

Influences in Choosing Life Goals

A life goal is not a gift from the gods. It is not inherited but learned. Parents, teachers, and associates may do much to shape an individual's life goal as may his general social environment with its war, famine, disease, estrangement of parents, or death of close friends.

A person develops his life goal slowly, often unconsciously, and may revise it from time to time. Sometimes a religious conversion or a personal tragedy may cause sudden dramatic changes.

Although it is usually not fully developed until maturity and sometimes not even then, the important elements begin to appear in adolescence. It is clear, then, that the period represented by the secondary school and college is of maximum importance in the development of a life philosophy—in the formation of a life goal.

The guidance needed for this phase of development lends itself especially well to group discussion, supplemented from time to time by individual counselling.

Here, again, is where teachers can be of great help, especially teachers of English, history, science, music and art. The lives of men and women who have made contributions in these fields can be studied and emphasis given to their special gifts, their purposes, and their motives.

The school will influence the life goals of its students whether it wishes to or not. The only question which remains is whether the influence is to be unconscious, disorganised, and negative or whether it will be conscious, systematic, and positive.

MAJOR LIFE GOALS

While, as has been explained, there may be many life goals, we may group them into three major categories—self-realisation, service, and satisfaction. This grouping does not suggest that other possible life goals might not be of comparable merit and importance, but rather that these three divisions lend themselves to illustration and comparison and therefore seem most useful for our present explanatory purposes.

Self-Concept as Guide to Life Goal

The importance of a life goal is forcible demonstrated in the findings of Roe and Super in their investigations of the factors that are associated with the choice of an occupation. Among these factors is the "self-image", or the "self-concept".

The self-concept may be described roughly as the elaboration of such statements as, "I am this sort of a person. These are my strengths and my weaknesses. These are the things I like to do."

Although a self-concept is far from being a life goal, it is a very important factor in the choice of a life goal. Self-realisation is becoming what one wants to be, and what one wants to be should take into consideration what one is—the present self-concept.

A life goal, however, is far broader and more comprehensive than the image of what one is now. The selection of an impelling life goal often serves to eliminate weaknesses and to utilise strengths not apparent to the individual; in short, it provides motivation.

In the two-way classification of occupations described by Roe, it can easily be seen how a clear life goal might help in the realistic choice of one of the occupational groups, but it would be of even greater significance in the choice of a level of work.

The relationship of the self-concept to the life goal is an instrumental one because, while the life goal should underlie and be basic to any valid occupational choice, the self-concept governs the selection of the best avenue or channel for attaining it.

There is real danger that the use of the self-concept may be restricted to the selection of an occupation. To be of maximum value it should include a clarification of factors and traits which may not be closely related to what is called "success on the job" but which are definitely essential to a successful life.

Guidance should help an individual relate his self-concept to his goals in such a way that he achieves "peace of mind" or "serenity of spirit".

Service as a Life Goal

Because a life goal brings together all the forces of the individual upon a single objective, it exerts a tremendous influence on the accomplishment of the objective chosen.

The result may be useful or disastrous to the individual himself or to society. History is full of examples of both.

Without question the life goal that has had the greatest influence for good is that of service to others. Service is the keystone on which any stable and enduring government is built.

In human history civilisation after civilisation has fallen because it has placed the selfish interest of the rulers above service to its people. Nearly every world religion is based on the concept of a supreme being and the obligation to serve one another.

Certain occupations, such as medicine, nursing, law, teaching, social work, and the ministry, are based directly upon service to others. And all have been of great benefit to society.

There are many organisations like Rotary, Kiwanis, Lions, and optimists which are distinctly service agencies devoted to high standards of professional, business, and civic life, to good citizenship, and to mutual assistance to fellow members. Many of these service clubs have direct connections with young people in school and college.

Satisfaction as a Life Goal

Satisfaction is a state of mind or an emotion that normally results from the successful attempt to reach a goal or satisfy a felt need. It is an essential element in a successful life and an invaluable asset in learning. It is imperative for every individual to have satisfaction somewhere in his life.

Satisfaction may also come from the effort to attain the goal even when the goal is not reached or the need satisfied. The very difficulty of attaining the goal becomes a challenge which may have value. As Ram said, "Keep the quality of effort alive within you by doing some gratuitous exercises every day".

Satisfaction in itself, however, cannot be a safe guide to the choice of an occupation or any other goal. Unfortunately satisfaction may also come from the effort to attain a harmful or undesirable goal.

Theft, rape, murder, oppression, cruelty give satisfaction to some people. It is the goal that is important, not the satisfaction in achieving it.

But within the group of useful and desirable occupations that are suited to the needs and abilities of the individual, the possible satisfactions are very important in determining choice.

Some occupations give opportunity for pride and satisfaction in the quality of the product and by the contribution that the worker makes to it.

In some others, however, the worker never sees the finished product but merely feeds an automatic machine that makes only a small part of it. In such situations whatever satisfaction the worker gets is from the wages received and, possibly, from his friendly relations with other workers.

The present tendency is to increase the proportion of occupations that involve complicated machinery. Thus the professions now give the greatest opportunity for satisfaction in work. As already pointed out, although satisfaction alone is not a safe guide for the choice of an occupation, it may be a real help in such a choice.

The types of activity which give satisfaction vary with different individuals. Some get their satisfaction in the production of articles made out of cloth, wood, metal, or plastic. Others get satisfaction from gardening, horticulture, farming, or forestry; and others, from working with people in such occupations as teaching, nursing, medicine, the law, and social work.

The hope of satisfaction may serve as a guide in choosing an occupation by permitting a comparison of the activities that give the individual satisfaction with those that are involved in various occupations.

The selection of a life goal is often very difficult for youth. It is hard to choose one which is suited to the abilities, needs, and interests of the individual and which has a reasonable promise of attainment.

Youth's limited experience does not provide sufficient background for a wise choice. Parents, teachers, and counsellors can help by suggesting types of life goals for consideration.

Schools Help Develop Life Goals

Although the school teacher and the counsellor are barred from exerting any influence regarding the religious beliefs and activities of the youth, the very knowledge that the youth is active in the church may help them to understand his attitudes and conduct. It might aid the counsellor in his attempt to give guidance toward life goals.

Especially in assistance in the selection of a life goal are the church and the school on common ground. In this country the basic ideals of character and conduct—honesty, integrity, obedience to authority, sincerity, industry, loyalty, and service to others—are evidences of good citizenship and are essential elements of good living.

The special contribution of the culture is to provide the religious incentive in the selection of a life goal and in the effort to attain the goal selected.

QUESTIONS FOR ANSWER

1. *Explain the meaning and implications of Life Goals.*
2. *Explain each of the three categories of Life Goals.*
3. *Write short notes on the following:*
   (a) *Difficulty in choosing Life Goals.*
   (b) *Self-concept as guide to Life Goals.*
   (c) *Satisfaction as a Life Goal.*

PART IV
AVENUES OF GUIDANCE

16

Academic Arena as an Avenue of Guidance: The Elementary School Stage

The childhood period between 5 to 10 years of age is most suited for the mental growth and development, therefore, he alike the budding child needs proper guidance for better life goods and achievements, the process of which we will, briefly, discuss hereunder:

INTRODUCTION

The elementary school is charged with the development of skills in the fundamental processes, but of equal importance is its responsibility for the encouragement of initiative, creativity, and leadership. In these early years of the school experience children develop self-concepts and values which determine their motivation for learning and personal development in the secondary school as well as in the later years of their lives.

It has long been the role of the elementary-school teacher to bear the chief responsibility for knowing the child and giving help in personal and social development.

Many factors have contributed to an increasing demand for organized guidance services in the elementary school, and there is a definite trend toward such services that will enhance the guidance role of the teacher and at the same time provide more adequately for the great diversity of pupil needs.

IMPORTANCE OF GUIDANCE IN ELEMENTARY SCHOOLS

Significant developments in recent decades have brought a recognition that organised guidance programmes are as important on the elementary as on the secondary level. Guidance is an integral part of the total educational programme, serving as a positive function rather than a corrective force, and to be most effective it must be a continuous process from the child's first contact with the school until he is ready for placement on a job or in some type of post-secondary education.

Guidance is no longer based on a concept of services designed to meet crises but rather on a concept of continuous development. This view emphasizes prevention and good mental hygiene and demands organised guidance services in the earliest years of the educational experience.

Preventive Measures Can Be Taken

The present emphasis upon the development and utilization of human resources is bringing increased demands for earlier and more effective identification of individual differences. This demand for earlier identification is gaining impetus with the growing recognition that guidance services in the elementary schools are especially effective because (1) the child is flexible and has had less time for problems to become deep-rooted; (2) the parents are more actively associated with the school; and (3) many years of more successful development lie ahead for the child who can be helped to understand himself and to find acceptable approaches toward the solution of his problems.

Readiness Can Be Developed

Research findings and developments in the curriculum field point up the necessity for increased guidance services in these early years of the school experience. The concept of readiness for learning includes the recognition that educational stumbling blocks may appear if curriculum experiences are offered too soon or too late. This concept demands the earliest and best possible identification of individual differences and calls for greatly improved systems of pupil records.

THE NATURE OF THE CHILD IN THE ELEMENTARY SCHOOL

All growth follows a pattern, and each child has his own built in-growth pattern and 'timetable'. Some mature very rapidly in all areas, and other lag behind their age group in one or more of the four areas of development—physical, mental, social, or emotional.

Research shows that children exhibit every conceivable combination and variation in their growth patterns. Some grow at the same rate in all four areas, while others grow unevenly.

Children may show rapid physical development with slow mental development. In addition, the same child may show both spurts and legs in his growth and development.

These differences are mainly the result of the built-in growth pattern but may be influenced to a limited extent by disease, nutritional deficiencies, or other extreme environmental deprivations.

The Child from Six to Ten

Middle childhood usually covers the years between six and ten. In this period the child is growing in all parts of his body but less rapidly than in early childhood. Muscular growth and coordination are uneven and incomplete, but manual dexterity and eye-hand coordination have developed sufficiently to allow the child to use his hands and fingers for writing, drawing, sewing, and playing musical instruments.

He still has better control over the large muscles than he does over the small. The child needs opportunities for active play to release pent-up energy and a balance of rest and relaxation to meet the increasing demands which school places upon him.

The mental development in middle childhood is characterized by learning to read and by the acquisition of many other knowledges and skills. Olson says there is evidence that these children learn best when they can be active while learning.

These children are becoming more independent, are learning to take more responsibility and to show increasing control of emotions. This is a period of emerging values with some concern about right and wrong.

The Child from Ten to Thirteen

Children in grades 4 to 6 have received only limited attention in research and in the study of human growth and development.

These children are active and want to be on the move. Physical growth is slow, and health is good.

Some, particularly the girls, may be maturing more quickly and may advance into the more rapid growth phase of prepubescence. The child of twelve or thirteen may show evidence of physical ungainliness and awkwardness of movement.

Enlarging hips, breast development, and menstruation may present problems of adjustment for those girls who are earlier matures. Voice changing and characteristic sex changes and developments in boys may appear in grade 5 to 6. These pupils want to be making things, want to be doing and performing in response to their need to try out their own powers.

This is the period when children are showing a tendency to draw away from adults and to turn towards their peers for companionship and for modes of living. Independence in ideas and activity is normal behaviour at this age.

These children need support from both adults and peers, for both help in defining acceptable limits of behaviour. In many cases children show fears and worries which centre in developing independence, parental and school expectations, and home problems. Competition may also be a threat to emotional well-being.

Later childhood is characterised by a desire to learn and by a wide variety of interests. The child is developing an understanding of cause and effect, forming concepts, and beginning to solve simple problems.

Implications for Education

In a summary of studies of how human beings grow and develop, we see the following:

Children are both similar and different

- Each individual grows according to his own time schedule and in his own style.
- Growth takes time; it can be encouraged but not forced.
- Both nature and nurture play a part.
- Growth of abilities in the same individual often varies.
- Growth is continuous, following an orderly sequence in each individual.

We also learn the conditions in the environment which encourage the proper development of human beings are:

1. Those which support physical well-being and stimulate growth—food, warmth, air, light, activity and rest, and safety;
2. Those which support emotional well-being—giving a sense of security and of worth or self-respect; and
3. Those which lead to increased ability to cope independently with life situations.

Finally, the emotional needs of all human beings must be kept in mind when we attempt to understand the nature of elementary school children. These are the need for belonging, achievement, economic security, love and affection; the need to be free from fear and relatively free from guilt; the need for self-respect and self-understanding.

THE ROLE OF THE TEACHER IN GUIDANCE

The interrelation between guidance and instruction in the educational process emphasizes the key role of the teacher in guidance. The teacher is uniquely responsible for the climate of learning in which the class as a group, and each pupil as an individual in the group, finds opportunity for learning and for personal development.

Johnston, Peters, and Evraiff say, "The school must be conceived of as the setting for learning experiences, and everything which helps to make that setting educational is a concern of the teacher." Teachers affect the lives and personalities of children, and their influence goes far beyond the academic area and what can be measured by achievement tests.

Ohlsen say, "If the teacher will accept each pupil as he is, with all his strengths and weaknesses, and will help him to improve where he needs to improve, the teacher will have many opportunities to help pupils understand and accept themselves and to aid them in defining reasonable life goals—two major aims of guidance. He may also influence the attitudes and feelings which contribute to making independent choice either easy or difficult."

The Teacher Studies Children

Child study is a basic guidance function and is accomplished through the use of both formal methods involving tests and cumulative records and informal methods based upon observations of the pupil in his classroom and in other settings.

The teacher learns much about the child as he studies the pupil's production, his oral and written work, his art work, and his reading record. The teacher seeks to observe hobbies and interests as an aid to motivation through understanding.

Observations of behaviour systematized through the use of the anecdotal record provide a rich source of data for child study. The teacher in an elementary school is in a strategic position to conduct child study, for he sees the child in many differing situations and has frequent opportunity for contacts with parents.

The first-grade teacher who must provide more formal learning experiences for children entering school for the first time faces a big task in studying the individual pupils in his class. Too frequently a reading-readiness score is the only objective evidence of individual differences.

Readiness for learning depends upon physical and mental factors, situational factors, and the self-system of the child. The child must see what is to be learned as meaningful and useful as it relates to his needs, goals, and self-concept.

The teacher must first look at the individuals in his class in order to determine each child's readiness for learning, the degree to which individual needs are being met, and how each child sees himself.

The teacher also looks at himself and raises the question, "How do I feel about each of these pupils? What are my personal needs which may influence my relationship with the group or with individuals within the class?

The Teacher Collects Data About Children

Early identification of individual needs makes educational planning more valid. Identification and planning, however, must be continuous and not a one-time experience.

Identification involves observation in many areas of behaviour, a study of developmental records, and interviews with parents and children. Kough and DeHaan provide teachers with techniques and procedures for observing behaviour. Their handbook provides descriptions of behaviours which can be observed as a basis for recognising children with special interests, abilities, or problems.

One of the most useful techniques for informal study is the anecdotal record together with the roster of observations kept by the teacher.

The teacher will also participate in the collection of data by more formal methods and will utilize all the data in the cumulative record of the child. Such data usually cover personal and family background, health, attendance, scholarship, and activities both in and out of school.

The standardized test, inventories, and rating scales may all be used in the elementary school to provide essential information for understanding children.

The cumulative record which the school develops in designed to help teachers function more effectively by grouping the data collected so that conclusions are more easily drawn. Effective use of pupil records is possible only when the information covers all the fundamental areas of human development and when it is so organised that developmental patterns are evident.

Then the record can be analyzed with a reasonable expenditure of time and effort. Cassell offers a plan of organisation for recording developmental data on a profile which makes it possible to recognise growth in some six areas of physiological, emotional, psychosexual, intellectual, social, and educational development. This or some similar plan lends continuity to records.

The Teacher Counsels

The teacher works with individuals as well as groups, and there is a kind of counselling which is a legitimate function of the classroom teacher. Johnston feels that the teacher's relationship with pupils in this class often leads to possibilities for establishing good counselling rapport.

Only in the classroom climate which is really conductive to learning can such a rapport be established, because it is based on respect for the individual and reflects attitudes and not processes.

Gordon reminds us that "the teacher-counsellor cannot be all things to all students. He must be closely aware of his limits and use referral processes when the counselling situation seems to be going 'out of his depth.'" Johnston says:

"The teacher's counselling role is not a therapeutic one, but he does aim at offering the student assistance in making more effective personal and environmental adjustments."

When the pupil is unable to relate to the classroom teacher, or when the case calls for techniques beyond the ability of the teacher, the child should be referred to the school counsellor.

Many teachers are including courses in guidance in their graduate programmes, and these teachers often possess skills which make for effective counselling. If a teacher finds it difficult to accept the basic philosophy of counselling, he cannot be expected to do counselling, as such, in his work.

Counsellors can serve as consultants to teachers, thus providing in service education in the area of referral procedures. The case conference involving teacher, administrator, nurse, counsellor, visiting teacher, and school psychologist offers an excellent opportunity to increase the teacher's skill in looking beneath symptoms to problems which need to be referred.

Although the teacher is the key guidance worker in the elementary school, he needs to recognise the guidance roles of other school personnel. The teacher is a member of a team whose function is to obtain the maximum development of each child in the school.

Johnston says, "No school is effectively staffed guidance-wise when there is n't someone in the school who can function as a counsellor and handle the kinds of cases which are referred by the classroom teacher."

THE ROLE OF THE COUNSELLOR

The counsellor, a regularly assigned member of the elementary school staff, is specifically charged with the responsibility for developing those aspects of the guidance function which demand an expenditure of time and the use of specialized competencies which the teacher ordinarily does not have. He is directly responsible to the principle and has only a staff relationship with the teachers and other members of the school staff.

Principal and counsellor working together plan an organised programme of guidance services which include the following:

1. in-service education for teachers,
2. consultation services for teachers and parents,
3. counselling services for children,
4. referral services for children,
5. follow-up and research activities, and
6. evaluation studies.

The Counsellor Gives In-service Education

An effective programme of guidance services provides in-service education for teachers in the development and interpretation of pupil records. Since the average teacher will have neither the time nor the training to develop records which are complete and so organised that an analysis can be made with reasonable expenditure of time and energy, the counsellor must provide assistance in the collection of data, in the methods of recording, and in the interpretation of the development record.

The development of a sound test programme is another aspect of the elementary guidance services. Counsellors can provide in-service education for teachers and can act as consultants in the development of the programme and in the interpretation of results.

The Counsellor Counsels

The Counsellor's chief responsibility is to provide counselling for all children with usual interests or needs. Teachers can be helped to recognise these needs so that the children may be referred to the counsellor.

The per cent of time devoted to counselling for personal adjustment will be greater in the elementary school than in the secondary school, and this is probably the greatest difference in guidance at the two levels.

Children, whether self-referred or referred by parents or teachers, may need help in many areas of personal development. The excessively shy child, the socially inept child, the child whose self-concept interferes with learning, the child whose behaviour interferes with work in the classroom, the child with educational deficiencies, and any child whose progress in school seems unsatisfactory—all find their way to the counsellor's office.

The counsellor's office should be an attractive, even if small, room, with toys, books, and manipulative materials readily available to the child. Here a youngster who is overwhelmed by the experiences he is handling or who has reached "an explosion point" may work off tensions with clay, finger paints, darts, punching bags and return to class ready to try again.

Toys play an important role in helping children verbalize and communicate. Teacher and child, sitting back to back, may hold 'conversations' over toy telephones even if the child is too shy to communicate in a face-to-face interview.

Furnished classrooms and doll houses, erector sets, dump trucks, fire engines, and a host of other toys provide opportunities for a child to play and talk as he works with the counsellor.

Whether the counsellor works with the individual child or with small groups, his office represents a neutral setting with many aids to help the child evaluable himself, set goals, and make choices.

Here the counsellor uses every competence he can muster. Training which includes a knowledge of how personality develops, an understanding of counselling theories and techniques, and some supervised practice in counselling is essential if the counsellor is to meet the needs of the children who find their way to his office.

Research indicates that many underachieving pupils have emotional problems and that counselling provided on a systematic long-term basis is essential before the pupil can begin to use his potentialities. Pupils respond more readily if counselling is available in the early years of school at the onset of underachieving.

The Counsellor Makes Referrals

The counsellor makes referrals of pupils to other school services and utilizes the resources available in the community. He helps to provide continuity of the educational experiences through articulation services at the time a child leaves the elementary school to enter junior high school.

Adequate counsellor services should contribute to the curriculum through carefully planned research and follow-up activities which reveal the needs of children in the school and which provide evidence of the success with which the school is meeting these needs.

THE TEAM APPROACH

A definite trend in guidance is toward a coordinated team approach under the leadership of the principal. Principals, teachers, counsellors, and other staff personnel working as a team should evaluate the guidance needs within the school and assess the effectiveness of the service designed to meet these needs.

Many staff people, including school social workers, school psychologists, nurses, doctors, speech correctionists, reading specialists, supervisors, and consultants, are available to the modern school. Their services can be most effectively used if the principal arrange systematic case conference procedures.

In such case conferences the teacher and the counsellor share with other team members the problems of children which they have identified by their close contact. Teachers get some support and consultative help in planning for these children.

Referrals for other services which are the result of these case conferences are usually more valid than referrals made without such conferences. The referral report is more detailed and often more accurate, and therefore the referral services will be more effective.

Guidance in the elementary school is the responsibility of every member of the school team. Under the leadership of the principal the team constantly evaluates its objectives and plans for more effective guidance services. Follow-up, research, and evaluation activities are essential aspects of the attempt to provide an educational climate in which each child work toward a healthy personality capable of achievement commensurate with ability.

QUESTIONS FOR ANSWER

1. *Write a note on the importance of guidance in Elementary Schools.*
2. *Explain the nature of the child in Elementary Schools.*
3. *Write a note on the role of the teacher in guidance in Elementary Schools.*
4. *Explain the role of the counsellor in respect of the pupils and teachers of Elementary Schools in providing effective guidance.*

17

Academic Arena as an Avenue of Guidance-2 : The Secondary School Stage

Guidance in secondary schools is of great value because at this stage student develop their own personality and being at adolescence period of age they start making choices, have guidance is essential because it provide a systematic effort to improve the quality of choices. Preventive guidance at this stage reduces the need for remedial guidance at later stage. Hereunder, we will discuss this aspect:

NATURE OF THE SECONDARY-SCHOOL STUDENT

Adolescents are in a Period of Change

he period represented by students in grades 7 to 12 is that of adolescence, when the transition from childhood to adulthood takes place. It is a period of profound physical, mental, social, and emotional change and growth, the nature and significance of which the youth himself does not understand. He is often a stranger to himself as well as to others. It is a period of rapid growth in height, weight, and physical strength and of a broadening of vision of the physical and social world.

There is an increasing feeling of personal independence which is mixed with a consciousness of the need—which he sometimes denies and tries to suppress—for companionship and help. It is so difficult for the adolescent to know himself that, even when offered help that he needs and knows that he needs, he often rejects it.

Adolescents Differ in Growth and Development

Adolescence begins with puberty, which is the stage of development at which the reproductive organs mature and the secondary sex characteristics develop. The onset of puberty is not uniform for all youth. It begins at different ages and lasts for different lengths of time.

Another factor making for differences is that 'spurts' of rapid growth—physical, mental, and social—come at different ages, and there are 'plateaus' that are not uniform in time of beginning or in length of duration.

The problems due to differences among students in extent of maturity are further increased because girls begin and complete the period of maturation before boys.

Misunderstanding often results from the use of tables showing the ages of maturing boys and girls. In most discussions the average ages of beginning and ending this period are considered to be key points and the fact that there are great differences within as well as between the sexes is overlooked.

Nor is there any clear evidence that a student who begins this period earlier or later than the average is 'abnormal' in the sense that something is wrong with his development.

He may be 'unnormal' without being 'abnormal'. Because of these differences in development and the fears and embarrassments associated with them the secondary school students is in special need of guidance.

Adolescents Differ in Attitudes and Interests

During adolescence there are changes in mental and social characteristics, in attitudes toward school toward teachers, toward parents, toward peers, and toward authority. Interests and attitudes toward literature and society change rapidly, and individuals in the same grade may not have the same interest or the same comprehension.

GUIDANCE NEEDS RELATED TO EDUCATION

Adjustment to Secondary School

Although the change from the six-year elementary school to the junior high school is not so abrupt as that from the eighth grade of the old elementary school to the first year of high school, there are several very important differences between the two schools.

Because of the departmental organization usually found in the junior high school, the pupil must adjust himself to a variety of teachers instead of to only one teacher. Instead of remaining in the same room for all classes, he moves from room to room. The character of the junior-high-school building itself is often quite different from that of the elementary school. The student is plunged into a different type of school life and school discipline.

Many of these same problems arise in the transition from the junior high school to the senior high school. Where the entire six years of the secondary school are housed in one building and considered as a six-year school, there is no problem of adjustment to a new building but other more important problems remain.

For example, a student may need help in deciding whether to leave school at the end of the compulsory attendance age or to remain for graduation. In certain areas it is the custom of some parents to transfer their children from a public to a private school for the last two years.

When this happens, there is need for some help in preparing the student for the changed life in the private school, especially if it is a boarding school.

Decisions about Leaving School

Soon after starting secondary school some children will begin to reach the place where further schooling of the kind available may not be desirable because each year brings them diminishing returns. How long to remain in school becomes an important problem for these students.

Research indicates that the 40 per cent of our students who do not graduate from high school are at a disadvantage for the rest of their lives, particularly with regard to employment.

It is essential, then, that every possibility of adapting the school programme to serve the individuals be explored before the reluctant conclusion is reached that leaving school is the best available method of "continuing education."

Learning Problems

Although the learning problems encountered in the secondary

school are not always new, many now become of increasing importance. Reading difficulties; rate of reading and comprehension; likes and dislikes of studies, teachers, and types of literature; differences in aptitude for different school subjects—all are very important factors in the student's adjustment to the secondary school.

A guidance programme will help diagnose the learning difficulty and plan steps to overcome it. The student may need remedial reading, help in arithmetic, a different course of study, a change of teachers, or perhaps prolonged counselling to overcome emotional barriers to learning.

Decisions about College

At graduation from the secondary school a decision must be made regarding enrolment in some type of post-high-school institution, such as business school, technical school, or college. Such a complex and crucial decision should be made with adequate guidance from teachers and counsellors.

At present it seems likely that, with the limited facilities of colleges and with the great increase in the number applying for admission, the problem of being accepted for college work will be a very serious one.

The unprecedented demand for trained men and women in science and mathematics for increased educational facilities and scholarships place an added responsibility upon the schools for the guidance of students who have the abilities to succeed in such specialized training and who have the desire and the ambition to enter this specialization.

The choice of a college is one of the very important problems facing parents and high-school students, and it merits far more consideration than is usually given to it. Colleges are not all alike in entrance requirements, cost, atmosphere, or opportunities offered.

Proximity to the home of the student is often a controlling factor. Some students do need a continuance of home influence, but others need to get away from home and learn to be independent. Some need a small college; others, a large one.

Two of the most frequent reasons for the choice of a college are that the father or the mother graduated from that particular college or that some friend, possibly the teacher or the counsellor, did. These reasons are emphasized by the propaganda organised by nearly every college and by the alumni.

The decision should be made on the basis of the needs of the student and the degree to which the institution meets these needs. When two institutions are equally suitable and equally good, other reasons may then properly enter into the decision.

The Question is altogether too vital, and means too much in the life of the young man or woman, to be decided upon any other basis than the needs of the individual.

Information about college entrance requirements should be known by students and parents long enough in advance of graduation from high school so that subjects necessary for entrance may be taken.

At present the unprecedented demand for college education and the limited facilities throughout the country have changed the question for many from "What college shall I choose" to "What college will take me?"

This condition has made it necessary to begin making plans several years in advance and to make application to several colleges instead of to only one. The competition after a student enters college is also so great that much emphasis is placed on meeting the scholastic demands of the college and on adjustment to college life.

This situation places an added responsibility on the secondary school for considering more carefully the type of college which is best suited to a student's ability and needs and for preparing him to adjust himself to the scholastic and social life of the college.

The difficulty, importance, and complexity of decisions about college argue strongly for the need for guidance services in secondary schools.

GUIDANCE NEEDS RELATED TO PERSONAL DEVELOPMENT

Emotional Development and Guidance

Emotional disturbances may occur in any stage of a person's development and in any part of the school system. Some have their origin or at least become more pressing in the secondary school.

Physiological development, bringing with it increased size and strength, sex impulses, responsibilities resulting from approaching maturity—all are very important causes of emotional changes and emotional instability.

Such emotional conditions are often the causes of much maladjustment and unhappiness. The student needs help in his growth toward "emotional maturity," that is, in the ability to direct his strong basic emotions into channels that lead to the attainment of ends that are socially desirable and individually satisfying.

Social Development and Guidance

The purpose of education is to help young people acquire the knowledge, develop the habits and skills, and attain the attitudes and ideals that are essential for adjustment to modern life and for its progressive improvement.

Although individual instruction may be more effective than group work in the acquisition of knowledge and in the development of useful habits and skills, providing such instruction is quite impossible.

Moreover, there are some distinct advantages in class or group organisation in learning to live and work together, to accept restrictions essential to effective learning, to respect the rights of others, and to cooperate with others in enterprises that are planned by the group and have value for all. Group work utilizes the social instinct of human beings.

Guidance has a major responsibility in assisting youth to organise or choose groups that have useful objectives and that are suited to the desires, needs, and abilities of the individuals of the group. Assistance to youth in social adjustments is a function of the entire school.

The administrator, librarian, teacher, and counsellor all have a definite responsibility for giving such help. Every pupil should feel that he is accepted by his teacher and by every other member of the school staff who has contact with him.

The entire atmosphere of the school should be permeated with this spirit even though corrections, restrictions and punishments may be necessary.

Pupils should always feel free to come to any member of the school staff for help. The desire to be accepted by someone is universal. We all want to have a feeling of belonging, to be needed and wanted. Nonacceptance or open rejection often results in reprisals and in destructive activities.

Guidance can also help in assisting in the organisation of such activities as student clubs in the secondary school. Very often the organisation of clubs that are constructive and useful prevents the formation of clandestine groups that have undesirable objectives.

In many schools certain clubs are purely traditional and, although once useful, do not now meet real needs. Such clubs should be eliminated or their purposes changed.

It has been suggested that the choice of a new member of any club be based on his mental ability as compared with that of the members of the group, that is, that a club made up largely of pupils of high mental ability should choose only those students who have high mental ability.

In some cases where the activities of the club demand high ability, this might be desirable; but in most cases this is not the case. Studies seem to indicate that the selection of a new member is more often based on personality traits than on mental ability.

Student organisations should be helped to realise that they are very important elements in the overall school programme and should be so organised and administered that they will be of maximum value to the entire student body and not merely self-perpetuating clubs for certain types of students.

The problems occasioned by organisations and other elements in the school programme designed to increase social adjustment call for guidance services.

The finest programme of clubs, classes, and activities will not help the student who has not been guided in making best use of his available opportunities.

QUESTIONS FOR ANSWER

1. *Explain the nature of secondary school student which make guidance very important for his proper development and social adjustment.*
2. *Explain how guidance needs are related to personal development at secondary school level.*

18

Academic Arena as an Avenue of Guidance-3: The College and University Stage

INTRODUCTION

The college and university education in India, by and large, is a mass education, therefore, the quality is suffering because students enter in university and college with any, guidance, hence, there is a practical need for adiquate guidance programme at this stage of our educational system. As suggested by many scholars—guidance has to be made an integral part of higher education to make it meaningful and purposeful for the students. The kind of guidance programme which may be introduced can be *inherent* (unintentional and unorganised), *informal* (intentional but not co-ordinated), and *professional* (well-organised). There is no doubt about this fact that inherent and informal programmes have their place in an educational institution.

But it needs hardly any emphasis that a programme, if it is to make its impact felt on the growth and development of students and enhance the quantity and improve the quality of the educational programme as a whole, there needs to be set up a well-organised structure covering the three major functions of the programme viz., *adjustmental, orientational* and *developmental*. It is true that a structure never guarantees the success of an operation, but there is no doubt that a poor structure can be a major obstacle to success.

THE ORGANISATIONAL SET-UP

The nature and organisational set-up of colleges and universities differ in our country at present, therefore, we can not suggest an uniform organizational set-up for guidance and counselling for all colleges and universities, hence, hereunder we are suggesting different set-ups for colleges and universities, which may be modified by the concerned college or universities as per their need and resources (*Note*: see last two pages of this chapter).

The Counselling Officer in the university should be in the Reader's grade while the Assistant Counselling Officer may be in the Lecturer's grade.

Each university should have a specialist coordinator of Guidance Services to help the counselling officers or Liaison Officers in different colleges.

Essential Activities

1. *Guidance and counselling committee:* A Guidance and Counselling Committee should be formed to serve in an advisory capacity or a policy making body for the programme. The committee can thrash out problems requiring group solution. It should plan monthly, quarterly and yearly programme, co-ordinate guidance activities and assess the work done.

The committee should consist of the Dean/Principal, Counselling/Liaison Officer, teachers representing different points of view, academic disciplines, interests and basic philosophies, student representatives, parents, Deputy Chief of UEIGB, Vocational Guidance Officer, etc.

It is essential to determine the limits of responsibility of the guidance committee and identify the specific role to be assumed by each faculty and staff member.

Clerical Assistance needs to be provided to the Counselling/ Liaison officer as a methodically organised guidance programme would require maintenance of a lot of record/information. It may range from a part time to whole time assistant depending upon the load of work.

2. *Counselling centre*: Every university and a large college should have a counselling centre headed by a trained professional counseling officer who should be a Ph.D or possess **Master's**

degree in Psychology and Counselling, with considerable counselling, experience.

The Centre should discharge the following functions:

(*i*) give assistance to individuals and small groups of students and staff members with special educational, vocational and personal problems;
(*ii*) give assistance to the university and constituent colleges in developing, advising and counselling programmes and consultation on special psychological problems;
(*iii*) provide psychological testing facilities for the university both for individuals and groups;
(*iv*) carry on research on the development of testing procedures and experimental programmes in counselling; and
(*v*) help in the training of post-graduate students in counselling and testing.

Counsellors can develop confidence in the Counselling Services by meeting new students at the time of orientation, visiting the hostel and giving talks to assemblies.

The Counselling Officer/Liaison Officer's Office

The Counselling Officer/Liaison Officer should be given a separate room which should afford him sufficient privacy. His office should be adequately furnished. It should have a small desk or table with a chair for the Counselling/Liaison officer and one or two extra chairs for the visitors.

A few other small items of furnishing such as a small book-shelf, a filing cabinet, an almirah, curtains for the windows and doors, a flower vase or table lamp or even an attractive unattractive room.

The Counselling/Liaison Officer should make the room as cheerful and pleasant, inviting, warm and attractive as possible so that the students like to visit it and feel welcome and at home.

3. *Occupational information room and its maintenance*: Occupational information room needs to be set up in every college and university. It should have adequate arrangements for the seating of the students who may visit it for consulting the occupational information material.

It should also have sufficient space for conducting group discussions and other guidance activities. There should also be some provision for individual guidance.

Occupational information room should be distinct and prominently noticeable. However, if a separate room cannot be spared, a portion of a room or a verandah may be utilised for the purpose.

Display of occupational information in an attractive manner is very important. Some suggestions are given below:

(*i*) *Presentation of the information should be attractive and motivating.* Contents should have relevance to the current needs of the students.

(*ii*) *Charts, posters and other visual aids should be at the eye level of the students.*

(*iii*) *Detailed information, if placed for reading, should be purposively arranged bearing close relationship with the materials displayed on the walls.* Wherever possible, classification system should be shown for the benefit of the students.

(*iv*) *Materials should not be crowded in a particular place; it should be evenly distributed over places* where students normally gather for receiving various services and need to stay for a reasonable time.

(*v*) *Material displayed should be reviewed frequently* with a view to updating the contents as also highlighting specific aspects of the information.

If the University Employment Information and Guidance Bureau exists on the campus of the university, the university alumni can use the same. But in a college, occupational information room forms an important part of the guidance programme.

Continuous Evaluation

Continuous evaluation of the programme will ensure its usefulness and make it respond to the needs of the student population.

4. *Adequate student record system*: An effective guidance and counselling programme presupposes information about the individual which is reliable, valid and comprehensive.

This is possible when the work of collecting information is done on a systematic basis. Maintenance of cumulative Record Card is one of the most important activities of a good guidance programme. This record should contain:

(*a*) Student's identification, family history, personal history, health condition, etc.,
(*b*) Test results,
(*c*) Problems inside and outside the college/university, emotional and social problems,
(*d*) Specific assets and limitations,
(*e*) Unusual talents,
(*f*) Academic and co-curricular progress,
(*g*) Placement,
(*h*) Follow-up.

Counselling officer with the cooperation of other members of the faculty should maintain this record.

GUIDANCE AND COUNSELLING SET UP IN UNIVERSITIES

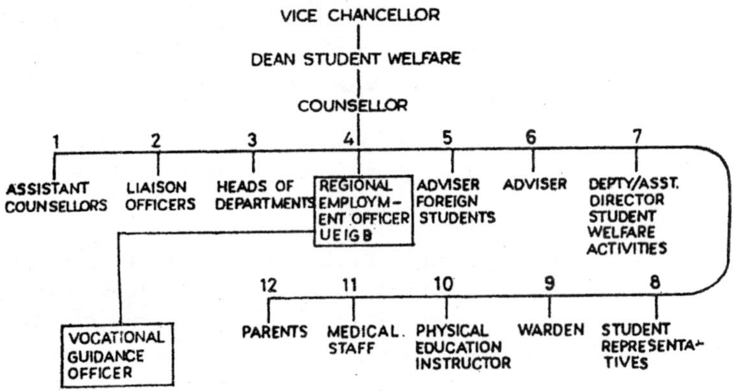

GUIDANCE AND COUNSELLING SET-UP IN COLLEGES

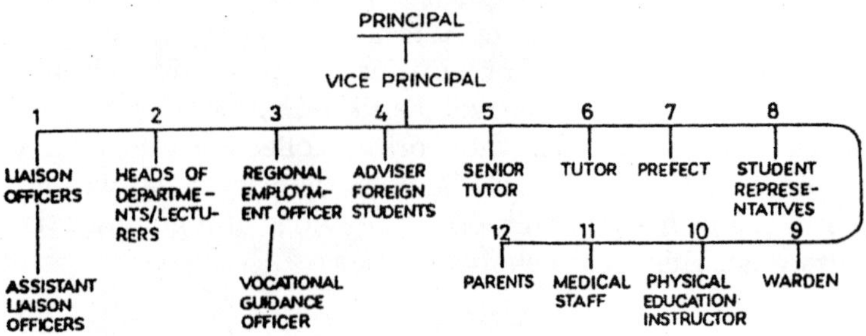

The Guidance Programme—Its Content

Below we give an outline of the desirable activities which could be taken up by a Counselling/Liaison officer in a university or a college.

(*i*) *Educational talks*: Talks on educational topics should be arranged by the Counselling/Liaison Officer. He himself or the members of the Guidance Committee or some highly educated and experienced persons from the community or some neighbouring institution may be invited to deliver such talks.

Some suggestive themes are adjustment with the institution, adjustment with peers, getting the best out of college/university education, studying effectively, preparation of notes, preparing and taking examinations, utilisation of library services, participation in co-curricular activities, good work habits, entry and success in a job, taking an interview, living in hostels, choosing your career.

(*ii*) *Orientation talks*: These talks are meant to give adequate information to the students regarding the courses of studies, the facilities available in the institution in the form of libraries, laboratories, workshops, playgrounds, hobbies, teaching personnel, freeships, free concessions, stipends, scholarships, etc.

The students should also be made familiar with information about courses and careers open to graduates/post-graduates, competitive examinations, correspondence courses, apprenticeship schemes, entry jobs which could be taken up fresh from the college/university without experience, courses and careers available abroad, changing occupational pattern, employment and occupational trends, guidance agencies at different levels, etc.

(*iii*) *Career talks*: Career talk means a talk about the details of a particular job. The talks may be delivered on themes such as avenues open to graduates and post-graduates, self-employment schemes, government service, scope of employment, methods of recruitment, discovering vocational interests and aptitudes, exploring vocations which interest you, planning your vocational programme, etc.

Talks on as many careers as possible should be arranged.

Every career expert should be provided with an outline of the career talk at a much advanced date so that he/she knows what to prepare.

(*iv*) *Career conferences:* Career conference is a group activity organised for the purpose of providing occuptional information of a preliminary or supplementary nature to a large number of students in a small or a big group. In a career conference, several speakers belonging to different professions come and deliver talks about their own fields to groups of students.

For example, a successful electronics engineer gives a talk on electronics engineering as a career to a group of students interested in this branch of engineering and a production engineer gives a talk to a group of students interested in production engineering as a career, and so on. The conferences may be organised twice a year.

(*v*) *Plant tours*: Visits to commercial establishments, industries, professional colleges, research institutions, etc. should be arranged as these provide the students with direct and first hand experience of the work done and the physical and social environment in which it is done.

To make the visit useful, the students should be prepared well in advance so that they know what to observe, which questions to ask and how to behave during the visit. A visit is more useful when followed by a group discussion in which students talk about, what they have seen and exchange ideas.

As many plant tours may be arranged as possible depending upon the resources of the institution and the time available.

(*vi*) *Screening of films and film-strips:* Film shows followed by group discussions are good means of disseminating information. The film can be obtained on loan from various agencies.

QUESTIONS FOR ANSWER

1. *Write a note on the need and nature of guidance programme in the colleges and universities in India.*
2. *Write short notes on:*
   (*a*) *Continuous evaluaction,*
   (*b*) *Contents of guidance programme, and*
   (*c*) *Essential activities of guidance programme.*

19

The University Employment: Information and Guidance Bureau (UEIGB) and University Students Advisory Bureau (USAB) as an Avenue for Career Guidance

BRIEF HISTORY

As stated earlier, a study group on Educated Unemployed, in 1956, recommended the establishment of the Bureaux in the universities to provide their alumni with employment information and career guidance. Later, in 1957, the scheme for the setting up of the Bureaux was prepared by the Directorate General of Employment and Training. The scheme envisaged bureaux to be primarily employment counselling agencies but they could also function as placement agencies for professional and highly qualified persons. It was also intended that bureaux would cater to the needs of all students of the universities whether still pursuing studies or about to leave after completing their education.

The first University Employment Information and Guidance Bureaux was set up at the University of Delhi in 1958. The experiment proved its utility and now each university has this facility. These establishments now function as per procedures and policies of the National Employment Service.

The University Grants Commission at its meeting held on 5th May, 1971 considered the question of giving financial assistance to universities for their University Employment Information-cum-

Advisory Bureaux and Career Advising Units in selected affiliated colleges and agreed to provide financial assistance upto the end of the Fourth Plan period to 41 bureaux and 75 career advising units whose proposals were approved by the Commission.

The Review Committee appointed by the University Grants Commission on September 2, 1976 recommended:

(*i*) The Vice-Chancellor and other university authorities as well as different faculties and departments should be actively associated with the activities of the bureau.

(*ii*) The bureaux should initiate research projects, programmes and studies which should be conducted in collaboration with various concerned departments of the university/colleges on local and regional basis for estimation of manpower requirements in various categories in the context of the developmental outlay in a district/region/state. The UGC should encourage such activities and provide necessary financial assistance for understanding such programmes, and projects on priority basis. COHSIP* colleges could be fruitfully involved for data collection and surveys.

Set up

The bureau in a university, as stated above, is an integral part of the National Employment Service and functions according to the procedures and policies laid down by the service. In order to gear the working of the bureau to the needs of the university, it has an advisory committee with the Vice-Chancellor as its chairman. The committee consists of, among others, heads of departments, principals of colleges, representatives of employers, the state and central governments, director of employment and training, deputy secretary to government, labour and employment department; deputy chief of UEIGB, representative of Director General of Employment and Training; Ministry of Labour, Government of India; president of Rotary Club or his nominee, student representatives and Liaison Officers of the colleges etc. The bureau functions under the guidance of the Vice-Chancellor of the university. A senior member of the teaching staff of the university works on a part-time basis and is paid Rs. 200 p.m. for this service by the state government. He is responsible to the Vice-Chancellor for the day to day work of the bureau. The staff for bureau which consists of 1 Divisional or Regional Employment Officer or Deputy Chief, 1 Technical Assistant, 2 clerks, 1 steno typist, 2 peons, is provided by the State Department of Employment. The university provides accommodation and furniture to the bureau at its own cost. The rest of the expenditure is borne by the state government.

The bureau maintains a Career Information Room for use of the visitors where guidance literature and other material considered useful for the university students is displayed. A visitor's register is also maintained to keep a record of those who use this room.

Functions

General

The bureaux are supposed to discharge the following general functions:

(*i*) To give employment information and advice to the university alumni;

(*ii*) To collect and disseminate information on higher education, technical and professional courses in India and abroad;

(*iii*) To provide help for admission in foreign universities.

(*iv*) To render employment assistance to graduates in professional and post-graduate courses and to answer enquiries regarding the availability of suitable applicants on its registers from employers and furnish particulars where called for;

(*v*) To provide information on scholarships, fellowships, grants and loans to students;

(*vi*) To assist students in finding part time and vacation employment;

(*vii*) To arrange group guidance by faculty members on social adjustments and other problems of students;

(*viii*) To give proper orientation to students to cultivate right attitudes towards work;

(*ix*) To arrange talks on employment opportunities to students of various faculties by specialists and employers;

(*x*) To mobilise community resources for making available guidance and employment to the students.

(*xi*) To arrange group programmes of vocational guidance;

(*xii*) To arrange visits of students for on-the-spot studies of occupations; and

(*xiii*) To conduct surveys and research pertaining to guidance and man-power, etc.

Registration

The following categories of applicants are registered at the bureaux:

(*i*) Persons holding Bachelor's or higher degree or equivalent diploma in a professional or specialist course, such as Engineering, Medicine, Agriculture, Veterinary Science, Technology, Law, Education, etc.

(*ii*) Persons holding a Master's or higher degree or post-graduate diploma or equivalent in other subjects except B.A./B.Sc./B.T./B.Ed.

Other graduates can be registered if they so desire but their index cards, after registration, are transferred to the local employment exchange where all further action is taken in respect of them.

(*iii*) National Register Card (C-1) is to be completed and sent to the CSIR in respect of the scientists and technical personnel who are eligible for registration in the special section of the National Register maintained by the CSIR.

(*iv*) University Employment Bureaux are to register not only their own alumni but also graduates of other universities resident in the area, who seek such registration.

Vacancies and submission

The Directorate General of Employment and Training and the State Appointments Branch Officers concerned circulate to the University Employment Bureaux vacancies that are appropriate for those registered with them. The bureaux are supposed to submit particulars of suitable candidates on their registers to the P and EO against vacancies notified by it. The P and EO considers these candidates for submission against notified vacancies at par with the candidates on its own register. The bureaux make direct submission against vacancies circulated to them by the Central Employment Exchange.

It is also open to the university bureaux to submit particulars of suitable persons in response to specific enquiries addressed to them by private employers.

Forms and Procedure

The University Employment Bureaux follow the same procedure and use the same forms as the National Employment Service. Where modifications are considered necessary, these are made in consultation with the DGE and T and the university authorities.

Statistics of the work of bureaux are rendered in the forms prescribed for the purpose. If an applicant submitted by the bureaux is placed against a vacancy circulated by the P and EO it is accounted for the POD placement by the P and EO and the bureau counts it as LOD placement.

Co-ordination

The DGE and T effects the necessary coordination at all India level in regard to registration and circulation of vacancies to University Employment Bureaux. At the state level, the State Appointments Branch Office (State Directorate of Employment Bureaux situated within the state) does this job.

University Employment Information and Guidance Bureaux and the Colleges

One of the channels of communication between bureaux and the college student community is the liaison units in colleges.

A number of bureaux have assisted the constituent and affiliated colleges in their jurisdiction in establishing career advising units under the charge of a teacher of the college concerned. The bureaux regularly feed these college units with occupational information literature. They organise training seminars for the Liaison officers. They also help them to arrange career and educational conferences, talks and exhibitions.

Improving the functioning of UEIGBs: It is being felt that although the bureaux have been functioning in our country for about four decades, they have not fulfilled the objectives for which they were set up. The lukewarm attitude of the universities as well as the state governments, lack of proper accommodation, furniture and equipment, and only a meagre budget are stated to be some of the reasons for this state of affairs. They need to make special efforts so that they matter in the university life. They should:

(*i*) Sponsor hobby clubs at the university and colleges which may be helpful in developing technical and professional skills of the students.

(*ii*) Give training for preparing the youth and suitably equip them so that they face with confidence the "ordeals" of "viva voce" and written tests, conduct mock interviews, organise periodic quiz contests regarding the questions set or topics commonly covered in the employment interviews, hold sessions on how to face the interview, give guidance on how to prepare for competitive examinations. The National Employment Service should activate the UEIGBs in its fold to render service on these lines.

(*iii*) Endeavour to create an awareness, motivation and acceptance of the importance of guidance on education and employment given by them to the university and college students.

(*iv*) Supply detailed, latest and up-to-date information on occupations, training, admissions, higher studies, apprenticeship facilities, scholarships, study facilities abroad, employment information, general trends in job market situations, etc. The bureaux should be veritable "data banks" on careers and courses of local, regional and national interest so that once a student visits the bureau, he finds something worthwhile to read, rather than be disappointed and goes frustrated, not to visit it again.

(*v*) Confer greater weightage to human angle in their activities. They should treat the students and job seekers calling for guidance not as mere cases but as 'individual personalities' passing through a crucial phase of life. The impression needs to be created that UEIGBs are honestly, sincerely and genuinely trying to help the students and job-seekers in solving their problems.

(*vi*) They should have a good reference library having information on the following aspects:

   (*a*) Syllabi of all India universities.

   (*b*) Facilities for research specialisation in different universities and research institutes in India and abroad.

(*c*) Scholarships available for specialised training courses.
(*d*) Facilities for study abroad.
(*e*) Relevant selected books and periodicals, etc.

(*vii*) Arrange group talks and screen films on career counselling.

(*viii*) Arrange mobile exhibitions for the benefit of students in the rural and urban colleges.

(*ix*) Undertake research projects, relevant to employment and unemployment aspects of the local area.

(*x*) Provide scientific and imperial base for man-power planning. This can be achieved by conducting studies and surveys on recruitment practices of employers, occupational aspirations of students, etc.

(*xi*) Have full time chiefs in the scale of university professor. They may be designated as the Director of Bureau.

(*xii*) They should maintain liaison with state and central ministries, Indian Council for Cultural Relations, United States Educational Foundation in India, British Council, principals of the colleges, heads of the departments of the university and other organisations.

(*xiii*) The Deputy Chiefs of the UEIGBs should be well-motivated and fully trained persons. They should undergo a special orientation course so as to equip themselves regarding the relevant job requirements.

(*xiv*) Arrange orientation courses for the principals as well as the liaison officers of the colleges where guidance facilities are provided so as to ensure the worthwhileness of the programme.

(*xv*) Start 'Earn While You Learn' programmes so that the students learn to use the leisure time in learning useful arts and crafts, develop dignity of labour and help them in defraying part of the expenses on education.

(*xvi*) Initiate new schemes as Talent Bank schemes—so as to select talented students from various departments of the universities and prepare them through special coaching for taking up senior management and executive posts in big industrial houses.

(*xvii*) Be housed in proper buildings and should have adequate furniture and other equipment.

These suggestions, if implemented, can revitalise the UEIGBs, will give them a facelift, and make their presence felt in the university life.

Student Advisory Bureaux

The Ministry of Education realised the need and importance of providing educational guidance for the deserving students. It set up 13 Students Advisory Bureaux which are functioning at the various universities. These bureaux:

(*i*) help in creating among the students keen desire to know and plan their future;
(*ii*) encourage them to increase their knowledge about educational developments, activities and facilities in India and abroad;
(*iii*) disseminate information on higher education, research and training in India and abroad to the students;
(*iv*) maintain educational information libraries for the use of students;
(*v*) supply application forms for admission into educational institutions and universities in foreign countries; and
(*vi*) hold orientation courses for the benefit of students passing out of the university.

These bureaux were set up to render service to the students pursuing higher studies in England for I.C.S., F.R.C.S., Bar at-Law etc. and such examinations. Later on their scope was widened to include other countries and the work of finding suitable employment for those who returned from foreign countries.

At this time, in some of the universities the Academic Adviser who heads the Student Advisory Bureau is under the Dean, University Instruction, and Deputy Chief who heads the University Employment and Information Bureau, is under another Dean. Thus the much needed coordination between educational guidance and counselling and vocational guidance and counselling becomes difficult.

The Education Commission (1964-66) recommended that the Student Advisory Bureaux and University Employment and Guidance Bureaux should be combined to form an information and employment centre which should function directly under the supervision of the dean of students. To improve the working of both the bureaux, the two need to be combined at the earliest.

QUESTIONS FOR ANSWER

1. *Write a note on the functions of the University Employment Information and Guidance Bureaux and justify how it can be termed as an avenue for career guidance for the students?*
2. *Write brief notes on:*
   (*a*) *Student Advisory Bureaux*
   (*b*) *University Employment Information and Guidance Bureaux and the Colleges.*
   (*c*) *Set-up of University Employment Information and Guidance Bureaux.*

20

Duties and Responsibilities of Guidance and Counselling Personnel

INTRODUCTION

Reputation and effective efficiency of each and every institution, organisation and socio-economic or socio-political or socio-cultural or socio-educational programme rests on the proficiency, efficiency, devotion and dedication of the personnel deputed to do the required job of the concerned establishment. This principle is equally and effectively applicable to guidance as well, therefore, the duty of each co-operating member of the guidance programme is:

1. to know exactly what are the general and specific kinds of services to be rendered by the institution;
2. to understand thoroughly the kind and extent of activities in which he should engage as related to the duties of his co-workers; and
3. to be prepared to deal with his specific responsibilities as effectively as he can with a minimum of duplicated or wasted effort.

Guidance, as discussed earlier, is an all-inclusive programme, intended to help the students achieve their optimum potential. It, as we know, is both a *generalised* and a *specialised service*. Naturally, therefore, in such a programme, the *total needs* of the students need to be met by the *total staff*.

One cannot assign the teaching-learning relationship to the teacher, the counselling relationship to the counselling officer and the smooth functioning relationship to the administrator. In fact, everybody who comes into contact with the student, contributes in one way or the other in his growth and development.

DISTRIBUTION OF GUIDANCE RESPONSIBILITIES

The size of the school or school system determines the number and kinds of duties that are allotted to one particular person. No matter what the distribution of duties, no matter how extensive or narrowly prescribed the job of a guidance worker may be, one guiding principle of responsibility should be understood and strictly adhered to: *Each member of the staff must know and stay with his particular job, refraining from engaging in guidance or counselling activities that rightfully are the respective responsibilities of his fellow workers, except as he cooperates willingly and intelligently with all or any of these others in situations that require such cooperation.*

The purposes to be served by the guidance and counselling programme may be stated to be as follows:

1. To collect facts necessary for understanding the growth experience, interests and needs of the individual pupil at successive school levels.
2. To organise and record these facts so that they can be interpreted and made available for the continuing use of educational personnel, parents and students.
3. To use an agreed-upon common terminology at all school levels when discussing a student's record with the student, his parents, college representatives and/or business and industrial personnel.
4. To make available pertinent educational, personnel, social, and occupational information through group guidance, individual counselling service and literature.
5. To provide for each pupil a personal counsellor to serve as a friendly consultant from whom the pupil may expect to receive reliable assistance with his educational, personal, social and occupational problems.
6. To plan cooperatively with each pupil a programme of experiences which will utilize his abilities, capitalize upon his interests and satisfy his needs.

7. To draw parents into the consultation and planning at every opportunity.
8. To utilize all available resources in school and community activities and facilities to assist in carrying forward the developmental plan.
9. To help pupils to make the transition from one experience level to the next as easily and efficiently as possible.
10. To make possible the revision of each student's plan as necessary, with emphasis upon the key points for restudy.
11. To provide for the continuous professional growth of all teachers and administrators in the understanding, improvement, and revision of the guidance and counselling services.
12. To promote better understanding by teachers, administrators and pupils of the constantly changing community opportunities which pupils may use while they are in school and specifically include in the planning for their life after leaving school.

Administrative Responsibilities

The fundamental responsibilities of an administrator in respect to the guidance programme include:

1. Knowledge and acceptance of the basic philosophy and principles of effective guidance services.
2. Leadership in the organisation and reorganisation of the services.
3. Encouragement of a guidance-pointed attitude among the members of the entire staff.
4. Provide suitable accommodation and facilities for the guidance service.
5. If there is whole time counselling officer, arrange time schedule in such a manner that all students could benefit.
6. If there is a part-time counselling/liaison officer, allow a relief of at least six periods in his teaching load so that at least the admission, orientation, student information and occupational information services are possible.
7. Make adequate provision in the budget for carrying on the guidance programme; by considering it a fit charge on the students' amalgamated fund.

8. Establish and maintain a cumulative record system.
9. Send teachers for in-service training.
10. Give desirable publicity to the programme to improve relation of the institution with home, community and world of work.
11. Offer special inducements and recognition to the members who make solid contribution to the programme.
12. Evaluate the guidance programme in cooperation with the staff to determine and promote its effectiveness and evolve measures to strengthen it still further.

New programmes like guidance will success in proportion to the zeal and enthusiasm shown by the administrator—as is the administrator so will be the guidance programme in an institution.

THE CO-ORDINATOR OF GUIDANCE SERVICES

For any guidance programme to function smoothly and successfully, it is imperative that the various services be coordinated by a director of guidance for the entire school system or by a dean, a chairman of guidance, a head counsellor, or a guidance co-ordinator attached to an individual school.

Responsibilities

The director of guidance of a whole school system can be regarded as a liaison officer who, working out of the central office, co-operates with the personnel of individual schools in providing special services for them and in helping guidance departments improve their programme offerings. The remainder of this discussion is concerned with the work of the school guidance co-ordinator or chairman.

With the approval of the principal and in co-operation with his staff, the co-ordinator establishes the guidance policies and implements them.

He assists other staff members in solving difficult problems of adjustment; he keeps the teachers informed about the activities of the programme, and enlists their co-operation in matters such as making referrals and administering remedial measures; he maintain an attitude of friendly interest in and co-operation with pupils; directly or indirectly, he supervises testing programs, pupil admissions, pupil programming, and out-of-class pupil activities; he meets and discusses with parents their children's interests, plans, and problems; and he serves as the liaison officer between the school and other community agencies.

Personal Qualities

A person who is interested in young people, who has leadership qualities, and who does not resent hard work and much apparent failure is guidance chairman material. The co-ordinator's responsibilities are many, his hours are long, and his degree of patience must approach that of Job. He must be all things to all people.

He must be able to meet a frown with a smile and to remain calm and emotionally controlled amidst unbridled emotionalism on the part of pupils, parents, or teachers; he must at all times be tolerant, understanding, objective, self-possessed, co-operative, and ready to pour oil on troubled waters.

At the same time, he must be a human being who has known what it means to endure suffering, to face disappointment, to take unjust criticism. His own experiences should serve to make him sympathetic toward the weaknesses of others.

Above all, he must know how to meet his own emotion-arousing problems of adjustment and to solve them with a reasonable degree of objective behaviour.

The co-ordinator should always maintain an attitude of cheerfulness born of sincerity and desire to serve. Although he may sympathize with an offender, he should not condone the offense.

By precept as well as by example, he should strive constantly to encourage attitude of honesty, industry, cooperation, and other high ethical standards among those with whom he is associated.

The Counselling Officer

The Counselling Officer is the nerve centre of the guidance programme—be it a university or a college. He should be a guidance-minded person with at least a year's full time course in Guidance and Counselling from a University. He should have a well-balanced lovable personality, a broad outlook, an understanding attitude, a genuine interest in helping students.

"The counsellor" in the words of Williamson, "should be clearly more than a competent technician; he should be viewed as a broadly informed and cultivated educator."

The counselling officer needs to discharge the following functions:

1. Arrange orientation programmes for the teachers to enlist their cooperation.
2. Arrange orientation programmes for freshers and also for those passing through the transitional period.
3. Prepare an uptodate list of the resources—informational, referral and energy-available to him and the proper method for calling on each particular resource and classify and fill the information properly.
4. Organise the Guidance Committee.
5. Set up an educational and occupational information centre.
6. Display the information collected in an attractive way.
7. Disseminate the information through educational and career talks, group discussions and film shows, etc.
8. Arrange talks by experts from different fields.
9. Organise career days, career weeks, career conferences, parents' days, etc.
10. Educate students regarding proper study habits and assist them in their development.
11. Introduce Cumulative Record cards and get them maintained with the cooperation of other members of the faculty and use these cards in guiding the students.
12. Arrange individual discussions with students and their parents for giving them educational and occupational information.
13. Arrange visits to places of work like industries, business establishments, offices, higher educational institutions etc.
14. Maintain an active relationship with schools, colleges, university and other regional, national and social agencies like Indian Council for Cultural Relations, United States Educational Foundation in India. Principals of Colleges, Heads of Departments of the University, University Employment and Information and Guidance Bureau, Employment Exchanges, University Health Centres, Medical Research Institutions, etc.

15. Maintain an active liaison with clubs like Lions Club and Rotary Club.
16. Refer the serious mental cases to clinical psychologists, psychiatrists or university health centres where the services of the clinicians are available, as his training and education does not equip him to deal with such cases.
17. Maintain complete secrecy about the discussion between him and the client.
18. Administer psychological tests.
19. Provide counselling service to his students.
20. Help in the placement of students.
21. Take up research projects relating to the field of educational, vocational and personal-social guidance in the colleges and universities and convey the findings to important relevant agencies.
22. Prepare guidance leaflets, brochures and monographs and get them printed for distribution to the students.

To be effective, the counselling officer should have six major qualities—belief in each individual; respect for individual human values; alertness to the world; open-mindedness; understanding of self; and professional commitment.

The Liaison Officer

In a small college, Liaison Officer—a part time guidance worker—can be appointed from the rank of teachers. Liaison officer, in single or groups as convenient to respective colleges, can take charge of the guidance programme in a college. He should be a guidance-minded person with some specialised training in guidance at least for three months.

The liaison officer should discharge the same duties as that of the counselling officer given above except the last five.

The progress and efficiency of the guidance services in colleges will mainly depend on the ability, enthusiasm and dedication of liaison officers and the attitude of the administrators and teachers to them and to their work.

The job, even if part-time, is important and needs to be done in a serious way. Depending upon the number of students and the load of work, the time can be fixed for the liaison officer.

The Teacher

Traxler and North have stressed that the teachers and counsellors should join hands for an effective guidance programme. They write, "Teachers and counsellors need to combine their efforts to help young people to understand themselves, to see the subject-matter of each field in relation to their own strengths and limitations, and to appreciate the need for developing broad abilities and skills to meet the vocational demands of tomorrow as hundreds of new occupations are developing to meet the new needs, and hundreds of others are rendered obsolete or relegated to places of minor importance. This is primarily a learning situation and the teacher, more than anyone else, can open doors through which the student may glimpse his own future."

The teachers are, in fact, the most useful allies of the counselling/liaison officers. It is they who have the closest, the most frequent and the most extended contacts with students in a natural situation.

Without their co-operation, guidance service can never become an integral part of any educational programme. Their part, in the over-all programme, is inevitable.

The teachers can help in the programme by:

1. playing a primary role in advising and orientation, in making known to the students the requirements and future job possibilities connected with their particular subjects;
2. providing vocational motivation to the subjects taught by them;
3. assessing the achievements of the students and thus enabling them to know better their strengths and weaknesses in certain subjects;
4. enabling the students to explore and develop interest by integrating the curricular and co-curricular activities and thus orienting them towards worthy goals;
5. co-ordinating the efforts of various agencies, parents and guidance workers and thus raising guidance to a scientific level;
6. detecting early symptoms of any abnormality in the students' make up and drawing the counselling or liaison officer's attention; and

7. rendering "mental hygiene first-aid" and helping students remain on the right track.

To be of solid help, the teacher should:

1. Study the needs, interests, abilities and problems of each student in his class.
2. Win the confidence of the students and help them in every possible way to evaluate their own growth.
3. Get acquainted with the parents and take an active part in Parent Teacher Association.
4. Instruct the students in appropriate methods of applying for posts.
5. Co-operate with placement organisations in their task of making specific suggestions and finding suitable openings.
6. Follow-up those students they advise by obtaining progress reports on their satisfaction.

Teachers have an important role in assisting the students conserve their native capacities and invest and use the same so as to bring greatest satisfaction to themselves and benefit to society.

The Tutor

In colleges, the first line of reference on guidance matters is the tutor, who is usually a teacher who does not actually teach the members of his tutorial group. This is a deliberate policy to remove guidance from the academic setting and to make it possible for a tutor to help with personal guidance without being hampered by any specific teaching relationship or overtones from the class-room situation. This places an extra responsibility on the tutor, namely that of developing a 'guidance' relationship with students he does not teach in a limited weekly tutorial period.

At some universities, the word 'tutor' is used in a different way. The tutor-guardianship scheme is close to a student advisory system; tutor here is a synonym for a teacher, and 'guardianship' implies a caring or helping relation to a ward.

The tutor can contribute to the guidance programme by:

1. Orienting the members of his group regarding the curricular, co-curricular facilities and ancillary services available in the institution.

2. Collecting different types of information about the student and assisting in the compiling of this information in the cumulative record.
3. Informing the members of his group regarding the occupational openings.
4. Arranging discussions on educational problems.
5. Orienting the members of his group regarding the facility of scholarships, grants, loans, freeships and concessions available, their eligibility and how to apply for them.
6. Recommending the genuine cases for help.
7. Acquainting the members with proper study habits and assisting them in their development.
8. Meeting the parents for solving the problems of the students.
9. Arranging visits to places of work like industries, business establishments, offices, higher educational institutions, etc.
10. Detecting symptoms of abnormality in the students' make-up and drawing the counselling or liaison officers' attention.
11. Rendering "mental hygiene first-aid" and helping the students remain on the right track.
12. Referring the serious cases to clinicians or psychiatrists.

Tutorial meetings can provide much needed close faculty student contacts.

The Warden

The warden, too, is an important link in the process of guidance and counselling. He/she can ensure that hostel is not just a place for passing the night, but is also a place of education. A hostel should develop a reputation for promoting scholarship as well as a place for making good leaders and good citizens.

Students coming to college from the rural areas, where they were recognised as individual members of the community, experience in college, particularly on university campuses, a vast impersonalism.

Life in the hotel, if correctly established, can well provide a bridge from the closer and quite personal environment of the house community to the recognisably less personal one of the educational institution. With an increasing number of students knocking at the doors of higher education, the sense of the impersonal threatens the very existence of the student.

It is here that the hostel warden can play a crucial role. He/she can give recognition and love to the inmate, help him/her build up self-confidence and self-reliance. He/she can establish rapport through directness of approach, friendliness in manner, voice and sympathy and thus, create in the residents a much-needed sense of belongingness to an institution.

It needs to be remembered that hostel is not to be an island, it cannot be isolated from the other counselling or cultural or social functions of the campus. Rather it has to be an integral part of both the curricular and extra-curricular activities of an institution, and a warden can make it so.

The warden can contribute to the guidance and counselling programme in ways more than one:

1. Orient the students regarding the customs and expectations of the hostel and help them anticipate some of the problems of group living and indicating the availability of help in the hostel so as to enable them to reach a satisfactory solution.
2. Provide help to those students who are handicapped by the lack of emotional stability or psychological resources which are needed in order to function well as students.
3. Collect all types of information regarding the resident in cumulative record and coordinate and use the information for the benefit of the student.
4. Take care of natural therapies which include day to day relations of residents in their rooms, in the mess and in co-curricular involvements.
5. Establish a good communication system, so that the students could express freely, participate in the activities without any reservation.
6. Encourage participation so as to develop self-discipline, initiative, sharing of common tasks within the framework of hostel and be well-adjusted residents.
7. Create a sense of belongingness among the residents through cultural programmes, informal evenings, dinner nights, celebration of days in the hostel.

8. Offer the student opportunity to achieve the kind of freedom, responsibility and skills which promise maturity and make the hcstel a place *par excellence* for achieving the adult role.
9. Protect the weak, temper the strong, encourage the shy, bring out latent talents of the residents, stimulate self-discipline and serve as an interpreter of administrative policies of the institution.
10. Give sound advice recognising the needs of the students—security, recognition and love.
11. Refer residents to experts when the occasion demands.

The warden is in a very good position of knowing the aptitudes and interests of the wards in co-curricular activities, emotional maturity, financial adequacy and ability to handle finances, ability to take individual responsibility, family background, social development and social maturity, vocational development, special telents like singing, dancing, sports etc.

This information is of utmost importance in "seeing through" the student and helping him/her "see himself/herself through." No wonder, warden is a very important person in the entire superstructure of guidance and counselling. The warden should have the essential qualities of politeness, patience and concern for the wards so that the wards develop an essential respect for him/her.

The Physical Education Teacher

Physical health is an important part of the make-up of a student. There are so many careers for which physical efficiency is one of the basic requirements. Even for tough courses of studies as Medicine, Engineering etc. good physical health is essential. Thus physical education teacher is also an important link in the chain of guidance personnel. He can contribute to the guidance programme by:

1. Giving the necessary data regarding the physical efficiency of the student, his performance in the physical efficiency tests, games and sports for the cumulative record.
2. Discovering the potentiality of the student in a particular game and arranging special training facilities for developing the same.

3. Bringing to the notice of the doctor the students with physical problems and handicaps for treatment.
4. Arranging coaching classes and demonstrations for the promising players.

The Librarian

The librarian too has an important role in the over-all guidance programme. He can contribute his share by:

1. circulating the latest information material among the teachers and students;
2. providing right type of books on educational, vocational and personal guidance to both teachers and students;
3. helping the counselling and the liaison officers in the classification, and filing of the occupational information material;
4. displaying the material received from time to time in an attractive manner.

The Psychologist

A psychologist with training and experience in education can utilize his specialised knowledge concerning child development, learning, learner-evaluation, and interpersonal relationships to help counsellors and teachers gain a greater understanding of their pupils, especially those who are exceptional.

Although in some schools psychologists serve as full-time members of the guidance department, it is more common for psychological services to be available to individual schools as the need for them arises.

The chief responsibility of a school psychologist is to administer, correct, and interpret the results of whatever standardized instrument of evaluation are used to determine the learning readiness of pupils or to discover something about their interests, attitudes, or behaviour trends.

The Psychiatrist

A young person's emotional difficulties may be so serious and deep-rooted that a school guidance staff or a psychologist is unable to cope with the problem. In a situation of this kind, the service of a well-trained psychiatrist is needed.

Every school should have the opportunity to obtain such psychiatric treatment for pupils who seem to be evidencing symptoms of incipient or serious mental illness.

Health Service Personnel

The part-time services of a physician are needed for periodic checks of the physical status of pupils. A periodic health examination by a physician is common in elementary schools. In many high schools the members of the health education department are responsible for this phase of guidance.

However, an increasing number of secondary schools are beginning to recognise the value of having a physician on call.

Vocational and Placement Counsellor

In some junior and senior high schools, interested and relatively well-qualified teacher-counsellors have the responsibility of giving vocational guidance and of placing pupils in jobs, either part time while they are attending school or full-time after graduation. Such an arrangement is rarely successful. The teacher counsellor must combine vocational guidance with a part-time teaching load.

The tasks of acquainting pupils with vocational opportunities, helping them in their vocational choices, locating jobs, and making appropriate placements are time-consuming. Pupils' class schedules and employers' convenience must be taken into consideration, as well as the teacher-counsellor's teaching periods.

The Parents

There are no two opinions about the fact that parents are the principal counsellors of the students. The favourable upbringing, plus the special help in the form of praise, admonition, reproof, and advice in difficult situations—all contribute to the guidance process.

The influence of parents on a student's life decisions is formidable. Any guidance endeavour on the part of the educational institution, therefore, should be based on this premise; for educators and other guidance personnel only supplement the counsel given to students by their parents.

Parents can play a very important role in the guidance programme by:

1. Getting maximum information regarding the educational and vocational possibilities for their children in the decades ahead.
2. Utilizing good principles of mental hygiene and right living in their families.
3. Helping the children in developing effective study habits, plan their activities and budget their time for maximum achievement.
4. Showing the children how to postpone immediate pleasure in favour of later gratification.
5. Getting all sorts of information regarding the facilities available and helping their children in utilizing the same.
6. Help their children in discovering, developing and directing all of the inherent potentialities.
7. A word of caution: Whereas it is true that students receive most help from their parents (as revealed by an All India Study, 1960-61) we have to be cautious as most of these parents are not equipped to handle their problems adequately. The said Report points out, "It is probably true that the parents themselves became the students' greatest problems by expecting them to perform at a much higher level than they are capable of. If these expectations are not realistic and are not based upon the knowledge of the ability and aptitudes of the young people, they may become a source of misunderstanding between the parents and the child and a cause of despair and frustration to the student." So it is important that parents are made guidance-conscious. For achieving this objective, Parents' clubs, Parents' Forums may be formed. Parents' Days may be organised. Parents' Group Conferences may be held from time to time. Parents' bulletins and Reports may be issued to keep them in touch with current happenings.

Guidance programme is a service to the individual student and indirectly the whole society. Understanding and active support from the administrator, counselling officers, Liaison officers, teachers, medical staff, parents, etc. is basic to the success of any guidance programme.

FUNCTIONAL COMPETENCIES

A. Competencies Needed to Work with Pupils

The ability to:

1. Advise a pupil concerning his choice of curriculum and of electives.
2. Select and interpret information to the pupil.
3. Direct the pupil to sources of information concerning educational, occupational, and personal problems.
4. Determine what information should be collected for all pupils.
5. Make case studies.
6. Appraise the work habits of the pupils.
7. Evaluate the personality patterns of the pupil and to determine both strong and weak areas.
8. Evaluate the socio-economic status of the pupil and of his background.
9. Give group tests of scholastic aptitude, reading, and achievement.
10. Appraise the pupil's present and past academic achievement.
11. Appraise pupil's interests and present activity patterns.
12. Help pupils identify and resolve problems.
13. Use and interpret techniques that measure pupil adjustment.
14. Make and interpret sociograms.
15. Describe significant pupil behaviour by use of anecdotal reports.
16. Evaluate the information a pupil possesses in relation to his educational occupational, and personal problems.
17. Create a satisfactory counselling setting.
18. Organise and direct a systematic testing programme.
19. Select or devise forms for the economical gathering and recording of information.
20. Organise records and establish procedures for effective and economical utilisation.
21. Utilize school resources to provide adequate remedial work.

22. Match job requirements with pupil abilities in individual pupil placement activities.
23. Use group procedures for guidance purposes.
24. Organise and direct a systematic programme of evaluation of guidance services.
25. Plan and develop an effective pupil follow-up programme.
26. Deal with emotionally upset pupils at least to the extent of recognising their situation and, if necessary, referring them to others.

B. Competencies Needed to Work with Staff Members

The ability to:

1. Gain the confidence and respect of the administrative, supervisory, and teaching staff.
2. Cooperative with others responsible for non-instructional services.
3. Organise, initiate, or improve a guidance programme.
4. Give leadership in guidance committee work.
5. Conduct teacher group conferences on problems related to guidance services.
6. Organise and lead group and forum discussions on pupil problems.
7. Organise and carry out a programme of in-service training.
8. Interpret and present effectively the results of a follow-up programme and attendant curriculum needs or changes.
9. Assist individual teachers with specific pupil problems.
10. Conduct research and evaluation studies on all phases of the guidance programme.

C. Competencies Needed to Work with Parents

The ability to:

1. Conduct effective home visitations.
2. Gain the confidence and respect of the parents.
3. Enlist the cooperation of parents in the solution of pupil adjustment problems.
4. Work with both pupil and parent in the pupil-parent conflict.
5. Organise and direct parent conferences.

D. Competencies Needed to Work with Community

The ability to:

1. Know when and how to make referrals.
2. Participate effectively in number of community activities.
3. Explain the entire school programme and to show how the guidance programme is a part of this programme.
4. Develop effective relationships with employers and other community groups.
5. Plan and direct community occupational surveys.
6. Explain in an effective manner the school's guidance programme to groups of adults.
7. Gain support of the community for the guidance programme.
8. Identify other guidance agencies in the community and to develop a guidance programme that utilizes the available services of these agencies.

THE COUNSELLOR AS A CONSULTANT

One person makes a difference in the social situations of which he is a part. The counsellor makes a big difference. The counsellor-consultant can make a still bigger difference. Many factors have combined to make the role of counsellor as consultant a desirable one.

Another factor in the development of the consultant role is the improved level of preparation of counsellors. As they perform vocational guidance at a more than perfunctory level and as they provide effective counselling for personal problems they perceive the need for further expansion of their role.

Moreover, their higher level of competence provides, a confident basis upon which to build the consultant role. Urbanisation and technological change are also factors in the development of counsellor-consultant role.

THE CONSULTANT ROLE

Webster's New World Dictionary defines a consultant as "1. a person who consults another person. 2. a person who gives professional or technical advice, as a doctor, lawyer, engineer, editor, etc."

However, the word *consult*, as a verb, means "to deliberate, consider, ask advice...to call together..." It is this latter connotation which is intended when the word consultant is used in this book.

The role is not that of expert or specialist who gives advice but that of expert in human communications and in interpersonal skill who uses dialogue in the study of a situation and continues with dialogue in proposing a solution. He is one who calls others together to deliberate, to consider, and to plan, cooperatively, programmes for pupil development.

The word *consultant* is often used to refer to the expert, the specialist who enters a situati n for a few days, evaluates it, and makes some pertinent recommendations.

Boy and Pine have given a description of the counsellor-consultant under the heading "Elementary School Counselling Consultants." They describe this professional as having five major areas of work:

1. working with children in terms of assessment placement, and individual and group counselling,
2. working with principals and teachers conducting conferences relating to pupils, in-service courses, interpreting the objectives of the pupil personnel programme,
3. working with other school personnel such as instructional materials managers, librarians, nurses, reading consultants, and speech therapists,
4. working with parents to consider educational programmes and problems, counselling with parents, organising workshops and discussion groups, and interpreting pupil personnel services, and
5. working with community agencies on referrals, participating in staff conferences, and being active in professional organisations.

Stripling and Lane in surveying the history and scope of guidance, indicate that one of the most effective ways of accomplishing guidance objectives is through consultation with parents, teachers, and other adults who are concerned with pupil growth.

The role of the counsellor-consultant has expanded as emphasis has shifted from the child to those who deal with child most intimately and for the most hours per day. In addition to working with parents and teachers, some see the evolving role as having responsibility for coordinating the pupil personnel services of the school.

Others see the one who exercises such leadership as being the one who should interpret the pupil personnel services to the public, not only so that the work can be done more effectively but in order to counteract successive waves of suspician and undue popularity and high expectation. Certainly, it seems much too early to attempt to formulate a concept of exactly what the role should be.

Today's school counsellor is involved in so many activities that often times he isn't sure what he is or what he is supposed to be. He bears the title counsellor but usually he hasn't time to involve himself in an inter-personal counselling relationship with a troubled student since he is too busy with programming, interviewing students who are academic failures, handling discipline problems, checking absences, arranging a co-curricular activities schedule, and handling a variety of other administrative duties.

The emerging role of the counsellor is that of concern about the network of interactions which characterise a learning milieu. Danskin, Kennedy, and Friesen refer to the circularity of learning processes as student ecology.

This student ecology takes cognizance of research results which indicate that the key determinants in the pupil's learning success are:

1. the socio-economic status of the home in which the pupil was reared,
2. the reference groups (peer groups) from which the pupil so largely derives his values, and
3. his intelligence and the manner in which it is used.

If this emerging role is to be effectively performed some modifications of the counsellors increases are required. It will be necessary for the counsellor to:

Spend much less time planning *future* educational and vocational programmes for students while spending much more time in exploring and probing *current* educational experiences of students. Planning for the future will flow from being alive to the present experiences.

Invest a much larger part of his total resources in observation of systematic research into the learning climate of the school. For this he will need time to reflect, discuss, and write, *without* the pressure of having to do the highly visible guidance functions.

Greatly enlarge the scope of his contacts with teachers and administrators. He would become the important "human development consultant" in issues concerning curriculums, activities, policies, etc.

Acting as a counsellor-consultant means dealing with people as the major forces in improving the learning environment of the school. Such action means that a generalist in interest of knowledge uses his specialist skill in dealing with people.

This specialist skill is the ultimate outcome of the counsellor-consultant's preparation and orientation. While most school workers are concerned with cognitive skills—the acquisition and methods of acquisition of subject matter—the orientation of the acquisition and methods of acquisition of subject matter—the orientation of the counsellor is toward the pupil.

To the counsellor the pupil is the subject matter to be learned. The counsellor must, however, remember that he himself is very much a part of that subject matter, he is irrevocably involved.

QUESTIONS FOR ANSWER

1. *Write a note on the responsibilities of the director of the guidance programme.*
2. *Explain the activities of school Counsellor.*
3. *Write a note on the Functional Competencies of guidance personnel.*
4. *Explain the role of Counsellor as a Consultant.*

PART V
DISCOVERY OF HUMAN RESOURCE AND CREATIVE TALENT

21

Basic Goal of Career Guidance: The Discovery and Utilization of Human Resources

INTRODUCTION

The growth and development of the nation basically depend upon discovery and maximum utilization of its human resource for which proper efforts—guidance to youth, be made. This aspect is being discussed, hereunder, in brief:

We have seen that in the twentieth century man has made effective and beneficial efforts for the discovery and utilisation of physical energy, which have been found everywhere—on the surface of the earth and in its interior, in the depths of the ocean, in the air above, in the sun, moon and stars and in intersteller space. Similar feverish search is on by the governmental and industrial enterprises for the discovery and utilization of human resources through guidance programmes.

GUIDANCE FOR THE SEARCH FOR TALENT

This emphasis upon research and the recognition of the importance of talent have set off the most widespread manhunt in history. Men and women of unusual ability with training in research are in great demand, especially those who have specialized in mathematics, physics, chemistry, and related fields.

Scientific and mathematical societies have been organised for the purpose of emphasizing the importance in our economy of training in these areas as a basis for research and encouraging more men and women of high ability to chose occupations in these areas. They are also seeking ways by which the basic training in these areas in secondary schools and colleges may be strengthened and higher achievements secured.

Many schools are now offering special college courses in mathematics, chemistry, and physics for students of high ability, and colleges are giving advanced credit for those who have taken these courses and admitting them to the advanced courses in college.

Research on gifted children has a high priority, and much emphasis is being given to the identification of bright children and the enrichment of their education.

It is easy to understand why the emphasis in seeking talent has been on mathematics and science, but it is unfortunate that more attention and effort have not been given to seeking out and stimulating unusual ability in other areas where it is just as necessary, such as in art, music, language, literature, public service, social sciences, and philosophy.

We are beginning to recognise the fundamental values of these areas and are taking steps to remedy what many think to be an overemphasis upon mathematics and science. It is a growing belief that the engineer, the chemist, the physician is also a citizen and has obligations to society beyond those of his specialty and that the narrowly trained person is, at best, only half a man. Education should be broad enough to make every man an effective citizen and a well-rounded member of society and for this national talent search examination is held all over India every year.

The Development of Talent

Guidance has a very important responsibility in this search for new sources of power and for men and women who have special talent. It is concerned not only with helping the individual discover his abilities and powers but with assisting him in their proper development and use for the best advantage to society.

Although guidance is centered primarily upon the individual and his developing the ability to find a way of life which is satisfying, it is also concerned with the needs of society.

Guidance workers are concerned with giving every student the best possible opportunity to develop whatever talents he has.

Both society and the individual benefit most when every child has an education suited to his interests and abilities.

GUIDANCE AND THE PHYSICALLY HANDICAPPED

The need of an individual for guidance depends on his ability to make his choices and to solve his problems without assistance. Some of the chief factors contributing to his lack of ability to make choices are inadequate background and inability to analyze and learn from experience.

A handicapped person may be described as one whose physical, mental, or emotional condition or characteristics or economic and social surroundings make it difficult or even impossible for him to participate in society up to his potential capacity and so to live a normal, useful, and satisfying life.

The removal or modification of handicaps may be accomplished by changing the individual or by changing the occupational and sociological conditions so that his effective participation in society may be realised.

One of the greatest triumphs of medicine, education, and social science in the past half century has been the progress that has been made in reducing or removing handicaps.

Each disabled person served by the programme receives the combination of the following services which best meets his needs.

1. *Diagnosis and counselling*. Physical examinations are conducted to determine the extent of his disabilities and to establish eligibility for rehabilitation. If he is eligible, counselling is provided to assist in planning a vocational rehabilitation programme.

2. *Medical, surgical, psychiatric, and hospital services*. These may be provided if the physical or mental impairment can be substantially corrected or improved and if the applicant is financially in need.

3. *Braces, limbs, hearing aids, or other prosthesis.* These are purchased for him if they are considered necessary to overcome the handicap and if he is in financial need.

4. *Vocational training*. This is arranged for him if he needs preparation for an occupation at which he can engage within the limitations of his handicaps. Normally, vocational training is provided after the completion of the high-school course and when

the individual has demonstrated a need for special training not readily available to him in order to enter employment.

5. *Maintenance and transportation.* This is provided during the training programme if it is found necessary to meet the expenses incurred in the training.

6. *Tools, equipment, and occupational licenses.* These are provided if found necessary during the training programme or to aid a person in establishing his own business.

7. *Placement on the job.* This is the goal for each person undertaking a vocational rehabilitation programme. Every effort is made by the rehabilitation staff and by cooperating agencies to assist in satisfactory placement.

8. *Follow-up on the job.* This is provided for several months to be certain that the placement is satisfactory both to the client and to the employer.

Values of the Rehabilitation Programme

It seems that even from a financial standpoint the rehabilitation programme has paid off. The estimated annual earnings of this group the first year after rehabilitation were nearly eight times their earnings the year before rehabilitation.

It is estimated that in the three years after rehabilitation, the rehabilitants will have paid back to the government in income taxes much more than the entire programme cost.

These figures suggest the great increase in available man power which has been brought about by the rehabilitation programme. Of much greater basic importance, however, are the values that have come to the rehabilitated person himself.

Before rehabilitation he has a sense of economic worthlessness and feels that he is a burden to others, but after rehabilitation he begins again to feel the joy of being a producer, of being independent, of being a help rather than a hindrance. The value to these persons and to society is incalculable.

Cooperation between Schools and Rehabilitation Agencies

Once of the most important phases of this programme is the cooperation between the Federal government and the states and especially the teamwork which exists in some states between the rehabilitation agencies and the public schools.

At present only a few school systems have developed programmes that are at all adequate to meet the needs of the older disabled students.

Most schools do not have sufficient financial resources or trained personnel for such services, but it is possible for the rehabilitation programme to provide help to these pupils when their formal education ends. Schools now generally have educational programmes for the handicapped child.

These programmes—for the mentally retarded, the crippled, or the child with sensory handicaps—are collectively known as "special education."

The proper cooperation between special education and rehabilitation will result in more effective educational and guidance programmes for the handicapped of all ages.

Teamwork such as this gives promise of the development of adequate services for all kinds of handicaps. It is not too much to hope that soon every child and youth with any kind of handicap will have available in his school sources of help in removing or reducing his handicap. Such an accomplishment would be of far greater significance than all the spaceships or artificial satellites that man can produce.

UNDERACHIEVERS

Closely related to the handicapped are the 'underachievers'. These are individuals whose achievement is below their proved ability. The present concern is chiefly with children and youth in schools, although some attention is given to college students who are underachievers.

It is estimated that 13 to 15 per cent of students in school or college are underachievers. Special attention is given to underachievers in the upper ability group, but those in the middle group are taken into consideration as well.

Research studies do not as yet determine all the causes of this underachievement. It seems certain, however, that the family is a very important factor.

One study found that higher achievement (less underachievement) was related to the following:

1. Homes not broken by death, divorce, and separation.
2. Higher educational level of parents.

3. Greater agreement on the life values of *parents*.
4. Parents who were concerned about the achievement of their children and who took positive action regarding their progress in school.

Other studies seem to indicate that high achievers possess certain personality traits. Among these are the following:

1. They have more positive character traits.
2. They are more reliable and have greater inclination to participate in extracurricular activities.
3. They have greater emotional health, fewer emotional disturbances (in many cases the underachiever had a higher degree of emotional disturbance than the achiever).
4. They are found to have more favourable behaviour traits.
5. In many cases bright children, as they grow older, tend to cover up their high ability because they do not want to be called "teachers' pets" or to seem brighter than their friends.
6. Their level of achievement is not temporary but remains fairly consistent.
7. Unlike underachievers, they do not tend to rationalize errors and underachievements in such a way that they do not feel responsible and make no effort to improve.

General Methods of Assistance

During the years from age five to eleven the school has the best opportunity to give assistance to the underachiever, for this is when evidence of underachievement first appears.

Teachers, administrators, counsellors, and parents should work together on a cooperative basis to identify the underachiever and to assist him. One of the best services a counsellor can give is to have faith and belief in the student and to feel that he can help him.

An imaginative and capable teacher can be of great help in understanding the student and in helping him to realize his situation and to develop the desire to achieve up to his ability.

Studies show clearly the importance of guidance in assisting youth to achieve the level of accomplishment suited to their abilities.

There are, however, some dangers in this process. It is not possible for every individual to attain this goal, nor is it always desirable. One must also consider other facets of his life than achievement in school alone—health, social obligations and development, citizenship, membership in a family, etc.

It is by no means unusual for an ambitious student, when the urge is for high achievement, to impair his eyesight and health or to miss the social and cultural values in college life.

Some people believe that unusual ability in music, art, literature, inventiveness, etc., is "God-given" and that this gift demands all-out effort to attain its full development.

There is no doubt that in the history of civilization there are many instances where this effort for achievement has been of immeasurable value. But there have been instances where it has been of immeasurable harm. Its value depends upon the nature of the ability. It may be good, or it may be evil.

There is also a tendency to forgive the evil conduct of a person who has given something of great value, a sort of book-keeping of comparing the "good that a man does" with the bad that he does. There are many cases where the great good that is given to the world has far less of an effect than the evil done.

QUESTIONS FOR ANSWER

1. *Write a note on the need of Guidance for the search of Talent and the process of Talent Development.*
2. *Explain the nature of Rehabilitation Programmes and their relationship with guidance for the Physically Handicapped.*
3. *Write a note on guidance of underachievers.*

22

Creative Talent and Goals of Career Guidance

INTRODUCTION

Highly creative individuals usually have very strong creative needs. They are attracted to the mysterious, to the unknown, and to the unexplained. They have a strong need to question, to explain, to test ideas, and to communicate the results of their testing.

Creative individuals, however, need outside encouragement to keep up their efforts. Society in general does not supply this encouragement, but teachers and counsellors are in a position to supply much of this support.

It should be recognised, however, that the goal of guidance is not to promote just individuality and creativity but to encourage healthy kinds of individuality, creativity, and conformity.

Many creative individuals, however, need guidance in achieving the balance between creativity and conformity so that they enhance one another. This is a guidance task for teachers and counsellors at all levels of education, because the creative personality does not emerge suddenly and dramatically. It must be nurtured through many crises.

Kris (1951), Maslow (1954), Rogers (1954), Stein (1956), Barron (1958), Kubie (1958), MacKinnon (1960), and others have discussed the essentials of the creative personality from various viewpoints.

Before suggesting some specific goals in counselling and guiding creative individuals, please review briefly some of the personality requirements which have been outlined in chapter 28 of this book.

By synthesizing the findings of various investigators, we might list the following as necessary conditions for the healthy functioning of the preconscious mental processes which produce creativity:

1. The absence of serious threat to the self, the willingness to risk.
2. Self-awareness—in touch with one's feelings.
3. Self-differentiation—sees self as being different from others.
4. Both openness to the ideas of others and confidence in one's own perceptions of reality or one's own ideas.
5. Mutuality in interpersonal relations—balance between excessive quest for social relations and pathological rejection of them.

Another general goal in guiding the highly creative individual of course is to help him counteract some of the many pressures which push him towards the mean. Evidences of the existence of these pressures and of the power of their influence are widespread.

Pressures from parents are especially difficult to deal with and the research evidence on this count is rather strong. Getzels and Jackson (1960b) found that the parents of both the highly intelligent and highly creative children are not interested in nurturing giftedness in their children. Parents prefer that their children be "well adjusted."

SPECIFIC GOALS

Rewarding Diverse Contributions

Research has repeatedly shown that people will develop along whatever lines they find rewarding. Whenever only two or three types of talent are rewarded or receive a major share of the rewards, the conditions for creativity cannot be met.

Teachers and counsellors must acknowledge spontaneously and respectfully the questions, ideas, and other requests or contributions of creative individuals rather than respond with shock, withdrawal, or arbitrary rejection.

Vocational counsellors have, of course, long accepted the goal of helping individuals find the niche where their unique talents will be rewarded. Schools, through their emphasis on developing well-rounded personalities and because of their remoteness from vocational placement, many neglect this goal.

It is natural for the counsellor to want to help a pupil consider as many opportunities as possible and discourage a vocational goal in which there are few employment opportunities.

This poses a difficult problem in guidance creative adolescents, since many of their vocational choices are likely to fall in the category of rare or unusual occupations.

Many pieces of evidence spell out the failure of educational institutions to find ways of rewarding divergent kinds of achievement. One of the more recent of these is a study byElizabeth Drews (1961b) of three types of gifted high school students; the studious, the social leaders, and the creative intellectuals.

The poorest teacher-grades were made by the creative intellectuals. In competitive examinations sampling a wide range of information, however, they performed better than either of the other two groups.

Recognising Value of One's Own Talent

Many creative individuals desperately need help in recognizing the value of their own talents. Otherwise, they will continue to despise what could be their most valuable assets.

This guidance goal is not an easily achieved one. It is indeed difficult to believe that a talent is of value when almost everyone ridicules its display. This is true even though the individual may receive very rich intrinsic rewards from the exercise of the talent.

It might seem to some that teachers and counsellors could accomplish this goal easily the administering tests to discover giftedness and then simply telling the individual the results.

In some cases this may be helpful, but inevitably the locus of evaluation will be the individual, not the teacher, counsellor, or psychologist. There are numerous other techniques whereby counsellors and teachers can help the creative individual recognise the value of his talents.

Avoiding Exploitation

Since highly creative individuals frequently do not recognise the value of their talents, especially when these talents are ridiculed, they are especially susceptible to exploitation of various types.

This may result in the ill-use of the talent, loss or debilitation of the talent, or unrewarded talents. Children recognise this possibility in their stories of divergent talent.

The psychological needs of exploited individuals are usually such, however, that they need guidance in recognising that they are being exploited. In the case of children, teachers and counsellors may have to intervene actively to prevent undue exploitation.

Accepting Limitations

Inevitably there will be limitations both within the environment and the individual. Parents, schools, and communities will be unable to provide all of the resources which creative children need to develop and test their ideas. The children will lack some of the abilities and skills they need to fulfill their dreams.

Both kinds of limitations must be accepted, not cynically or with resignation, but creatively. In an early study of the psychology of inventors. Rossman (1931) found that this characteristics differentiates inventors from non-inventors.

Non-inventors only curse the defects of their environment and of themselves. Inventors, however, take a more constructive approach, saying, "This is the way to do it."

In the case of the school counsellor and the creative individual, the "record player" may be a hearing aid, a pair of eye glasses, a prosthetic device, a wheel chair, or a similar aid or help may be needed in accepting creatively such limitations as tallness or shortness, a long nose, stuttering, or other differences.

Developing Minimum Skills

Quite obviously the psychological conditions described in the introduction cannot be maintained, if the individual does not possess the minimum skills necessary for survival and for entry into situations where creativity can be expressed.

Many possible causes might be cited for the failure of highly creative individuals to develop some of the fundamental skills essentials to any kind of achievement. Perhaps one of the most frequent, however, is the popular fallacy that gifted children do not need guidance and good instruction.

Buhl (1961) in his study of creative engineering students found that members of this group were encouraged as children to make decisions regarding clothes, friends, and activities. They were also given guidance and encouragement and plans and goals to work toward achieving. The researcher found these characteristics to a far greater degree in the backgrounds of the jet aces than in those of their less successful colleagues of the same rank and similar training and experience.

Utilising Opportunities

Frequently questions are asked concerning the role of chance in scientific discovery (Taton, 1957). Certainly many great discoveries have resulted from the exploitation of a chance occurrence or unexpected incident. Because of their problems of adjustment, creative individuals may be blinded and fail to see such opportunities. It should be the teacher the counsellor's goal to help free such individuals from this blindness.

Developing Values and Purpose

Studies of outstanding individuals in various fields almost always reveal that such persons seem to be impelled by feelings of mission or purpose. They believe that what they are doing is tremendously worthwhile, and they are thereby aroused to all-out efforts.

When learning and thinking are made to be "tremendously important and worthwhile," schools will become exciting places. Even gifted children may achieve more than we thought possible.

Since the values of creative individuals as different from those of their teachers, it may be that the school counsellor is the only person in some schools who can assist them in finding and holding to their purpose.

Holding to Purposes

If pressures continue unabated over too long a period, even the strongest personality is likely to 'break'. In the case of the highly creative individual, this 'break' may include the sacrificing of his creativity or his purpose.

One of the problems of the teacher and the counsellor is to help creative individuals to accept the necessity for tolerating discomfort for long-range goals and purposes. This is an especially difficult feat to accomplish if guiding highly creative children from the lower socio-economic classes where immediacy and inability to delay gratification are strong.

In studies of talent, commitment to a purpose or a creative career seems to be tremendously important in success. In guiding creative talent, teachers and counsellors may have to help such individuals develop a commitment to some purpose or career which they regard as important.

In general, it is not necessary for teachers and counsellors to push talented children, although some may need help in finding ways of self-discipline. Commitment to a purpose or goal frequently helps them achieve this discipline and stick to a line of development until they have achieved something worthwhile.

Avoiding Equation of Divergency with Mental Illness or Delinquency

Many highly creative children need help in recognising that divergency should not be equated with mental illness or delinquency. Since our culture does generally equate them, the counsellor may have to explain away their misconceptions and attitudes. The widespread existence of this misconception is reflected in the stories of children.

Flying monkeys in the stories are frequently thought to be crazy or devils or under the spell of witches. Lions that won't roar and cats that won't scratch are thought to be mentally ill.

In our studies of highly creative children, we find many evidences that they feel that their parents and teachers do not understand them. Their teachers themselves admit that they do not know these children as well as they know highly intelligent (IQ) pupils (Torrance, 1959a). For some creative individuals only a school counsellor may be able to provide this understanding.

Reducing Overemphasis on Sex Roles

The inhibiting effects of overemphasis or misplaced emphasis on sex roles was discussed earlier. It is mentioned again since this overemphasis interferes so strongly with the achievement of the general goals outlined at the beginning of the chapter. The primary creativeness described by Maslow, McPherson, and others requires that the individual be able to accept his softness and femininity as well as his intellectual autonomy.

For "regression in the service of the ego," one must have a sense of being in touch with his feelings and being free to have subjective experiences which imply how it was to have been a child and to have felt feminine, receptive, and helpless. He must also have the intellectual independence to be able to maintain his "anchors in reality," as he regresses.

Becoming Less Obnoxious

Both our experimental and longitudinal studies (Torrance, 1960b) and studies of outstanding creative persons reveal that highly creative individuals do in fact possess characteristics generally considered somewhat obnoxious.

They do, in fact, create problems for their parents, siblings, peers, teachers, and supervisors. Many of your elementary school authors recognize this problem.

We also need to help children recognise that outstanding talents may threaten others and make them uncomfortable and afraid. Our young authors recognise this and offer some interesting philosophies.

The performance of important services and courageous deeds on behalf of the larger social group is seen by our juvenile authors as one way of reducing the social pressures on divergent individuals.

In the terms employed by Pepinsky (1959) Roger had built up a "credit rating" with his peers through his service to them, and they had accepted his divergency.

In conserving creative talent, the problem resolves itself into one of helping the child maintain those characteristics which are essential to his creativity and at the same time help him acquire skills for avoiding or reducing to a tolerable level the social sanctions against him.

Stein (1958) on the basis of his study of research chemists, has offered a set of helpful principles whereby creative research chemists can become less obnoxious without sacrificing their creativity.

This model probably asks too much of the gifted child, but at least it provides a model which may be useful in guiding him in becoming less obnoxious without sacrificing his creativity.

Reducing Isolation

Considerable attention has been given in professional literature to the problems stemming from the isolation of gifted children.

Isolation has been a favourite technique for handling individuals having almost any kind of divergent characteristic.

As already reported, research has shown that highly creative children are especially estranged from teachers and peers. This must be especially difficult for the highly creative individual because of his unusually intense need to communicate.

Teachers and counsellors must help the creative child learn to tolerate his separateness or they must help him in his search for someone with whom he can communicate. In some cases, the counsellor may become the person to whom the creative child communicates. In others, it may be a teacher or principal.

Several current streams of research (Drews, 1961; Torrance and Arsan, 1961) suggest that various kinds of homogeneous groups may provide means by which the isolation of highly creative children may be reduced and communication increased.

Coping with Anxieties and Fears

Neither gifted children (Torrance, 1959c) nor creative scientists (Roe, 1959) are free of handicapping anxieties and fears. Many creative children desperately need help in coping with their anxieties and irrational fears. Otherwise they may fail to be fully functioning mentally; they will be afraid to break away from the safest, most frequently travelled paths.

An unusually frequent theme in the stories of animals and persons with divergent characteristics is the fear that one's own talent v. ill bring injury or destruction.

LEARNING TO COPE WITH HARDSHIPS AND FAILURE

All of the studies of eminent individual with which I am familiar emphasize the role of coping with hardship and failure. This comes out clearly in the recent study by the Goertzels (1960) and in an earlier study by Anne Roe (1952). On the basis of these and other studies, some workers advocate that we deliberately and calculatedly subject gifted children to hardships.

It is my own opinion that gifted children should learn how to cope with hardship and failure, but they should not be forced to do so deliberately. Gifted children are resistant to and are embittered by hardships which seem to them unfair, wasteful of their energies, and unnecessary.

If they are encouraged and permitted to explore, experiment, test ideas, initiate projects on their own, and assume responsibility, they will encounter enough hardships and failures in the natural course of events. This is especially true if freedom to try out ideas without penalty is permitted against a background of high standards.

The importance of skills in coping with hardships is reflected in Anne Roe's (1952) finding concerning the disproportionate number of her eminent subjects whose fathers had died during the subject's childhood. It is also reflected in one of Peter Freuchen's (1954) stories of his first year with the Thule, Greenland, Eskimos.

On one occasion Freuchen was deploring the plight of certain orphan children in the tribe who had to fight for survival. The chiefs of the tribe scolded Freuchen, telling him not to feel sorry for these orphan children because they would be the future leaders of the tribe.

They pointed out to him that each of the present leaders had been an orphan. They also explained that they realised that they should permit their own children to experience more difficulties and hardships but that they had grown soft and would not permit their children to expose themselves to cold, danger, or similar hardships.

In most societies it takes some kind of accident or adverse circumstance to force adults to permit their children to attempt to master the skills of coping with difficulties.

QUESTIONS FOR ANSWER

1. *Explain the necessary conditions for healthy functioning of the preconscious mental processes which produce creativity.*
2. *Write a note on specific Goals of guidance for creative talent.*

23

Career Guidance: The Need for Identification of Creative Talent

The concept of guiding creative talent deserves an independent book but as per need of this book on career guidance. We are discussing this aspect very briefly:

Progress and development of the nation depends upon national talent. It is said that democracies collapse only when they fail to use intelligent imaginative methods for solving their problems and thus it is rightly believed that Greece failed to heed such a warning by Socrates and gradually collapsed. Here it can be said that the nation which has more creative talent makes maximum progress in minimum time and with minimum resources, hence, we are including the concept of guiding creative talent in this book for effective career guidance.

LEGITIMATE CONCERNS OF EDUCATORS

Why should counsellors, teachers, and administrators be concerned with the problems of creative individuals? What business is it of theirs whether or not one is highly creative? Doesn't everybody know that the highly creative person is 'a little crazy" and that you can't help him anyway? If he's *really creative,* why does he need guidance anyway? He should be able to solve his own problems. He's creative, isn't he?

Unfortunately, these are attitudes which have long been held by some of our most eminent scholars and which still prevail rather widely.

Most of the educators perk up when they discover a child with a high Intelligence Quotient or a high score on some other traditional measure of intellectual talent. They are impressed! Most of them are rather impressed if they discover in a child some outstanding talent.

There are very legitimate reasons why educators should be concerned about assessing and guiding the growth of the creative thinking abilities.

CREATIVE THINKING ABILITIES

Hereunder, we will discuss only a few of these abilities:

Mental Health

Schools are legitimately concerned about the mental health of children, adolescents, college students, and adults. They would like to be able to help their students avoid mental breakdowns and achieve healthy personality growth. These are legitimate concerns of education. But what does all this have to do with creativity?

Actually, it has a great deal to do with creativity. There is little question but that the stifling of creativity cuts at the very roots of satisfaction in living and ultimately creates overwhelming tension and breakdown (Patrick, 1955). There is also little doubt that one's creativity is his most valuable resource in coping with life's daily stresses.

Fully Functioning Persons

Schools are anxious that the children they educate grow into fully functioning persons. This has long been an avowed and widely approved purpose of education. We say that education in a democracy should help individuals fully develop their talents.

Recently there have been pressures to limit this to intellectual talents. There has been much talk about limiting the school's concern to the full development of the intellect only.

Even with this limited definition of the goals of education, the abilities involved in creative thinking cannot be ignored. There has been increasing recognition of the fact that traditional measures of intelligence attempt to assess only a few of man's thinking abilities.

In his early work Binet (1909) recognised clearly this deficiency. It has taken the sustained work of Guilford (1959a) and his associates to communicate effectively the complexity of man's mental operations.

Certainly we cannot say that one is fully functioning mentally, if the abilities involved in creative thinking remain undeveloped or are paralysed. There are the abilities involved in becoming aware of problems, thinking up possible solutions, and testing them.

Educational Achievement

Almost no one disputes the legitimacy of the school's concern about educational achievement. Teachers and guidance workers are asked to help under-achievers to make better use of their intellectual resources and to help over-achievers become better 'rounded' personalities. But, how do you tell who is, an under-or over-achiever?

In my opinion, recent findings concerning the role of the creative thinking abilities in educational achievement call for a revision of these long-used concepts.

We are finding (Getzels and Jackson, 1958; Torrance, 1960c) that the creative thinking abilities contribute importantly to the acquisition of information and various educational skills.

Of course, we have long known that it is natural for man to learn creatively, but we have always thought that it was more economical to teach by authority.

Recent experiments (Moore, 1961; Ornstein, 1961) have shown that apparently many things can be learned creatively more economically than they can by authority, and that some people strongly prefer to learn creatively.

Traditional tests of intelligence are heavily loaded with tasks requiring cognition, memory, and convergent thinking. Such tests have worked rather well in predicting school achievement. When children are taught by authority these are the abilities required.

Recent and ongoing studies, however, show that even traditional subject matter and educational skills can be taught in such a way that the creative thinking abilities are important for their acquisition.

It is of special interest that the children with high IQ's were rated by their teachers as more desirable, better known or understood, more ambitious, and more hardworking or studious. In other words, the highly creative child appears to learn as much as the highly intelligent one, at least in some schools, without appearing to work as hard.

Our guess is that these highly creative children are learning and thinking when they appear to be "playing around." Their tendency is to learn creatively more effectively than by authority. They may engaged in manipulative and/or exploratory activities, many of which are discouraged or even forbidden. They enjoy learning and thinking, and this looks like play rather than work.

Vocational Success

Guidance workers (school personnel doing guidance functions) have traditionally been interested in the vocational success of their clients. Indeed, the guidance movement got much of its impetus form this concern. Of course, it has long been recognized that creativity is a distinguishing characteristic of outstanding individuals in almost every field.

It has been generally conceded that the possession of high intelligence, special talent, and technical skills is not enough for outstanding success. It has also been recognised that creativity is important in scientific discovery, invention, and the arts.

Social Importance

Finally, educators are legitimately concerned that their students make useful contributions to our society. Such a concern runs deep in the code of ethics of the profession. It takes little imagination to recognise that the future of our civilization—our very survival—depends upon the quality of the creative imagination of our next generation.

Democracies collapse only when they fail to use intelligent, imaginative methods for solving their problems. Greece failed to heed such a warning by Socrates and gradually collapsed.

What is called for is a far cry from the model of the quiz-programme champion of a few years ago. Instead of trying to cram a lot of facts into the minds of children and make them scientific encyclopedias, we must ask what kind of children they are becoming.

What kind of thinking do they do? How resourceful are they? Are they becoming more responsible? Are they learning to give thoughtful explanations of the things they do and see? Do they believe their own ideas to be of value? Can they share ideas and opinions with others? Do they relate similar experiences together in order to draw conclusions? Do they do some thinking for themselves?

We also need more than well-rounded individuals. We ordinarily respect these well-rounded individuals, broad scholars, and men of many talents.

Dael Wolfle (1960) has made a case for those who develop some of their talents so highly that they cannot be well-rounded. He argues that it is advantageous to a society to see the greatest achievable diversity of talent among those who constitute the society.

HOW TO HELP OR GUIDE CREATIVE TALENTS THE SCHOOL

Many will say, "Surely, schools have a right to be concerned about mental health, full mental functioning, educational achievement, and vocational success. They ought to be concerned that coming generations contribute productively to our society. *But* how can school guidance workers contribute to the creative growth necessary for these things?"

This is a legitimate question. Parents and peers play such important roles in the encouragement or discouragement of creative expression and growth, what can school guidance workers do?

There are at least six special roles which school guidance workers can play in helping highly creative children maintain their creativity and continue to grow.

Each of these is a role which others can rarely fulfill. Our social expectations frequently prevent even teachers and administrators from effectively fulfilling these roles.

Thus, in some cases, only counsellors, school psychologists, and similar workers will be able to fulfill these roles. In many cases, however, teachers and administrators can supply these needs, if they differentiate their guidance roles from other socially expected roles.

The six roles which I have in mind are:

1. providing the highly creative individual a 'refuge',
2. being his 'sponsor' or 'patron',
3. helping him understand his divergence,
4. letting him communicate his ideas,
5. seeing that his creative talent is recognised, and

6. helping parents and others understand him. We shall now discuss each of these roles briefly.

Provide a 'Refuge'

Society in general is downright savage towards creative thinkers, especially when they are young. To some extent, the educational system must be coercive and emphasize the establishment of behaviour norms. Teachers and administrators can rarely escape this coercive role.

Counsellors and other guidance workers are in a much better position to free themselves of it. Nevertheless, there are ways teachers and administrators can free themselves of this role long enough to provide refuge, if they are sensitive to the need.

From the studies of Getzels and Jackson (1958), we know that highly creative adolescents are estranged from their teachers and peers. Minnesota studies indicate that the same holds true for children in the elementary school. The reasons are easy to understand.

Who can blame teachers for being irritated when a pupil presents an original answer which differs from what is expected? It does not fit in with the rest of the grading scheme. They don't know how the unusual answer should be treated. They have to stop and think themselves. Peers have the same difficulty and label the creative child's unusual questions and answers as 'crazy' or 'silly'.

Thus, the highly creative child, adolescent, or adult needs encouragement. He needs help in becoming reconciled and, as Hughes Mearns (1941) once wrote, in being "made cheerful over the world's stubborn satisfaction in its own follies."

The guidance worker must recognise, however, that the estrangement exists and that he will have to create a relationship in which the creative individual feels safe.

Be a Sponsor or Patron

Someone has observed that almost always wherever independence and creativity occur and persist, there is some other individual or agent who plays the role of 'sponsor' or 'patron'.

This role is played by someone who is not a member of the peer group, but who possesses prestige and power in the same social system. He does several things.

Regardless of his own views, the sponsor encourages and supports the other in expressing and testing his ideas and in thinking through things for himself. He protects the individual from the reactions of his peers long enough for him to try out some of his ideas and modify them. He can keep the structure of the situation open enough so that originality *can* occur.

It is true contention that the school counsellor or guidance worker is in a better position than anyone else in the social system to play this role, especially if such a role for him is sanctioned by the teachers and principal.

Since few elementary schools have counsellors or guidance workers, this role is usually assumed by principals. It is a difficult role for a principal, however. Think of the role conflicts which must be involved in the following case of a principal whose school participated in a research project on this subject.

In an experiment conducted on a Monday, one had observed the exceptional creative talent of Tom, a fourth grader. Before leaving the school, the researcher asked the teacher about Tom. She volunteered the information that he had had a struggle with most of his teachers, but that he had a very successful experience in the third grade.

On Friday, the researcher returned to the school to conduct the experiment in some other classes. In the meantime, the principal had observed this boy's class for an hour. During the mathematics class. Tom questioned one of the rules in the textbook.

Instead of having Tom try to prove his rule and perhaps modify it or explain the textbook rule, the teacher became irate, even in the presence of the principal. She fumed, "So! You think you know more than this book!"

Tom replied meekly, "No, I don't think I know more than the book, but I'm not satisfied about this rule."

To get on safer ground, the teacher then had the class solve problems in their workbook. Tom solved the problems easily and about as rapidly as he could read them. This too was upsetting to the teacher. She couldn't understand how he was getting the correct answer and demanded that he write down all of the steps he had gone through in solving each problem.

Afterwards, the teacher asked the principal to talk to tom. The principal explained to Tom that many things came easy to him, such as solving problems, and perhaps he really didn't need to write out all of the steps.

The principal also explained that there are some other things like handwriting which came easier to others than to him and that he might have to work harder than some of the others on these things.

Apparently, this principal had been able to provide enough of the 'patron' role to permit him to keep alive his creativity up to this time. Soon afterwards, Tom's family moved to a nearby suburb and he was duly enrolled in a new school.

On Tom's very first day in the new school, the principal of the new school called the principal of the school from which Tom had transferred. He wanted to know immediately if Tom is the kind of boy who has to be squelched rather roughly. His former 'patron' explained that Tom was really a very wholesome, promising lad who needed understanding and encouragement. The new principal exclaimed rather brusquely, "Well, he's already said too much right here in my office!"

We can certainly sympathize with the new principal. He must support his teachers and maintain good discipline in the school. It is frequently difficult for a principal to play the 'sponsor' or 'patron' role. It is far more harmonious with the position of the school counsellor. Nevertheless, it is a role which administrators and teachers may have to play. Otherwise, promising creative talent may be sacrificed.

Help Him Understand His Divergence

A high degree of sensitivity, a capacity to be disturbed, and divergent thinking are essentials of the creative personality. Frequently, creative children are puzzled by their own behaviour. They desperately need help in understanding, themselves, particularly their divergence.

There are crucial times in the lives of creative children when being understood is all that is needed to help them cope with the crisis and maintain their creativity.

Let Him Communicate His Ideas

The highly creative child has an unusually strong urge to explore and to create. When he thinks up ideas, or tests them, and modifies them, he has an unusually strong urge to communicate his ideas and the result of his tests. Yet both peers and teachers named some of the most creative children in our studies as ones who "do not speak out their ideas."

When we see what happens when they do "speak out their ideas," there is little wonder that they are reluctant to communicate their ideas. Frequently, their ideas are so far ahead of those of their classmates and even their teachers that they have given up hope of communicating.

All school guidance workers need to learn to perform this function more effectively. They must genuinely respect the questions and ideas of children to sustain the highly creative child so that he will continue to think.

See that His Creative Talent is Recognised

Information from many sources indicates that much creative talent goes unrecognised. In studies at all educational levels (Torrance, 1960c), you will recall that over 70 per cent of those in the upper 20 per cent on tests of creative thinking would be eliminated if only an intelligence or scholastic aptitude test had been used. Therefore, the teacher/guidance worker must recognise the creative talent of the child at the earliest.

Help Parents Understand Their Creative Child

One of the most tragic plights we have witnessed among highly creative individuals stems from the failure of their parents to understand them. Frequently destructive or incapacitating hostility is the result of this failure. When teachers fails to understand highly creative children, refused to learn, delinquency, or withdrawal may be a consequence.

In some cases, the quiet and unobtrusive intervention of the counsellor offers about the only possibility whereby parents and teachers may come to understand them and thus salvage much outstanding talent.

Guidance workers need to help parents and teachers recognise that everyone possesses to some degree the ability involved in being creative, that these abilities can be increased or decreased by the way children are treated, and that it is a legitimate function of the home and the school to provide the experiences and guidance which will free them to develop and function fully.

Of course, these abilities are inherited, in the broad sense, that one inherits sense organs, a peripheral nervous system, and a brain.

The type of pursuit of these abilities and the general tendency to persist in their search is largely a matter of the way parents and teachers treat children's creative needs.

Guidance workers can, as I see it, help parents to guide highly creative children in two major ways. The first concerns the parent's handling of the child's unusual ideas and questions, and the other involves helping such a child become less obnoxious without sacrificing his creativity.

The school should help parents recognise that criticism—making fun of the child's ideas or laughing at his conclusions—can prevent his expression of ideas. The parents experienced eyes and ears can help the child learn to look for and to listen to important sights and sounds. The parent should stimulate the child to explore, ask questions, and try to find answers.

Many parents attempt too early to eliminate fantasy from the thinking of the child. Fantasy is regarded as something unhealthy and to be eliminated. Fantasies such as imaginative role playing, fantastic stories, unusual drawings, and the like are normal aspects of a child's thinking.

Many parents are greatly relieved to learn this and out of this understanding grows a better parent-child relationship. Certainly we are interested in developing a sound type of creativity, but this type of fantasy, it seems to us, must be kept alive until the child's intellectual development is such that he can engage in sound creative thinking.

Counsellors and administrators can be sympathetic with teachers and parents who are irritated by the unending curiosity and manipulativeness of highly creative children. Endless questioning and experimenting can be inconvenient.

Parents may not appreciate the child's passion for first-hand observation. Persistent questioning can be very annoying. A mother of a three-year old complained. "He wears me out just asking questions. He won't give up either, until he gets an answer; it's just awful when he gets started on something!"

Counsellors, teachers, and administrators can help parents recognise the fact that there is value in such curiosity and manipulativeness and that there can be no substitute for it. Parents should be encouraged to help the child learn to ask good questions, how to make good guesses at the answers, and how to test the answers against reality.

Most parents find it extremely difficult to permit their children to learn on their own—even to do their school work on their own. Parents want to protect their children from the hurt of failing. Individual administration of problems involving possible solutions to frustrating situations has shown that the imagination of many children is inhibited by the tremendous emphasis which has been placed on prevention.

Certainly teaching of all kinds of failure is important, but overemphasis may deter children from coping imaginatively and realistically with frustration and failure, which cannot be prevented. It may rob the child of his initiative and resourcefulness.

All children learn by trial and error. They must try, fail, try another method, and if necessary, try even again. Of course, they need guidance, but they also need to find success by their own efforts. Each child strives for independence from the time he learns to crawl, and independence is a necessary characteristic of the creative personality.

QUESTIONS FOR ANSWER

1. *Explain the legitimate concerns of educators for recognising Creative Talent of the Child at an early stage in education.*
2. *Explain the role of guidance to recognise the Creative Talent of the Child at the earliest.*
3. *'The role played to guide creative talents will not only ensure best career to the Child but it will lead to the progress and development of the nation' Justify this statement.*

24

Career Guidance: The Process of Identifying Creative Personality

Career guidance will be much more effective if one is able to identify not only the potentialities of the concerned person but also his creational talent, which may be inner aspect of his personality, therefore, this chapter is devoted to understand the process which may lead to identification creative aspect of individuals personality with a view to ensure best and most suitable career for the concerned individual.

INTRODUCTION

In the earlier chapter we have stressed the need to recognise the creative talent of the child at the earliest stage. The child with creative talent develops into a creative personality in due course of time, which is distinctive from other in the peer group, therefore, the society should identify his personality accordingly because his creative personality will be a vital factor in his creative achievement which will contribute not only for his personal good but for the good of the society.

There has long been general agreement that personality factors are important in creative achievement. Even in the matter of measuring the creative thinking abilities, there have been persistent and recurrent indications that personality factors are important even in test performance.

For example, Hargreaves (1927) hypothesized that the 'unknown' common factor found in his measures of imagination is cognative in nature. Guilford and his associates (Guilford, Christensen, Frick and Merrifield, 1957) have also been interested in determining what relationships might exist between measures of traits of temperament and motivation to measures of factors of ability within the areas of creative performance.

They found a large number of significant correlations between the non-aptitude traits and the measures of ideational fluency and originality. Ideational fluency appears to be related to impulsiveness, self-confidence, ascendance, greater appreciation of originality, and inclination away from neuroticism.

Those having higher originality scores tend to be more interested in aesthetic expression, in meditative or reflective thinking, and appear to be more tolerant of ambiguity, and to feel less need for discipline and orderliness.

PERSONALITY STUDIES OF HIGHLY CREATIVE ADULTS

There has been a great variety of empirical studies (Stein and Heinze, 1960) in which individuals identified as being highly creative on some criterion were contrasted with comparable individuals on personality measures derived from traditional personality tests such as the Minnesota Multiphasic Personality Inventory, Thematic Apperception Test, Rorschach and others.

The following list of characteristics differentiate highly creative persons from less creative ones:

1. Accepts disorder,
2. Adventurous,
3. Strong affection,
4. Altruistic,
5. Awareness of others,
6. Always baffled by something,
7. Attracted to disorder,
8. Attracted to mysterious,
9. Attempts (difficult jobs (sometimes too difficult),
10. Bashful outwardly,
11. Constructive in criticism,
12. Courageous,
13. Deep and conscientious conventions,
14. Defies conventions of courtesy,
15. Defies conventions of health,

16. Desires to excel,
17. Determination,
18. Differentiated value-hierarchy,
19. Discontented,
20. Disturbs organisation,
21. Dominant (not in power sense),
22. Emotional,
23. Emotionally sensitive,
24. Energetic,
25. A fault-finder,
26. Doesn't fear being thought 'different',
27. Feels whole parade is out of step,
28. Full of curiosity,
29. Appears haughty and self-satisfied at times,
30. Likes solitude,
31. Independence in judgment,
32. Independent in thinking,
33. Individualistic,
34. Intuitive,
35. Industrious,
36. Introversive,
37. Keeps unusual hours,
38. Lacks business ability,
39. Makes mistakes,
40. Never bored,
41. Nonconforming,
42. Not hostile or negativistic,
43. Not popular,
44. Oddities of habit,
45. Persistent,
46. Becomes preoccupied with problem,
47. Preference for complex ideas,
48. Questioning,
49. Radical,
50. Receptive to external stimuli,
51. Receptive to ideas of others,
52. Regresses occasionally,
53. Rejection of suppression as a mechanism of impulse control,
54. Rejection of repression,

55. Reserved,
56. Resolute,
57. Self-assertive,
58. Self-starter,
59. Self-aware,
60. Self-confident,
61. Self-sufficient,
62. Senses of destiny,
63. Sense of humour,
64. Sensitive to beauty,
65. Shuns power,
66. Sincere,
67. Not interested in small details,
68. Speculative,
69. Spirited in disagreement,
70. Strives for distinct goals,
71. Stubborn,
72. Temperamental,
73. Tenacious,
74. Tender emotions,
75. Timid,
76. Thorough,
77. Unconcerned about power,
78. Somewhat uncultured, primitive,
79. Unsophisticated, naive,
80. Unwilling to accept anything on mere say-so,
81. Visionary,
82. Versatile,
83. Willing to take risks, and
84. Somewhat withdrawn and quiescent.

NEW AND EXISTING INSTRUMENTS FOR IDENTIFYING CREATIVE PERSONALITIES

In his (the researcher Mr. E. Paul Torrance of Minnesota University) opinion, present instruments for personality study are not suitable for use in guiding the creative development of either children or adults. Instruments built upon the best knowledge now available concerning the problems, development, and adjustment of creative individuals are needed.

In the meantime, however, teachers and practicing counsellors will probably have to accept creatively the limitations of existing instruments, observational data, and the like. As a researcher, however, I shall turn my own energies towards the search for new instruments.

Creativity research has yielded results which provide counsellors with some very useful guides for maximizing the usefulness of existing instruments such as the Strong Vocational Interest Blank, the Allport-Vernon-Lindzey Study of Values, and the Minnesota Multiphasic Personality Inventory.

Some of the most useful research findings involving these instruments come from the studies of MacKinnon (1960) and his associates at the University of California Institute for Personality Assessment and Research.

A finding obtained in their first study of graduate students and repeatedly confirmed in investigations of other groups is that individuals who rated high on originality reveal a characteristic pattern of scores on the Strong Vocational Interest Blank.

The more original subjects, with slight variations from sample to sample, rate high on such scales as architect, psychologist, author-journalist, and specialization level; and low scores on such scales as purchasing agent, office man, banker, farmer, carpenter, veterinarian, policeman, and mortician.

Mac-Kinnon interprets these findings as indicating that creative individuals are less interested in small details and the practical and concreate aspects of life, and more concerned with meanings, implications, and symbolic equivalents of things and ideas.

A consistent finding from the use of the Minnesota Multiphasic Personality Inventory occurs in the realm of sexual identification and interests. All of MacKinnon's highly creative male groups show unusually high peaks on the Masculinity-Feminity Scale. For example, he found a mean standard score of 72 for his group of creative architects. These creative men were not characterised by markedly effeminate manner or appearance.

MacKinnon reports that in applying an adjective check list to describe these men, his staff frequently checked both 'masculine' and 'feminine.' They showed an openness to their feelings and emotions, a sensitive awareness of self and others, and wide-ranging interests, many of which are regarded as feminine in our culture.

In one of Minnesota studies (Torrance, 1959c) involving the 1959 Summer Guidance Institute, an interesting supplementary result was obtained. Beginning with the male counsellors having standard scores of 55 or above on the Masculinity-Feminity Scale, the researcher identified two patterns: an independent pattern involving low social introversion, high manic and high psychopathic deviate, and a dependent pattern involving high scores on the neurotic triad and psychasthenia.

ASSESSMENT OF CREATIVE MOTIVATIONS

Personal-Social Motivation Inventory

Although the researcher drew items from many sources and constructed some of our own, we relied most heavily upon the earlier work of the Runners (Runner Associates, 1954; Runner, 1954). Early in their work with the *Runner Studies of Attitude Patterns*, they devised a scale which they originally labelled "Creative Attitude." Later they incorporated it into their Individualist scale.

Although they have accumulated a wealth of evidence of validity in industrial and educational situations, they have not yet published any of these interesting data.

Kenyon Runner (1954) has, however, characterised the individualist pattern in a way that is interesting. He lists the following as being the more common and observable attributes of the individualist:

1. Seeks change and adventure. Any system he follows will be his own system.
2. Inclined to sloppiness and disorganisation. May give meticulous attention to things important to him personally.
3. Tendency not to plan activities, inclined to wait for developments, and changes plans quickly. Doesn't expect to be able to predict in detail and probably won't try.
4. Questions rules and authority.
5. Inclined to be chummy with strangers, not confining social activity to any certain groups. May talk too much or refuse to talk if he is interested in something else.

6. Thinks of people as individuals; is tolerant and open-minded and has faith in goodness of people as individuals.
7. Holds conformists in some disdain.
8. Disciplines himself to accomplishment of specific results; acts impulsively and fails to stick to any one course of action.

Following leads from the Runners and from the theoretical formulation of Tumin (1953), the researchers assembled a 189-item inventory entitled Personal-Social Motivation Inventory.

Tumin (1953), researchers hypothesized five motivations inimical to creative productivity: an excessive quest for certainty, power, meaning, and social relations, and pathological rejection of social relations.

The items in this Inventory require 'True' or 'False' responses in terms of the subject's present attitudes and motivations. The following are examples of items in the Creative Attitude Scale.

I enjoy trying out a hunch just to see what will happen.

I like to work on problems in which the outcome is unpredictable.

I feel that it is always wiser to stick to the tried and true way of doing things.

A variety of studies are underway with adults and the items are being adapted for use with children and adolescents. Already teachers ranking in the upper half on the Creative Attitude Scale have their pupils engage in a larger number of creative activities in grades three through six than their colleagues, and that their pupils show high scores on this scale.

DISCREPANCY BETWEEN "WILL DO" AND "CAN DO"

Educational and vocational counsellors have always been harried by the discrepancy between what people *can do* and what they *will do*. This problem is accentuated when we attempt to predict creative behaviour; the "will do" becomes even more important than in ordinary predictions.

Counsellors have for a long time sought to improve the usefulness of measures of capacity by combining with them measures of motivation—interests, needs, wants. Some have sought assistance from various indicators of mental health, attempting to correct the crippling effects of maladjustment. The research proposes another concept for increasing ability to predict what individuals *will do* and in helping them achieve what they *can do*—the concept of risk-taking or testing the limits.

McClelland (1956) explored a similar idea in his paper at the 1955 Utah conference on the identification of creative scientific talent. He attempted to make a case for the hypothesis that the successful scientist, like the successful salesman or business entrepreneur, has a higher need for achievement, in part because high achievement motivation will predispose him to take moderate calculated risks in which the success or failure of the enterprise will depend upon his own efforts.

Holland (1961) in his studies for the National Merit Scholarship Corporation developed some similar ideas and is experimenting with a revision of the Torrance-Ziller measure of risk-taking tendencies in predicting the performance of scholarship winners.

Holland takes some of his leads from research findings which suggest that creative performance at the high school level occurs more frequently among students who are independent, intellectual, expressive, asocial, consciously original, and who aspire for future achievement.

On the basis of the negligible relationship he found between academic aptitude and creative performance at a high aptitude level, Holland concluded that we must use non-intellectual criteria in the selection of students for scholarships and fellowships. He feels that further efforts to improve existing intellectual measures are likely to be unproductive.

PERSONALITY STUDIES OF HIGHLY CREATIVE CHILDREN

In general the study of the personalities of highly creative children has not been considered a very worthwhile or attractive pursuit. Investigators have been afraid that children identified as creative may not develop into creative adults. Given the creative adult, we may obtain some fairly reliable information about his childhood experiences, but we can never study his personality as a child.

When fellow investigators criticize my interest in the study of the personalities of highly creative children, I assure them that I know fully well that many of these children will not be creative adults.

In fact, I know that many of the children who stand out as highly creative in the second and third grades, especially boys, will not be highly creative as fourth graders. Some of them will never again show a high degree of creativity. Thus, I am interested in studying the personalities of children to see if I can find in them the trends, elements, or characteristics which lead to the eventual abandonment of this talent.

Two studies (Weisberg and Springer, 1961; Torrance, 1959) provide a wealth of leads concerning the personality of the highly creative child and his problems. The most thoroughgoing of the two is the one by Weisberg and Springer (1961) of thirty-two gifted fourth graders and their families. The criterion tests used included the Ask-and-Guess Test, Tin Can Uses, and Circles from the Minnesota battery.

Their personalities were studied through psychiatric interviews. Rorschachs, and the Draw-a-Family technique. Judgments of the children and their parents by the psychiatrists on the basis of the interviews were made on six-point scales. Various studies express the following:

From the statistical analysis of the comparative data, three personality characteristics stand out as differentiating the highly creative children from less creative but 0equally intelligent children. First, the highly creative children have a reputation for having wild or silly ideas, especially the boys.

Their teachers and peers agree on this point. Second, their work is characterised by the production of ideas "off the beaten track, outside the mold."

This comes out as a highly differentiating characteristic both when we use the number of non-essential details in the drawings, and when we use the number of unique or unusual details.

Third, their work is characterised by humour, playfulness, relative lack of rigidity, and relaxation. This provides an interesting confirmation of the findings described above by Weisberg and Springer (1961) on the basis of psychiatric interviews and by Getzels and Jackson (1959).

The three characteristics which emerge strongly would appear to be of considerable importance to teachers and counsellors in their efforts to understand and guide the highly creative youngster.

In spite of the fact that these children have many excellent ideas, they readily achieve a reputation for having silly, wild, or naughty ideas. It is difficult to determine what effect this derogation of their ideas has on their personality development, as well as upon the future development of their creative talents.

The uniqueness of their ideas makes this a really difficult problem, because there are no standards, as in answer books and manuals. Although their humour and playfulness may win some friends for them, it does not always make them "easier to live with."

In fact, it may make their behaviour even more unpredictable than otherwise and this probably makes their presence in a group upsetting. Recognizing and understanding these three characteristics are important because each apparently has an important role in making an individual 'creative.'

PERSONALITY STUDIES OF HIGHLY CREATIVE ADOLESCENTS

Two studies of the personalities of highly creative adolescents may be cited to supplement the two childhood studies just described. One is the study by Getzels and Jackson (1958, 1959, 1960, 1961) in which they differentiated highly creative adolescents (grades seven through twelve) from highly intelligent ones. The other is an exploratory investigation of the personalities of gifted adolescent artists (eleventh and twelfth grades) by Hammer (1961).

It will be recalled that in the Getzels-Jackson study the school achievement of the highly creative and the highly intelligent groups was equally superior to the total school population from which they were drawn. This was in spite of the fact that there was a 23-point difference in average IQ between them.

The high IQ student was rated as a more desirable student than the average student but the highly creative was not. On their fantasy productions, the more creative made significantly greater use of stimulus-free themes, unexpected endings, humour, and playfulness.

On the basis of these findings, Getzels and Jackson have suggested that an essential difference between the two groups is the creative adolescent's ability to produce new forms and to risk joining together elements usually seen as independent and dissimilar.

They also suggested that the creative adolescent seems to enjoy the risk and uncertainty of the unknown. The high IQ adolescent prefers the anxieties and delights of 'safety' to the anxieties and delights of growth. These differences are reflected in the occupational choices of the two groups.

Sixty-two per cent of the creatives chose unconventional occupations, such as adventurer, inventor, writer, and the like. Only 16 per cent of the highly intelligent subjects chose such occupations; 84 per cent of them chose 'conventional' occupations, such as doctor, lawyer, engineer.

Getzels and Jackson (1961) also interviewed rather intensively the parents of their two groups of subjects. The parents of the high IQ students tended to recall greater financial difficulties during their childhoods and at the present expressed greater real or imagined personal insecurity than those of the highly creatives.

The parents of the high IQ adolescents also seemed to be more 'vigilant' with respect to their children's behaviour and their academic success. They are more critical of both their children and the school than are the parents of the highly creative adolescents.

The high IQ parents focus their concern on immediately visible virtues such as cleanliness, good manners, and studiousness. The parents of the creatives focus theirs on less visible qualities such as the child's openness to experience, his values, and his interests and enthusiasm.

In the second study by Hammer (1961) of the personalities of gifted adolescent artists, an attempt was made to contrast the genuinely creative with the merely facile personality. In an intensive study of eighteen high school artists in a workshop, five were identified as "truly creative" and five as 'merely facile."

On the basis of elaborate psychological studies, Hammer found that the "truly creatives" differed from the "merely faciles" in that they exhibited deeper feelings, greater original responsiveness, preference for the observer role over the participant role, stronger determination and ambition, integration of feminine and masculine components, greater independence, rebelliousness, and self-awareness, stronger needs for self-expression, greater tolerance for discomfort, and a fuller range of emotional expression.

Teachers, counsellors, and administrators should recognise that highly creative adolescents may exhibit vastly different personalities in school and in the rest of their world, as exemplified in the biographies of some of our most creative scientists and inventors.

It is heart-breakingly apparent in the stories of many of the highly creative adolescents about whom parents and teachers write and/or tell me. For example, the mother of one rather obviously creative boy of thirteen years has described to me in beautiful contrast her son as he is at school and as he is in the rest of his world.

After a steadily declining academic record, he was retained in the seventh grade "to teach him a lesson." His teachers, counsellors, and principals have described the boy to his parents as extremely bright, very bored, lazy, daydreaming, and very withdrawn but not rebellious. One teacher declared to the mother, "I'll make him work, if I have to break his spirit to do it—and ridiculing and shaming him is the only way with children like him."

He is not permitted to participate in science clubs because he doesn't have a 'B' average. Instead, the principal insists that he play football and be "better rounded." The boy whom the parents and others outside of school sees "never daydreams; loves to learn and is always getting books from the library; works hard, many times almost collapsing from trying to work out an experiment late into the night."

In the world outside of school, "he has energy enough for ten people" and has an outgoing, bubbling personality and a keen sense of humour. He talks of quitting school when he is sixteen and his parents wonder if this might possibly be his best chance to get out of the trap in which he finds himself.

QUESTIONS FOR ANSWER

1. *Give stories of two personality studies of highly creative adolescents as mentioned in this chapter, in your own words.*
2. *Explain the methods of assessment of creative motivations.*
3. *Explain the methods of study of personality studies of highly creative children.*
4. *Write a note on the characteristics of highly creative person, which differentiate them from less creative ones.*
5. *How do you evaluate the discrepancy between "WILL DO" and "CAN DO" in respect of determination of creative personality.*

25

Career Guidance: How to Face Problems of Maintaining Creativity?

Creative person being a social being under social influence or account of some other situations may drift from the original form of his creative personality, therefore, there is great need to face the problems of maintaining creativity of the creative personality. Hereunder, we will consider this aspect very briefly from the point of view of career guidance for better results:

INTRODUCTION

It is rightly said and believed that it is easy to achieve something than to preserve and maintain the same. It is more true in respect of creative talent because maintaining creative talent does not only need one's continuous and sustained effort but a proper sponsor or patron for a long period of time, hence, there is practical need of proper guidance for maintaining creativity of the individual concerned, because he being out of step from others in the social group faces many problems. Hereunder, we discuss the problems in maintaining creativity.

Inescapably, the individual who thinks of a new idea is in the very beginning a minority of one. Even when matters of demonstrable fact are involved, as in the Asch (1955) experiments, there are very few people who can tolerate being a minority of one.

Since creativity involves independence of mind, non-conformity to group pressures, or breaking out of the mold, it is inevitable that highly creative individuals experience some unusual problems of adjustment.

Thus, the highly creative child must either repress his creativity or learn to cope with the tensions that arise from being so frequently this minority of one. Repression of creative needs may lead to actual personality breakdown. Their expression leads to loneliness, conflicts, and other problems of adjustment. Since teachers, administrators and counsellors need to understand both types of problems.

PRECAUTIONS AGAINST DIVERGENCY

Teachers, parents, and peers feel threatened when highly creative children express their creativity. Some of the questioning, experimenting, and wild ideas are annoying. In many respects, however, the annoyance can be tolerated more than the threat which this creative behaviour poses. Adults do not know how to evaluate these unusual ideas or respond to the many questions.

Creative behaviour may be interpreted as aggressive or even hostile, and certainly it soon becomes just that, if ideas and questions are rejected. Thus, one of the problems becomes that of helping the creative child maintain his aggressiveness without being hostile, as Roarer had become.

This tale brings out another problem concerning the parents' expectation of counsellors and school psycholgists—the expectation that they will use some kind of magic. Frequently, counsellors, psychologists, and teachers are expected to play an aversive role.

Such a role is frequently expected of the mental hygiene clinic. Guidance workers must be alert to these expectations and prepared to play more positive roles.

About two-thirds of the stories about flying monkeys tell similar tales of conformity or of destruction. Some cultures, however, are more indulgent of divergency than others. Stories written by gifted children in special classes are far more hopeful in outlook than those of gifted children in regular classes.

In about seventy per cent of the stories of pupils in classes for high achieving children, the flying monkey is in some way able to persist in his flying. The stories written by children in a small Oklahoma town composed of Indians, whites, and a few Negroes also reflect this tolerance of divergency. In seventy-four per cent of their stories, the flying monkey succeeds.

The following story by a gifted Long Island boy illustrates some of the dynamics of the plight of the gifted child who lacks some quality regarded as highly important by his society. It especially communicates the depth of the anxiety of the parents under such conditions.

Freddy was born in a cave in Rocky Mountains. He lived there with his mother, father and his ten brothers and sisters.

The first thing a lion is supposed to learn is how to roar. His ten brothers and sisters learned how to roar very well, but Freddy wouldn't roar because he was a friendly lion. First, his mother tried to teach him. She tried and tried for ten days, after which she fainted. Then his father tried to teach him for eight months, but still Freddy wouldn't roar. So finally they gave up and ordered Freddy to go and find another place to live...

> When freddy walked into the jungle all of the animals ran and hid in the bushes. Freddy was very sad. He tried to make friends with the monkeys but they ran up the trees. He tried to make friends with the zebras but they ran away as fast as possible. All of a sudden there was complete silence as all of the animals waited for Freddy to roar. When he didn't roar, the animals were very surprised. Slowly one by one the animals came out from behind the bushes and down from the trees and started to form a circle around Freddy. Then one of the animals brought up enough courage to go over and touch him. When Freddy didn't do anything, the animals went over to Freddy and started to play with him. Freddy and the animals became good friends. Until this day, Freddy hasn't roared.

This story may possibly reflect the childlike optimism that it is possible to escape the rejection of divergency.

MAINTAINING CREATIVITY MAY ALIENATE FRIENDS

Many highly creative children find quite early that the use of their creative talents alienates them from their friends. In the stories of flying monkeys, the exercise of the talent for flying quite frequently brings about isolation, warnings by parents that the other animals won't like the monkey, and the like. In the stories of silent lions, many are afraid to roar because they will either scare away their friends or alienate others in their society. The following such story illustrates a number of the dynamics of this problem:

> One sunny day, the king of the jungle and his wife were blessed with a cub. The king was so happy that he even gave cigars to his enemy, the monkey. Many animals came to see the cub.

The cub was growing and his parents were getting worried. He was five and he hadn't roared once. His father decided that he was old enough to go to school and then may be he would roar. The king hired a teacher to teach his son, John, who would soon rule the jungle. John did fine in arithmetic, spelling, and other subjects. But in roaring class he refused to roar! His teacher was startled; his mother fainted; and his father was amazed.

That night John and his father went into the study to talk. John's father asked, "Why won't you roar, son?"

John replied, "it scares all of the animals." John then told of his adventure when he was two years old. He had roared his loudest. He saw the monkeys and the other animals he had wanted to be his friends with run away. His father understood and told him that he should learn to roar louder to scare the bad animals. John said that he would make the bad good without roaring. A creative talent child may behave like this.

CREATIVE CHILDREN MAY NOT BE WELL-ROUNDED

The highly creative child is likely to have lagged in some phase of his development. Many investigators in a variety of fields have been disappointed in finding that outstanding individuals in the field under study are not well-rounded, "all-American" boys. For example, verbal abilities frequently will be below some of their other abilities. They may even have difficulty in learning to read or write.

Perhaps the most inventive and imaginative child we have tested is a boy who has had unusual difficulty in learning to read, yet his store of information and his ability to use it imaginatively in solving problems and developing ideas is fantastic.

Because verbal skills are highly valued in our society, tremendous pressures are placed on children to be "well-rounded" in this area. The relentlessness of these pressures is symbolized in many of the stories about lions that won't roar, ducks that won't quack, and dogs that won't bark. Some of the authors of the stories deplored the relentless pressures exerted by adults.

One referred to those who exert such pressures as "chasers and quackers." Some children resist pressures to become well-rounded because they feel that they can win and maintain respect in more acceptable ways than the commonly approved and expected ways of the society.

CREATIVE CHILDREN MAY DIVERGE FROM SEX NORMS

Our over emphasis or misplaced emphasis on sex roles and efforts to establish sex norms during early childhood and throughout the educational ladder makes many problems for highly creative children.

We have usually thought that this emphasis takes its toll only on the creativity of women. It has been pointed out frequently that rarely do women become scientific discoverers, inventors, or composers.

Over emphasis or misplaced emphasis on sex roles, however, does exact its toll on the creativity of both sexes and does create serious problems of adjustment for highly creative individuals of both sexes.

Creativity, by its very nature, requires both sensitivity and independence. In our culture, sensitivity is definitely a feminine virtue, while independence is a masculine value.

Thus, we the researcher may expect the highly creative boy to appear to be more effeminate than his peers and the highly creative girl to appear more masculine than here.

Roe (1959), Barron (1957), and I (1959b), have all cited evidence in support of this phenomenon. In our longitudinal studies we are finding interesting examples of children who sacrifice their creativity in order to maintain their 'masculinity' or their 'femininity', as the case may be.

This cultural block to creativity comes out in many places. The researcher first observed it in his Product Improvement Test in which children are asked to think of all the ideas they can for improving common toys so that they will be more fun to play with.

In the first grade, boys excelled girls on the fire truck, but girls excelled boys on the nurse's kit. Many of the boys refused to think of anything to make the nurse's kit more fun, protesting, "I'm a boy! I don't play with things like that!"

Some of the more creative boys, however, first transformed it into a doctor's kit and as such were quite free to think of improvements. By the third grade, however, boys excelled girls even on the nurse's kit, probably because girls have been conditioned by this time to accept toys as they are and not to manipulate or change them.

The inhibiting effects of sex-role conditioning also showed up in our experiments involving small groups working with science toys (Torrance, 1960b). Girls were quite reluctant to work with these science toys and frequently protested, "I'm a girl; I'm not supposed to know anything about things like that!"

Boys demonstrated and explained about twice as many ideas as girls in experiments involving these materials. We know already, however, that this situation can be modified significantly (Torrance, 1960b). In 1959, we found these phenomena operating quite strongly in one school. Later I had the opportunity to report these and other results to both the teachers and parents in this school. In 1960, we conducted some experiments in this same school in which we used a different but similar set of science toys.

This time, we found none of this reluctance on the part of girls; there was no difference in the expressed enjoyment of the activity of boys and girls, the mean performance of girls and boys was almost identical. In one way, however, the situation remained unchanged. The contributions of boys was more highly valued by peers than those of girls.

Apparently, the school climate has helped to make it more acceptable for girls too.

Another problem may be seen in the negative identification which apparently exists between Roarless and his father. Because of early, unpleasant relationships with the father, Roarless identifies himself as being play around with science things, but boys' ideas about science things are still supposed to be better than those of girls.

The social consequences of failure to achieve the behavioural norms associated with sex and social roles are well understood by children by the time they reach the fourth grade, if not before.

Thus, if roaring makes him like his father, Roarless is motivated to avoid roaring.

CREATIVE CHILDREN PREFER TO LEARN ON THEIR OWN

Many creative children prefer to learn on their own, but schools have been slow in providing such opportunities. Last year we conducted an exciting study in which we found that children would do a great deal of writing on their own, if properly motivated. In another (Fritz, 1958), it was found that gifted children in a split-shift school showed more growth in language development; science, and social studies than they did on a full-day schedule.

Only in spelling was there significantly less growth among the split-shift children (seventh graders). In still another, we found that children in a split-shift school engaged in a larger number of learning activities on their own.

Since we have generally assumed that children do not learn on their own, we have seldon provided them with opportunities to do so, learning situations left 'open' become quite excited about what would happen, if we should do so more frequently.

CREATIVE CHILDREN LIKE TO ATTEMPT DIFFICULT TASKS

Frequently highly creative children strongly desire to move far ahead of their classmates in some areas. They often make their teachers afraid that they are not 'ready.' Fortunately, however, educators of gifted children are rapidly revising many of their concepts about what can be taught at various levels of education. This terrifies many. The following recent headlines reflect such a fear:

"Caution urged in Changing Primary into High Schools"
"Can We Rush Primary Education?"
"Don't Turn Grade Schools into High Schools, Educators Warn at Parley"
"Reading for Kindergarten, Languages Too Soon Attacked"

Some of the panic may have been eased by a recent report of the Educational Policies Commission of the National Education Association and the American Association of School Administrators (*Contemporary Issues in Elementary Education*, 1960).

Bruner's (1960) exciting book, *The Process of Education*, should give educators some very useful guidance in working out this problem. Along with revisions about readiness, Bruner develops the concept of "structure of knowledge" and offers interesting ideas about intuition and motivation.

About readiness, he says, "Experience over the past decade points to the fact that our schools may be wasting precious years by postponing the teaching of many subjects on the grounds that they are too difficult... The essential point often overlooked in the planning of curricula... [is that] the basic ideas that lie at the heart of all science and mathematics and the basic schemes that give form to life and literature are powerful." For this purpose, Bruner suggests "the spiral curriculum," one that turns back on itself at higher and higher levels of complexity.

A common experience in the lives of many highly outstanding individuals has been their ability to cope with failure and frustration. Certainly, almost all highly creative scientists, inventors, artists, and writers attempt tasks which are too difficult for them. Had they not attempted such tasks, it is quite unlikely that their great ideas would have been born.

CREATIVE CHILDREN MAY UNDERTAKE DANGEROUS TASKS

In learning on their own and in testing their limits through attempting difficult tasks, creative children may also undertake dangerous tasks. This poses difficult problems for parents, teachers, playground directors, and school administrators who have responsibilities for the safety of children. I have frequently wondered if the solution to this problem doesn't lie in the technique of the parents of the jet aces of the Korean struggle.

We found that the parents of these aces both exercised more control and permitted more testing-the-limits and risk-taking behaviour than did the parents of the non-aces. They exercised control until skills were adequate and then permitted wide testing of the limits. Their children then could say in sincerity, "This would be dangerous for most boys or most pilots, but for me it is quite safe."

CREATIVE CHILDREN ARE SEARCHING FOR A PURPOSE

It has been said that most outstanding creative achievers seem to be possessed by a purpose and to be "men of destiny." Creative children need some purpose which is worthy of the enthusiastic devotion they seem capable of giving.

Perhaps this has some implications not only concerning the need for helping children discover their potentialities but for helping them achieve their self-concepts creatively rather than by authority.

We also need to help highly creative individuals accept themselves, remembering that they may even despise an outstanding 'gift,' if their giftedness makes them different from others. This makes far too many gifted children willing to emasculate themselves and consciously or unconsciously hide or destroy their talents.

CREATIVE CHILDREN HAVE DIFFERENT VALUES

Counsellors and teachers should recognise that the values and attitudes of the highly creative student are likely to be different from those of other students. The very fact that he is capable of a high order of divergent thinking, has unusual ideas, and is independent in his thinking in itself is likely to make his values and attitudes different from the norms of his peer group.

Some of these differences have been highlighted in the Getzels and Jackson (1959) study. They found that for the high IQ group, the rank-order correlation between the qualities making for adult success was .81 (showing great similarity); for the high creativity group it was .10 (indicating little or no similarity).

Among the highly intelligent, the correlation between the qualities they desired and the qualities they believed teachers favour was .67 (moderately similar); for the highly creative group, it was minus .25 (actually somewhat dissimilar). In other words, the highly creative adolescent desires personal qualities having little relationship to those he believes make for adult success and are in some way opposite those he believes his teachers favour.

Thus, counsellors and teachers should recognise that the desire to emulate the teacher is absent or weak among creative students. The desire to emulate peers is also weak.

SOME CREATIVE CHILDREN CAN'T STOP WORKING

Many people misinterpret the motivations of highly creative individuals who can't seem to stop working. Few creative individuals can stand the pressure of working only a forty-hour week. This is interpreted as an attempt to outdo others, rise to a position of power or favour, or such.

Creative individuals, however, do not usually care for power and some of the other usual rewards. The exercise of their creative powers is itself a reward, and to them, the most important reward.

The creative individual is unable to stop working because he can't stop thinking. To him, there is nothing more enjoyable than work in which he can use his creative powers.

CREATIVE CHILDREN SEARCH FOR THEIR UNIQUENESS

Counsellors and teachers may become irritated with creative children who seem to create problems for themselves by trying consciously to be different—searching for their uniqueness.

Barron (1958) maintains that creative individuals reject the demands of their society to surrender their individuality because "they want to own themselves totally and because they perceive a shortsightedness in the claim of society that all its members should adapt themselves to a norm for a given time and place."

One way in which the creative individual searches for his uniqueness is through his vocational choice. Getzels and Jackson (1960), for example, found that their highly creative subjects gave a greater number of different occupations and more 'unusual' or rare occupations than their highly intelligent subjects.

THE PSYCHOLOGICAL ESTRANGEMENT OF CREATIVE CHILDREN

From the foregoing it should be obvious that a large share of the highly creative child's adjustment problems are likely to be centered in his psychological isolation and estrangement from his peers and teachers. It will be no news to counsellors that peer groups exercise rather severe pressure against their most creative members.

In no group thus far studied have we failed to find relatively clear evidence of the operation of these pressures, though they are far more severe in some classrooms than in others.

When we select the most creative members of each sex in each classroom and match them for sex and Intelligence Quotient with other children in the same classroom, three characteristics stand out as differentiating the highly creative children from the less creative ones.

First, there is a tendency for them to gain a reputation for having wild or silly ideas. Second, their work is characterised by its productivity of ideas "off the beaten track." Third, they are characterised by humour and playfulness. All of these characteristics help explain both the estrangement and the creativity.

QUESTIONS FOR ANSWER

1. *Explain the nature of problems faced by creative talents in maintaining their creatability.*
2. *Write short notes on the following:*
   (*a*) *Creative Children and Values.*
   (*b*) *Creative Children and difficult tasks.*
   (*c*) *Creative Children's search for a purpose.*

PART VI
EMERGING WORLD OF WORK
CAREERS AND GUIDANCE

26

Emerging Careers in the New World of Work and the Role of Institutions of Higher Learning

INTRODUCTION

Life without work is no life. Any person without work is a burden on earth, therefore, work is considered as worship. Thomas Carlyle has rightly said that *"Blessed is he who has found his work; let him ask no other blessedness."* In the present work the concept and nature of work for better career has changed the road to this goal passes through institutions of higher learning. We will consider this aspect of career formulation, briefly as hereunder:

Work is said to be the central and essential part of man's life; it motivates him, sustains him and makes the living meaningful and purposeful. Without work, all life goes rotten. But when work is soulless, life stifles and dies. "If any would not work, neither should he eat". —*St. Paul*

Charles Winnick has written, "Work has a profound role in establishing a person's life space, emotional tone, family situation, object relations, and where and how he will live."

ROLE OF INSTITUTIONS OF HIGHER LEARNING IN THE WORLD OF WORK

We are living in an era where the traditional forms and processes of teaching and learning are changing rapidly. The ancient ideal of the institutions of higher learning being a kind of *cloister or an ashram* where seekers of knowledge could abstract themselves from the persistent problems of daily life, and concentrate on higher values and principles, is no longer meaningful.

One of the important aims of institutions of higher learning is to prepare the youth for work, to equip them for occupations, as well as prepare them for cultivated intellectual and human lives. The institutions of higher learning—the universities and colleges, come into contact with students in the formative stages of their life.

The students not only study the prescribed syllabus but also acquire the intellectual equipment with which they face the problems of life. One of the persistent life problem before them is to enter into the world of work.

In the new industrial and technological era, institutions of higher learning have to ensure that their products suit adequately to the needs of the market which constantly requires higher levels of education, skill development and professional specialisation. They have also to ensure that their products are employable.

Therefore, all levels of education, must quickly move to assume greater responsibilities for preparing men and women into the changed and changing world of technological work.... Technology has created a new relationship between man, his education and his work, in which education is placed squarely between man and his work. Technology today, in fact, dictates the role that education must play in preparing man for work.

It is also being increasingly felt that all engineering, technical and vocational courses need to be made industry-oriented. They say that courses should not be just institutions-based, rather the professional trainees should be given the feel of work.

The Education Commission (1964-66) recommended: "Practical training for full time degree students should commence from the third year of the course, and should be properly prepared and supervised in cooperation with the industry. Wherever possible sandwich type of courses should be adopted."

"For colleges and institutes of technology to become more concerned with the needs of the industry, research design projects sponsored by industry or government should be made a part of the curriculum."

It is a valuable advice which we can ignore at our own peril.

A clear linkage and working arrangement between education and the world of work is also necessary to control lopsided development of educational facilities. This would enable us to make education an effective instrument for occupational preparation of the labour market entrants and harness manpower resources effectively.

Future development of educational facilities in agriculture, science, engineering and technology and expansion of other vocational and technical courses needs to be so planned as to meet the requirements of employment market and the new technology.

There should be close coordination between the institutions of higher learning and the world of work due to the challenge posed by super-industrialism and tremendous increase in the rate of scientific activity which necessitate estimating and forecasting technical man-power requirements at all levels.

The development of science and technology, new fields of knowledge such as electronics, instrument technology, aeronautics and astronautics and nuclear power generation, and advanced research in various areas need careful planning for which institutions of higher learning and world of work must join hands.

We cannot get away from the idea that good higher education is one of the stepping stones to a good world of work. Institutions of higher learning have to shoulder the responsibility of feeding the entire economic system in a country, coordinate education with man-power requirements, estimate and forecast the future requirements, plan and adjust its plans and programmes to suit the present and emerging requirements. They cannot afford to remain in the ivory towers quite oblivious of what is needed for the changing world of work.

Expanding Nature of World of Work

There has been tremendous scientific development in our country during the past few decades. A number of scientific research organisations as the Indian Council of Agricultural Research (1929), The Council of Scientific and Industrial Research (1942), The Department of Atomic Energy (1954), The Defence Research and Development Organisation (1958) etc. have been set up.

These research facilities have created, during the past few decades, innumerable well-staffed hierarchies of scientific workers. These national laboratories are a source of gainful careers to qualified scientists.

A number of research organisations financed by private endowments, industry, professional associations, universities and centres of advanced learning, too, have been occupied with scientific research.

Typical examples are: The Tata Institute of Fundamental Research (TIFR), Mumbai; The Bose Institute, Kolkata; The Birbal Sahni Institute of Palaeobotany, Lucknow; The Ahmedabad Textile Industry's Research Association, Mumbai; The South Indian Textile Research Association, Coimbatore; The Indian Jute Industries Research Association, Kolkata; The Maharashtra Association for Cultivation of Science, Poona; The Sri Ram Institute for Industrial Research, Delhi, etc. All these are offering jobs to outstanding youngmen and women.

The tremendous technological and scientific development and growth is throwing up new occupational outlets. More and more persons are specialising in the rapidly expanding new fields like Nuclear Physics, and Nuclear Power Generation, Electronics Engineering, Computerisation, etc.

There has been tremendous technological development during the past three decades which has resulted in huge industrial growth and expansion.

Today, the country is producing its own supersonic fighter aircraft, heavy electrical transmission equipment, railway engines, sophisticated instruments and equipment, engineering goods and machinery, light and heavy armaments, etc. The country has, in fact, come a long way in the field of industrialisation.

Industrialisation has not only created innumerable new job opportunities, but has also thrown up new occupations, in the wake of development of improved technological processes and new raw materials.

Fuel and gas, petroleum, chemical and plastics, technologies and electronics, agriculture, forging and heat treatment, hydraulics and dam engineering and naval architecture, etc. have developed into distinct specialisations as a result of these developments.

Green and white Revolutions, too, have caused a number of occupational changes. Agriculture has been mechanised. It now requires application of technical know-how and use of new agricultural machinery and implements.

Agricultural research, development and extension work is offering employment to numerous graduates and specialists in various fields of agriculture as agronomy, agricultural botany/chemistry/economics/entomology/microbiology/marketing/extension/sociology, mycology and plant pathology, plant breeding and genetics, plant physiology, etc., horticulture, floriculture, fisheries, veterinary science and animal husbandry, animal nutrition, animal pathology, dairy science, warehousing, water conservation, soil science, poultry farming, etc. etc.

Agricultural revolution has also opened up new and steadily expanding avenues of self-employment—agro-service centres, customs service units, agro industries, rural industries, forest based industries, etc.

Increasing urbanisation has also resulted in greater housing, educational, transport and recreational activities and is throwing up innumerable service industries and occupations to cater to the demand of the urban population.

There is a steady growth in the number of workers in transport, catering and hoteliering, construction, education and service occupations.

The establishment and seemingly unending growth of local transport, electricity, water, milk, gas, petroleum and petroleum products and food and food products supply system and public health, sanitary and fire services are also the necessary off-shoots of urbanistion.

Then, there are numerous other 'social' services to tackle sociological problems arising from urbanisation; law and order, magistracy and judiciary, housing and slum clearance, town planning and development, delinquency and vagrancy, beggary and immoral traffic, unemployment, labour unrest and dispose, etc.—all these offer various career openings.

In addition to all these, the break up of occupations and jobs has created new occupations at the national level. Three decades ago, there were not many engineering occupations other than those of the popular civil, mechanical and electrical engineers.

The National Classification of Occupations (NCO), 1968 lists 82 occupations of engineers and technologists at the degree and specialisation level. And by the time, this book is being written, some new branches might have emerged.

It is obvious that the occupational pattern is fast changing. New occupations are emerging, some old ones are disappearing. It is obligatory for the institutions of higher learning to keep themselves posted with the latest information regarding the developments in occupational pattern, and the surplus and shortage occupations to avoid the imbalance in demand and supply; to predict the occupational outlook; to forecast the man-power requirements and plan and adjust the educational facilities accordingly.

Institutions of higher learning should also keep a close contact with the Directorate General of Employment and Training, Institute of Applied Man Power Research, Planning Commission, Directorate of Man Power, etc. to keep themselves equipped with research on occupational outlook, manpower forecasting and manpower projection and demands.

The Present Dilemma

The greatest dilemma of the present is that the contact between institutions of higher learning and those responsible for using their products is not effective. The institutions do not know where to modify their programmes in more functional directions.

The passive absorption of knowledge and the uncertainty of being able to use it in a career is unwelcome to young people of intelligence anywhere. The underlying unease amongst students does not help them to get the most from institutions of higher learning nor does it enable them to make a rational and constructive contribution to the economy.

There is also the lacuna as far as the products of institutions of higher learning are concerned. Employers complain that their products are inadequately equipped.

The graduates even in specialised subjects are unable to cope with their work without substantial further training, and graduates recruited for responsible jobs lack the qualities and skills of good management. Some ex-students also complain that they were taught much that is of no use to them!

Why close Liaison between Institutions of Higher Learning and the World of Work?

Close liaison between institutions of higher learning and the World of Work is needed to:

1. help students to understand the world of work and to appreciate where they are likely to stand in it;

2. help students to enter appropriate employment;
3. help employers to pick suitable young workers;
4. reveal the quantitative and qualitative needs of the world of work to students and the faculty;
5. bring the work of institutions into as practical a relationship as possible with the needs of the economy;
6. ensure the proper quality of products;
7. involve and associate employers in the work of the educational establishments which, in the end, will provide them with their key staff; and
8. check the imbalance between supply and demand in various sectors of economy.

GUIDELINES FOR BRINGING INSTITUTIONS OF HIGHER LEARNING AND THE WORLD OF WORK CLOSER

It is of utmost importance that institutions of higher learning and world of work are brought closer and there exists a two-way traffic between the two. Here are some suggestions to bring them closer.

1. *Industry-university interaction*: There is an urgent need for improving the mutual confidence at various levels between Industry and Universities. To achieve this objective, the following points of contact need to be established:

A. Representation should be given to people from Industry and Government—on various academic bodies like Board of Studies and Research Boards. Besides, individuals from each side should interact frequently, discuss and identify areas of mutual interest.

B. University science and engineering departments should establish visiting committees with strong participation of industrial research and development managers. These committees could advise on research in curricula, industrial openings for staff and post-graduate students, summer openings, etc.

C. There should be interaction between people from both sides in teaching and research programmes. Some courses should be tailored to the needs of industry and offered at the post-graduate level.

D. These courses should be over and above the core or basic courses which are a must for every post-graduate students. Talent from industry should be used for teaching such courses in situations where the industry has competent persons.
E. Competent persons from industry should be appointed as visiting professors so as to enable them to participate in the teaching programmes of the university.
F. Industries should be motivated to offer fellowships to post-graduate students who take specially designed courses or do thesis research in fields of importance to the industry.
G. Contracts in the major and medium size industry in the public and private sector can play very important role in developing progress of mutual interest and benefit. The universities should make available their facilities to industry at a reasonable charge.
H. Students should be allowed to work in industrial research centres/laboratories for post-graduate research degrees, provided appropriate facilities are available.
I. Universities should explore all avenues for securing sponsored research projects from industry in areas of mutual interest.

2. *Development and research:* The institutions of higher learning are supposed to conduct research of a *pure and fundamental* nature; the industrial establishments mostly conduct *applied* research. They can join hands to the benefit of both. For instance, an engineering college having certain facilities which the industry may not have, may even design and develop prototypes for the industry.

Universities and professional institutions are generally equipped with sophisticated apparatus which can be utilised for industrial advancement. They can carry out performance tests on the products of industries. The information collected can prove useful for applied research and fundamental investigations.

The institutions of higher learning may also enter into the field of technical and general consultancy and may take up assignments like job evaluation, analysis of wage structure, incentive schemes etc.

3. *Research on manpower problems and requirements:* Institutions of higher learning like universities, institutes of technology, various

institutes of research can undertake studies and research projects on behalf of government agencies, industrial establishments, government undertakings and also send the members of their faculty in deputation to serve in them for short terms.

The research in manpower requirements will enable them to make reliable man-power estimates, forecasts and projections and thus the cobwebs, which at present blur the understanding, can be removed.

Such type of studies is being conducted by a number of universities in foreign countries. These studies can be of immense use to manpower planners in our country also.

4. *Analysis of productivity, skill and occupational composition of labour force:* Institutions of higher learning can analyse the levels of productivity and manpower composition in various industries and their units. This will help build up reliable national estimates of productivity, skill composition and other related matters in the different sectors of the economy.

A detailed micro-analysis on productivity manpower mix can provide a firm and dependable basis for manpower planning. Such studies can provide valuable data regarding the ratio between technical and non-technical personnel in various sectors and levels of employment, the preparation of various categories of manpower to total employment in different sectors and the extent to which manpower availability has been affected by in and out migration of personnel.

The institutions of higher learning are in the best position to take up these studies.

5. *Collecting data about employment trends of their products*: India has risen to the second place in the world in terms of college enrolment, immediately following the United States. There are also significant changes in the pattern of enrolment of students. These changes are, to some extent, due to the tremendous demand for educational facilities that is building up in the country.

If institutions of higher learning are able to build up reliable statistics regarding the employment history of their alumni, it will be helpful to determine from time to time the emerging pattern of the utilization of educated manpower in the country. All this information will provide valuable guidelines for manpower and educational planners.

The regular flow of such information would serve as an early warning signal indicating the manpower categories which the economy is finding difficult to absorb.

6. *Formation of an apex body at national level*: An apex body at the national level in relation to manpower requirements should be set up at the earliest. This apex body may be formed under the aegis and guidance of DGE&T without prejudice to its autonomy. It may consist of the representatives of DGE&T, UGC ICAR, ICMR, NCERT, national laboratories etc.

The data regarding manpower requirements should be speedily circulated to college and universities for curricular adjustment and future planning.

7. *Creating a sense of dedication and commitment*: Institutions of higher learning can educate and train high level and middle level manpower; inculcate in their products a sense of dedication and commitment so essential for successful completion of plans and projects so ambitiously launched by the country.

8. *Redesigning the courses of studies*: The institutions of higher learning can make provision of new courses to meet the emerging needs, redesign the old ones to suit the new requirements so that the products of these institutions get the intellectual equipment to meet the contemporary challenge.

The employing agencies can also make conscious evaluation of the adequacy of their employers' educational qualifications with reference to job requirements and they may take the initiative and approach the institutions for formulating special courses, and modify the existing ones.

9. *Sandwich courses or work-experience*: The campus theoretical studies need to be supplemented with practical and mechanical reference and thus raise the theoretical appreciation of the tasks. There should be an effective link between institutions of higher learning and the vast world of work so that the institutions can give practical slant to their courses, and employers can help their workers gain the much needed theoretical base for their jobs.

The system of 'cooperative courses' under which a student will obtain practical experience by actually working in an industry for specified period should be extended to as many fields of technical education as possible.

10. *Compulsory vocational paper*: A compulsory vocational paper may be introduced in the colleges to pave the way for graduates to take the advantage of self-employment schemes.

Research projects—Institutions of higher learning can undertake research projects on problems arising in the various fields of world of work. Market research, application of modern mathematical techniques into business planning, ergonomics, industrial relations, incentive schemes, selection techniques, etc. might be taken up.

Such projects could produce results of great commercial value for which leading firms would be prepared to pay. Thus both the institutions and the students involved would benefit.

11. *Job studies*: Institutions of higher learning can take up job studies to help prepare the young men and women for the world of work. These studies should include information on what people do in their jobs, what decisions they make and what knowledge and techniques they use.

First hand studies of jobs can prove of immense use for familiarising the students with the world of work and ultimately help in proper choices.

12. *Employment surveys*: Institutions of higher learning can undertake employment surveys to find out:

(*a*) The number of students who found jobs within one year of graduation either by direct selection or through competitive examination;
(*b*) The number of students who found jobs after securing additional skills outside the institutes; and
(*c*) The number still unemployed in each category.

This information can prove of immense use to manpower planners and also enable the institutions to judge the extent to which the various kinds of courses command value in the labour market. It is likely that institutions may discover new intake and training needs and as a result feel the need for starting new courses. These surveys may also indicate to employers genuine concern on the part of the institutions to seek the real needs of the economy.

To make the surveys comprehensive and useful, discussions should be arranged with members of Chambers of Commerce—Rotary clubs, Lion clubs, etc.

13. *Entrepreneurial development courses*: These should be introduced at the college and university level with active cooperation of financial institutions and banks, government departments and promotional agencies.

14. *Inclusion of case histories of successful entrepreneurs in the courses*: Case histories of successful big, medium and small entrepreneurs should be included in the courses of studies to serve as beacon lights and motivate the young students for venturing into new paths.

15. *Self-employment cells*: Such cells should be opened in colleges and universities to provide students with necessary information on self-employment opportunities. In the changing economy, it is necessary that the youth is weaned away from illusive 'glamour' of white-collared jobs. A sizable fraction of enterprising youth need to be initiated into careers of self-development.

Efforts need to be made to make self-employment an acceptable and worthwhile proposition to our young men, identify the deserving cases fit to take up self-employment, educate them on how to proceed about the job of setting up a venture, help them through the cooperation of the concerned agencies in this sphere to prepare technically sound and economically viable projects, sponsor their cases to the banks for loan assistance, and guide them to overcome the teething troubles through effective follow-up after the commencement of venture.

16. *Continuing education*: Facilities for continuing education should be provided in the institutions of higher learning to those engaged in the labour force. Refresher courses, seminars, workshops, advanced courses may be arranged for the labour force like the engineers, technologists, scientists, medical specialists, etc.

Facilities should also be offered for persons in employment who desire to acquire additional knowledge which has been found necessary in the light of their experience in employment.

For example, an engineer may undergo an advanced course in Mathematics and a Mathematician that of economics. Besides, they can make provision for specialised courses to satisfy the requirements of the users of manpower.

17. *Setting up of information centres*: A chain of information centres in terms of procedures, policies, economic information, statistical data, technical library facilities should be set up in each state at the state headquarters, at the industry concentration centres, and colleges, so that the students could get the latest and most reliable information.

18. *Recruitment on the campus*: This is another way of establishing a close liaison between institutions of higher learning and the world of work. Employers may be encouraged to visit the institutions to interview students either to fill specific vacancies or to review applications from students interested in employment in their firms.

Facilities may be arranged by the authorities and the occasion might also serve for informal talks by the employers with heads of departments and discussions with the faculty, etc.

There is also the practice of visit to the institutions of higher learning by recruiting and selection teams of the leading firms to select boys and girls of recognised and proven ability. Thus, the most brilliant and meritorious get into good jobs without any difficulty.

19. *Meeting*: Meetings of staff of institutions and employers can also go a long way in bringing them closer. These will enable them to understand each others' problems and outlook, and to help them find ways of assisting each other.

If some students are also invited to these meetings, that can also prove useful as it will help them to understand the world of work and to appreciate where they are likely to stand.

20. *Career conferences*: These can also be or immense use in familiarising the students with the world of work. Talks by employers or by selected young employers (particularly ex-students of a college or university), 'live' exhibits of young people doing their jobs, facilities for individual students or groups to visit enterprises with suitable preliminary briefing and follow-up discussion, offer employers the chance to influence young people towards a sensible and appropriate choice of career and to open their minds to possibilities which they may not have thought of.

21. *Open days*: Institutions may throw their doors open to guardians and the public on some specific days in a term/year so that people could understand and know what they are doing. Employers of the different sectors could be special invitees, both direct and through their organisations.

QUESTIONS FOR ANSWER

1. *Write a note on the role played by Institution of Higher Learning in the development of the world of Work.*

2. *Discuss in detail expanding nature of the world of work and its impact on the working of Institution of Higher Learning and Career prospects of students.*
3. *Write a note on the guidelines for bringing Institutions of Higher Learning and the world of work closer and state how it will ensure better career for students.*

27

Forward Look: Prospects of Some Emerging Careers in the New World of Work Identified

The preceding chapter identified the nature of the present world of work, which is likely to be more complex and thus needing more and specialisation, therefore, the present career, scenario is likely to be phase of micro specialisation. Hence this chapter is devoted to the identification of prospects of some of the emerging careers in the new millennium.

The IT revolution has transformed our lives and opened a universe of opportunity. The 'E' phenomenon is prefixed to almost every aspect of our lives from E-Education to E-Business. Every career today has at E-perspective. However, while we cannot avoid being an E-person, let us not forget that people matter! A judicious blend of hi-touch with hi-tech will contribute to your success in any career.

INFORMATION, COMMUNICATION, ENTERTAINMENT (ICE)

This is the age of Information—Communication—Entertainment (ICE)

We are witnessing a Communications Revolution which has led to a massive expansion in broadcasting with the introduction of more television channels, direct broadcast satellites, T.V./Computer link ups, cable T.V. and rapid growth in both All India Radio and other broadcasting services particularly FM.

The unprecedented proliferation of satellite television channels and the entry of multinational media networks have resulted in a wide spectrum of job openings for directors, producers, engineers, technicians, journalists, writers, researchers, computer animators, actors, V.Js. anchor persons, news readers, script editors, videotape editors, set designers etc.

The popularity of the FM radio in the metros and the proliferation of radio stations has once again made careers in broadcasting an attractive proposition. You could work for the FM stations as a Radio Jockey (RJ), marketing executive, sound engineer or correspondent. All India Radio with its wide network and reach also offers a number of job openings.

Undoubtedly, the ICE careers are among the top careers of the new millennium. The reach of the electronic media is phenomenal, literally beyond one's imagination. Given the vastness of this field, it is hardly surprising that innumerable opportunities exist for anyone with the inclination to enter it.

You can enter mass communication, journalism as well as advertising from any subject stream. However effective communication skills, creativity and general awareness are vital.

SOME LEADING INSTITUTES/UNIVERSITIES OFFERING COURSES

After 10+2

- Xaviers College, 30 Park Street, Kolkata-700016 (Mass Communication)
- Xavier Institute of Communication (XIC), St. Xavier's College, Mumbai-400001 (Mass Communication)
- Sophia College for Women, Mumbai. (Mass Communication)
- Indraprastha College for Women, Delhi University, New Delhi (Mass Communication)
- Lady Sri Ram College, Delhi University, New Delhi (BA Hons, Journalism)
- Communication and Culture Media Education Programme. Loyola College, Madras (Mass Communication)

After Graduation

- International Institute of Information Technology
  Course name: M. Tech (Bioinformatics) Duration: 2 Years
  Selection criteria: All India: Contact International Institute of Information Technology Gachibowli, Hyderabad, Andhra Pradesh.
- Chitrabani, 76 Rafi Ahmed Kidwai Road, Kolkata-700016.
- Mass Communication Research Centre, Jamia Millia Islamia, Jamia Nagar, New Delhi-110025.
- Indian Institute of Mass Communication, Aruna Asif Ali Marg, JNU campus, New Delhi-110067
- Mudra Institute of Communication, Shela, Ahmedabad-380058.
- Satyajit Ray Film and Television Institute, F.M. By Pass Road, P.O. Panchsayar, Kolkata-700094.
- National Institute of Design, Paldi, Ahmedabad-380007.
  Course: Diploma in Communication Design with specialisation in Graphic Design, Animation Film Design, Video Programming.
- Film and Television Institute of India, Law College Road, Pune-411004.
- NIMT Institute of Mass Communication
  Course Name: Post Graduate Diploma in Audio and Video Journalism
  Duration: Admission 2004-2005 Selection criteria: Written Test, GD and Interview. Contact: NIMT Institute Of Mass Communication, GT Road, Post Office, Mohan Nagar, Ghaziabad, Uttar Pradesh.

Design

Design has become the cornerstone of every enterprise today. *The fashion industry* is flourshing with a global demand for Indian designer creations. In the field of design a creative idea is the starting point, the seed. If you can come up with a world class idea and actually execute it, you have a "pot of gold" says Professor Krishna Palepu of Harvard Business School. The prospects in the field of design are vast and include *product design, textile design, ceramic design, interior design, fashion design, fashion retailing, gem and jewellery design and communication design. The latter has three sub-divisions namely graphic design, animation film design and video programming.*

Designers should be creative, artistic and imaginative. They should be able to analyse problems, think in a clear logical manner and come up with original solutions.

SOME LEADING INSTITUTES/UNIVERSITIES OFFERING COURSES

After 10+2

- National Institute of Design, Ahmedabad, Paldi, Ahmedabad-380007.
  Course: Product Design, Furniture Design, Textile Design, Ceramic Design.
- National Institute of Fashion Technology, Hauz Khas, New Delhi-110016.
  Branches at: Bangalore, Kolkata, Chennai, Delhi, Gandhinagar, Hyderabad, Mumbai.
  Courses: Fashion Design and Information Technology (FDIT), Fashion Design.
- Sophia Polytechnic, Bhulabhai Desai, Mumbai-400026.
- J.J. School of Art, Mumbai.

After Graduation

- National School of Design, Paldi, Ahmedabad-380007.
  Course: Product Design, Furniture Design, Textile Design, Ceramic Design.
  Diploma in Communication Design with specialisation in Graphic Design, Animation Film Design, Video Programming.
- National Institute of Fashion Technology, Hauz Khas, New Delhi-110016.
  Branches at: Bangalore, Kolkata, Chennai, Delhi, Gandhinagar, Hyderabad, Mumbai.
  Course: Apparel Marketing and Merchandising (AMM). Garment Manufacturing Technology (GMT).
- IIT Mumbai
  Course: M. Des Programme in Industrial Design and visual Communication.

Services Sector

With Tourism as the fastest growing industry in the globalised world, *travel and tourism* related business as well as *the hotel and catering industry* require suitably trained professionals.

The recent opening up of the *Insurance sector* will result in a demand for many more personnel in this field as also in the case of *banking and investment*.

A more organised and quality conscious health care sector requires *hospital managers/administrators*. This has been identified among the top ten careers of the new millennium. Hospital Management courses are open to non-science graduates as well.

As the *"Education for All"* movement gains momentum in India and the world moves from the industrial era to the knowledge era there is a great opportunity for private enterprise in *Education and Training*. More and more 'quality' schools promoting excellence in education are being set up. They require committed teachers and principals whose salaries are enviable!

IT enabled services 'outsourced' services like tele-shopping centres, medical transcription, maintenance of data bases, insurance claims processing and records for multinationals require thousands of English speaking computer literate graduates.

For a career in the Services Sector, you should have good organizational, communication and social skills along with the requisite professional training to do well in this sector.

SOME LEADING INSTITUTES UNIVERSITIES OFFERING COURSES

Hotel Management

After 10+2

- **National Council for Hotel management and Catering Technology**, Pusa, New Delhi, Training institutes in 19 cities.
  Kolkata Branch: P-16, Taralota Road, Kolkata.
- **Welcomgroup Graduate School of Hotel Management Administration** at Manipal, Karnataka.
- **International Institute of Advanced Studies**, EC 37 Salt Lake City, Kolkata.

- **Institute of Advanced Management, Hotel Management College**, AE-486, Salt Lake City, Kolkata.
- **The Maulana Azad Educational Trusts, Indian Institute of Hotel Management,** Assisted by The Taj Group of Hotels, Maulana Azad Educational Campus, Rauza Bagh, Aurangabad-431001.
- **Woodland College of Hotel Management**, Bangalore.
- **M.S. Ramiah College of Hotel Management**, Bangalore.

Insurance

After 10+2

- **University of Bombay**, MG Road, Fort, Mumbai-32, *Course:* B.A. in Acturial Science.
- **The College of Vocational Studies**, Delhi University, Sheikh Sarai Phase-II, New Delhi, *Course:* B.A. in Insurance.

After Graduation

- University of Kalyani, P.O. Kalyani, Nadia Distt. West Bengal, *Course:* P.G. Course in Acturial Science.
- Amity School of Insurance and Acturial Science, Noida *Course:* P.G. Diploma in Insurance Management (1 year) P.G. Diploma in Acturial Science (2 years full time or 3 years part time).
- I.C.F.A.I. School of Finance & Management, 52, Nagarjuna Hills, Punjagutta , Hyderabad. *Course:* M.B.A. (Insurance)-2 years (leading to the Certified Risk and Insurance Manager—CRIM (designation).
- Asia Pacific Institute of Management, New Delhi *Course:* P.G. Diploma in Insurance Management (1 Year), Certificate course 3 months.
- Narsee Monjee Institute of Management Studies, Vile Parle, Mumbai, *Course:* P.G. Diploma in Insurance.
- Jaipuria Institute of Management, Gomti Nagar, Lucknow *Course:* P.G. Diploma in Insurance Management.

Hospital Management

Some Medical Colleges have introduction Post Graduate Courses of Hospital Management namely, **All India Institute of Medical Sciences**, New Delhi, **Armed Forces Medical College** in Pune **Nizam Institute of Medical Science** in Hyderabad, Kasturba Medical College in Manipal and **Sher-I-Kashmir Institute of Medical Sciences**, Jammu and Kashmir. The minimum qualification is M.B.B.S.

Other Hospital Management courses for non-medical graduates are offered by:

After 10+2 (with PCB at plus two)

- Devi Ahilya Bai University, Khandwa Road, Indore-452001. *Course:* Bachelor of Hospital Management.

After Graduation (from any subject stream)

- Devi Ahilya Bai University, Khandwa Road, Indore-452001.
  Course: Master of Hospital Management.
- Tata Institute of Social Sciences, P.O. Box No. 8313, Deonar, Mumbai-400088.
  Courses: Master of Health and Hospital Management.
- Symbiosis Centre of Health Care (SCHC), Senapati Bapat Road, Pune-411004 (Maharashtra).
  Course: Post Graduate in Hospital and Health Care Management.
- Indian Institute of Health Management and Research (IIHMR), Jaipur 1, Prabhu Dayal Marg Sangarani Airport, Jaipur-302011.
  Course: Masters of Health Administration, Master of Hospital Administration.

SCIENCE AND TECHNOLOGY

Today as a *research scientist* you can have a rewarding career. Information and Communication systems are broadening the scope, accelerating the pace and increasing the synergy of scientific discovery and technological applications. It has also led to great improvements in medicine and engineering. *Hardware and software are developing at an unprecedented pace.* The *biotechnology frontier,* specially developments in the field of *genetics* has already achieved significant break throughs in agriculture and human health care.

Biotechnology could eventually eliminate food shortages, improve health and life expectancy. *Bioinformatics*—the convergence of telematics and micro-genetics will be a basis for a major jump in evolution. The biotechnology sector will be the driving force of the markets. Thus IT and the Life Sciences are fast converging into a single technological and economic force. Herein lies a vast career opportunity.

Some of the other key areas are:

- *Robotics*: the automation of dangerous and dull work is increasing in surgery, security, health care, space, mining laboratory and fast food.
- *Nanotechnology*: (machines whose parts are measured in millionths of a millimetre) promises to lower unit cost and spread the benefits of technology.
- *Neuroscience*: is one of the new interdisciplinary fields which combines cellular and molecular biology with physics, chemistry, psychology and physiology.
- *Cognitive Sciences*: related to neuroscience, this specialisation is less about brain biology and more about reasoning, behavior, language and logic.
- *Space research*: is generating an extraordinary number and range of inventions which have lowered costs of many technologies from satellite communications to medical diagnostic techniques.
- *Environmental Science*: The new millennium will witness a greater emphasis on quality of life of which health is a vital component. Therefore, environmental professionals will be required to deal with pollution of various kinds. Moreover, more and more industries are becoming environmentally conscious and giving serious attention to environmental audits which have become mandatory. Keeping these developments in view, the demand for environmental specialists is expected to grow.

In order to carry out any type of scientific work, you must be capable of clear logical thought with the ability to implement practical experiments and techniques. No scientific advance is possible without inspired thought and a strong curiosity to find out why something has happened or how it is possible to make it happen. This calls for a great deal of patience and accuracy apart from good written and oral communication skills.

Scholarships for Science and Technology

The HRD policy of the government as reflected in the new S&T policy is to encourage talented students of science to take up research by providing attractive scholarships and prospects for growth. If you are a topper in 12th Standard (within top 20 ranks of the Board/University examination or equivalent) and decide to pursue a research career in Science and join B.Sc./Integrated M.Sc. or an equivalent programme in my branch of science viz. Physics, Chemistry, Mathematics and Biology in any college/ University of your choice, you have an excellent opportunity to become an IISc Young fellow. If selected Indian Institute of Science (IISc) will continue partially towards payment of your tution fees and purchase of books. You will be invited to spend one month during May-June every year in the research laboratories of IISc and you will be paid travel and stay expenses. If you maintain a high academic record, you may be considered for admission to the integrated Ph.D./Regular Programme and IISc after you complete your studies. At the same time there is no obligation on your part to join IISc after B.Sc./Int. M.Sc.

After post graduation, if you are interested in Research, you can appear for the CSIR, UGC, GATE and Net examinations. The first two provide openings for *Junior Research fellowships* (JRF). After two years work is evaluated and you can be selected as Senior Research Fellow (SRF).

INFORMATION TECHNOLOGY

After 10+2

- Indian Institute of Information Technology (IIIT), Kolkata, Techno Campus, 12 Block-EP, Sector V, Salt Lake, Electronic Complex, Kolkata-700091.
- Indian Institute of Information Technology (IIIT), Language Technologies Research Centre, Gachibowli, Hyderabad-50001.
- Indian Institute of Information Technology (IIIT), Nehru Science Centre, Kamla Nehru Road, Allahabad-211002.
- Indian Institute of Information Technology and Management (IIITM), Gwalior, Gola Ka Mandir, MITS Campus, Gwalior-474005.

- Vellore Institute of Technology (VIT), Vellore-632014 (Tamil Nadu).
- Dhirubhai Institute of Technology, Ahmedabad.

After Graduation

- Indian Institüte of Information Technology (IIIT), Bangalore, 1st Floor, "INNOVATOR", International Tech. Pack. Whitefield Road, Bangalore-560066.

BIOTECHNOLOGY

After 10+2

- IIT—Kharagpur.
  Course: 4 years B. Tech. programme in Biotechnology & Biochemical Engineering.
- IIT-Delhi, Kharagpur & Guwahati.
  Course: 5 years integrated programme in Biomedical Engineering and Biotechnology.
- Don Bosco College of Science and Management Affiliated to Bangalore University, Wayanamac Education Trust, 475, 9th Main Road, 39-C, Cross, 5th Block, Jayanagar, Bangalore.
  Course: B.Sc. Genetics/M.Sc. Biotechnology.
- Faculty of Science, Andhra University, Visakhapatnam 530003 (A.P.).
  Course: 3 years B.Sc. in Biotechnology.
- University of Madras, Faculty of Science, Centenary Building Chepauk, Trilicane, P.O. Chennai-600005 (T.N.)
  Course: 3 years B.Sc. in Biotechnology.
- Osmania University, Hyderabad-500007 (Andhra Pradesh)
  Course: 3 years B.Sc. in Genetics.
- Vellore Institute of Technology, Deemed University, Veloore-632014.
  Course: 4 years B.Tech. programme in Biotechnology.

After Graduation

M.Sc. Programmes in Biotechnology. The entrance examinations are conducted by JNU, New Delhi for admission to 25 Universities including the following:

- Benaras Hindu University, Varanasi.
- Calicut University, Kerala.
- Devi Ahilya Vishwavidyalaya, Indore.
- Goa University, Goa.
- G.B. Pant University of Agriculture and Technology, Pantnagar (Nainital).
- Guri Nanak Dev University, Amritsar.
- Himachal Pradesh University, Shimla.
- University of Hyderabad, Hyderabad.
- Jawaharlal Nehru University, New Delhi.
- M.S. University of Baroda, Baroda.
- Madurai Kamraj University, Madurai.
- Panjab University, Chandigarh.
- Pondicherry University, Pondicherry.
- Poona University, Pune.
- Punjabi University, Patiala.
- Tezpur University, Tezpur (Assam).

Science and Technology Research: Some of the leading institutes are listed below:

- Indian Institute of Science, Bangalore.
- Agharkar Research Institute, Pune.
- Shri Chitra Tirunal Institute of Medical Sciences and Technology, Thiruvananthapuram.
- Indian Association for the Cultivation of Sciences, Kolkata.
- Jawaharlal Nehru Centre for Advanced Scientific Research, Bangalore.
- Raman Research Institute, Bangalore.
- Bhabha Atomic Research Centre (BARC), Mumbai.
- Variable Energy Cyclotron Centre (VECC), Kolkata.
- Tata Institute of Fundamental Research (TIFR), Mumbai.
- Saha Institute of Nuclear Physics, Kolkata.
- S.N. Bose National Centre for Basic Sciences, Kolkata.

Space Science

Space Science research is mainly carried out in the areas of astronomy and astrophysics, planetary atmosphere and aeronomy, earth sciences and solar system studies and theoretical physics. The activities are carried out mainly at •Physical Research

Laboratory, Thiruvananthapuram, • Space Applications Centre, Ahmedabad and •ISRO Satellite Centre, Bangalore.

Environmental Sciences

After 10+2

- Delhi University, South Campus, New Delhi.
  Course: B.Sc. (Life Sciences/Environmental Science).

After Graduation.

- Indian institute of Social Welfare and Business Management, Management House, College Square (W), Kolkata 700073.
  Course: Post Graduate diploma in
  Environmental Management.
  Energy Management.
- Jawaharlal Nehru University.
  Course: M.Sc./M.Phil/Ph.D. in Environmental Sciences.
- Indian Institute of Technology, Mumbai.
  Course: Master of Technology (M.Tech.)
- Salim Ali School of Ecology, Pondicherry University, Pondicherry.
  Course: M.Sc. Ecology.

Correspondence Course

- Indian Institute of Ecology and Environment,
  A-15, Paryavarhan Complex, Saket, Maidangarhi Road, New Delhi.
  Course: 2 years Post-graduate programme in Ecology and Environment.

BUSINESS MANAGEMENT

Future organisations will depend on *"intrapreneurial managers"* for their profitability. An intrapreneur is an entrepreneur within an organisation. Another emerging trend is *business consulting*.

We are witnessing a corporate boom which has pushed up the demand for management professionals. According to the Centre for Monitoring Indian Economy, there are 1,125 companies in India whose turnover exceeds Rs. 100 crore, comprising 74 banking companies, 30 financial services companies, 886 manufacturing companies and 135 service providers.

Their collective requirement for fresh management graduates from the top business schools is greater than the supply. The total number of entry level managers needed by corporate India every year stands at 2,735. The top 20 Business school produce only about 1,740 managers every year—resulting in a demand-supply gap of about 36 percent.

At the same time courses in business management have mushroomed across the country in universities as well as specialised institutes. However, the knowledge base and skills of the students they churn out leaves much to be desired. Thus it is advisable to pursue a management course in one of the top ranking business schools.

Business management encompasses a very wide occupational area. Moreover, the occupations are not confined to one industry but exist in all sectors of the economy.

Leadership qualities, resourcefulness, dynamism, an extrovert personality, interpersonal and communication skills contribute in a big way to your success in this field.

SOME LEADING INSTITUTES/UNIVERSITIES OFFERING COURSES

After 10+2

- Sukhdev Singh College of Business studies, Jhilmil Colony, Vivek Vihar, New Delhi-110095.
- Apeejay School of Marketing, 54, Tuglakabad Institutional Area, Next to Batra Hospital, Mehrauli-Badarpur Road, New Delhi-110062.
- Centre for National Economic Planning & Industrial Entrepreneurship.
  (Affiliated to the Indian Institute of Planning and Management), 133/4 Qutub Enclave, Phase II, New Delhi-110016.
- EMPI Business School, Campus: CSKM Educational Complex, Satbari, Mehrauli, New Delhi-110030.
- Guru Gobind Singh Indraprastha University, Kashmere Gate, New Delhi-110006.
- Mithibai College, Mumbai.

- Narsee Monjee College, Vile Parle, Mumbai.
- Jai Hind College, Churchgate, Mumbai.
- S.K. Somaiya College of Arts & Commerce, Vidyavihar, Mumbai.
- H.R. College of Commerce & Economics, Churchgate, Mumbai.
- Sydenham College of Commerce & Economics, Churchgate, Mumbai.
- International Institute for Professional Studies, c/o Devi Ahilya University, Taxila Campus, Indore (M.P.)-452001.
- Institute of Management Studies, Ghaziabad, KH-3; Kavi Nagar, Ghaziabad-201002.
- Amity Business School, Post Box No. 503, Sector 44, Noida-201301.

After Graduation

- Indian Institute of Management (IIM), Ahmedabad.
- Indian Institute of Management (IIM), Bangalore.
- Indian Institute of Management (IIM), Kolkata.
- Indian Institute of Management (IIM), Lucknow.
- Indian Institute of Management (IIM), Indore.
- Indian Institute of Management (IIM), Kozhikode.
- Xavier Labour Relations Institute (XLRI), P.O. 222, Jamshedpur-831001.
- Jamnalal Bajaj Institute of Management Studies, Mumbai.
- Indian Institute of Social Welfare and Business Management, College Square West, Kolkata.
- S.P. Jain Institute of Management & Research, Bharatiya Vidya Bhawan, Mumbai.
- Faculty of Management Studies, Delhi.
- Management Development Institute, Mehrauli Road, Sukhrali, Gurgaon-122001.
- Indian Institute of Foreign Trade, New Delhi.
- Mudra Institute of Communication, Shela, Ahmedabad-380058.
- Narsee Monjee Institute of Management Studies, Vile Parle, Mumbai.
- Institute of Management Technology, Ghaziabad.
- T.A. Pai Management Institute, Manipal-576119, Karnataka.
- Symbiosis Institute of Business Management, Senapati Bapat Road, Pune.

- IIT, Delhi.
- IIT, Mumbai.
- IIT, Bangalore.
- NITIE, Mumbai.
- Xavier Institute of Management, Bhubaneshwar.
- University of Punjab, University Business School, Chandigarh-160014.
- Goa Institute of Management, Panaji, Goa.

Law

Globalisation has increased the demand for *corporate lawyers*. A potential area for specialisation is cyber law. The expansion of internet has created the demand for cyber lawyers. Another emerging and potential area for specialization is biotechnology law.

Any legal system needs trained people who can understand and interpret it and give advice to clients. The laws are administered through the courts and offences are broadly divided into criminal (related to breaking of laws) and civil (disputes). Within each area there is a graded court structure. Apart from practicing as a civil lawyer or criminal lawyer, you can specialise in Business Law, Corporation Law, Environmental Law, Patent Law, Tax Law, International Law. Real Estate Law, Labour Law, Cyber Law etc. According to the Bar Council over 1500 lawyers enroll every year and the demand for lawyers is steadily increasing.

All legal jobs call for trustworthiness, discretion and integrity of character as well as a thorough knowledge of the language of practice. Those legal jobs which involve contact with the public or appearances in court require excellent communication skills. Most legal work demands close attention to detail alongwith an ability to think logically. The profession also calls for a knowledge of human nature and an understanding of the motives of human conduct.

SOME LEADING INSTITUTES/UNIVERSITIES OFFERING COURSES

After 10+2

- National Law School of India University, Post Bag No. 7201, Nagarbhavi, Bangalore-560072.

- University Law College, 1 Palace Road, Bangalore-560009.
- National Law Institute University, P.O. Box No. 369, Head Post Office, Bhopal.
- Symbosis Society's Law College, Senapati Bapat Road, Pune-411004.
- ILS Law College, Law College Road, Pune-411004.
- University of Calcutta, Department of Law, Senate House, 87, College Street, Kolkata-700073.
- Department of Law, University of Chandigarh, Sector 14, Chandigarh.
- National Academy of Legal Studies & Research University, University of Law, 3-4-761, Barkathpura, Hyderabad.
- The W.B. National University of Juridical Sciences, Aranya Bhawan, 10A Block, Salt Lake City, Kolkata.

After Graduation

After graduation the following law faculties are considered to be the best:

- Faculty of Law, Delhi University.
- University of Calcutta, Department of Law, Senate House, 87, College Street, Kolkata-700073.
- Law College, Pune.
- Govt. College of Law, Mumbai.
- Faculty of Law, BHU, Varanasi.
- Faculty of Law, Madras University.
- Faculty of Law, AMU.
- Faculty of Law, Allahabad University.
- Univ. College of Law, Hyderabad.
- Faculty of Law, Cochin.

NGO Sector

With the emergence of civil Society, governments are shrinking and their roles are being largely confined to regulatory activities. Development activities aimed at eradicating poverty are increasingly being undertaken by non-governmental organisations. Hence, specialisations in Social Work, Anthropology, Human Rights, Gender, Developmental Economics and HRD have good job prospects in the social sector.

Today, a degree in Social work is a much sought after professional qualification by those who wish to develop a career in the area of socio-economic development. In promoting developmental efforts, the strength of NGOs lies in identifying, targetting and meeting the basic human needs of grassroot communities as well as in mobilising communities. Thus social work as a career requires specialised skills in optimising a community's development with people's participation and in catering to the more vulnerable groups in society such as elderly people, those with physical or mental handicaps, children at risk and people who are mentally ill. Other areas of specialisation are labour welfare, industrial relations, family welfare, counselling services etc. Social workers are also involved in conducting research studies, data evaluation, project formulation, training activities as well as programmes of awareness of raising gender sensitisation etc.

After 10+2

After plus two you can opt for a Bachelor's in Social Work (BSW). This degree however, is offered by very few colleges/universities. Nirmala Niketan, Mumbai and Jamia Milia Islamia, New Delhi offer well known courses of BSW.

If you wish to train as a professional social worker it would be advisable to do a Masters degree in Social Work (MSW). This degree is open to graduates from all subject streams and is offered in over 30 institutions/university departments in the country to graduates from any discipline. The top institutes like the Department of Social Work, University of Delhi, Jamia Milia Islamia, New Delhi, Tata Institute for Social Sciences, Bombay hold admission tests/interviews.

After Graduation

- Tata Institute of Social Sciences Mumbai, Post Box No. 8313, Deonar, Mumbai-400088.
- Indian Institute of Social Welfare and Business Management, College square West, Kolkata.
- Jamia Milia Islamia University, New Delhi.
- Madras School of Social Work, Casa Major Road, Egmore, Chennai (Tamil Nadu).
- Delhi School of Social Work, 3 University Road, New Delhi.
- Institute of Social Service, Nirmala Niketan, New Marine Lines, Mumbai.

- Xavier Institute of Social Sciences (XISS), Purulia Road, Ranchi-834001, Jharkhand.

E-Governance

Electronics governance is what we are heading towards in place of bureaucracy and red 6 tapism. This will involve new styles of leadership, new ways of debating and deciding policy, a new way of listening to citizens and new ways of organising and delivering information and services.

It is anticipated that the *Alagh Committee* which is reviewing the selection criteria and examination pattern for the civil services will suggest suitable reforms.

SELF-EMPLOYMENT AND ENTERPRISE

There is tremendous scope of *self employment and enterprise* in all the above mentional areas. Working life-long or a lifetime employment—the choice is yours! What is important is to rise above stereotypes and select a career which brings out your creative best. This will result in job satisfaction, maximum contribution and career growth.

Note

1. *The careers enlisted and discussed in the preceding pages are just a tip of iceberg and thus only symbolic. The emerging careers are countless.*
2. *The names of institutions mentioned in the preceding pages as leading avenues of higher study for specialised courses of study are too just symbolic, because at present itself there are many more such institutions in each and every part of India and apart from these recognised names many more institutions are opening up, thus, bridging the gap between demand and supply.*

QUESTIONS FOR ANSWER

1. *Write short notes on the followings:*
   (*a*) *Careers in Service Sector.*
   (*b*) *Careers in Science and Technology.*
   (*c*) *Careers in Biotechnology.*
   (*d*) *Careers in Business Management.*

28

Some Low Profile Areas with High Profile Career Opportunity

The new world of work has transformed many low profile area into areas of high profile career opportunities. Hereunder, we will discuss, symbolically, only some of these areas for the benifit of career counsellors and job seekers alike:

CAREERS IN CERAMIC TECHNOLOGY

Ceramics now is not restricted to pottery alone but has moved on to many varied fields. Ceramic engineers design and develop products which range from a flower vase to the ceramic nose cones for missiles.

In the current scenario, many industries in the consumer goods sector depend on ceramic materials. These include bricks, cement, tiles, glassware, pottery, spark plugs. The electronics industry needs ceramics for electrical insulators, diodes, capacitors magnetic materials and computer memory packages.

Space technology needs it for high temperature tile insulation and composite materials. The aerospace industry uses ceramic spark plugs and the nuclear industry needs nuclear fuel rods.

Given the demand, ceramic engineers and designers seem set to make hay as their need is felt in all walks of life. Ceramics, in short, has application in any industry which uses heat-resistant materials.

Eligibility

A career in ceramics needs a background in Physics, Chemistry, and Mathematics, along with a degree in Ceramic Technology/ Engineering is the preferred qualification to work in the industry.

After Class XII with PCM, go for a four-year B. Tech. (Ceramics). It is also possible to do a Diploma in Ceramic Technology after Class X.

A Bachelor's degree in Ceramic engineering or materials science will only get an entry-level job. Some firms ask for a degree in materials engineering, physical chemistry, physics, or metallurgy if the under-graduate programme has included ceramics. For a job in R&D, a post graduation in ceramics in required. For top executive positions in administration or management, a doctoral degree in ceramic technology, materials science or business administration will help.

The Indian Institute of Ceramics, Calcutta offers a correspondence course while the Indian Institute of Technology offers a five-year M.Tech. degree programme. The Regional Engineering College at Rourkela offers a graduate engineering degree in ceramics. The Anna University and the Allagappa College of Technology conduct a graduate course in ceramic technology. The College of Ceramic Technology conducts a four-year Bachelor course in ceramic technology.

Personal Traits

Technical knowledge should be coupled with social and communication skills. One must have good communication skills an innovative outlook and problem solving skills. Gift of the gab will be an added asset when you have to build a rapport and interact with artisans, technicians, managers, production workers and customers. One should be a good team player and possess an innovative streak as well as a keen analytical ability, an eye for detail and design.

Job Opportunities

The industry usually has two types of workers—ceramic technologists and ceramic designers. The designers use sand and clay for basic ceramic materials, while the other hand technologists use materials produced by complex chemical processes.

Ceramic engineers are employed in industries producing glass, cement, enamel retractories, porcelain, iron and steel and in industries manufacturing special ceramics for power and nuclear energy projects, aerospace, R&D laboratories and defence establishments.

Ceramic engineers deal with research, development and design of materials and products. They specialise in specific product lines like glassware, electronic equipment, fibre optics, plumbing fixtures, bulbs, drain and sewer pipes and so on. Ceramic industries, nuclear energy ancillaries, electronics industry and the defence establishment are some of the places where the engineers find employment.

Ceramic engineering graduates begin as junior or assistant technologists. A technologist may advance to supervising engineer, chief engineer or plant manager.

The ceramic technologist engaged in research may be given increasingly responsible assignments with corresponding salary increases and may progress to positions such as supervisor, project engineer or director of research. Ceramic technologists are often challenged to develop innovative processes to create utilitarian ceramic items out of ordinary, inorganic and non-metallic materials. They find employment in research, product development and ceramic engineering companies, in telecommunication, medicine and refractory and cement industries, research institutes.

Many ceramic technologists work in the nuclear field, as ceramic fuel material make nuclear power generation possible. Ceramic technologists can specialise in whitewares (porcelain and china dinnerware or high voltage electrical insulators), structural materials (brick, tile, and turbine blades), electronic ceramics (magnetics, memory systems, and microwave devices), protective and refractory coatings for metals, glass products, abrasives, and fuel elements for nuclear energy. They use scientific knowledge to anticipate new applications to replace existing products.

Ceramic Designers are responsible behind the new products being released by companies and have to look for buyers' expectation with regard to functionality and aesthetic looks to win over competitors and get recognition for products. A whole range of products from automobiles to consumer durables, from transportation and large industrial vehicles to medical equipment and instrumentation are being innovated and upgraded by designers. Moreover, designers must be creative and artistic with a good imagination. To achieve maximum satisfaction, they should be able to express ideas through drawings, and must have good colour sense and appreciation of aesthetics. Ceramic designers can work with ceramic manufacturers, freelance or set up design studios of their own. Ceramic artists can display their work at galleries and exhibit centres.

Ceramic marketers either have their own retail or business outlets where ceramic products are sold. They form a vital link between the manufacturer and the customer. They often help the manufacturer decide the newest product range to be introduced in the market by gauging customer reaction.

Remunerations

Depending on the company, starting salary may range from Rs. 6,000 to Rs. 8,500 a month if you are a degree holder. If you are a diploma holder your starting salary will range from Rs. 4,000/- to Rs. 5,000/- a month. Life, health, and accident insurance and retirement benefits are usually offered to ceramic technologists on a contributing or employer-paid basis. Some employers also offer stock options, profit-sharing plans or pay annual bonuses.

Career Prospects

There is a shortage of ceramic technologists. To maintain a competitive edge in the market, ceramic companies will often hire ceramic technologists to serve in vital business and management areas. Since Ceramics are a part of almost all industries, one can get into any industry of one's choice. This is an area where one may find employment abroad too.

One of the top research projects of ceramic technologists is the development of a ceramic engine which would replace the present diesel, gasoline, and turbo engines.

This new engine would withstand extremely high temperatures, would be much lighter, would be more efficient, and would not wear out like metal engines.

Eastern Region

- College of Ceramic Technology, 73, AC Banerjee Lane, Kolkata-700010.
  B.Sc. (Tech.)—4 years.
- Indian Institute of Ceramics, C/o Central Glass & Ceramic Research Institute, Kolkata-700032.
  Correspondence course equivalent to B.Sc. (Tech.).

* University College of Science & Technology, 92, Acharya Prafulla Chandra Road, Kolkata-700009.
  B.Sc. (Hons.), B.Tech. Ceramics.
* Regional Engineering College, Rourkela-769008.
  BE Ceramics.

Northern Region

* Benaras Hindu University, Institute of Technology, Varanasi-221005
  B. Tech, M.Tech.

Western Region

* Indian Institute of Technology, Mumbai-400076.
  5 years Dual degree programme in M.Tech Ceramics & Composites.

Southern Region

* PDA College of Engineering, Gulbarga-5805102
  B.E. in Cement and Ceramics Tech.
* Anna University, Allagappa College of Tech, Guindy, Chennai-600025.
  B.Tech. Ceramics.

CAREER IN FISHERY SCIENCE

Fisheries aims at breeding fish, ensuring the continuance of genetic specie strengths, saving species from extinction etc. Scientific fish culturing not only improves the quality of fish but also meets the increased global demand for quality fish and canned foods.

The job involves working in laboratories besides working in fish farms. It involves assessing the impact of the change in habitat on fish.

A major branch of Fishery Science is Aquaculture—the farming of aquatic organisms (e.g., fish, aquatic plants, etc.) in natural or controlled marine or freshwater. Developing innovative technologies for use in aquaculture such as aerators, pumps, feeding equipment etc. also a part of it. Hence you would be responsible for developing new aquacultural species besides creating cost effective solutions in aquaculture. You will then market the products and even export them abroad.

Requirements

Fishery Science can be studied at the B.Sc. level after completing 10+2 with Biological Science, M.Sc. in Fishery Science can be done after completing B.Sc. in Zoology.

Personal Traits

A curious, inquisitive mind would help in research areas. The ability to come up with new advanced ideas. High stamina and energy levels, and being able to work in disagreeable weather conditions are other requisites.

Job Opportunities

Opportunities lie in Government agencies, State Departments of Agriculture and organisations such as the Central Marine Fisheries Research Institute (CMFRI), Recruitment to these institutions is through the State Public Service Commission. Private research companies in India and abroad are also entering this area with large investments.

Several corporate houses have also entered fish food processing and marketing, for which specialists in Fish Processing Technology or Fisheries Resources and Management are preferred.

If you have good research skills, then you can find employment in organisations such as the Central Institute of Fisheries Technology (CIFT), the National Fisheries Development Board and others. One can also get involved in supervision of fish research centres: Domestic and export marketing; Research and preservation of marine life; Hatchery Management etc.

Remuneration

Starting salary ranges from Rs. 5,000-7,000 a month. Government jobs don't offer much growth but stability is provided that is not seen in the fish farming industry.

Research positions in private firms are lucrative and range from Rs. 18,000-20,000 per month. But these are usually reserved for doctorate holders with experience.

Career Prospects

India is the fourth largest shrimp supplier to the US. India holds the seventh position in the world in fish exports. But the fact is that agriculture is not considered hot and fishery science is almost unheard of.

CAREERS IN OCEANOGRAPHY

Oceanography is the study of the seas, its coastlines, coastal waters and the ocean bed. An oceanographer collects and studies data of ocean waters through waves, currents, tides, marine life, mineral and oil deposits in the ocean bed. "The information is used for preparing maps, charts and graphs. He uses high-tech devices, such as satellite sensors and acoustic measurement for under water study," said Prof. Mayank Singh, a marine biologist.

Different Fields: Oceanography can be divided into:

Physical Oceanography: It deals with mathematical formulations to explain changes taking place in oceans.

Geological Oceanography: It involves understanding the processes that shape the ocean basins and determines the structure and composition of the earth's crust.

Chemical Oceanography: It involves understanding the processes that control the distribution of elements and their compounds in the ocean.

Physical Oceanography: This field is about finding out which chemicals are beneficial to marine life and how pesticides, petrochemicals, metals and radioactive materials contaminate the ocean.

Qualifications: Graduation in pure sciences with post-graduation (PG) in an oceanographic subject is a necessary prerequisite to enter this field. In India, this subject is not taught separately. "One can enter by completing B.Sc./BE or M.Sc./ME/M.Tech in marine biology, marine biotechnology, marine geology, marine science, marine zoology, botany, marine geophysics, applied geophysics, ocean engineering, marine technology or geotechnology," says Prof. Singh.

Careers: Oceanographers are chemists, physicists, biologists, or geologists who bring their skills to ocean studies. Marine-related professions include biologists, mathematicians, physicists, geophysicists, computer scientists, meteorologists, chemists, geologists, engineers, and public policy experts.

Students interested in biology, chemistry, geology or physics, can choose marine biology applied marine biology, marine chemistry or geological oceanography. Students having a penchant for biology can combine this with chemical or physical oceanography in marine biology or oceanography. Those who are interested in physical sciences can choose ocean science, which offers a wide choice.

If one wants to excel, a Ph.D. is must. Oil and gas extraction, maritime trade, aqua culture and fisheries, defence, renewable energy generation and waste disposal are some fields which come under ocean sciences. The increasing demand for seafood, sea-based medicines and grooming of ecofriendly industries has increased the demand for such professionals.

"Areas where salaries are lucrative are physical oceanography, marine technology and engineering and computer modelling. The greatest demand is for physical and chemical oceanographers and for ocean engineers," says Prof. Birendra Sahu, a geophysicist.

Another area of growth is exploratory geology. Remote sensing also offers job avenues. Most openings are in environmental conservation organisations. Companies engaged in exploration work, the Geological Survey of India, National Institute of oceanography, Indian Navy, Coast Guard and meteorological departments require these professionals. Oceanographers are also self-employed.

Salaries: A researcher generally receives a stipend of approximately Rs. 6,000 to Rs. 10,000. The starting salary after post-graduation can be between Rs. 8,000 and Rs. 12,000 per month. With a Ph.D., this can go to anything between Rs. 14,000 and Rs. 16,000. "One of the added advantages is that one gets to travel a lot. With research projects on hand, one gets opportunities to visit beautiful locations. But the problem is that there is a severe shortage of equipment. This results in a lack of practical experience," says Prof. Sahu.

COURSES IN OCEANOGRAPHY

The National Institute of Oceanography, Goa .
A range of courses are offered here.

College of Fisheries, Pusa Rajendra Agricultural University, Bihar.

Course: B.Sc. (fisheries).

Qualification: Higher secondary (physics, chemistry and biology).

Beharampur University.

Course: M.Sc. (marine sciences).

Utkal University, Orissa.

Course: M.Sc. (marine zoology).

Goa University, Teleigao Plateau, Goa.

Course: B.Sc. and M.Sc. in marine science.

University of Chennai.

Course: M.Sc. in marine geology and ocean life sciences.

Mangalore University.

Course: M.Sc. in marine geology.

Andhra Pradesh University.

Course: M.Sc. in marine science.

Central Marine Fisheries Research Institute.

Course: M.Sc. in marine science.

College of Fisheries.

Course: B.Sc. and M.Sc. in fisheries.

Central Institute of Fisheries Education.

Mumbai, Maharashtra Diploma in Fisheries.

M.Sc. in fisheries.

Kerala Agricultural University.

Course: B.Sc. and M.Sc. in fisheries.

Cochin University of Science and Technology.

Course: M.Sc. in marine biology.

University of Mumbai.

Course: B.Sc. in aquarial science.

University of Goa.

Course: B.Sc. in aquarial science.

College of Fisheries.

Course: B.Sc. and M.Sc. in fisheries.

Cochin University of Science and Technology.

Course: M.Sc. in marine biology, Oceanography, marine geology .

Mangalore University.

Course: M.Sc. in marine geology.

University of Chennai.

M.Sc. in ocean life sciences.

B.Sc. in botany or zoology.

Andhra Pradesh University.

Courses: M.Sc. in marine sciences, M.Sc. in meteorology and oceanography.

Berhampur University.

Course: B.Sc. and M.Sc. in marine sciences.

Goa University.

M.Sc. in marine science.

Utkal University, M.Sc. in marine zoology.

Indian Institute of science, Bangalore.

Course: M.Tech and Ph.D. in oceanography, students with master's degree in science are admitted.

CAREERS IN ENVIRONMENTAL SCIENCES/STUDIES

With a rise in awareness about clean environment along with the growth in industrialisation and urbanisation, jobs in environmental sciences are attracting a lot of attention. Those who wish to enter a field to provide the world with clear air, fresh water and fertile soil, must move in this direction. Within the field, hazardous management technology is also emerging as a lucrative area of specification.

Environment scientists study the causes behind river pollution, water contamination, sewage treatment and hospital waste management. IIT-Delhi offers an M.Tech in environmental science and engineering and an inter-disciplinary M.Tech in energy and environment management. An M.Tech degree in environmental engineering is offered at Delhi, Kanpur, Kharagpur and Chennai IITs, but it's offered only to those who are B.Tech in civil engineering. Students at the M.Tech programmes are admitted through Graduate Admission Test in Engineering (GATE).

"We are witnessing a shortage of energy resources around the globe. This is forcing us to look for alternative resources like thermal and hydel power, solar, wind, ocean and bio-mass energy. Both Indian and multinational companies are investing heavily in renewable energy sources.

To carry out their jobs, they require environment scientists to find the root cause of problems and offer solutions", says Ramakant

Chugh, an environment scientist. Opportunities are available at Central Pollution Control Board, State Pollution Control Boards as environment consultants and pollution control, water management and sewage management bodies. The starting salary ranges from Rs. 12,000 to Rs. 18,000 MNCs pay higher sums to experienced people.

Institutes offering courses in environment and hazardous management.

- Tropical Forestry Research Institute, Jabalpur.
- Centre for Social Forestry and Eco-habilitation, Allahabad.
- Indian Council of Forestry Research & Education, Dehradun.
- Centre for Ecological Sciences, IISc., Bangalore.
- Forest Research Institute, Dehradun.
- Centre for Forestry Research and Human Resource Development, Chhindwara.
- Institute of Forest Productivity, Ranchi.
- Institute of Rain and Moist Deciduous Forest Research, Jorhat.
- IIT-Mumbai.
- Jawaharlal Nehru University.
- Centre for Environmental Management of Degraded Eco Systems, University of Delhi.
- Institute of Wood Science and Technology, Bangalore.
- Temperate Research Institute, Shimla.
- Indian Institute of Forest Management, Bhopal.
- Delhi College of Engineering.
- Guru Gobind Singh Indraprastha University.
- Wildlife Institute of India, Dehradun.
- Centre for Environment Education, Bangalore.
- Annamalai University, Tamil Nadu, Diploma in Energy Management Technology.
- Centre for Mining Environment, Indian School of Mines, Dhanbad.
- IIT, New Delhi.
- CPR Environmental Education Centre, Chennai.
- G. B. Pant Institute of Himalayan Environment and Development, Almora.

CAREER IN LEATHER TECHNOLOGY

India is one of the biggest leather producing nations in the world. The leather industry is the fourth largest export earner in the country. A lot of institutes offering specialised courses in leather technology have come up. There are certificate as well as diploma courses in designing and production of leather.

Due to certain reasons, leatherwear has always been in vogue and commands high prices. For youngsters, it's considered hep to wear leather apparel.

Nature of Work

"With multinationals coming in hordes, the industry is all set to witness a boom", says Sanjeev Shukla, an industry expert. Leatherwear includes items like footwear, belts, bags, purses, upholstery, baggage, and gift items, "But despite competition from foreign companies, Indian companies too are expanding their market share. In fact, they have floated branded products which have found favour with the public," he adds.

The biggest problem facing the industry is a dearth of trained professionals. "But with technical advances, qualified professionals are in demand," says Shukla.

Before entering the industry, one needs to decide on the stream of interest: designing or production. "This is important as a lot depends on your interest. If you can visualise new designs according to market demand, you should enter the designing field. Otherwise go in for the production line," says Rashmi, a student of leather technology.

"A person can begin working with leading leather manufacturing companies and tanneries," adds Rashmi. If one happens to be in the production line, however, the work can be strenuous, especially if working in tanneries and production houses.

Careers

Designers work with footwear companies as technical designers and stylists. While technical designers train themselves in pattern-making, cutting, designing, stylists design products keeping market demands in mind. They are also employed by leather garment production houses and boutiques.

Remuneration

Fresh recruits can expect a starting pay package ranging between Rs. 6,500 and Rs. 11,000. "If you hold an MBA degree, chances of going up the ladder of success are easy," says Shukla.

Study Institutes

- Muzaffarpur Institute of Technology, Anna University.
- Bharath Institute of Science and Technology.
- Priyadarshini Engineering College.
- Harcourt Butter Technological Institute.
- BR Ambedkar Regional Engineering College.
- Footwear Design and Development Institute.
- Central Footwear Training Institute.
- National Institute of Fashion Technology.
- AVI School of Fashion and Shoe Technology.
- Central Footwear Training Institute.

CAREERS IN EARTH SCIENCES/GEOGRAPHY

For those of us who had been always fascinated by questions like how rainbows are formed, rainfall and hurricanes happen, how the weather changes, being a geographer could well be a truly satisfying career option.

For, geographers study the earth, its constituents, atmosphere and inhabitants. They also study the various regions of earth and the climatic differences across earth. Besides, the characteristics of the land in different regions and the principles of land and ocean development, earth's resources like minerals and water, distribution of resources over region, and its utilisation.

Geographers interpret the climatic conditions in different regions, their effect on the natural resources and development of human civilisation, plant and animals. Study of local weather conditions and the seasonal progression also come into their ambit. Apart from this, they are involved in global monitoring of environment and weather forecasting.

As a geographer, one can also get into urban and regional planing and development, housing development, town planning, transport planning, environmental planning and monitoring.

Geographers these days use a range of technologies and sophisticated devices in their study. For example, Geographic

Information Systems, Remote sensing, Spectrographic imaging devices, and Synthetic aperture radar for studying formation of rain clouds, movement of storm, etc. Specialisation in various fields of Geography includes Economic Geography, Cultural Geography, Environment Control, Political Geography and Natural Resources, Other specialisation areas include Cartography, Geographic Information Systems (GIS), Geomorphology, Meteorology, Climatology, Remote sensing, and other related areas.

Job profiles include those of Cartographers, Climatologists, Research scientists, Environmental analysts, GIS specialists, Urban planners, Regional Planners, Population scientists, Resource analysts, Remote sensing specialists, etc.

Requirements

An MA/M Sc. in geography is a must. After post graduation, one could do a Master's degree in Planning/Remote Sensing/GIS (M Tech level courses) with Mathematics as a subject in BA/BSc.

For academic careers, one has to do well with a Ph.D.

Job opportunities

Jobs are available in universities research organisations like the National Geophysical Research Institute, Hyderabad and National Institute of Oceanography, Goa; NGOs; Government Ministries and departments like Ministry of Environment, Ministry of Urban development; pollution control boards; municipal and urban development corporations; housing developmental corporations.

Money and other benefits

In university departments and colleges starting salaries are about Rs. 12,000-14,000 a month, going up to a maximum of Rs. 25,000 a month. Government jobs fetch Rs. 10,000 a month initially, going up to a maximum of Rs. 25,000 a month. NGOs generally pay less, about Rs. 6,000 a month.

CAREERS IN PLASTIC SURGERY

Not everyone may be born beautiful, but many would certainly like their looks to be different. Given the chance and the resources, people would pay a fortune to get the look they desire. That's what many celebrities any way do, investing a lot of money in plastic surgery to get the perfect blend of facial and body features. Not just Aishwarya Rai, Michael Jackson or even Sushmita Sen, but a whole host of people, not necessarily in showbiz, talk about plastic surgery as more and more persons are becoming conscious of good physical features.

As a profession, plastic surgery definitely gives one a chance to work with the most beautiful people in the glamour industry. They also get to work on that most important ingredient of a person's mental makeup—self-confidence. Plastic Surgeons not only perfect smiles, whiten stained teeth, implanting silicones, etc. but also change the overall personality of individuals.

Plastic surgery comes from the Greek plastikos, meaning to mould or give form. Plastic surgical procedures fall under two major categories—reconstructive and cosmetic.

Reconstructive procedures restore the form. In many cases, they correct the function of abnormal body parts. This is the vital branch of plastic surgery, where the doctors deal with accident victims, burn injuries and people with physical deformities.

Cosmetic surgeons, on the other hand, work with wannable Miss Indias, models and film stars. Their operations enhance the physical appearance. Procedures such as face lifts, nose reshaping for appearance fat suction, etc fall under this category.

The various types of cosmetic surgery, include Rhytidectomy (face lift), Rhinoplasty (nose surgery), Blepharoplasty (eyelid surgery), Hair transplants, Breast enlargement, Breast reduction, Abdominoplasty (tummy tuck), Chemical Peels and Dermabrasion and Liposuction.

While plastic surgeons perform most of the procedures, surgeons ophthalmic surgeons do blepharoplasties; gynaecologists offer abdominoplasties and dermatologists perform chemical peels. All doctors learn some surgery in their medical training. So legally, anyone with a medical degree can perform cosmetic surgery.

Requirements

Despite this, plastic surgery remains a super specialisation in medicine, involving many years of training. As an MBBS student, you will have to put in four and a half years for the degree and then serve in a government hospital or college for about a year. Only then will you be eligible for the Master's degree course in surgery. Here you can specialise in either General Medicine, ENT, Opthalmic, or Orthopaedic surgery. After this you will have to take up a super speciality course or Master of Chirurgiae (MCh) in Plastic Surgery.

A course in plastic surgery, offered as a super speciality in Mumbai government-run colleges lasts three years, the fee for which is between Rs. 10,000-12,000 per annum.

Personal attributes

Good aesthetic sense tops the list. A plastic surgeon is in a way an artist who shapes the nose, eyes, smiles and what have you.

Apart from the artistry, you should have extremely good communication skills as well. The communication skills help in putting across the limitations of this field to the people who come with starry dreams and are spellbound by the prospect of "miraculous" physical transformations. Many people think plastic surgeons are magician who can convert ugly ducklings into gorgeous swans. You have to explain that it is not all that easy.

Plastic surgeons also, for most part, have to deal with people suffering from inferiority complex. They need to refer such persons to psychologists.

Job Opportunities

After becoming a certified Plastic Surgeon, the preferred option or the first option should be to work under a renowned plastic surgeon. The job, under a senior, will give you hands-on training and help you to learn the tricks of the trade. This way, you earn a reputation for yourself.

Sometimes, the work under the senior may be without remuneration, but the positive aspect is that you are learning or implementing whatever you have studied at medical school. Some plastic surgeons may pay you in the range of Rs. 10,000-20,000 a month.

The next option is to be a consultant with a hospital. For this you need recommendations from well-known doctors, and get published in medical journals to be eligible.

If you want to pursue a career in academics then you could try the option of working as a lecturer with an academic institution. Otherwise you can start your own practice immediately after doing your course. But starting your own practice needs initial investment to the order of Rs. 50,000-80,000 in the premises including equipment. Besides you have to be ready for a wait to be recognised as a plastic surgeon, since it takes sometime, even years to establish yourself in the field.

Money and Other Benefits

There aren't too many plastic surgeons around, but no one should not expect to earn potfulls immediately after finishing the course. In the learning years, you are only learning the tricks of the trade.

Working as a lecturer with an academic institution after M.Ch earns you Rs. 7,000-8,000 per month.

With your own practice, your earnings usually depend on the references you get from other doctors and the locality where you set up practice.

Career Prospects

Prospects for a plastic surgeon are very bright to say the least. With people becoming more and more conscious of their looks, skilled surgeons with steady hands and steely nerves are very much in demand the world over. There is not much work in the field of reconstructive surgery but as far as cosmetic surgery is concerned plastic surgeons have never ever been more busy. The trend is expected to only increase, as long as people have an urge to look good.

CAREERS IN URBAN MANAGEMENT

With Burgeoning populations eroding beauty and the aesthetics of cities comes the need to have planned urban centres. Given the pace of globalisation, cities at present are absorbing nearly one-third of the total population. The rapid growth is both the cause and effect of growing economic importance of the cities. Demographers forecast that around 2035 more than half of India's population would live in the cities. The then is the most important rationale for studying the issues involved in urban management.

Urbanisation not only stretches a city horizontally, but also imparts it a vertical reach. Large complexes are being built in cities at enormous costs. In the absence of scientific management and maintenance, these complexes deteriorate with time. Consequently, "estate management" has developed as a serious and attractive profession.

"Urban management is not only about construction but about every aspect of city life. The objectives of this course are: To understand the administration, planning and implementation process of urban local government; the basic concepts and actual practices of public finance, issues related to the sustainability of urban local bodies and also to equip the students with key management techniques, "says S.P. Jakhanwal, director, Amity School of Urban Management. He adds: "The course also assists in an all-round development of Urban Managers in design, planning, technology and Management of Natural/Human/ Financial resources and basic services."

"The course also aims at creating awareness among professionals about the urban environment.

As metros expand, a very high order of capital is needed to create the commensurate urban infrastructure. Thus another objective of the urban management course is to facilitate direct involvement in developmental works at various levels by providing research and consultancy services. By generating resources, it also aims to provide learning grounds for students and teachers.

The quality of urban life could easily be compromised till urban local bodies learn to tap sources of finance other than the Government. Besides this, urban finance managers need to promote projects incorporate the latest technical know-how and the Government authorities have to encourage such projects. Urban management courses tackle these needs by infusing greater professionalism in students to be a part of the system and help in the overall development of the urban centres.

Objectives

- To generate awareness of the forces shaping urbanisation.
- To equip students with strategies of planning, financing and management of urban infrastructure.
- To equip them with skills to prepare and evaluate urban projects.

- To improve their capabilities to develop synergies amongst different stakeholders of urban development and between the forces of urbanisation and globalisation.

Eligibility

Graduate in any discipline. Various modules help graduates of different fields acquire an edge over others.

"For Trends and Patterns of Urbanisation, a person with a background in geography would fare well. An MBA is helpful in Decentralisation: Empowerment of Local People—Constitutional amendments, Local Self-Governments. For Urban Infrastructure, engineering, while for Urban Finance a background in economics is essential," says Mr. Jakhanwal.

Job Prospects

With increasing urbanisation in Asia, Africa and other developing countries, jobs in this field are bound to increase. The scope can be gauged from the fact that the level of urbanisation in India till now has been only about 30 per cent. In Asia, it is around 38 per cent and Africa about 39 per cent. Another factor is that by 2015, the world would have 358 metro cities (with population of more than 1 million) and Asia would have around 153 of them. Similarly there would be 27 mega cities (with population of above 1 crore) in the world, of which 15 would be in Asia. That means Asia will emerge the favourite field for Urban Managers. A tag of Urban Management would certainly boost career prospects in Asia and other developing countries.

Job Profile

An urban manager is responsible for strategising, planning, marketing and financing of urban development. He is required to answer questions like: How to improve facilities in urban centres? He needs to look into where the city is expanding, in its slums or the posh areas. What needs to be done to improve life in slums and how to get the finances to get the work done. As the Government alone cannot bear urbanisation costs, some support has to come from private financers or banks. And an urban manager has to get the project prepared to get it funded by the bank," says Mr Jakhanwal.

Employment Opportunities

An urban manager can get employment with urban development authorities, municipal corporations, municipalities, district boards, financing institutions such as HUDCO, HDFC etc. and developers.

CAREERS IN ARCHITECTURE—DESIGNING THE SURROUNDINGS

Anyone with aesthetic sense, taste, style, sense of harmony and space can think of becoming an architect. It is a challenging job and not merely about the designing shelters but also fulfilling the psychological needs of people occupying it.

With people being fascinated by awe-inspiring foreign locales in Bollywood, the importance of landscape architecture has also increased.

Only bricks and cement do not make a construction beautiful. To make a dream come true, a landscape architect deals with planning and design of cityscape, including layout of shops, parking spaces, recreational buildings, roads and so forth. The haphazard development of cities has led to many problems. Thus, making it important for the Government to use the services of landscape architects. Moreover, people are increasingly becoming conscious of employing landscape architects to design their houses and other buildings.

Landscape Architecture is a fine art, which creates and preserves beauty of habitations. Several residential and commercial complexes are being designed and planned by landscape architects, as this phenomenon has only come up very recently.

Job Pofile

They are involved in planning, designing and construction of the outdoors such as planning and designing parks, highways, housing complexes, commercial centres, plazas, recreation facilities etc. They construct outdoors in a way that would best complement the natural surroundings and work to integrate functionality and aesthetics with nature by blending scientific, architectural and engineering skills.

They also work in areas such as natural resource conservation and preservation of historic monuments. they may also redesign streets to limit traffic and to improve pedestrian access and safety.

Job Prospects

Landscape architecture is a highly specialised area. The school of Planning and Architecture, New Delhi, offers a post-graduate degree in L.A. Initially, one can work as an assistant to a senior landscape architect. Employment is available in both private organisations as well as the Government. After gaining experience one can start one's own private consultancy business. But, growth would be restricted to big cities for some years. One can also work abroad, where the profession is already advanced and pays handsomely.

At present landscape architects are not part of town planning. But sooner or later, their services would be approached with more seriousness as congestion and pollution would become a regular feature in our city life.

Personal Traits

A keen visual sense, an eye for beauty, a scientific bent of mind and ability to as similate knowledge from different streams of study like soil, ecology, geology, hydrology and the like. Above all, love for the nature.

Besides an aptitude and inclination for architecture, one should also be interested in art and nature.

A certain amount of business acumen is also necessary, as a lot of co-ordination has to be done not only with clients, but with other professionals as well.

Today, in developed countries, landscape architects are working in specialised areas such as the construction and beautification of playgrounds, gardens, hotels and resorts, shopping centres, public houses and hospitals. In India too, several such projects are increasingly being undertaken and therefore the demand for Landscape architects is growing.

Remuneration

One can get anywhere between Rs. 7,000 to Rs. 12,000 in both government and private organisations. With experience it is bound to increase.

CAREERS IN MUSEOLOGY/ARCHAEOLOGY

Do you see a future in the past? Or are deeply interested in showcasing our heritage, or perhaps making the natural would interesting for kids and adults alike? If so, consider a career concerned with the science of museums; Museology.

Museology is the branch of knowledge concerned with the study of the purposes and organisation of museums. The role of museology is museum-specific, its emphasis is on development of museums and in evolving fresh methods and techniques to improve their working.

An increased awareness of our cultural heritage has given greater prominence to activities such as preservation, restoration and excavation of ancient monuments and the art material. This has created a need for persons having skills in various related fields of history. It is expected that in times to come, persons having specialised knowledge in the field of history will be in a better position to find jobs in the public and private sectors.

A museum provides a window into a place's cultural resources and civilisational achievements. Museums can be classified on the basis of their collections, who runs them and the area they serve, the audiences they cater to and the way they exhibit their collections. It is better for the student to understand the place s/he wants to join. Museums offer a variety of career opportunities to individuals. Some of the positions that they offer are:

The person in charge of a particular collection is the CURATOR, whose responsibilities, however, go far beyond caretaking. S/he is specialist in the particular academic discipline relevant to the collection. The curator is directly responsible for determining and overseeing all policies and care, preservation and academic interpretation of objects.

An Archivist administers unique original documents in all material media. S/he advises museum staff on principles and methods for documenting museum activities and for creating orderly and useful filing systems of records. S/he acquires, maintains and supplies manuscripts and other permanent records of historical and administrative importance for reference. An archivist appraises public records and documents transferred to the archives. S/he recommends weeding material while safegurding records by modern means such as fumigation, lamination and microfilming, etc.

Trained archivists mostly find jobs in the National Archives of India.

A collection manager is most often found in natural history and history museums, where the size of the collection is large.

A conservation scientist has the responsibility of acts of conservation in the research section of the museum. S/he may serve as the immediate assistant to the chief of conservation.

A conservator is responsible for the physical well being of a collection. His responsibility is two-fold: Examination and treatment of the collection material and protection of the collection from further deterioration.

Deputy Director/Assistant Director, Associate Director: He is in charge of specific areas of a museum like administration, education or exhibitions, curatorial and research departments. S/he also manages human resources and personnel matters.

The deputy director's position takes on a variety of configurations depending upon the desires and predisposition of the director and on the size and scope of the museum. This position is often designated as being in charge of a specific area of museum activities such as administration, education or exhibitions or research departments. This position may also manage HR and personnel matters.

Museum Educator: Essentially, the museum educator provides a broad spectrum of learning experiences for museum's diverse public, leading the way to reach out to a wider circle. The educator develops, implements, evaluates and supervises the museum's educational programmes based on the mission of the museum.

Marketing Manager: Marketing is a relatively recent phenomenon as museums strive to cope with financial crises, prove their accountability, make their services and products for the community better known and reach new and diverse audiences. The marketing manager is responsible for conducting market research, developing a marketing plan, and organising the staff to accomplish it. The marketing manager usually reports directly to the director of the museum and works closely with the development and public relation officer.

Docents, or guides/volunteers are the voices of the museum. Their function is to serve as catalysts in the interaction between the objects and the observers. The docent is an educator and should acquire the ability to mediate, interpret and encourage visitors to participate actively in learning through organised educational guided tours and programmes. The docent leads visitors in encountering, experiencing and enjoying objects and artifacts.

One has to be an enthusiastic professional, with an analytical mind and a strong drive to succeed. It is better if students choose a path right from their schooling. Anyone can follow a path of developing interest in history, and finally can get into museum studies.

There are around six universities that have museology as their academic curriculum. A student of history can choose the course to increase employment opportunities.

Eligibility

For MA in museology, a degree in history, history of arts, archaeology or diploma is museology.

Some universities offer PG Diploma in museology to the students who have completed M.Sc., M.A. (history, or archaeology) or BA (history). Some universities offering PG Diploma in Museology are Aligarh Muslim University and Barkatullah University. For Ph.D. in museology, post-graduation in museology or museum studies is required.

Some institutes also offer the minimum eligibility for such courses is 10+2. Some institutes that offer short-term courses are the National Museum of in Inst. of History of Art (Delhi), Bhartiya Kala Nidhi, Institute of Archaeology, ASI, Activities of the National Archives are increasing. Hence they are opening branches in important towns and cities of the country. The junior level posts such as assistant archivist are filled through employment exchange or advertisements. However, gazetted level posts are referred to the UPSC. Persons holding junior posts, after gaining prescribed experience become eligible for senior positions.

NATIONAL MUSEUM INSTITUTE

The need to initiate a museum university led to the establishment of the National Museum Institute of History of Art, Conservation and Museology (NMIHACM) in 1988, with the status of a deemed university. The institute was formed as an autonomous organisation by the Department of Culture on the recommendation of the UGC.

The institute disseminates advanced teaching in the realm of art-covering its history conservation and museological parameters-leading to post-graduate and doctoral degrees. This is to provide trained professionals to museums all over the country.

There are six universities in India which have Museology Departments. Most are without any museum and the required infrastructural facilities such as laboratory, slide library, documentation centre, etc.

The National Museum Institute fulfils the criteria of infrastructural facilities like a formidable conservation laboratory, a multi-disciplinary collection of art-objects, library of art-books and slides, workshop, photography department, educational unit etc.

CAREERS IN OUTSOURCING INDUSTRIES

Outsourcing is the latest mantra in India. But is no way alien to India, having been around since 1960s. The only difference is that since 2000 outsourcing has expanded to cover IT-enabled services as well, while earlier it was only about time-sharing, IT operations, alliances/tie-ups.

It would not be wrong to say that if the 1990s had been dominated by the software companies, the beginning of the 21st century certainly belongs to the outsourcing companies.

What is Outsourcing?

Outsourcing literally means long-term contracting of no-core business processes to an outside provider to help achieve increased shareholder value. "It is a practice seen in every field but IT professionals are particularly familiar with the term. Some forms of outsourcing may include both IT management and business operations. The approach of outsourcing is about turning over functions such as payroll, accounting, billing or even real estate management to a third party. Though these business processes may depend on IT. They are separate from the core IT operations, such as data centre activities or network management," says Gursharan Singh Sidhu, Executive resourcing, Access computers, which is outsourcing for Accenture.

Why Outsourcing?

Why indeed would a company prefer to outsource certain

functions despite being able to employ sufficient staff itself?" Actually outsourcing helps corporates to shed part of the responsibility. It helps their executive to be free of some day-to-day process management responsibilities. It is seen that, usually, executives spend more time managing details than strategy. Once a process is successfully outsourced, the ratio can be reversed. Executives get more time to explore new revenue streams, to accelerate other projects, and to focus on customers," says Manoj Kulashreshtha of ASM Infosystems.

Outsourcing also helps save money. Outsourcing companies can reallocate resources to other projects and leverage investment in technology.

"It also increases capabilities. In addition to doing things more efficiently, companies can expand abilities to deliver new products and services to customers. Then there are factors of scalability and scope as well. Companies wanting to grow internationally must continuously invest in infrastructure and find talent around the world," says Aali Iqbal, ASM Infosystems.

Why India?

In order to meet the growing international demand for lucrative, customer-interaction centres, many organisations worldwide are outsourcing these services from locations like India.

"A culmination of factors—dramatic improvement in connectivity from India, huge investments in telecom infrastructure, and an economic slump in the US which forced companies to look at every cost cutting option—has today resulted in the outsourcing sector growing at a faster pace than software services. So much so that despite lack of infrastructure, they are also coming up in a big way in smaller cities," says Sidhu.

Many companies provide a comprehensive menu of outsourcing services across a range of functions—including claims processing, in payroll, finance, procurement and customer support. Also, India has one of the largest pool of low-cost English speaking scientific and technical talent. This makes India an obvious choice as an outsource destination.

"Dell, Sun Microsystems, LG, Ford, GE, Oracle are just some of the big names that have announced plans to scale up operations in India. Others like American Express, IBM and British Airways are leveraging the cost advantage India has while setting up call centres. Several foreign airline and banks have too have set up business process operations in India," says Shoab Rais, ASM Infosystems.

Potential in Indian Outsourcing Industry

Accenture is on a hiring spree in India. Many other outsourcing companies are increasing their staff two fold. The business in India is booming with more and more American and European companies moving their backroom operations as well as software development centres here, to tap the country's skilled but low-cost labour force.

"Even the Government is coming up with a campaign to position outsourcing as a career of choice. The move is being taken to ensure that the fast-growing sector did not face manpower shortage."

The outsourcing industry in India has been growing at a rate of 70 per cent per year. It is now worth US$ 1.6 billion, employing 100,000 people. And as McKinsey analysts put it, outsourcing has to grow only 27 per cent till 2008 to deliver $17 billion in revenues and employment to a million people.

"The philosophy behind is specific, do what you do best and leave everything else to business process outsourcers. Companies are moving their non-core business processes to outsource providers. It saves precious management time and resources and allows focus while building upon core competencies. The list of functions being outsourced is getting longer by the day. Call centres apart, functions outsourced span purchasing and disbursement, order entry, billing and collection, human resources administration, cash and investment management, tax compliance, internal audit, pay roll...the list gets longer everyday" says Aali Iqbal.

Eligibility and jobs

Eligibility differs for different fields. For Technical Processing (Purchasing and Disbursement, Billing and collection) requirement is finance professionals if it is related to finance; MBA or insurance professionals if it is related to insurance or other general fields even graduate with 3 years of experience are required.

For accountancy, the eligibility is B.Com with 3 years experience or even finance professionals. For call centres, the minimum eligibility is 12th pass and even housewives can get work. The important criterion for getting a Call centre job is good communication skills.

Vendors Active in Outsourcing

Automatic Data Processing and Paychex in payroll, as well as Concord EFS, First Data Corporation, Global Payments, and Total System Services are involved in payment processing. These are some of the larger, more established outsourcing firms.

The well known IT outsourcing firms—Computer Sciences Corporation, Electronic Data System, Fiserv, and IBM—have all established large, billion-dollar plus outsourcing organisations and should benefit from its growth. These lines of business, however, are still relatively small given their revenue percentage (10 per cent-15 per cent) but should be an increasingly important contributor to growth over the next several years.

The Big 5 consultants—Accenture, IBM, Bearing Point, Cap Gemini Ernst and Young, and Deloitte—have made particular strides in outsourcing, leveraging their process improvement-oriented consulting practices.

Motivation Factors for outsourcing:

- Factor Cost Advantage.
- Superior Competency.
- Utilisation Improvement.
- Economies of Scale.
- Business Risk Mitigation.

Benefits derived from outsourcing can be summarised as follows:

- Productivity improvements.
- Access to expertise.
- Operational cost control.
- Cost savings.
- Improved accountability.
- Improved HR.
- Opportunity to focus on core business.

Services Provided by Outsourcers

Offshore outsource service providers in India render facilities as Business Service Providers.

A strong and skilled work force of the companies ensure total solution to various business needs such as Book Keeping, Inventories, Data Entries etc.

General Services

- Receivables and Payables.
- Inventory Management.
- Order Processing.
- Budget Analysis.
- Cash flow Analysis.
- Reconciliation.
- Data Entry.
- Payroll Processing.
- Quick Book Accounting.
- Financial Statement Preparation and Accounting Services.

Web-Based Services

- Live online sales and order entry.
- E-commerce transaction support.
- Internet-based research.
- Web Design/Development.

Who is Interested in Outsourcing Services?

- CFO who are looking at every option to further cut costs.
- IT Executives under pressure to reduce costs and improve quality.
- Human Resources executives seeking lower transaction processing costs.
- Finance and Accounting executives considering new processing options.
- Customer Care executives building the next-generation virtual global contact centre.
- Sourcing executives with cost cutting and offshore mandates.
- Shared Services executives looking to leverage an offshore advantage.
- Outsourcing Providers seeking new ways to reduce cost and improve services.
- Venture Capital Firms targeting the IT and IT-enabled services markets.

- Consultants working with clients to develop and implement an BPO strategy.

CAREERS IN RUBBER INDUSTRY

With a view highlight the careers offered by rubber industry. We, hereunder, record an interaction with Dr. N.M. Mathew, Director of the Rubber Research Institute of India in Kattayam, Kerala, which was published in 'Avenue' on Oct. 21, 2003, in which he considers Rubber Industry as "An Industry that is one revolution ahead."

- **How big is the rubber industry in India?**

The Indian rubber industry is worth Rs 15,000 crore. In India, both natural and synthetic kinds of rubber are produced. The industry is expanding at a fast rate.

- **Brief us about the rubber Research Institute of India?**

It is the research department of Rubber Board, a statutory body constituted by the Government under the Rubber Act 1947. As the name suggests, its main function is R&D. It was established in 1955 and deals with research in natural rubber.

- **What kind of people are required by the rubber industry?**

The rubber industry is facing a severe shortage of quality manpower. This is due to the gravitation of students towards IT.

- **What kinds of jobs are in the offing?**

There is a demand for people in the production, R & D and quality control departments. Those who have a diploma or degree in rubber technology can enter this industry. Normally, students neglect this sector, but it's important to note that this would be one of the hottest fields in the not so distant future. Recruitment takes place at three levels: Manufacturing, R & D and quality control. But first we need to understand the process. First, rubber polymer is mixed and processed with chemical substances in a laboratory. One draws up a formula to initiate the manufacturing process. Then comes the product development, which involves the design of various new rubber products and planning is done with the aid of engineers, draughtsmen.

One is required to make prototypes and test them to see if they comply with the requirements. After the rubber polymer has been mixed with chemicals in a large mixer, the rubber compound is moulded into intermediate forms, which are fed into machines until the final product is tested. For production, one has to have a bent towards agriculture. People with a botany background are suitable for production. They work mostly on rubber plantations.

- **Why are most courses in rubber technology located down south?**

It is partially true. Many reputed tyre companies have set up manufacturing units down south, creating such an impression, in fact, a lot of institutions in north India offer courses in rubber technology.

- **How should one go about to get a job?**

After BTech, a person can start as a trainee, but he can also be employed directly. The salary could be anything between Rs. 10,000 and Rs. 15,000 at the start. After gaining experience, it could go up to Rs. 40,000. And it's not just rubber technologists who find jobs in the Industry. Mechanical, chemical and electrical engineers are also recruited here in large numbers.

COURSES IN RUBBER TECHNOLOGY

Anna University, Chennai:
BTech Rubber (Post-BSc 70 per cent in PCM).
LD College of Engineering, Ahmedabad.
BE in rubber technology.
IIT Kharagpur:
MS (rubber technology).
MTech for two years PhD.

Offers specialisations in rubber technology, adhesion and adhesives, elastomers, nanocomposites, plastics, polymer modification, polymer degradation and failure, polymer blends, alloys and composites, reactive processing, rheology, thermoplastic elastomers, waste utilisation, polymer chemistry, liquid crystallic materials and nano composites.

Cochin University of Science and Technology

One of the premier academic institutions, CUSAT offers post-graduate level courses.

Government Polytechnic, Mumbai in association with All India Rubber Industries Association.

Diploma programme in rubber technology. Admission requirements: High School or Class 12 in science with 50 per cent marks for open and 45 per cent for reserved category.

The course includes studies in engineering chemistry, engineering drawing, elements of mechanical and electrical technology, Introduction to polymer science, applied mathematics, machine drawing, rubber chemistry, communication practice, vulcanisation system, rubber and its compounding ingredients, rubber physics, mould design, latex technology, basic machine tools and operations, rubber compounding and processing, development of soft skills. Testing of rubbers, rubber machinery, metrology and quality control production management, project work and seminar, rubber product manufacturing, thermoplastic rubbers entrepreneurship, inplant training.

Duration: 2½ years.

Offers diploma and degrees in civil, mechanical and electrical engineering.

Offers diploma level, post-diploma, post-graduate diploma and advanced diploma programmes.

Indian Institute of Technology, Delhi

The course includes introduction to polymeric materials, rheology and of polymers, polymerisation processes and kinetics, performance properties of polymers, high performance polymers, major project part design of products and polymer and rubber technology.

Post-graduate programme: Inter-disciplinary M.Tech. in polymer science and technology.

RUBBER INDUSTRY—BASIC UNDERSTANDING

India is the world's fourth largest producer of natural rubber. The Rs. 12,000 crore Indian Rubber Industry provides direct employment to around 80,000 people, and is a source of indirect employment to nearly three lakh. There are about 6,000 manufacturing units, which produce over 36,000 domestic and industrial end products. The industry also exports goods worth Rs. 15,000 crore per year to 80 countries, including the USA and Germany.

"Rubber and its products have made a deep impact on our lives. We are the fourth largest consumers of rubber products in the world. Unlike other major rubber producing countries, where the market is export-oriented, India, along with China and Brazil, consumes its entire domestic output for industrial purposes," says an industry expert.

Career

For a career in the rubber industry, one should have a BTech degree or diploma in plastic technology, chemical engineering, rubber technology or mechanical engineering. One can also pursue an MTech in plastic technology after MSc. in chemistry or physics.

"The tyre industry is the biggest employer in this sector. Hundreds of young graduates are recruited every year, and with India's auto sector making its mark globally, the industry would be recruiting on a large scale in the coming years," says an expert.

Besides the tyre industry, jobs are also available with various rubber-processing units. If we include small scale as well as unorganised sectors, the turnover of the industry crosses Rs. 30,000 crore, with lakhs of people employed in it.

"It's important to remember that the field involves the use of chemicals. One may have to work in unhealthy environments at times." says, Dr. N.M. Mathew, Director, Rubber Research Institute of India in Kottayam, Kerala.

Institutes offering courses in rubber technology are IIT, Kharagpur; BIT, Ranchi; Cochin University of Science and Technology, Cochin; Laxminarayan Institute of Technology, Nagpur; MIT, Anna University, Chennai; Kamaraj College of Engineering and Technology, Tamil Nadu; Sri Krishnadevaraya University, Andhra Pradesh; Rubber Research Institute of India, Kerala; Cochin University of Science and Technology, Kochi; Government Polytechnic, Mumbai and Indian Rubber Institute, New Delhi.

Marketing and sales executives would also be required in large numbers but the industry prefers people with science background.

"An MBA degree surely helps one to rise fast in the company hierarchy," says Mathew.

Research and development is coming up as a major thrust area for rubber technologists as polymer substances are increasingly being used for a host of products like spacecraft, optical fibres, textiles and household utilities.

The industry also recruits quality managers who are entrusted with the job of testing the quality of raw materials and finished products.

"For a career in the rubber industry, it is important to have a thorough knowledge about polymer science, natural and synthetic rubber production and processing, tyre technology, non-tyre products and chemical engineering," says S.C. Roy, vice-chairman, Indian Rubber Institute, One must be able to solve problems logically and should be able to master both chemical and engineering problems. Physics and Chemistry are the basis of training in rubber technology.

"There has been a transition in recruitment strategies in the last few years. Instead of recruiting experienced people, companies are now absorbing people who are conversant with the latest technologies," points out Ravindran, Director General, Automotive Tyre Manufacturers Association (ATMA).

In some states, rubber technology is taught along with plastic technology, which broadens the job scope. Grouped together, it forms part of a larger field called polymer science.

Over the last decade, polymer sciences has attracted multi-crore investments from some of the biggest industrial houses in India. Companies such as Reliance, Spic, Finolex and others have set up plants to produce raw materials and research laboratories to develop new products.

"We require quality manpower. It's true that the industry, in the past, could not attract talent, but with the scenario is changing with the rise in demand for tyres, spare parts and other rubber products."

The automotive tyre and tube manufacturing sector has dominated industry from beginning. Even though its share has declined due to the expansion of the non-tyre sector, the industry still remains the single largest producer with an annual turnover of Rs. 9,500 crore," says Mr. Ravindran. Over the years, polymer sciences has attracted multi-crore investments from some of the biggest industrial houses in India.

A rubber technologist researches, develops and tests various end products apart from planning rubber process management systems. He is also responsible for implementing and monitor these system. "We are facing competition from countries like Malaysia and Sri Lanka, but we have managed to keep our nose ahead due to cheap labour and good R & D facilities," says Mr. Mathew.

CAREERS AS EDUCATORS OF SPECIAL CHILDREN

A Ray of Hope for the Educators and Needy

The RCI approved courses could open the next big avenue for students wanting a professional career.

The Rehabilitation Council of India (RCI), a statutory body under the Ministry of Social Justice and Empowerment, feels that the range of professional courses it runs can help meet the demand for special educators in the upper primary and primary schools across the country.

In the Tenth plan, the HRD Ministry has emphasised the need for at least one special educator for persons with a disability in an upper primary school in every block in the country. The Persons with Disability (PWD) Act 1995 also makes free education to a disabled child up to 18 years by a trained teacher a statutory obligation for the State and the Central Governments. Considering the number of upper primary schools in the country, the demand for special educator is anywhere near 2 lakh trained teachers.

The RCI launched the foundation course in 2002 to train in-service teachers and has trained around 4,000 of them across the country so far. The huge demand for trained manpower can only be met by having more professionals with Diploma and B.Ed. Special Education degrees.

This is very encouraging for 10+2 students and graduates in small towns and big cities alike as they can opt for such courses. The RCI is already running several diploma courses in special education and rehabilitation which are very popular in southern States, Gujarat and Maharashtra.

The latest National Sample Survey (NSS) suggests that 2 per cent of the population in the country is disabled. The RCI feels that about 7-8 lakh professionals are needed to serve the requirement in the next 5-10 years. The NSS also implies that about 84 per cent of urban disabled children do not have access to schools and about 94 per cent of disabled children in rural areas do not have access to schools.

MORE DETAILS

Many of us sympathise with physically and mentally challenged people, but how many of us manage to do something about our emphathy? Till a few years back, there used to be an acute shortage of educators for these special children. But now, special education is gaining importance in Indian society and a lot more people are getting trained for it.

Despite being a neglected sector in India, the outlook towards special education is changing quite fast. Many special schools are opening up and the less advantaged children have more choices now with professionally qualified special educators.

There are many specialised courses to train children with different handicaps. These courses are available right after Class XII. To enter the field, in-service teachers can pursue a one-year specialised course.

Overview

Most special education teachers instruct students at the elementary, middle, and secondary school-level, though some teachers also work with infants and toddlers. They design and modify instruction to meet a student's special needs.

Special education programmes for various types of disabilities include specific learning disabilities, speech or language impairments, mental retardation, autism, deaf-blindness etc. Students are classified under one of the categories, and special education teachers work with specific groups.

Depending on the disability, teaching methods are evolved, including individualised instruction, problem-solving assignments, and group or individual work.

Special education teachers help students develop emotionally and be comfortable in social situations.

With technology playing an important role in special education, educators now use specialised equipment such as computers with synthesised speech, interactive educational software programs as well as audiotapes.

Areas of Work

Educators work largely in educational or medical set-ups. Job openings are available in Special schools such as the Spastic Society of India; NGOs; hospitals and clinics; rehabilitation centres; therapy clinics, and as private tutors.

Career growth

Although the field is uncommon, the advancements in people's approach as they are becoming more broad-minded and understanding will boost the career. Trained professionals find a lot of job satisfaction in this field as their knowledge touches a fellow human being's life in a manner that is perhaps most unique.

Remuneration

Remuneration depends on three factors:

- The level of professional qualification.
- Nature of work (work with visually/mentally challenged students etc.).
- Nature of organisation employed in.
- With a recognised postgraduate degree in the area of specialisation, educators can expect to start with a salary of Rs. 5000-8000.

Diversification

Special educators can diversify into mainstream education and training. The paramedical sector is also an option.

Personal Traits

This profession demands more than most as one has to deal with needs deserving special attention. The jobs not only demand a high degree of patience and high levels of concentration, but also great emotional stability and physical fitness. Moreover, persistence excellent listening and communication skills are also required.

Attributes, however, differ with the kind of students one is dealing.

For educators working with mentally challenged students: Alertness, objectivity, warm personality and physical stamina.

For educators working with physically challenged students: Physical stamina and knowledge of physiotherapy.

For educators working with blind students: Strong articulate voice, good language skills and knowledge of Braille.

For educators working with deaf and dumb students: Knowledge of sign language and positive body language. These qualities are essential as one has to motivate students and understand their needs. Creativity is also required from the teacher in the teaching methods.

Although teachers need to show sympathy, they should not indulge in pity. A balance is needed between love and discipline. Even handling parents of these children is a challenge since they are over-protective about their child.

Study Routes

Training for teaching children with special needs is a specialised course. Most courses are of one year duration for teachers. There are 3 years graduate courses after 10+2 for training teachers for mentally challenged children.

Entry Routes

Class XII (any subject) followed by graduation in special education.

Or, graduation in any subject followed by B.Ed. and a one year course in special education.

Class XII (PCB/M) followed by graduation, B.Sc. in Speech Therapy, followed by postgraduation in the subject.

Graduation (any subject) and diploma in Special education.

Working Conditions

Despite emotional satisfaction, the work is stressful due to heavy workloads and tedious administrative tasks. Occasionally, teachers may have to work with medical therapists and physiologists to take care of the children.

Courses

- Bachelor's Degree in Mental Retardation
  Offered by the National Institute for the Mentally

Handicapped (NIMH), Manovikas Nagar, Secundarabad affiliated to Osmania University, Hyderabad.
Duration: 3 years
Eligibility: 10+2 with a minimum of 50 per cent aggregate marks.

- Diploma in Special Education (Mental Retardation)
  Offered by North Eastern Regional Training Institute for the Mentally Handicapped, Guwahati,
  Chetna Institute for the Mentally Handicapped (Teacher's Training Centre) Bhubaneshwar.
  Duration: 1 year
  Eligibility: Graduation
- Bachelor's Degree in the Education of the Hearing Impaired
  Offered by the Ali Yavar Jung National Institute for the Hearing Handicapped (AYJNIHH), Mumbai affiliated to the University of Bombay, Mumbai.
  Duration: 1 year
  Eligibility: In service teachers' (graduates with B.Ed. and teaching experience).
- B.Ed. (Special Education: Hearing Impaired)
  Offered by Sri Padmavathi Mahila Visvavidyalaya, Tirupathi (A.P.)
  Duration: 1 year
  Eligibility: Graduation
- Advanced Diploma in Special Education Offered by Jamia Millia Islamia, New Delhi.
  Duration : 1 year
  Eligibility: B.Ed./Diploma in Education with a graduate degree.
- B.Ed. (Special Education)
  Offered by University of Mumbai, Fort, Mumbai.
  SNDT Women's University, Mumbai
  Duraion: 1 year
  Eligibility: Graduation
- Diploma Course for Secondary School Teachers of the Visually Handicapped Offered by the National Institute for visually handicapped (NIVH), Dehradun.
  Eligibility: Graduation/Sponsored seats available , Duration: 18 months.

CAREERS FOR GEOLOGISTS

Geologists study the composition, structure and the history of the earth's cruist, besides they examine rocks, minerals and fossils to identify and determine the sequence of processes that affect the development of the earth. By applying the laws of chemistry, physics, biology and mathematics, geologists also locate and estimate probable gas and oil deposits using aerial and satellite photographs, research data and survey results. With geological reports, maps, charts and diagrams, they analyse engineering problems at construction projects, such as dams, tunnels and large buildings.

Geologists test soil and rocks to determine geological characteristics, using optical, x-ray, heat, acid and precision instruments. They also measure the characteristics of the earth, using seismographs gravimeters, magnetometers and pendulum devices.

Specialisation for geologists is in the following areas:

- *Mineralogy*—Involves testing soil samples for various minerals to determine, their quality and quantity.
- *Petrology*—Involves mapping and prospecting for oil.
- Hydrology—*Study of water resources.*
- *Palaeontology*—Hunt for dinosaur bones and other extinct creatures.
- *Structural Geology*—This involves testing the soil to determine the feasibility of undertaking projects such as dams etc.
- *Geochemistry*—This is concerned with the chemistry of earth's materials. One will use principles of chemistry to research the earth's chemical composition. And also to determine the chemical characteristics of minerals and fossil fuels.
- *Geophysics*—It involves applying principles of physics to study earth's gravitation and electro-magnetic field.
- *Marine Geology*—Research and study of the ocean bed and ocean-continent interactions.
- *Seismology*—Study of earthquakes—analysing their behaviour and forecasting.

One can also specialise in environment geology and

geomorphology (study of the origin of landforms) and historical geology (study of rock layers and sedimentation).

Requirements

Ability to enjoy exploration and outdoor work; data collection and comparison skills. Good mathematical, analytical and observational skills. Initiative and leadership.

Courses

Many universities offer graduate and post-graduate courses in geology. At the master's level, one can specialise in Geophysics, Applied Geology, Mineralogy, Mineral Processing, Petroleum Engineering, Geotechnology, Natural Resources, Marine Geophysics, Marine Geology, etc. IIT (Kharagpur) offers a five-year integrated course in Exploration. Geophysics after Class 12. MTech in geology or Geophysics after clearing BTech/BE/MSc.

Jobs

The first prerequisite to enter this diverse and exciting field is a science background. "To get a job, one needs to have a master's degree in geology. One can become a surveyor with the Geological Survey of India (GSI) after clearing the UPSC exam, through which nearly 40-50 people are recruited every year. Other organisations employing geologists include Central Ground Water Board, Coal India, Mineral Exploration Authority, Oil & Mineral Gas Corporation and Hindustan Zinc besides several other organisations engaged in mineral explorations," says Prof. Ramanathan, a geologist. "Specialisation is the key as it widens job avenues. One can join ISRO and lend expertise to projects," he adds.

Geology also offers immense scope for research for those inclined to do that. The Centre for Earth Studies, National Institute of Hydrology, Wadia Institute of Himalayan Geology and Indian Institute of Tropical Meteorology recruit geologists as researchers and teachers. For that, one requires a doctorate degree. In private sector, there are openings as consultants.

Many universities offer graduate and post-graduate courses in geology. At the master's level, one can specialise in geophysics, applied geology, mineralogy, mineral processing, petroleum engineering, geo-technology, natural resources, marine geophysics and marine geology.

One can earn around Rs. 12,000 as a surveyor in a Government organisation, while geologists involved in exploration work get between Rs. 16,000 and Rs. 21,000 a month. For instance, if one is working for an MNC as a consultant in an oil exploration project, it's financially quite lucrative.

Remote sensing analysis is an ever better prospect, with salaries ranging from Rs. 50,000 to Rs. 65,000 per project.

Geological software developers get an initial salary of around Rs. 16,000, which can go up to Rs. 55,000. After MSc., one can start with a salary of around Rs. 6,500. After PhD, the remuneration could be anything between Rs. 8,000 and Rs. 12,000.

Human Qualities

To excel in this field, you need to possess effective oral and written communication skills. One should be able to visualise three-dimensional figures and enjoy exploration and outdoor work. One should have the aptitude for accurate details, good data collection, comparison skills and stamina.

The presence of good mathematical, analytical and observational skills is also essential. One should be able to adapt to various working conditions since the job entails both lab work and field projects in far-off lands. An ability to work in a team is, like other professions, important too.

New Trends

"Hydro-geology is an upcoming field. With scarcity of water emerging as an important issue, water harvesting has caught everyone's attention. Interdisciplinary fields of geology are in demand nowadays" says Prof. Mahmood. "Another upcoming field is urban geology, which deals with issues like controlling damage from earthquakes and waste management," adds Prof. Ramanathan.

Another new field is geological software development. This deals with computer programming to recreate the various geological processes on a computer. Remote sensing analysis and geological software development provide the maximum scope of a high-paying job abroad.

A master's degree is usually needed for junior college teaching and a PhD is required for teaching at the university level.

Employment for graduates depends on their speciality Jobs include exploration or mining environmental consultants, geologists in Government Geological Surveys, petroleum geologists, research scientists in industry or Government research institutions, as well as positions in education and environmental management.

Technological advances have greatly increased demand for many natural minerals which are essential in manufacturing and processing goods. The discovery of these mineral resources, their management and search for new resources, are all dependent on geologists.

Money and Other Benefits

One can make around Rs. 10,000-12,000 as a Surveyor in any Government organisation. Research positions pay more or less the same. Geologists, involved in exploration, get anything between Rs. 15,000-20,000 per month.

Consultants on oil-rigs or working MNCs make as much as $500-600 an hour.

Another high-paying job is Remote Sensing Analysis, where each project fetches up to Rs. 45,000-60,000.

Geological Software Developers get starting salaries of around Rs. 15,000, going up to Rs. 50,000 a month.

Research opportunities are also good. After doing MSc, one can secure a job paying about Rs. 6,500 per month or a research scholarship for Rs. 5,000-6,000 per month. After PhD one can get about Rs. 8,000-12,000 per month.

Admission Procedure

The examination for geologists is conducted by the Union Public Service Commission (UPSC).

The Geological Survey of Indian puts the recruited condidates through a training programme and an internal examination before posting them to any part in the country.

Post-graduates in geology/applied geology/marine geology/mineral exploration/hydrogeology or associates in applied geology of the Indian School of Mines at Dhanbad are eligible to appear in the examination.

Candidates should be between 21 and 30 years. The examination comprises five papers.

CAREER IN VARIOUS GEOLOGICAL FIELDS

The biggest employer for geologists is the Government of India. One can become a surveyor with the Geological Survey of India (GSI) through the UPSC examination consisting of five papers: including English (1), hydrogeology (1) and geology (3). Specialists work for organisations like the ONGC, Coal India, etc. Similar openings also exists with the Central Ground Water Board.

Employment is also possible with the Indian space and research organisation and lending expertise in remote sensing projects.

Geology offers ample scope for academic research. The Centre for Earth Studies National Institute of Hydrology, Wadia Institute of Himalayan Geology and Indian Institute of Tropical Meteorology recruit geologists for research as well as teaching. Of course, at this level one requires a doctoral degree in the subject. Openings in the private sector are too few and far between for consultants. A new field that one can branch into is Geological Software Development, which deals with computer programming to recreate various geological processes on computer.

- Marine geologists study the ocean floor and physical oceanographers study the physical aspects of oceans such as currents and their contact with the atmosphere.
- Petroleum geologists conduct exploratory tests to locate natural gas and oil deposits, both onshore and offshore. They also advise on the commercial viability of exploration projects.
- Geohydrologists locate, assess and analyse sources of water, identify agents of water pollution, advice on sitting and constructing reservoirs.
- Mineralogists analyse and classify minerals and precious stones in rocks and mineral deposits through chemical and physical analysis for use by industries.
- Hydrologists identify, measure and analyse water sources.
- Palaeontologists study fossils found in geological formations to trace the evolution of plant and animal life and estimate their age.
- Seismologists interpret data to locate earthquakes and earthquake faults.

- Stratigraphers study the distribution and arrangement of sedimentary rock layers to understand the distribution of land and sea.
- Engineering geologists carry out investigations before the foundations and earth works for large civil engineering projects are constructed.
- Environmental geologists deal with questions such as disposal of waste of all types and evaluate the environmental impact of construction projects.
- Geomorphologists study processes such erosion and glaciation.
- Geology education and research involves geologists in teaching and academic research in universities.

COURSES IN GEOLOGY

IIT Kharagpur

Offers a five-year integrated course in geophysics after Class 12. If one has cleared BTech/BE/MSc, he can do MTech in geology or geophysics.

IIT Roorkee

The Department of Earth Sciences runs three post-graduate courses, viz. MSc (applied Geology), MTech (applied geology) and MTech (applied geophysics) with specialisations like petroleum geology, earth resources technology, seismic exploration and well logging). Research programmes leading to doctoral degree in Earth Sciences are also conducted. Courses on computer programming form an integral part of the curriculum.

IIT Mumbai

The Department of Earth Sciences offers a programme leading to an MSc degree in applied geology. It also offers academic programmes leading to the MSc (applied geology), MTech (geoexploration) and doctoral degrees.

UPSC

Geologist examination is conducted by the Union Pubic Service Commission.

•

Geological Survey of India Training Institute (GSITI)

Headquartered in Hyderabad, the GSITI has six training centres at Hyderabad, Lucknow, Ranchi, Raipur.

Zawar and Chitradurga.

The Institute conducts orientation courses for geologists, geophysicists, analytical chemists, drilling engineers and surveyors.

It also conducts basic and refresher courses in photo-geology and remote sensing engineering geology, glaciology, geochemical exploration, petrology, palaeontology, environmental geology and quaternary geology; inter-disciplinary courses in geology, geophysics and geochemistry; advanced courses in geological mapping, mineral exploration, rock mechanics, geophysical methods and digital image processing.

It also conducts training courses in geological mapping and glaciology sponsored by the Department of Science and Technology under SERC School Scheme.

University of Mysore

MSc geology, MSc applied geology PG Diploma in hydro-geology. The intake is 20, 15 and 12 respectively for the three courses.

Anna University

The following courses are offered: MSc in applied geology, MPhil, PhD.

Specialised courses are offered in geo-tectonics, exploration geophysics, applied geochemistry, hydro-geology, mining geology, photo geology and remote sensing, engineering geology, environmental geology and petroleum geology. Other universities which offer courses in geology are Delhi University and Jadavpur University.

Geology streams which are in demand nowadays are petrology, sedimentology, structural geology and resource geology. Other fields which are coming up are urban geology and hydro-geology.

CAREERS IN HOTEL INDUSTRY

Today, the Hotel Industry is the fastest growing sector of the Indian economy owing to industrial growth and promotion of tourism. Career avenues are varied and there are plenty of job opportunities for trained and suitable hotel management personnel. Emerging trends in the growth of tourism and the expansion of the accommodation sector has necessitated a substantial increase in the additional requirement for trained manpower. Coupled with this is the demand for manpower in special areas such as airline and railway catering, industrial catering, etc.

This is a service oriented industry requiring skill based proficiency in addition to management, personnel and communication abilities. The skills include cooking, banking, serving at a table, making a bed or taking a reservation. These form an integral part of the training. In addition to this, a three year diploma or degree course in Hotel Management covers principles of management, financial management, Communications, Computer applications, sales and marketing, food production theory, nutrition, hotel law, a foreign language, etc. The practical aspect of the course provides hands on training where you operate actual systems and procedures in a hotel. If you join a hotel directly you will receive on the job training.

Work Environment

Everyday presents a new situation. It is not like any other business where you can plan your day, here you have to excel in tackling diverse situations. The work environment is unenviable. You are in air conditioned elegant surroundings. The whole atmosphere is professional and productive. You meet with corporate executives, famed personalities and people from different countries. Thus you have a good social reach. There is never a dull moment as there is job variety. The emoluments compare favourably with the best in the country. At the same time the working hours are long and you could be in the morning, afternoon or night shifts as the hotel operates through 24 hours. If you are placed in the night shift you will have to adjust your routine accordingly and sleep during the day! You have to be a good stress manager and you cannot afford to be temperamental even if harrassed by an irritating guest! You have to serve and it has to be "service with a smile"! Moreover, even if you are a manager you have to be willing to use your hands and do manual work if the situation so requires as the hotel atmosphere demands a tremendous dignity of labour.

Personal characteristics

According to Mr. R.K. Sexana, Principal. Indian Institute of Hotel Management, Lucknow, you should be an extrovert with strong qualities of leadership and have the ability of getting on well with people and dealing tactfully and diplomatically with dissatisfied customers. As you are very much in the public eye you should have a smart appearance and good social skills are essential. Also important are organisational ability business skills, competence in financial matters and interest in and knowledge of the practical skills related to hotel work such as cookery. The work can be hectic so you do need stamina!

Training

Training opportunities are available after plus two and after graduation. After plus two, selections through an entrance examination and interview are made by the following institutes/ colleges:

- *National Council for Hotel Management and Catering Technology, Pusa, New Delhi.* A joint Entrance Examination is held admission to a three year diploma course in Hotel Management by this Institute for admission to 15 years government sponsored Institutes of Hotel Management and Catering located at Ahmedabad, Bangalore, Bhopal, Bhubaneswar, Kolkata, Chandigarh, Goa, Hyderabad, Jaipur, Lucknow, Chennai, New Delhi, Srinagar, Thiruvananthapuram.
- *Welcomgroup Graduate School of Hotel Management Administration at Manipal, Karnataka.* This is affiliated to the Mangalore University and offers a three year programme leading to a Bachelors degree in Hotel Management (BHM). It is recognised by the International Hotel Association, Paris.
- *Institute of Professional Sciences and Management, (College of Hotel Management) Mangalore, Karnataka.* This is also affiliated to Mangalore University, is an affiliate of the International Hotel Association, Paris and offers a three years BHM programme.
- *Srinivas College of Hotel Management, Mangalore* G.H.S. Road, Mangalore-575001 Phone (0824)-425966;

E-mail: a.s.rao@bgl.vsnl.net.in. The College offers a three year BHM course and also post graduate diploma in Tourism and Hotel Management which is one year programme.

- *Asan Memorial Institute of Hotel Management and Catering Technology, Chennai,* offers a three year diploma course in Hotel Management and Catering Technology.
- *International Institute of Advanced Studies, Kolkata.* This Institute is affiliated to the Council of Hotel, Restaurant and Institutional Education, USA and conducts a number of courses related to the Hotel Industry.
- *Institute of Advanced Management, Hotel Management College, AE-486, Salt Lake City, Kolkata-700064 (Ph.) 3377726* is affiliated to the confederation of Management. U.K. and offers a two year diploma in Hotel and Catering Management.
- *The Indian Institute of Hotel Management, Aurangabad.* This is run by the Taj Group of Hotels and has a three year diploma in Hotel Management. Here the Hotel is attached to the Institute and run entirely by the trainees.
- *Merit Swiss Asian School of Hotel Management.* 22, Havelock Road, Ooty-643001, Nilgiris (Ph.) 0091-42343601-642486, E-mail: dean@md3.vsnl.net.in
- *International Institute of Hotel Management,* EC 07, Salt Lake City, Kolkata-700064 (Ph.) 3219546 Fax: 3346674
- *Saptagiri College of Hotel Management,* (Affiliated to Mangalore University), Kavoor, Mangalore-575015, Karnataka. (Ph.) 0824-481672 (7 lines) E-mail: Somayaji@saptagiri.com
- *Woodland College of Hotel Management,* C/o The Principal, Admissions, K.K.R.M. College, Woodlands Hotel Complex, 5, Raja Ram Mohan Roy Road, Bangalore-560027, (Ph.) 080-2225111, E-Mail: kkrmcollege@excite.com
- *M.S. Ramaish College of Hotel Management.* M.S. Ramaish Nagar, Msrit Post, Bangalore-560054, (Ph.) 080-3442829
- *Army Institute of Hotel Management & Catering Technology,* C/o ASC Centre (South), PO Agram, Bangalore-56007 (offers a degree course in bachelor of hotel management-BHM-open only to children of service Army personnel, or regular army pensioners).
- *Guru Govind Singh Indraprastha University,* Kashmere Gate, Delhi-110006—Website: http//ggsipu.nic.in. The

university offers Bachelors of Hotel Management & Catering Technology. This is a four years course.

- *Oberoi Centre for Learning and Development, 1 Sham Nath Marg, New Delhi-110054*, (Admits graduates from campuses of select colleges, hotel management institutes, or their own hotels).

Apart from the above recognised courses many more Institutes for Hotel Management are opening up thus bridging the gap between demand and supply.

After graduation, executive—training programmes are offered by a number of Five Star Hotels like Oberoi, Taj, Meridien, Asian Hotels. The Oberoi School of Hotel Management set up in 1996 offers a three-year management programme for graduates or diploma holders in hotel management. There are five seats and the selected executive trainees get a stipend of Rs. 4,000 to Rs. 5,000 a month. The school is recognised by the International Hotel Association of Paris. The Indian Tourism Development Corporation selects 55 management trainees every year. Hotel Management trainees generally get a stipend and have to execute a bond to serve the hotel for a given period. These hotels look out for "bright young people with pleasant outgoing personalities and a natural flair for hospitality." In addition, you should be a graduate, in your early twenties and fluent in English. Working knowledge of a foreign language is definitely an asset.

After from training opportunities in India which undoubtedly meet with international standards you can also seek admission to Hotel Management Institutes abroad. Schools in Austria, Switzerland, France, Germany and England and US particularly the School of Hotel Administration, Cornell University are the best and recognised worldwide. The courses are of one to three years duration. Information regarding these courses is available at the concerned Embassy/High Commission. If you study in Europe, it is essential to be fluent in the language spoken in the country. *Les Roches* in Switzerland which is managed by the Swiss Hotel Association conducts the course in English.

Institutes Abroad

— The Hotel and Tourism School, Les Roches, CH 3961 Biuche, Crans Montana, Valais, Switzerland.

— Leeds College of Technology, Coverly Street, Leeds, Yorkshire, UK.

— Cornell University School of Hotel Management and Administration, Statler Hall, Ithaca, NY 14850, USA.
— Michigan State University School Hotel Restaurant and Institutional Management, 424, Eppley Center, East Lansing, Michigan 148822, USA.

Entrance Examinations

The entrance examinations generally comprise objective type questions on analytical reasoning, logical deduction, numerical ability, scientific aptitude. English language and general awareness. The interview is a personality test to assess your suitability for the career-confidence, self-assurance, etiquette, manners, communication skills, general awareness, physical appearance and health.

Job Opportunities

Job opportunities for successful students of Hotel Management are plentiful in hotels, restaurants and clubs, food service for airlines, hospitals, the armed forces, institutional catering and consultancy firms, designing and marketing of institutional equipment and products, hotel marketing and sales, the management of resorts and teaching. You can start your own business and became a successful entrepreneur.

Once you join a hotel you will be assigned work in one of the following departments of the Hotel:

Accommodation, which is concerned with upkeep and sale of rooms and includes:

- Front Office and lobby services and housekeeping.
- The food and beverage department.
- Public Relations—Sales and Marketing
- Minor operating departments like health club, beauty parlour, business center, shopping arcade, etc.

Remunerations

The salaries match the best in any industry along with a pleasant working environment. Monthly remuneration at different levels is approximately:

General Manager	:	Rs. 30,000 to 50,000 plus perquisites
F & B Manager	:	Rs. 20,000 to 25,000
Front Office Manager	:	Rs. 6,000 to 10,000

Lobby Manager	:	Rs. 6,000 to 10,000
Restaurant Manager	:	Rs. 6,000 to 10,000
Executive Chief	:	Rs. 15,000 to 20,000 or more
Sous Chief	:	Rs. 8,000 to 10,000
Executive Housekeeper	:	Rs. 10,000 to 15,000
Assistant Housekeeper	:	Rs. 8,000 to 10,000

The creditable aspect of the hotel career path is that everyone can aim for the top position of General Manager irrespective of the level they joined. What matters is experience and performance.

QUESTIONS FOR ANSWER

1. *Write a note on the career prospects in ceramic industry.*
2. *Discuss different fields of oceanography and career prospects which oceanography holds for meritorious candidates.*
3. *Write short notes on the following industries to high light the requirements of jobs, nature of jobs and career prospects:*
   (*a*) *Leather Technology*
   (*b*) *Rubber Industry*
   (*c*) *Outsourcing Industries*
4. *Write a note on the nature of career prospects Plastic Surgery and Museology.*
5. *Discuss the career prospects of Geologists and name five major institutions of higher learning in Geology.*
6. *Write a note on the career prospects of a student of Hotel Management.*

29

Forward Look on the Impact of Emerging World of Work on Career Guidance

In the last three chapters we have discussed the nature of the emerging world of work and the role of institutions of higher learning in the formulation of careers of job seekers to suite the requirements of the new world of work, which has created uncountable new careers as discussed in the earlier two chapters.

It will not be wise to see the impact of the new world of work on economic aspects of national and individual life because it has remifications of various nature and, hence, the entire social structure, social value system, moral and cultural concepts, socio-political priorities have undergone are undergoing the sea-change. All these aspects determine the aims, objective, goals and nature of education, therefore, educational system and concepts are bound to adjust accordingly and, hence, there will be great need of qualitative career guidance to enable the individuals to properly decide his life goals.

In view of the above we have opted to devote this chapter to discuss the future need and nature of career guidance as well as to enable the individuals to make right choice of careers as per his abilities and capabilities and decide his life goals accordingly.

EMERGING NEED OF GUIDANCE

There is an urgent case for the introduction of guidance services in our colleges and universities-there can be no two opinions. What is needed today is a clear-cut, straight-forward and viable national policy about the programme-its pattern at different levels.

And this needs to be decided at the highest echelon involving the Ministry of Education and Social Welfare, Ministry of Labour and Employment, and University Grants Commission. The goals and Expectations of education and guidance with particular relevance to our immediate and long-term requirements need to be refocussed; unnecessary duplication of work by different agencies needs to be avoided; untouched areas need to be ensured to achieve the best results so that what we introduce in our country in the form of guidance and counselling service in colleges and universities is a well-knit integrated structure suiting Indian requirements.

What is needed today is to improve whatever little we have, and introduce the programme in right earnest. The task is by no means easy. Policy-makers, administrators, teachers and students have to be involved; certain attitudes and beliefs have to be re-evaluated and changed; new concepts with particular relevance to our requirements have to be established; confidence has to be won; services of trained personnel in the new area of development have to be enlisted and above all money has to be found.

All these are challenges in themselves. Discussions need to shift from indifference and wavering to firm, commitment; and the decision to transfer from future tense to present tense that is something has to be done ere and now.

SOME STRUCTURAL REFORMS NEEDED

1. *Agency at the National Level*—Some agency at the national level needs to be set up to act as an Advisory Body, a coordinator and a clearing house of knowledge. A separate Department of Guidance and Counselling needs to be created in the UGC exactly on the lines of Department of Psychology and Foundations of Education in the NCERT to initiate, coordinate and look after the guidance and counselling programme in the universities and colleges.

Directorates of College Education in each state should have under them guidance wings having guidance specialists to supervise and evaluate the guidance services in colleges.

2. *University Employment Information and Guidance Bureaux under the National Employment Service and Student Advisory Bureaux set up by the Ministry of Education should be combined*—It was

recommended long back by the Education Commission (1964-66). This step is long over-due to avoid unnecessary duplication of work and wastage of resources. This needs to be taken up now and very soon.

3. *Appointment of Counselling Officer*—The Education Commission (1964-66) had recommended the appointment of at least one counsellor for every one thousand students on the roll. It further had recommended that smaller institutions may share a counsellor who will work in each of the institutions on a part-time basis. Some immediate steps need to be taken for the appointment of counselling officers.

4. *Training of Counselling Officers*—Adequately qualified persons to run the programme in our colleges and universities is our immediate requirement. Some selected universities should immediately take up the task of training the personnel to work as counselling officers. The course of studies for the said course should have adequate practical slant to enable the trainees to create favourable atmosphere for the programme to take roots. Only dedicated and committed persons will be able to create guidance consciousness among the students and the staff, parents and the general public. The counselling officers should be persons who could meet new opportunities, new issues and new challenges. They must be able to increase and broaden the pathways along which the students may move and find new horizons, particularly in the new set-up when vocations are finding their way to colleges and universities.

To make an early start, short-term courses may be arranged for interested teachers jointly by the Department of Psychology and Education in the Universities. The minimum of the programme can be started immediately.

Selected teachers from colleges may be deputed for full term courses to the universities offering such courses.

Every college and university has some faculty members who do not have sufficient teaching load-(the subject taught by them may be new or many students do not go in for that subject).

Such teachers may be given training to carry on the guidance and counselling programme in addition to their work. This will be like killing two birds with one stone—the programme could be started and the teachers would also be profitably occupied.

5. *Counselling Centres in the Universities*—Initially the UGC should provide for a counselling centre at each university. The

services of these centres should be made available to the respective constituent and affiliated colleges.

Required counselling sessions should be held at convenient places on a scheduled basis as is being done by the mobile unit of the counselling centre of Indiana University, Bloomington, Indiana.

6. *Phased programme*—The programme may be started in a phased manner. First of all, we should confine our efforts to the under-graduate student body.

Secondly, we should start with certain colleges, certain hostels, certain groups. It is better to attempt a limited amount successfully than to scatter one's efforts fruitlessly.

Similarly, we should emphasise services with the widest coverage. In every institution there will be important problems common to large groups as well as problems concerning individuals. Problems as lack of information about the library and how to use it; how to read effectively; how to study can be dealt to a considerable extent in groups.

In the early stages, when resources like personnel, equipment and money are scarce, to take up individual cases, especially those which require professional psychologists or psychiatrists should not be contemplated.

7. *We should start with the aspects of the programme that cost little or nothing*—For example, we can make a start with orientation service-a service of highest importance and value to the student; a welcome to the campus, with real depth of meaning but which can be supplied at virtually no cost.

This service requires intelligent organisation and coordination, but does not involve any expenditure.

With the money already provided for the maintenance of colleges and universities, a good orientation programme could be developed. When the values of other services are gradually recognised, additional money from the colleges and universities will be forthcoming.

8. *Guidance and Counselling complex in a college or university*—In a small town, the guidance and counselling complex may be set up in the already existing colleges in every town. The biggest college should have this arrangement and in a city which happens to have a university, the Guidance and Counselling complex should be set up there.

This complex should specially take up the task of preparing the students for interviews, for jobs and various competitive examinations. That way the service will find its way in the life of the institutions and it will become a much sought-after service.

The complex should initiate research projects, programmes and studies which may be conducted in collaboration with various concerned departments of the university/college on local and regional basis for estimation of manpower requirements in various categories in the context of the developmental outlay in a district, region/state.

The UGC should encourage such activities and provide necessary financial assistance for such programmes and projects on a priority basis. Colleges should be fruitfully involved for data collection and surveys.

9. *Financial Provision*—Whenever a new facility has to be added, the biggest problem before the administrators and educational planners is how to provide for it? It is true, provision for guidance and counselling service cannot be made cheaply; sufficient funds have to be allocated for the salaries of the counselling officers and the supporting staff, allowances of the Liaison officers in the colleges, tools and equipment.

While making provision for student welfare services, a separate allocation needs to be made by UGC for the Guidance and Counselling Services as it also is a very important student welfare service. A part of the students' amalgamated fund-say 5 per cent—may be spent on this programme.

The part-time guidance workers—Liaison officers and Assistant Counselling officers could be paid their allowances out of this fund, if possible. If the institution is not in a position to pay that, special provision must be made by UGC as is being done in case of NSS workers.

Let there be fair distribution of resources on different student welfare schemes. The states should finance the Guidance Wing in the College Directorate.

A college or a university—sufficiently rich should start counselling centre on its own.

If lack of financial resources alone prevents a college or a university from starting a counselling centre, some philanthropic trusts such as Mahatma Gandhi Memorial Fund or Nehru Memorial Fund should be approached for funds.

An effective guidance and counselling programme staffed with adequate qualified personnel and equipped with adequate tools does cost money. Of course, there is no hard empirical evidence that the cost of guidance and counselling services are in the long run self-liquidating.

Studies do suggest that potentially an effective programme of guidance can make significant contribution to student development. The real question, therefore, may not be "can the college or university or even the state afford guidance"? but rather "can the college or university or state afford not to have guidance?"

It needs to be pointed out that if one counselling officer could prevent the wastage of four student years each costing rupees four to five thousand a year, he would be earning his keep. Similar savings of graduate salaries foregone as a result of failure of delay would benefit student as well as the tax payer.

It should be apparent that it is not the question whether the facility of guidance and counselling for college and university students should be provided or not, but only a question of how soon and how sound!

AN OBSERVATION

The above discussion leads us to infer that there is a great need of more stress on proper programme of guidance and counselling at every stage of our educational system and similarly a great need to introduce structural reform in the implementation of the programme of guidance and counselling in our educational institutions.

It is unfortunate that our efforts to revamp the educational system of the country, our efforts were misdirected and a result of which instead of having compulsory elementary education for all the children of the nation, we opted to enlarge the area of higher secondary and higher education aimlessly.

We did not plan higher education as per need of the country and hence people without deciding the goals of life opted to become graduates, the result is that we have the largest army of unemployed graduates in the world. If this process continues for long then our socio-political, socio-economic and socio-cultural structure of society will collapse, because these unemployed graduates do not have a definite goal of life as they did not have the same for their education.

We observe that most of the unemployed or under-employed graduates not only feel frustrated with their status in the society, but feel inseure and unsuitable, hence, same of the opt for adopting unsocial or anti-social personality and virtually turn into white-collar criminals. Therefore, the prim need of society is to provide proper guidance and counselling to this young generation of adults to enable them to look after their children properly, give them proper education as per their abilities and capabilities as well as per needs of the emerging world of work. With this aim in mind we, suggest the nature of guidance and counselling programme for the adults.

QUESTIONS FOR ANSWER

1. *Write a note on the need of guidance in the emerging world of work.*
2. *Why we should reform our structure of guidance and counselling? Give reasons.*
3. *What reforms are needed in the structure of our guidance activities?*

30

Emerging World of Work: The Need of Guidance for Adults

As discussed in the earlier chapter, hereunder, we discuss various aspects of guidance and counselling as per need of the emerging world of work and socio-educational and socio-economic structure in our country.

Uneducated or less educated or those adults who have the urge to know more about the ever changing conditions and opportunities that comprise our modern complex stage of civilization need adult education and accordingly guidance too for achieving self-realization in and adjustment with their various life activities.

AREAS OF ADULT ADJUSTMENT

The young adult, the middle-aged man and woman, and the older person experience problems of adjustment that are peculiar to their age pattern, their hopes, and their ambitions.

The Young Adult

Need for further formal education; problems of courtship, and marital and family adjustment; job placement, and job efficiency and satisfaction; leisure-time and recreational activities-these represent some of the major areas of adjustment among younger adults.

The young person between the ages of eighteen and twenty-five usually is forward looking and hopeful for the future. If his educational experiences and the guidance he received during childhood and adolescence were adequate for his developing needs, he enters adulthood relatively well prepared to take on responsibilities. He feels secure in his ability to cope with whatever may lie ahead of him.

He may be at loose ends socially, having lost contact with his school friends. He may have neglected to associate himself with others of his own age through participation in community sponsored social and recreational organisations.

It is during this period that the young adult begins to assume specific citizenship responsibilities as he fist exercises his voting rights. Hence he may become the victim of political ideologies that intrigue his youthful enthusiasm.

No matter how well-prepared vocationally a young man or woman is when ready to start occupational activities, there are many work adjustments that need to be made.

Seeking and finding the right kind of job and becoming accustomed to new fellow workers, administrators, and work activities are not always easy. These experiences can cause serious emotional upset.

As the young worker becomes better acquainted with the conditions and activities of the job, he may discover that he is not satisfied with them and wants to change, or he may become so interested in his work that he is fired with ambition to improve his efficiency or to advanced his position. In either case he is likely to be motivated to continue his education beyond his formal study activities.

The Middle-Aged Adult

Usually by the time a man or woman reaches the forties, he or she has developed a relatively fixed pattern of life. The person may have become increasingly engrossed in day-by-day activities and interests that deal chiefly with provision of the necessities and some luxuries for himself and his family. It is likely that he or she has made certain more or less satisfying adjustment in social and occupational activities.

This is a dangerous age in the life of many men and women. The realisation that they are not getting any younger stimulates in them the desire to make up for lost time. Old age may seem to be just around the corner. Hence they may attempt to throw themselves headlong into new experiences with what may seem to be a return of youthful vigor and enthusiasm.

Rarely does such a course of action provided the satisfaction that is expected of it. Habits that have become relatively fixed cannot be changed suddenly and definitely. Moreover, the physical constitution of the middle-aged or older person cannot take the 'beatings' that it once took.

The Older Adult

A generally increasing life span and changed attitudes toward 'old age' are factors to which an individual needs to adjust while he still is young and vigorous. Preoccupation of grown children with their own families and adult activities; the forced or voluntary retirement from occupational activity; the possible onslaught of physical disorders peculiar to this age period; the death of former associates; and the degree of financial security that has been achieved constitute problems of adjustment that may be difficult for the elderly to solve unaided.

This is the age period, however, during which the man and woman who have lived rich and full lives during their earlier years now may find time for participation in many satisfying and worthwhile activities. There are books to be read, places to be visited, philanthropic and community projects to be engaged in, and social relationships to be enjoyed for which little time was available during the 'busy' years. The above classification of adults covers all those who completed their education in last thirty years or after 1974 or born in 1955 or after. We hereunder, suggest the nature of guidance and counselling the adults:

An adult's needs and interests usually are not concerned so much with the future as with the present. What he does now, of course, may affect what happens in the future, but it is the present that is of primary concern to him.

Guidance services for an adult must take into consideration his existing conditions and their background, and must render assistance that can be of immediate value to him.

Types of Guidance

Guidance services made available to an adult, as on lower age levels, must enter into every phase of his life pattern. The adult may need guidance toward the achievement of well-adjusted marital and family relations.

His hole pattern of sex-stimulated thought and behaviour may give rise to serious emotional conflict unless he has been helped from childhood on to develop whole some attitudes and forms of conduct.

Satisfactory worker adjustment is important to both the employer and the employee, but sometimes it is difficult to achieve. Hence many business and industrial organisations maintain a well-organised personnel department for orientation on the job and for the rendering of adjustive services to those employees who may experience occupational or personal problems of adjustment.

Last but not the least, the physical and mental health of all adults should be the primary concern of the individual himself and of society as a whole. Our hospitals for the physically or mentally ill are overcrowded. Physical health guidance is becoming increasingly effective.

Medical research, the dissemination of information concerning diseases and the taking of precautionary measures and the work of health clinics are bringing about a commendable improvement in the physical health of the citizens.

Mental health is not a static condition; once arrived at, it cannot be effortlessly maintained. Mental health consists of—it is—a dynamic balance. It is an emotional equilibrium amidst stresses and pressures in relation to which we must progressively find adjustment.

The following are some of the aspects of life in relation to which each of us continuously seeks to maintain his balance:

On the one hand there are:	*Which, on the other hand, must be balanced against:*
1. One's assets	1. One's liabilities
2. One's assets	2. Others' assets
3. The giving of a affection, sympathy, and understanding	3. The receiving of affection, sympathy, and understanding
4. Enjoyment of work	4. Enjoyment of play
5. Enjoyment of activity	5. Enjoyment of rest and quiet
6. Enjoyment of working co-operatively	6. Enjoyment of working alone
7. The enjoyment of success	7. Ability to accept failure
8. Seeing failure as due sometimes to one's own limitations	8. Seeing failure as due sometimes to environmental difficulties

(Contd.)

On the one hand there are:	*Which, on the other hand, must be balanced against:*
9. The ability to think	9. The ability to feel
10. The ability to be a leader	10. The ability to be a follower
11. The ability to use one's abilities to the utmost	11. The ability to recognise that there are powers beyond our control
12. The ability to recognise conscious factors as important in our motivation	12. The ability to recognise unconscious factors as important in our motivation
13. A respect for the mind	13. A respect for the body
14. One's own sex	14. The opposite sex
15. One's worth simply by virtue of being a person	15. The vastness of the universe
16. The importance of the years one lives	16. The past before one was born and the years that will follow one's death

Balance successfully maintained (or re-established), in terms of the stresses suggested above, not only is mental health, but also insures the future mental health of him who can maintain it.

COUNSELLING PERSONNEL FOR ADULT GUIDANCE

Teacher-Counsellors for Adults

Every teacher of adults is a counsellor whether or not he devotes all of his time to classroom instruction. An adult is more likely than a younger person to ask questions of a teacher in whom he has confidence. Since many who teach courses in adult education are part-time employees and since the courses are given at hours convenient for busy people, the instructors selected can be those who not only are qualified as teachers but also are interested in others and have some counselling potential.

The classes should be small enough to permit the teacher to give special help to every student. Adult learners usually are co-operative because they want to gain something other than credit from their participation in learning activities.

Among the types of problems that may be brought to the attention of the teacher by his adult students are these:

1. How can a newcomer to a community become acquainted with his neighbours?

2. Is it desirable to center one's social life in people who are in the same business or profession as oneself?
3. Why is it important to have fiends of both sexes?
4. In order to be popular, must one always subordinate his personal interests to those of the group?
5. Should children be included in all the social activities of their parents?
6. Could there be a central agency for community service for housewives?
7. Should married people include their older relatives in their social activities?
8. What are the leisure-time activities in the community in which one could engage with enjoyment?

If the adult is unmarried he may be interested in conferring with the teacher or counsellor on questions like these:

1. Can one discover before marriage whether or not the other person will be a good husband or wife?
2. What should the young man or woman do if the chosen mate receives family disapproval?
3. Should a girl of twenty marry a man of forty?
4. What should a man or woman tell the other concerning previous romantic experiences?
5. Should parents help a young couple financially?
6. Should a man and woman break old friendships when they marry?

If a couple are in their early years of marriage, they may be interested in answers to questions of this kind:

1. How can a satisfactory and healthful sex life be achieved?
2. Should a couple be expected to give up social activities after children are born?
3. To what extent should a wife show interest in her husband's occupational work?
4. Should a husband help with the household chores?
5. Is it desirable to have relatives of either mate live with the couple?
6. What should one mate do to correct the faults of the other?

During the middle years of married life one or the other of the mates may want advice concerning these matters:

1. How can husband-wife quarrels be reduced to a minimum?
2. Are children necessary to a happy marriage?
3. Need the fact that a woman has reached her menopause interfere with marital happiness?
4. What should a person do upon discovering that his mate no longer loves him?
5. To what extent should the middle-aged couple engage in social activities together?

Questions might be asked at any age about the adjustments to older people or of them. Among the questions asked are these:

1. Should aged parents live with their children?
2. Should the care of old people be the responsibility of their families or of society?
3. For whom are the problems of old age more difficult—a man or a woman?
4. What forms of recreation are desirable of older men and women?
5. how can a person best prepare himself for his declining years?

When men and women are concerned with their vocational welfare, they may raise questions such as the following with their teachers or counsellors.

1. Which is more important-economic security or happiness on the job?
2. What are reliable media for discovering good job openings?
3. What is the best way of selling oneself to a prospective employer?
4. Should a person accept a job away from home if this necessitates leaving his family and friends?
5. If a man has a family to support, should he remain in a steady job which he does not enjoy or should he take a chance in a new venture?
6. How friendly should an employee be with his employer?
7. How can a worker adjust to an employer whom he dislikes?
8. As an employer, what can one do with a disgruntled but skillful worker?

The type of questions concerning social activities about which adults might seek guidance are:

1. Should every adult join a social or political club?
2. In order to be popular with a group, to what extent should one subordinate his personal interests to those of the group?
3. What type of leisure-time activities are available for night workers?
4. What social activities should be shared by all members of the family?
5. Should a central community service be established for the social welfare of housewives?
6. Could more publicity be given to community and civic activities, so that more adults may know about them?

COUNSELLING SERVICE FOR ADULTS

As we know, counselling services for adults were established after World War II in order to provide educational and occupational counselling for returning servicemen.

As the veteran demands for counselling decreased, these services were expanded for the benefit of the general adult population. At first, such programmes were affiliated with colleges, school systems, or community agencies.

Later many of them were separated from established institutions but continued their counselling activities as low-fee, private agencies. Unfortunately, we still lack a sufficient number of adult counselling centers to serve the many adults and out-of-school youth who have begun to recognise the practical value of expert assistance in solving their educational, vocational, and personal problems.

Informal Versus Organised Guidance

Most teachers of adults are interested and concerned about the vocational plans of their students. Some are qualified to give informal but excellent advice in areas of relatively simple decision-making. To meet student demand for adequate guidance in more serious problem-solving situations, however, school-sponsored adult education programmes must include organised counselling services conducted by trained personnel.

The Interview

The focal point of adult counselling, as in the guidance of children and adolescents, is the individual conference or interview. Many of the educational and vocational problems on the adult level are similar. Yet, the social, economic, and personal factors which enter into the satisfactory solution of a particular individual's problem are numerous and varied.

Hence, to render effective assistance, the counsellor needs to have accumulated a background of information on the counselee as well as to discover other pertinent facts during the course of the interview or series of conferences.

The counsellor's interview approach mist be tactful and cautious. No matter how eager he is for help, the adult counselee tends to resent actual or imagined probing by the counsellor; he is sensitive about "baring his soul" to another adult, perhaps younger than he is. Sometimes, the more serious the problem, the more likely is the individual to be unco-operative. The experienced educational or vocational counsellor then refers the case to an appropriate specialist or community agency.

Guidance Toward Continued Education

Trained persons know how to encourage these older adolescents and young adults to further their best interests and meet their responsibilities as maturing individuals.

Not only have many opportunities been provided for continued learning by adults after they supposedly have completed their formal schooling and have moved into the field of productive activity but also, in increasing numbers, individuals are taking advantage of those opportunities.

So many are the offerings in programmes of adult-education that, contrary to his earlier school experiences, the adult student now is able to select a course or courses in light of his immediate interest rather than to fulfill graduation requirements.

If an adult is taking a course associated directly in a practical way with his existing interests and responsibilities, he generally experiences no difficulty in giving it his full attention. The parent who is attending a course on child-care dovetails the content of the course with his or her daily activities as he attempts to apply in parents-child relations some of the principles or practices discussed in class.

In the same way, a worker whose study activity is aimed at the improvement of the work in which he is engaged during the day attempt to carry study material into workroom practices.

On the adult level, study difficulties are more likely to accompany attempts to master subject matter that is unrelated to one's daily activities or one's cultural interest. Systematic studying is not always easy for the adult.

Study engaged in for the purpose of providing for future or anticipated needs, the content of which is unrelated to one's present life pattern or interest but the mastery of which may be required, is not done without a great deal of effort.

Qualities of a Group Leader

In order for the group leader to function effectively as a mentor and guide it is imperative that he possesses certain confidence-instilling characteristics. Among other qualities he

1. has a genuine interest in his students,
2. knows them and their interests and idiosyncrasies,
3. endeavours to work co-operatively with his students,
4. gives attention to each individual at each class session,
5. has so thorough a mastery of his subject matter that his approach is functional, inspiring the students to share his enthusiasm and interest,
6. presents subject matter in such a way that much of it can be learned during the class period,
7. avoids arousing any feeling of shame, inadequacy, or failure in the mentally slower students,
8. displays a keen sense of humour,
9. shows concern for the health and safety of his students,
10. discourages inconsequential digression but motivates worthwhile discussion, and
11. maintains a high level of student interest and participation throughout the course meetings. To the teacher who brings to his work these attitudes and behaviour patterns will come the rewards that accompany satisfaction in any line of endeavour; the payment in appreciation from his students will be immediate, heartwarming, and lasting.

COMMUNITY GUIDANCE SERVICES

Value of a Guidance Center

A community guidance center may be organised for the purpose of giving personal and professional guidance to out-of-school youth and adults. A number of these were started by the Veterans' Administration and are serving as the nucleus for services that are being carried on now that veteran needs have been reduced. These centers are becoming integral parts of the community service programme. They are being made available to all out-of-school citizens in the community.

The services of this type of guidance programme should be articulated with the activities of other community agencies. Each agency, however, should be allowed to continue its specialized service, in co-operation with the others.

In discussing the specific needs that can be met by community guidance services, R.H. Mathewson reports:

Among the specific services which the guidance center may provide in meeting needs expressed by adult clients are the following:

Useful information about educational, vocational, economic, and other opportunities or services in the community.

Aid to the individual in making maximum use of opportunities and services in relation to his own needs.

Specialized aid for persons with handicaps and disabilities.

Professional help with problems of emotional disturbance or disorder.

Locating suitable employment.

Assistance in dealing with economic, financial, and legal difficulties.

Help in adjusting to difficulties in home and family living; marriage problems.

The personnel in charge of the guidance center should be equipped especially to deal with adults and their problems. No guidance counsellor should find himself in a position similar to that which was reported by a graduate student in a course dealing with improvement of instruction in colleges and universities. After taking two inadequate courses in guidance, he had been assigned to assist other adults in meeting their personal problems.

When he interviewed the first counselee, he was frightened because he realised that he could not cope with the adjustment problem posed and had to be frank about it. To be effective, guidance deserves better counsellor preparation than this student had. Individuals should not be pleased in responsible positions unless and until they are qualified through training and experience to deal with the type of problems that arise on the adult level. Specialists should be available in appropriate agencies, and referrals should be permitted.

QUESTIONS FOR ANSWER

1. *Explain the need and functions of guidance for adults.*
2. *Write a note on the functions and responsibilities of teacher counsellor for adults.*
3. *Write a note on informal and formal counselling services for adults.*
4. *Write short notes on the following:*
   (*a*) *Guidance in adult education,*
   (*b*) *Community guidance services for the adults.*

Bibliography

Anastasi, Anne. *Psychological Testing.* London: London: Collier Macmillan Publishers, 1982

Anne. Roe. *Psychology of Occupations.* New York: John Wiley and Sons, 1956.

Arbuckle, Dugld S. *Counselling: Philosophy, theory and Practice,* Boston: Allyn and Bacon Inc., 1965.

Beck, Carlton, E. *Philosophical Foundations of Guidance.* Englewood Cliffs, new Jersey: prentice Hall, 1964.

Bernard, H.W. and Fullmer, D.W. *Principles of Guidance: A basic Taxt* (Indian Ed.). New Delhi: Allied Publishers Private Ltd.

Bennett, Margaret E. *Guidance and Counselling in Groups.* Second Ed. New York: McGraw Hill, 1963.

Bulletins 1-12 Educational Psychology Unit. NCERT, New Delhi.

Cattell, B.B. *Abilities: Their Structure; Growth and Action.* Boston: Houghton Mifflin Co., 1971.

Chauhan, S.S, *Principles and Techniques of Guidance,* New Delhi: Vikas Publishing House, 1982.

Crow, Lester D., and Crow, A. *An Introduction to Guidance Principles and Practices.* New Delhi: Eurasia Publishing House, 1962.

Cottle, W.C. *Interest and Personality Inventories.* New York: Houghton Muffling Co., 1968.

Cottle, W.C. and Downie, N.M. *Preparation for Counselling.* Second Ed. Englewood Cliffs. N.J.: Prentice Hall, 1970.

Cronbach. L.I. *Essentials for psychological Testing.* New York: Harper, 1970.

Downing, Lester N. *Guidance and Counselling Services.* New York: McGraw Hill, 1964.

Education Commission Report 1964-66. New Delhi: Ministry of Education, Government of India, 1966.

Effectiveness of Services Rendered by University Employment Information and Guidance *Bureaux.* New Delhi: CERTES, Jan. 1973.

Erickson, Clifford E. *A Basic Text for Guidance Workers.* Englewood Cliffs: Prentice Hall, 1955.

Frank, H. Krouse. *Counselling Technique with Youth.* Ohio: Charles and Mervil, 1960.

Freeman, Frank S. *Theory and Practice of Psychological Testing*. New Delhi: Oxford and IBH Publishing Company, 1965.

Fuster, J.M. *Psychological Counselling in India*. Bombay: Macmillan, 1964.

Fletcher, F.M. and Riddle, W. "The Guidance Movement in India." *Personnel and Guidance Journal*, 1962, 70.

Garret A, *Interviewing: Its Principles and Methods*. New York: Family Service Association of America, 1962.

Hahn, M.E. and Maclean, M.S. *Counselling Psychology*. New York: McGraw Hill, 1955.

Hamrin, S.A. *Initiating and Administering Guidance Services*. Bloomington: Mcknight and Mcknight Publishing Company, 1959.

Hansen, James C. *Counselling Process and Procedures*. New York: Macmillan, 1978.

Hatch, Ramend, N. and Steffle, Buford. *Administration of Guidance Services*. Englewood Cliffs. New Jersey: Prentice Hall, 1958.

Hollis, Joseph William, and Hollis, Lucide. *Organisation for Effective Guidance*. Chicago: Science Research Associates, 1965.

Hoose, William N. Van (ed.). *Counselling and Guidance in the 20th Century*. Boston Houghton Mifflin Co., 1979.

Humphrey, J. Anthony and Traxler, Arthur E. *Guidance Services*. Chicago. Science Research Association Inc., 1954.

Jones, A.J. *Principles of Guidance and Pupil Personnel Work*. New York: McGraw Hill, 1963.

Khoshed, A.W. *Guidance Movement in India*. Guidance Services Series, No. 4, New Delhi: NCERT, 1963.

Knapp, Robert H. *Practical Guidance Methods for Councellors, Teachers and Administrators*. New York: McGraw Hill Book Co., Inc. 1953.

Knight R, *Intelligence and Intelligence Tests*. (2nd Edition) London: Methuen and Co. Ltd. 1943.

Kroth, J.A. *Counselling Psychology and Guidance*. Springfield, Illinois: Charles C. Thomas, 1973.

Krumboltz, J.D. and Thoresen, C.E. *Counselling Methods*. New York: Holt, Rinehart and Winston, 1976.

McCully, C.H. "The Counsellor-Instrument of Change." *Teachers College Record*. 1965, 66, 405-412.

Mahler, C.A. *Group Counselling in the Schools*. Boston: Houghton Mifflin, 1969.

Matarazzo, J.D. *Wechsler's Measurement and Appraisal of Adult Intelligence*, Baltimore: Williams and Wilkins, 1972.

Mathewson, Robert H. *Guidance Policy and Practice*. New York: Harper and Row, 1962.

Miller, Carroll H. Foundations of Guidance. New York: Harper and Brothers, 1961.

Miller, Frank W. *Guidance-Principles and Services*. Ohio: Charles E. Merrill Books, 1961.

Munson, Harold L. *Foundations of Developmental Guidance*. Boston: Allyan and Bacon, 1971.

Murphy, G. "The Cultural Context of Guidance." *Personnel and Guidance Journal*. 1955, 34, 4-9.

NCERT Interest Inventory (Senior Form). Delhi: NCERT, 1974.

Occupational Pattern of India, Public Sector, 1968.

Ohlsen, M.M. *Group Counselling (2nd ed.)* New York: Holt Rinehart and Winston, 1977.

Pasricha, Prem. *Guidance and Counselling in Indian Education*. New Delhi: NCERT, 1976.

Patterson, C.H. *Theories of Counselling and Psycho-therapy*. New York: Harper and Row, 1973.

Counselling and Guidance in School: A First Course. New York: Appleton Century Crafts, 1966.

Pepinsky, Harold B. and Pepinsky, Pauline Nichols. *Counselling Theory and Practice*. New York: The Ronald Press Company, 1954.

Peters, H.J. and Hanson, J.C. (Ed.) *Vocational Guidance and Career Development*. New York: Macmillan, 1968.

Pinto, Diana V. Counselling: Theory, Research and Practice. Chicago: Rand McNally College Publishing Company,

Rao, Narayan. *Counselling Psychology*. New Delhi: McGraw Hill Publishing Company Limited, 1981.

Roeber, E.C., Smith, G.E. and Erickson, E.E. *Organisation and Administration of Guidance Service (2nd ed.)* New York: McGraw Hill. 1955.

Robinson, F.P. *Principles and Procedures in Student Counselling*. New York: Harper and Row, 1950.

Shertzer, Bruce Stone, Shelly, C. *Fundamentals of Guidance*. Boston: Houghton Mifflin Co. 1976.

Shrivastave, K.K., Principle of Guidance and Counselling Kanishka Publisher Distributors, New Delhi, 2003.

Singh, Amarjit. *Is Intelligence Inherited? A Critical synthesis and Review of Research Findings*. New Delhi: NCERT, 1978.

Schwarz, P.A. and Krug, R.E. *Ability Testing in Developing Countries: A Handbook of Principles and Techniques*. New York: Praeger, 1972.

Slocum, Walter L. *Occupational Careers: Sociological Perspective*. Aldine Publishing Co., 1968.

Smith, G.E. *Counselling in the Secondary Schools*. New York: MacMillan, 1955.

Smith, H.M. and Erickson, L.O. *Guidance Services in Elementary Schools*. Washington: Government Printing Press, 1966.

Smith, M.R. (Ed.) *Guidance-Personnel Work-Future Tense*. New York: Teachers College Press Columbia University, 1966.

Spearman, C.E. *The Nature of Intelligence and Principles of Cognition*, London: MacMillan, 1923.

Stewart, N.R. and Others. *Systematic Counselling* Englewood Cliffs, N.J.: Prentice Hall, 1978. Tec.

Strang, Ruth. *Counselling Technique in College and Secondary School*. New York: Harper and Brothers, 1937.

Super, Donald E. *Psychology of Careers*. New York: Harper Row, 1957.

Thomas, F. Station. *Dynamics of Adjustment*. New York: MacMillan Co., 1953.

Thorndike, R.L. and Hagen E. *Measurement and Evaluation in Psychology and Education. (3rd Edition)*. New Delhi: Wiley Eastern Pvt. Ltd., 1969.

Tolber, E.L. *Counselling for Career Development*. Boston: Houghton Mifflin, 1974.

"*Introduction to Counselling*. New York: McGraw Hill, 1959.

Traxler, A.E. and North, R.D. *Techniques of Guidance*. New York: Harper and Row, 1957, 3-4.

Tyler, L.E. *The Work of the Counsellor*. New York: Appleton Century Crafts, 1969.

"*Personality Assessment*." London: Methuen Co. Ltd., 1964.

Warters, Jane. *Techniques of Counselling*, (3rd Ed.) New York: McGraw Hill, 1964.

Weitz, Henry. *Behaviour Changes Through Guidance*. New York: McGraw Hill, 1964.

Williamson, E.G. *How to Counsel Students*. New York: McGraw Hill, 1939.

Wren, Gilbert C. *The Counsellor in a Changing World*. Washington: American Personnel and Guidance Association, 1962.

Zeran, Franklin. R and Riccio, Anthony C. *Organization and Administration of Guidance Services*. Chicago: Rand McNally and Co., 1962.

APGA-ACES, Standards for the Preparation of Secondary School Counsellors, *Personnel and Guidance Journal*, Vol. 46 (1947), 96-106.

Arbuckle, Dugald S., "The Self of the Counsellor," *Personnel and Guidance Journal*, Vol. 44, No. 8 (April 1966), 807-12.

Arnez, N. L., "Effect of Teacher Attitudes upon the Culturally Different," *School and Society*, Vol. 94 (March 19, 1966), 149-52.

Aubrey, Roger F., "The Legitimacy of Elementary School Counselling; Some Unresolved Issues and Conflicts," *Personnel and Guidance Journal*, Vol. 46 (December 1967), 355-59.

Axline, V., *Dibs, In Search of Self*, Boston, Houghton Mifflin Company, 1965.

Baller, Warren R., and Don C. Charles, *The Psychology of Human Growth and Development*, 2nd ed., New York, Holt, Rinehart and Winston, Inc., 1968.

Barker, R.G., "Ecology and Motivation," in *Nebraska Symposium on Motivation*, Lincoln, Nebraska, University of Nebraska Press, 1960.

Barry, R., and B., Wolf, *Motives, Values and Realities, A Framework for Counselling*, New York, Teachers College Press, Teachers College, Columbia University, 1965.

Bennett, Margaret C., *Guidance in Groups*, McGraw-Hill Book Company, Inc., New York, 1955.

Bennett, Margaret E., *Guidance and Counselling in Groups*, McGraw-Hill Book Company, New York, 1963.

Bentley, J.C., "Role Theory in Counselling: A Problem in Definition, "*Personnel and Guidance Journal*, Vol. 44, No. 1 (September 1965), 11-17.

Bienstock, Herbert, "The Employment Outlook: What The Statistics Show," *New Generation*, Vo. 50, No. 1 (Winter 1968).

Blocher, Donald H., *Developmental Counselling*, The Ronald press Company, New York, 1966.

Bordin, Edward S., *Psychological Counselling*, New York, Appleton Century-Crafts 1968.

Borow, H. (ed.) *Man in a World at Work*, Boston, Houghton Mifflin Co., 1964.

Bradford, L.P., J.R. Gibb, and K.D. Benne, *T-group Theory and Laboratory Method*, John Wiley & Sons, Inc., New York, 1964.

Brammer, L.M., and E.L. Shostrom, *Fundamentals of Counselling and Psychotherapy*, 2nd ed., Englewood Cliffs, New Jersey, Prentice-Hall Inc., 1968.

Brown, J.S., *The Motivation of Behavior*, New York, McGraw-Hill Book Company, 1961.

Burton, W.H., *The Guidance of Learning Activities*, New York, Appleton Century Crofts, Inc., 1944.

Butler, J., Lecture, Portland, "A Psychiatrist Looks at the School Counsellor," NDEA Counselling and Guidance Institute, January 7, 1966.

Casell, Arnold, Florence Ilg, and Louise Ames, *Youth: The Years from Ten To Sixteen*, Harper & Brothers, New York, 1956.

Clark, A.W., and P. Van Sommers, "Contradictory Demands in Family Relations and Adjustment to School and Home," *Human Relations*, Vol. 14 (1961), 97-111.

Coleman, J., *Adolescents and the Schools*, New York, Basic Books, 1965.

Combs, Arthur W., and Donald Snygg, *Individual Behavior* Harper & Brothers, New York, 1959.

Cottingham, Harold D., *Guidance in Elementary Schools*, Mcknight & McKnight Publishing Company, Bloomington, Illinois, 1956.

Cruickshank, William M., *Psychology of Exceptional Children and Youth*, Prentice-Hall, Inc., Englewood Cliffs, N.J., 1955.

Diamont, L., A. H. Todd, and D.T. Robinson, "School Counsellors as Therapists," *The School Counsellor*, Vol. 13 (1965), 110-116.

Dinkmeyer, Don C. (ed.) *Guidance and Counselling in the Elementary School*, New York, Holt, Rinehart and Winston, Inc., 1968.

Donahue, Wilma et al, (eds.) *Free Time: Challenge to Later Maturity*, University of Michigan Press, Ann Arbor, Michigan, 1958.

Frank, Lawrence K., and Mary Frank, *Your Adolescent at Home and in School*, The Viking Press, Inc., New York, 1956.

Freeman, V.J., et al., "Family Group Counselling (as Differentiated from other family Therapies)," *International Journal of Group Psychotherapy*, Vol. 13 (1963).

Fromm, Erich, *Man for Himself*, New York, Holt, Rinehart and Company, 1947.

Fullmer, D.A., and H.W., Bernard, *Counselling: content and Process*, Chicago, Science Research Associates, Inc., 1964.

Fullmer, D.W., and H.W. Bernard, *Family Consultation*, Boston, Houghton Mifflin Co., 1968.

Goldstein, A.P., K. Heller, and L.B. Sechrest, *Psychotherapy and the Psychology of Behavior Change*, John Wiley & Sons, Inc., New York, 1966.

Gordon, Ira J., *The Teacher as a Guidance Worker*, Harper & Brothers, New York, 1956.

Havighurst, Robert J., *Human Development and Education.*, Longmans, Green & Co., Inc., New York, 1953.

Hill, George E., *Management and Improvement of Guidance*, New York, Appleton, 1965.

Hodgkinson, H.L., *Education in Social and Cultural Perspectives*, Englewood Cliffs, N.J., Prentice-Hall, 1962.

Hoppock, R., *Group Guidance*, New York, McGraw-Hill, 1949.

Huxley, Julian, *Evolution in Action*, New York, Harper, 1953.

Ilg, Frances L., and Louise Bates Ames, *Child Behavior*, Harper & Brothers, New York, 1955.

Jersild, Arthur T., *The Psychology of Adolescence*, The Macmillan company, New York, 1957.

Johnson, Walter F., Buford Stefflre, and Roy A. Edelfelt, *Pupil Personnel and Guidance Services*, McGraw-Hill Book Company, Inc., New York, 1961.

Kemp, C. Gratton (ed.) *Perspectives on the Group Process*, Houghton Mifflin Company, Boston, 1964.

Kluckhohn, C., and H.A. Murray (eds.) *Personality in Nature, Society, and Culture*, 2nd ed., New York, Alfred A. Knopf, 1953.

Knowles, R.T., and B. Shertzer, "Attitudes Toward the School Counsellor's Role," *Counsellor Education and Supervision*, Vol. 5 (1965), 9-20.

Larrabee, Eric, and Rolf Meyerson (eds.) *Mass Leisure*, Free Press, Glencoe, Illinois, 1960.

Leary, T., *Interpersonal Diagnosis of Personality*, The Ronald Press Company, New York, 1957.

Lloyd-Jones, E., R. Barry, and B. Wolf (eds.) *Guidance in Elementary Education: A Case Book*, Bureau of Publications, teachers college, Columbia University, New York, 1958.

Loughary, J. W., et al., (eds.) *Counselling, A Growing Profession*, American Personnel and Guidance Association, Washington, D.C., 1965.

Mahler, C.A., *Group Counselling in the Schools*, Houghton Mifflin Company, Boston, 1969.

Maslow, A.H., *Motivation and Personality*, New York, Harper and Row, Publishers, 1954.

Masserman, J.H., *Individual and familial Dynamics*, New York, Grune and Stratton, Inc., 1959.

Menninger, William C., *Enjoying Leisure Time* Science Research Associates, Inc., Chicago, 1950.

Miller, Carroll, H., *Foundations of Guidance*, Harper & Row Publishers, Incorporated, New York, 1961.

Mortensen, Donald G., and Allen M. Schmuller, *Guidance in Today's Schools*, John Wiley & Sons, Inc., New York, 1959.

Norris, Willa, Franklin R. Zeran and Raymond N. Hatch, *The Information Service in Guidance*, Rand McNally & Company, Chicago, 1960.

Ohlsen, Merle, M,. "Counselling Children in Groups," *The School Counsellor*, Vol. 15 (1968), 343-49.

Overstreet, Harry A., *A Guide to Civilized Leisure*, W.W. Norton & Company, Inc., New York, 1934.

Passow, A. Harry, *Planning for Talented Youth*, Bureau of Publications, Teachers College, Columbia University, New York, 1955.

Patterson, C.H. (ed.), *The School Counsellor; Selected Readings*, McGraw-Hill Book Company, New York, 1967.

Patterson, D.G., "The Genesis of Modern Guidance," *Educational Record*, Vol. 19 (1938), 36-46.

Pepinsky, Harold B., and Pauline Nichols Pepinsky, *Counselling: Theory and Practice*, The Ronald Press company, New York, 1945.

Peters, Herman J., and Gail F. Farwell, *Guidance: A Development Approach*, Rand McNally & Company, Chicago, 1959.

Robinson, Francis P., *Principles and Practices in Student Personnel Work*, Harper & Brothers, New York, 1950.

Roe, Anne, "Personality Structure and Occupational Behavior", in H. Borow (ed.) *Man in a World at Work*, Boston, Houghton Mifflin, 1964.

Roe, Anne, *The Psychology of Occupations*, John Wiley & Sons, Inc., New York, 1956.

Rogers, C,R., *Client-Centered Therapy*, Boston, Houghton-Mifflin Co., Boston, 1951.

Seagull, Arthur, "The Counsellor as Consultant: What can Teachers Teach Him?" *Personnel and Guidance Journal*, Vol. 46 (April 1968), 808-10.

Sherif, M., and C.W. Sherif *Reference Groups*, New York, Harper, 1964.

Super, Donald E., *Career Development: Self-Concept Theory*, New York, College Entrance Examination Board, 1963.

Super, Donald E., *The Psychology of Careers: An Introduction to Vocational Development*, Harper & Brothers, New York, 1957.

Thurman, H., *Disciplines of the Spirit*, New York, Harpers & Row, 1963.

Index